THE
DERMAdoctor
SKINSTRUCTION MANUAL

THE SMART GUIDE TO
HEALTHY, BEAUTIFUL SKIN
AND LOOKING GOOD
AT ANY AGE

Simon & Schuster
New York   London   Toronto   Sydney

AUDREY KUNIN, M.D.,
WITH BILL GOTTLIEB

Note to Readers

This publication contains the opinions and ideas of its author. It is intended to provide helpful and informative material on the subjects addressed in the publication. It is sold with the understanding that the author and publisher are not engaged in rendering medical, health, or any other kind of personal professional services in the book. The reader should consult his or her medical, health, or other competent professional before adopting any of the suggestions in this book or drawing inferences from it.

The author and publisher specifically disclaim all responsibility for any liability, loss, or risk, personal or otherwise, that is incurred as a consequence, directly or indirectly, of the use and application of any of the contents of this book.

 Simon & Schuster
Rockefeller Center
1230 Avenue of the America
New York, NY 10020

Copyright © 2005 by Audrey Kunin, M.D.
All rights reserved, including the right of reproduction in whole or in part in any form.

SIMON & SCHUSTER and colophon are registered trademarks of Simon & Schuster, Inc.

Designed by Nancy Singer Olaguera

Manufactured in the United States of America

ISBN 0-7394-5855-8

Dedicated to the five people truly responsible for the creation of the *"DERMAdoctor"*:

My mother, Estey, who always wanted me to be a dermatologist and obviously I listened (doesn't that speak volumes about her influence?)

My father, Bob, the best father anyone could wish for, who has been my model for achieving success

My wonderful husband, Jeff, the man behind the image and my not-so-silent silent partner who lives and breathes for his family

My remarkable son, Matthew, his father's clone and my bright boy; a child who amazes us daily through his sense of adventure, enthusiasm, and joie de vivre

My beautiful daughter, Sophie, the ultimate girlie girl with her dazzling smile, who lives for dress up, princesses, and the color pink

Thank you for your encouragement and love.

ACKNOWLEDGMENTS

DERMAdoctor in all of its manifestations—the Web site, the product line, and now *The DERMAdoctor Skinstruction Manual*—could not possibly exist without a literal cast of millions.

To those who've toiled tirelessly to make DERMAdoctor.com a success—my staff, our freelancers, and those who have contributed their time and talents—I extend my heartfelt gratitude and thanks.

To Bill Gottlieb, a supreme professional who simply wanted to know if I'd ever thought of writing a book and then got things done, my admiration and respect go out to you.

For my agent, Chris Tomasino, you've gotten me through my angst, my writer's block, and my personal struggles to accomplish something I never dreamt possible.

My editor, Sydny Miner, you've become a friend and mentor in the world of publishing. I can't begin to thank everyone at Simon & Schuster for being so incredibly enthusiastic about and supportive in the creation of this book.

And to the millions of DERMAdoctor enthusiasts around the world, you have given back to me far more than I could ever give to you. You have let me know that I have been able to positively and personally touch your lives in a manner I could never have imagined prior to the dot-com era.

CONTENTS

PART II
BEAUTIFUL SKIN IS ALWAYS IN

INTRODUCTION

My mother always wanted me to be a dermatologist.

Good hours and good pay, was what she'd say. But I was convinced that I would be *anything* but. Who wanted to treat acne and warts all day long? Yet, despite my best intentions, I fell in love with dermatology.

A medical school rotation in dermatology at the Santa Clara Valley Medical Center in San Jose opened my eyes to the fact that dermatology had a lot going for it. I could care for children and adults and perform as little or as much surgery as I liked. Plus, I discovered that skin conditions weren't even remotely limited to those in my own childhood (warts) and adolescence (acne)—they affected *everyone*.

Upon my arrival back at the Medical College of Ohio that summer, I found myself under the tutelage of Drs. Walter and Dorinda Shelley, naively unaware that these two experts were considered pioneers in dermatology. Their offbeat and unique insights into dermatological therapy widened my understanding of how medicine is often as much an art as a science. Working with them solidified my interest and fanned my enthusiasm.

But while I have to begrudgingly accept the fact that my mother was right about my eventual career choice, even she never predicted the nontraditional use of my degree—a use that has allowed me to help millions of people seeking skin care solutions. Here's what happened . . .

Back in 1998, in the midst of the dot-com boom, I didn't even know how to turn on a computer. However, my husband, Jeff, whose passions included both business and the Internet, saw an unmet need—and www.DERMAdoctor.com was born. It was a great opportunity to provide skin care items online, as well as thoughtful advice and expertise. But our business start-up wasn't like that classic IBM commercial where the orders start rolling in. Rather, it was the *e-mail* that was overwhelming. Perhaps this occurred because it was next to impossible to obtain an HMO referral to see a specialist . . . or maybe it was the average sixteen-week wait to see a dermatologist . . . or it could be that so much of rural America was underserved by specialists. Whatever the reason, I got literally thousands of questions. And responded to every one. After answering similar questions over and over again, I started writing articles in order to provide complete descriptions of the conditions I was being asked about. As a result, the skin care information on DERMAdoctor.com grew and grew.

By the end of 1999, a recurrent theme had surfaced. Conditions previously not addressed by the cosmetics and skin care industries, like keratosis pilaris (a.k.a. chicken skin bumps), were continually being queried. Critiques of products in widely recognized categories were also accumulating.

Friends from medical school remember that I had wild dreams about starting a cosmetics company, marrying dermatology with beauty. It was time to dust off my dream and launch my targeted line of skin care solutions: DERMAdoctor Specialist Skin Care. It took four years and countless hours of self-education (and frustration!) before our first product hit the market.

Traditionally, skin care has been quite sterile, clinical, and predominantly masculine. Since I was essentially a mirror image of my own target audience, I knew that clinical skin care could use a feminine approach, even a touch of fun and whimsy. After all, most skin conditions are chronic. I was searching for something I could enjoy using day after day, something I'd enjoy looking at in my medicine cabinet (I prefer my skin therapy to be not only luxe but pretty), *and* something that was highly effective. I figured everyone else would be seeking the same thing.

Now more than five million people a year in America and around the world turn to DERMAdoctor.com and DERMAdoctor Specialist Skin Care for answers. However, I felt there was another unmet need in the marketplace—the need for a truly practical and comprehensive do-it-yourself skin care book.

It is not my intention to encourage people to diagnose themselves and replace the dermatologist. Rather, I wish to empower them to take the best possible care of their skin. DERMAdoctor.com has consistently positioned itself to be *the* definitive source of skin care information, educating consumers on up-to-date prescription medications, procedures, and workups. Sometimes seeing a physician needn't be your first response to a problem. Chicken skin bumps? There is no reason not to begin treatment at home. Poison ivy on Saturday night? Good luck getting into the dermatologist come Monday morning, not to mention dealing with the agonizing itching in the meantime.

Personalized skin care begins at home and can help prevent problems down the road. *The DERMAdoctor Skinstruction Manual* is one of your best tools and resources for at-home skin care.

Textbooks are boring. Magazines may not offer enough information for you to make an informed medical decision. *The DERMAdoctor Skinstruction Manual* provides information that's interesting, sometimes funny, occasionally poignant, and always up to date, with the best that medicine has to offer. It's about what really works or doesn't work. It's what you need to know about a treatment, a condition, an issue. It's about self-empowerment. And it's me and you, talking one on one about how I really treat skin issues; it's how I sit down, girlfriend to girlfriend, and discuss what really matters.

The DERMAdoctor Skinstruction Manual is how I relate to people. I was never good at the "mill" that medicine has become. I would find myself spending twenty or thirty minutes or more with each patient, having an in-depth discussion about their skin condition and treatment options. That's not going to get me far in a practice in this day and age, but that in-depth approach has allowed me to develop the material you'll find here.

Also, this book reflects what is going on in my life. Whether it's my personal experience with my surgically induced menopause or my son's outbreak of chickenpox, my life and *The DERMAdoctor Skinstruction Manual* are closely intertwined.

When I was a child, my mother often turned to Dr. Spock's book on child care, searching for information on tonsillitis and other disorders. I like to think of *The DERMAdoctor Skinstruction Manual* as that kind of resource—convenient, all-encompassing, accessible, and entertaining.

Everyone has a skin condition. It doesn't matter if it's your first case of acne or your first issue with crow's-feet. *The DERMAdoctor Skinstruction Manual* allows you to make educated decisions and find appropriate solutions for your skin. It shares all the skin care secrets and tips that I have long recommended to my own patients. When you have this book in your home library, the skin doctor is always in.

PART I

YOUR PRESCRIPTION FOR BEAUTIFUL SKIN

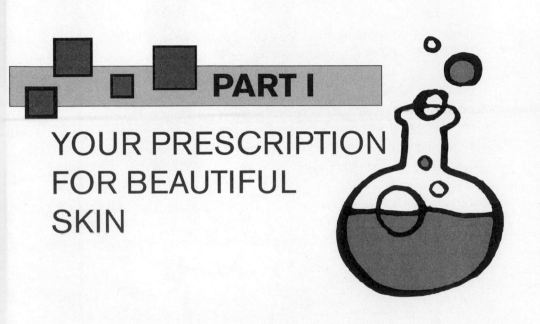

ACNE

No One Needs to Suffer

It's rare to escape the acne experience. Approximately forty-five million young adults between the ages of twelve and twenty-four have acne. And that number doesn't even include the millions of acne patients in their twenties and thirties who are *more* likely to develop acne than their teen counterparts.

A strong genetic predisposition is the source of most acne, exacerbated by hormonal changes (most women already know this!); stress associated with school, jobs, and starting families; and, occasionally, poor skin care habits.

HOW DOES ACNE FORM?

Acne is a disorder of keratinization—the development of the cells lining the sebaceous (oil) glands.

Instead of easily exfoliating themselves onto the surface, the cells become sticky, bind together, and plug the glands. But the sebaceous glands continue to secrete sebum, automatically triggered by DHT, the active form of testosterone. The excess sebum and lack of oxygen beneath the plug create a perfect environment for *Proprionibacterium acnes* (*P. acnes*), the bacteria that live on the skin. Too many *P. acnes* bacteria contribute to the inflammation within the gland.

Eventually, a combination of persistent plugging, excessive oil buildup (envision an expanding water balloon), and inflammation produced by bacterial overgrowth causes the gland to rupture. On the surface, this manifests as an inflamed acne papule or cyst.

FOOD AND ACNE: WAS MOM RIGHT?

Until recently—and contrary to what your mother may have told you—dermatologists have been taught that diet doesn't lead to acne (with the possible exception of nuts).

Yet a study done at Colorado State University suggests otherwise. The Kitivan Islanders of Papua New Guinea and the Ache hunter-gathers of Paraguay, both of whom traditionally eat low-carbohydrate diets, are acne-free. In contrast, in North America and western Europe, 79 to 95 percent of teens struggle with acne, and 40 to 54 percent of adults twenty-five and older still break out. Is diet the difference?

The theory behind these findings rests on known physiology. A diet with foods high in the "glycemic index" (those loaded with quick-digesting sugars and starches) sends insulin levels skyrocketing, triggering sebum production and, indirectly, acne.

So perhaps Mom's warnings about those potato chips, chocolates, and other junk food had some kernel of scientific truth. Not because the foods are oily, but because they're loaded with refined carbohydrates. Should you shun all the goodies? From a realistic standpoint, it's unlikely to happen. (I certainly don't have that level of permanent willpower!) Instead, go for a healthy, well-rounded approach.

NOT ALL ACNE IS CREATED EQUAL

There are different types of acne lesions. These are:

- Open comedone (the blackhead)
- Inflamed papule
- Pustule (the whitehead)
- Painful nodular cysts

Dermatologists also give acne a "grade" for severity, based on an estimate of the total number of lesions. Grade 1 is the mildest, with very few lesions. Grade 4 is the most severe. (A grade also allows the dermatologist to track improvement or lack thereof.)

Treatment is based on the types of lesions and the grade.

TREATING ACNE

Every dermatologist has her favorite acne regimens that have proven successful for her patients.

When a patient comes to my office, I evaluate the types of lesions and the grade, then determine the therapy. The goal of all acne treatments is to:

- Kill the bacteria
- Reduce unnecessary oils
- Unplug the pores
- Reduce inflammation

Many acne treatments conveniently provide more than one benefit, helping simplify the process. I allow six to eight weeks for any therapy regimen to show considerable (notice I didn't say "miraculous") improvement. If a patient does not improve enough, I will often change her medication. (Anyone who finds herself on the same medication for a year while continuing to break out shouldn't hesitate to talk to her doctor about a change!)

Prescription Systemic Therapy

Systemic therapy (pills) is best for inflammatory acne and practically mandatory for acne cysts. There are three categories of oral medication:

- Antibiotics (help kill bacteria and reduce inflammation)
- Hormonal therapy (reduces DHT)
- Accutane (considered the closest thing to an acne "cure")

Antibiotics

P. acnes bacteria thrive on excess sebum and in a low-oxygen environment. The result of bacterial growth is the production of highly inflammatory free fatty acids, which cause whiteheads, red bumps, and painful cysts. Antibiotics are used not only to kill *P. acnes* but also to reduce inflammation.

A stray monthly pimple doesn't warrant a long-term commitment to antibiotic therapy, but a patient plagued by blemishes—whether numerous or resistant to topical therapy—may qualify.

Several types of antibiotics are commonly used. They include:

- Tetracycline
- Minocycline
- Doxycycline
- Erythromycin
- Bactrim (sulfa)

The tetracycline family (tetracycline, minocycline, doxycycline) is considered the most effective group of antibiotics for acne therapy.

Tetracycline is most commonly prescribed in doses of 500 milligrams (mg), taken twice daily.

Minocycline (Minocin) is a more aggressive member of this antibiotic family and is given in a dosage of 50 milligrams, once or twice a day. It also is much more expensive. I reserve minocycline for patients who don't respond to tetracycline and patients with primarily cystic acne.

Doxycycline is similar to minocycline. However, I have not personally had nearly the response rate to this medication as I have to Minocin, so I tend to favor the latter.

The tetracycline family may cause increased sensitivity to the sun. These drugs are *not* to be used if pregnant or nursing, nor are they appropriate for patients younger than thirteen years of age, as they can cause permanent discoloration of dental enamel.

Erythromycin is not as effective for treating acne and tends to cause significant stomach upset. (To reduce nausea, take it on a full stomach.) I save this for patients unable to take tetracycline or its family members and for preteens.

Sulfa is highly effective, but allergies to this antibiotic are very common, so it is infrequently prescribed for acne therapy.

Hormonal Therapy

All women produce androgens (male hormones), including testosterone; a balance of androgens and estrogen (female hormones) create harmony for the skin, like a biochemical yin and yang. But when androgens outweigh estrogens, it's blemishes galore.

A woman can make too much testosterone, as in polycystic ovary syndrome (PCOS). She can make too little estrogen to "mask" the testosterone. Or—by far the most common cause of what's called androgenic acne—the cells in her skin and hair follicles can have a genetically predetermined sensitivity to "normal" levels of androgen.

However, it's not the testosterone itself that's causing the problems—it's DHT, a metabolite of the hormone. As explained earlier, DHT triggers an increase in sebum production. It also enlarges the sebaceous glands. Control the DHT and you control the acne. Hormonal medications can do that job.

Birth Control Pills. In order to treat acne hormonally, the medication must:

- Prevent the formation of androgens;
- Reduce the level of androgens circulating in the bloodstream; or
- Block the androgens from reaching their cellular receptors.

Birth control pills do all three of these things. They help prevent the formation of active androgens. They increase sex hormone binding globulin (SHBG), which binds to androgens and prevents them from going anywhere. They decrease the levels of circulating testosterone. And the progestin (the synthetic form of progesterone) in an oral contraceptive competes for binding sites on androgen receptors.

The only oral contraceptive the FDA has approved for the treatment of acne is Ortho Tri-Cyclen. This medication went through the rigorous testing and studies required by the FDA to prove that it was indeed beneficial for acne.

Spironolactone. Many women are turning to noncontraceptive antiandrogen options in the treatment of their acne, like the diuretic spironolactone (Aldactone). This drug—used to reduce water retention and control high blood pressure—has a molecular structure that mimics androgens. This allows it to bind to androgen receptors, blocking true androgen and helping to control acne. There are downsides to spironolactone use, however, including symptomatic low blood pressure, irregular menstrual cycles, spotting, and higher levels of potassium in the bloodstream. (If you take the drug, it's important to avoid binging on foods high in potassium, like bananas.)

Yasmin. For women who want the benefits of an antiandrogen but don't want to be on a diuretic, or for those who want to be on birth control pills but hate those extra few pounds of water retention that tend to go hand in hand with birth control pills, a new-generation oral contraceptive, Yasmin, may be a solution.

Yasmin contains drospirenone, a progestin that is structurally very similar to spironolactone. Because of this resemblance, Yasmin may be a beneficial "off-label" drug for addressing androgenic acne *and* can help you avoid those extra few pounds.

Injectable Steroids

The stray acne cyst can be rapidly resolved with a small shot of steroid solution known as triamcinolone (Kenalog). The upside: a quick fix for those "little emergency" situations like weddings and proms. The downside: this is simply not the way to treat widespread, recurrent acne. Nor is it pleasant to experience the infrequent side effect of a "sink" spot because of fat atrophy at the injection site. (Fortunately, it fills in over several months.)

TOPICAL THERAPY

A hot topic in acne therapy is how to best handle breakouts with topicals. Some consumers don't want to take pills; others, for various reasons, can't take pills. Most simply want to get clear skin fast and are willing to incorporate any agent into their routine that maximizes treatment.

Topicals are as varied in their actions as systemic therapies. They are invaluable for treating minor outbreaks and supplementing systemic therapy.

Synthetic Retinoids

These derivatives of vitamin A are indispensable in acne therapy. Similar in action to Accutane, they work to normalize the keratinization process. (For more information on Accutane, see the sidebar on page 9.) They can help eliminate blackheads, dry up excess oils, and squelch papular and pustular acne. But, unlike with Accutane, these benefits are only temporary.

Prescription retinoids are the most potent. But if for some reason they can't be used, a nonprescription retinol (like Afirm) can be beneficial. Prescription options include:

- Tazarotene (Tazorac)
- Tretinoin (Retin-A, Avita)
- Adapalene (Differin)

Retinoids are extremely potent. To avoid irritation, make sure to follow these steps:

- At the beginning, use just every other night.
- Wait thirty minutes after washing before application.
- Apply a *pea-sized* amount of cream or gel to your finger.
- Dab the cream or gel around the area to be treated and rub it in well.
- Avoid getting the substance in your eyes and wash your hands well afterward.
- Do not layer with any other skin treatment or moisturizer.
- Reduce frequency of use if your skin becomes irritated.

ACCUTANE: IF YOU TAKE IT, TAKE IT SERIOUSLY

Many patients with the most severe form of acne—grade 4 cystic acne—fail to be helped by traditional "aggressive" therapy. For these patients, Accutane has been a blessing.

This vitamin A derivative in capsule form is the closest medication to an acne "cure." It helps normalize the factors within the sebaceous gland that contribute to the formation of acne in the first place.

The therapy is limited to five months. The success rate is high.

Accutane, however, is a drug to be taken seriously.

It can have significant side effects, similar to what occurs with a vitamin A overdose. Problems can include: dryness of the skin, eyes, and mucous membranes; chapped, cracked lips; increased triglycerides; low red-blood-cell count (anemia); low white-blood-cell count (lowered immunity to infection); low platelet count (increased risk of bleeding); liver enzyme abnormalities; hair loss; pressure buildup behind the eyes; headaches; nausea; depression; and, most seriously, birth defects.

Pregnancy *must* be avoided while on Accutane and for one month after discontinuing treatment. To ensure this, two methods of birth control should be used. (It is important to understand, however, that the medication does *not* affect the ovaries, eggs, sperm, or any future pregnancies.)

While a patient is on Accutane, blood work is done every two weeks for the first month of use and monthly for the final four months of use. This monitors any possible changes in blood counts, liver and kidney function, and triglyceride levels.

Whether over-the-counter or prescription, vitamin A topicals should not be used while pregnant or nursing. They also may increase sun sensitivity; wear sunscreen with an SPF of 30 daily.

Topical Antibiotics

A myriad of prescription topicals possess bacteria-killing abilities. These products can help treat whiteheads and small inflammatory acne lesions and are typically applied twice a day. Some options are:

- Clindamycin (Cleocin T)
- Erythromycin (Erycette, Emgel)
- Metronidazole (MetroGel, MetroLotion, MetroCream, and Noritate)
- Sodium sulfacetamide (Plexion Lotion & Cleanser)

Benzoyl Peroxide (BPO)

Benzoyl peroxide is a tried-and-true acne treatment. Its benefits derive from its bacteria-thwarting abilities.

Strengths range from 2.5 to 10 percent. Benzoyl peroxide can be found in both over-the-counter and prescription treatments—often at the same levels! Gels, creams, lotions, soaps, masks, and even shaving creams provide formulations for every need. Recent variations have married benzoyl peroxide with other ingredients.

Some prescription-only options include:

- Benzamycin (combination of BPO and erythromycin)
- Clinac BPO (combination of OC Eight Mattifying Gel and benzoyl peroxide)
- Benzaclin (combination of BPO and clindamycin)

Some over-the-counter products are:

- BenzaShave 5% medicated shaving cream
- Peter Thomas Roth BPO 2½% Medicated Shaving Cream
- PanOxyl Bar 5%
- Peter Thomas Roth BPO Gel 10% and Sulfur

Benzoyl peroxide can be a useful aid in acne therapy, but don't go overboard. It can cause dryness, redness, and irritation if overused.

There are even an unfortunate few people who are allergic to it. Pay attention to what your skin is telling you and reduce your use should any irritation develop.

Azelaic Acid

Azelaic acid is a naturally occurring dicarboxylic acid found in grains like wheat, rye, and barley. Studies show that it possesses antibacterial activity against *P. acnes,* and it may also help normalize the keratinization process within the sebaceous glands.

Look for it in prescription acne medications like Azelex 20% Cream.

NDGA

Is there any topical medication that can reduce DHT, the hormone that revs up the sebaceous glands, causing oily skin and acne flare-ups?

Scientific research says yes.

The ingredient is NDGA—nordihydroguaiaretic acid, a natural plant-derived lipoxygenase inhibitor (which means it inhibits inflammation). Some studies suggest that the botanical NDGA possesses the ability to reduce the activity of 5 alpha-reductase, the enzyme responsible for changing testosterone into DHT.

DERMAdoctor's own 2n1 rosacea cream contains NDGA. It can help make your acne regimen more tolerable and effective by improving the appearance of redness caused by acne, inflammation, and other treatments, as well as visible blemishes. And since it isn't yet another topical antibiotic, it is complementary with other acne therapy.

Sulfur

Sulfur helps inhibit the growth of *P. acnes* and unclog pores. You can find it as a solo ingredient, in either over-the-counter or prescription options. In combination with sulfa, it's approved for use in prescription acne rosacea and seborrheic dermatitis (dandruff).

Some prescription-only options include:

- Sulfacet-R (sulfur and sulfa)
- Rosula (sulfur, sulfa, and urea)
- Ovace (sulfur and sulfa)
- Plexion (sulfur and sulfa)

Some over-the-counter products are:

- Rezamid Acne Lotion (sulfur and resorcinal)
- Sulforcin Acne Treatment Lotion
- Peter Thomas Roth BPO Gel 10% and Sulfur

PROCEDURES

Dermatologists may include procedures in their approach to acne. Most commonly, "acne surgery" is performed. This essentially refers to the use of a comedone extractor being firmly applied around a blackhead to push it out of the skin.

Other options include chemical peels, microdermabrasion, and (an old-time procedure) the application of liquid nitrogen to an acne cyst.

In my approach to acne therapy, I have personally found procedures rather limited and turn to them only to supplement other treatments.

Shedding Light on Acne

Those who make their way to a dermatologist often credit summer sunlight as helpful in reducing acne severity, and studies support the benefits of sunlight in acne therapy. But with today's heightened concerns about skin cancer (not to mention wrinkles!), indiscriminate use of medical ultraviolet phototherapy is not the treatment du jour. Leave it to medical science to find another way to get that summertime-like improvement.

The Acne Blues. P. acnes bacteria produce natural by-products called porphyrins. Porphyrins are exquisitely vulnerable to a high-intensity, narrow band of visible blue light. When porphyrins are exposed to this light (or, to a lesser extent, natural sunlight, which contains a less intense form of blue light), a chemical reaction toxic to P. acnes takes place. Kill the P. acnes, improve the acne.

Commercially, this process is called Acne PhotoClearing and is marketed under the name ClearLight, which has been approved by the FDA for the treatment of mild to moderate inflammatory acne—small, red papules and pustules (whiteheads). ClearLight is unlikely to resolve blackheads or cysts, minimize pore visibility, or reduce oiliness.

Remission with ClearLight usually lasts between four and eight months. Repeated series of ClearLight may be required for maintaining a clear complexion. And not all cases of acne are triggered by *P. acnes,* so the procedure isn't for everyone.

Smoothbeam Laser

This laser takes aim at the literal root of the problem: the sebaceous gland. In a series of treatments, the heat of the Smoothbeam alters the structure and function of the glands.

Results are fairly impressive. Improvement can be seen as early as three weeks—and after four treatments some patients achieve 98 percent clearance! However, those results aren't permanent. In one study, at a twenty-four-week follow-up, 100 percent clearance was seen in just one of twenty-seven patients.

FUTURE TREATMENTS

Two candidates in the "acne pipeline" include topical versions of oral medications already used to treat severe cases of cystic acne.

Isotrex. Essentially Accutane mixed in a protective sunscreen base, Isotrex is available in Canada and Europe. (For more information on Accutane, please see the sidebar on page 9.) I have read mixed reviews from Canadian and European dermatologists. It will be interesting to see if this medication makes its way through the FDA and onto the U.S. market and how it will truly perform.

I have seen some first-time patients who had been given "homemade" forms of this product by other doctors, which consisted of them poking holes in the Accutane capsule and applying the liquidy gel straight to the skin. All this method accomplished was to locally irritate and dry the skin without helping clear the acne lesions.

Atrisone. The topical form of the oral medication Dapsone, Atrisone is typically used in the treatment of certain forms of blistering disorders and systemic infections. It has both antibiotic and anti-inflammatory actions. It is occasionally prescribed for severe cystic acne when Accutane cannot be used or has not been effective. Atrisone sounds promising in the initial reports and is currently in clinical trials. Should the FDA approve it, Atrisone would offer an entirely new category of acne therapy.

11 IMPORTANT POINTS TO REMEMBER ABOUT ACNE TREATMENT

1. Blackheads. For best results, use some form of topical retinoid.
2. Cysts. They respond best to pill therapy.
3. Consistency of treatment. Steady treatment results in a better outcome.
4. Six to eight weeks. That's the amount of time to allow for any therapy to take effect before you give up on it.
5. Don't pick. It can lead to scar formation.
6. Don't scrub the face or have facials. If you're acne-prone, these actions may traumatize sebaceous glands and lead to further flare-ups.
7. Bangs. Keep them off your forehead.
8. Hands. Keep them off your face. Keeping hands and hair off your skin will help minimize distributing pore-plugging oils.
9. Apply products lightly. Don't apply an acne cream, lotion, or gel heavily, like a mask (unless it is one). There is no reason your product needs to be seen in order to work.
10. Heavy skin care products like cocoa butter. Avoid them. They will smother the skin and aggravate your acne.
11. Makeup. Remove it when you're at home. Let your skin breathe!

EVERYDAY SKIN CARE FOR ACNE PATIENTS

Acne is not caused by a lack of cleansing, but removing pore-plugging, bacteria-nourishing oils, as well as surface cellular debris, goes a long way to minimizing breakouts.

Glycolic acid (an alpha hydroxy acid, or AHA) and salicylic acid (beta hydroxy acid, or BHA) help dissolve grease and grime, lifting away cells plugging the pores. Glycolic acid tends to be more versatile and can be found in cleansers, treatments, and toners. BHA often assists glycolic acid in AHA-BHA products.

Thanks to the plastic industry, polymers have been created to surround and lift core-plugging oils away from the skin, without causing irritation or parching. They help keep the skin free of shine all day long.

Here are the types of products dermatologists advise their acne patients to use in routine skin care:

- Glycolic acid (an AHA). Try M.D. Forté Glycare Cleansing Gel and M.D. Forté Glycare I.

- Salicylic acid (BHA). Try Peter Thomas Roth Beta Hydroxy Acid 2% Acne Wash or Sal Ac Wash.
- Combination AHA-BHA products. Try M.D. Forté Glycare Perfection Gel, Peter Thomas Roth AHA/BHA Acne Clearing Gel, or Peter Thomas Roth AHA/BHA Face & Body Polish.
- Oil control. Try DERMAdoctor Tease Zone Oil Control Gel with Sebum-Sequestering Micro-Particles or OC Eight Mattifying Gel.

FINAL THOUGHTS

Too many acne sufferers go untreated for far too long. No one need suffer with acne—today there are more effective therapy options than ever. If you have acne that doesn't respond to over-the-counter treatment, please see a board-certified dermatologist.

Ask the DERMAdoctor

QUESTION

I do a pretty good job of keeping my mild acne under control, but sometimes one or two pimples just pop up—particularly right before an important event like a presentation at work or a party! (Must be the stress.) What's the best way to camouflage a pimple?

The DERMAdoctor:

First, you need to treat it. I recommend dabbing on a product with acne-fighting benzoyl peroxide, like Peter Thomas Roth BPO Gel 10% and Sulfur. Another possibility is an AHA-BHA product, like M.D. Forté Glycare Perfection Gel.

For those who like to carry around their emergency "zit fix" in their purse, Cellex-C Skin Perfecting Pen is a great way to dab your way to an invisible blemish, especially when you start out early. The natural botanicals have a drying effect and create an environment hostile to the bacteria. If none of these is on hand, try spotting the blemish with toothpaste. Select one that is white, free of cinnamon flavoring, and not packed with tooth-whitening peroxide.

Once you've dried it out, it's time to cover it up. One of the trade secrets of makeup artists who work on movie stars is Visine. The same stuff that "gets the red out" of your eyes can help get the red out of your face. After you've done your best to dry out the pimple, soak a cotton swab in Visine. Then hold the swab to the affected area for about ten seconds. The redness will disappear.

Next, get out that concealer. Green-tinted concealers are great for camouflaging redness. One to try: T. LeClerc Liquid Concealer-Tilleul. The green works to neutralize the redness. Don't overdo it or you'll make the blemish more obvious that it was before you tried to get rid of it. Use a small amount and tap lightly. Apply a small (repeat: *small*) amount to the blemish; then, using your ring finger (it exerts the least amount of pressure of all your fingers), lightly tap the concealer into the blemish.

When you apply your regular makeup, be careful not to smear the concealer, and always set your makeup with loose powder. This will reduce the chance of removing the concealer. You want to make your face look as uniform as possible, so that the pimple doesn't stick out and announce its presence to the world.

ACNE SCARS

There Is a Solution

Years after women outgrow their adolescent acne, the scars persist. But advances in acne therapy and dermatologic surgery have made it unnecessary for any acne patient to endure acne scarring.

AN OUNCE OF PREVENTION

Prevention may sound like a glib answer to the question of how to handle acne scars. But since an estimated ten million Americans become scarred to some extent by acne each year, intervention is the absolute best solution.

Who will develop acne scars, and how severe will scarring be? Without a crystal ball, much of that remains unknown. What we do know is that genes play a definite role in the likelihood of acne severity and subsequent scar formation. And the more severe the acne, the more severe the scarring.

Ninety-five percent of acne patients will develop scarring to some degree. The earlier that treatment is initiated, the better the odds are that scar formation will be mild. Delaying acne therapy by three or more years increases one's risk of more extensive acne scarring.

For the lucky majority, acne scars are a minor annoyance, difficult for others to see. For the unlucky minority, acne scarring can cause devastating long-term emotional suffering. Teens may become depressed and withdrawn, losing self-confidence. (Acne scarring has even been cited as a risk factor for male suicide.)

Newer acne therapies make it needless for *anyone* to suffer from acne or go on to form scars. (For more information, please see the previous chapter, "Acne.") Early medical intervention is the key to preventing unnecessary disfigurement. While this doesn't mean that everyone suffering from a single blemish should rush to schedule an appointment with a dermatologist, I can't stress enough that acne unresponsive to over-the-counter therapy options should be evaluated by a specialist.

PIH: THE GREAT FAKE OUT

I lost count long ago of the number of acne patients returning for their initial six- to eight-week follow-up concerned about their new acne scars—when in actuality there wasn't a scar in sight. What they were noticing was actually *color change*. This postinflammatory hyperpigmentation (PIH) is not acne scarring. It is the normal aftermath of the skin's inflammatory process.

For those with pale skin tones, this residual color change is generally pink, red, or purple. Patients with darker skin tones may notice brown or black spots where their acne once was.

PIH can fade on its own. Unfortunately, the darker the PIH, the longer it may take to resolve. It may also require intervention to hasten the resolution process. While PIH is not a true scar, when it lasts past a year it certainly seems like a permanent problem.

Mederma

Mederma, an over-the-counter cream derived from onion extract, is helpful for treating newly healed wounds and resolving acne, hastening the resolution of reddened spots. Mederma has a gel base that should not cause an acne flare-up. But it is important not to cake it on heavily, as acne-prone skin may not tolerate any product that smothers it. There is no point in aggravating your acne in your efforts to eradicate the discoloration.

Restoring an Even Complexion

For brown areas, bleaching with hydroquinone may be incorporated into an acne or skin care regimen. Prescription bleaches containing both hydroquinone and glycolic acid, such as Glyquin and Lustra-AF, are highly effective in resolving undesirable skin discoloration. Glyquin contains a higher percentage of glycolic acid and is free of the irritant metabisulfite. Both contain a sunscreen. Effective nonprescription ways to achieve an even complexion include the use of DERMAdoctor Immaculate Correction (contains a botanical nonhydroquinone lightening complex) and ScarGuard Lightener (contains 2 percent hydroquinone).

Sun Avoidance

Avoiding overexposure to the sun is crucial for many reasons, but when you're waiting out the "fade game," an oil-free, oil-reducing sunscreen—like DERMAdoctor Body Guard Exquisitely Light SPF 30 or M.D. Forté SPF 20—goes a long way to speeding the process. Ultraviolet light will darken the skin, preferentially darkening areas of abnormal discoloration. Sun protection prevents this process, giving bleaching treatments a chance to work without interruption.

WHAT CAUSES AN ACNE SCAR?

As an acne cyst forms, the neck of the sebaceous gland expands, filling with bacteria, cells, and sebum that are unable to pass through to the skin's surface. Eventually the cyst ruptures, depositing this "foreign matter" deep within the dermis, where it is quickly attacked by white blood cells responsible for fighting infection.

This forceful inflammatory response can have three results, creating three different types of scars. The most common outcome is loss of tissue as collagen is destroyed. Skin overlying the collapsed dermis sags, having lost its underlying support. The result is a soft, saucer-shaped depression (pockmark) or jagged ice-pick scar. This scenario is more typical on the face and is seen in both women and men.

Less frequently, excessive scar tissue (a keloid) is formed as fibroblasts (the dermal cells that produce collagen) are triggered into hyperactivity. Keloids most commonly arise on the male torso.

Patients are often surprised to discover that another type of skin change is, in fact, a form of acne scarring. Tiny, firm, white bumps surrounding hair follicles on the upper arms or upper torso are known as follicular macular atrophy. These scars can last indefinitely.

Aging often affects scar visibility. After the age of forty, 1 percent of the body's dermal collagen is lost each year. With this additional loss of collagen, acne scars can become more noticeable.

CHOOSING THE RIGHT TREATMENTS

Nobody wants to miss out on the "best" treatment. But when it comes to treating acne scars, there is often no single "best" solution that applies to an individual or to every scar. Differences in location, depth, size, and number of scars all affect treatment decisions. And combination therapy, incorporating more than one type of treatment, frequently improves the overall outcome.

THERAPY FOR KELOID SCARS

A keloid is an excessive tissue growth in response to skin trauma. You don't have to sustain a large wound in order to form a keloid. It takes just an acne bump, minor scratch, or pierced ear for a thick, raised, and rubbery keloid to form. Keloids can be overwhelmingly large, even becoming the size of a baseball. Fortunately, this excess is rare.

Keloids are never easy to treat. However, a variety of options continue to come to the market.

Silicone-based topicals are currently popular. Consider ScarGuard or Kelo-cote to help reduce keloid thickness and discomfort.

Steroid creams, injections, and impregnated tapes can also be beneficial for treating keloidal scars. Cortisone helps shrink thickened, raised fibrous scar tissue.

The pulse-dye yellow-light laser, discussed in this chapter, helps treat keloidal scars, flattening and reducing redness as well as helping control itching of the raised scar.

Interferon injections can help soften a keloid and smooth it out.

Pressure dressings and massage may help reduce some keloids but are not considered a terribly effective form of treatment.

What is your perception of the scars? Do they cause you great anxiety, or is their appearance something you'd simply like to improve, if possible? These questions, along with cost, your expectations, and the amount of effort you plan to devote to the treatment, will also be factored into the physician's decision-making process.

Luckily, a number of new procedures are now available that complement or surpass previous scar-revision techniques. Individually designing a program aimed at the patient's unique situation will help maximize improvement.

Laser Treatments

There are two major categories of lasers used in acne scar therapy: ablative (resurfacing) lasers and nonablative lasers.

Ablative lasers literally remove the outer layers of the skin, burning away scar tissue and stimulating the dermal collagen to tighten, thereby reducing the amount of scar visibility. The ultrapulsed carbon dioxide laser, erbium:YAG laser, and pulsed-dye yellow-light laser are most frequently used in laser resurfacing.

Because the skin is injured during these treatments and unprotected tissue is exposed, great effort must be put into wound care and infection prevention. The skin may remained reddened for several months to a year afterward. Total Block Clear SPF 65 protects delicate, healing skin from both UV and visible light.

Nonablative lasers trigger changes within the dermis without injuring the epidermis. They are the "lunchtime" form of laser therapy. Smoothbeam is the newest FDA-approved laser for this treatment. Smoothbeam targets and heats the sebaceous gland and the surrounding collagen. Dermal collagen tightens in response to the heat, resulting in less visible scarring.

A topical anesthetic (like L.M.X. 4 Topical Anesthetic Cream) is applied about an hour before the procedure. The surface of the skin is cooled with liquid nitrogen to prevent the laser from damaging the epidermis. During the session, a patient will feel both the cold spray and some amount of stinging and heat. The procedure takes about an hour. Typically, three sessions are performed, about a month apart.

Another nonablative laser, the N-Lite, has been used to trigger collagen formation. Three or more treatments may be required to obtain acceptable improvement.

Filler Substances

Filler substances are well suited for shallow, saucer-shaped acne scars. The market has seen an increase in both the number and the quality of filler substances used to help instantly "plump up" acne scars. Restylane, Hylaform, Cosmoderm, Cymetra, Fascian, Artecoll, and bovine collagen are all available. Expect to pay anywhere from $350 to $500 for a 1-milliliter syringe of your chosen filler substance.

Perhaps a filler agent is simply out of your price range or medically out of the question, or you simply want to bolster the results you've already received. DERMAdoctor Faux Fillment softens the appearance of mild, saucer-shaped acne scars for up to twenty-four hours by plumping unsightly dermal defects.

Fat transplantation utilizes a patient's own fat, which is removed by a small liposuction cannula, prepared, and reinjected into the der-

PREVENTING SCAR FORMATION

Wouldn't it be easier if you didn't have to get the scar in the first place? Then you wouldn't have to worry about how to fix it.

Prevent Infection. Infection is a major contributor to increasing your chances of developing a bad scar. To prevent infection, you should cleanse all open wounds with hydrogen peroxide and apply a topical antibiotic ointment like Polysporin twice daily.

Don't Pick. You've heard it time and time again. Don't pick at your skin! This includes squeezing your acne bumps, popping your chickenpox, scratching open your mosquito bites, and digging at those ingrown hairs.

Help the Healing Process. Say you've treated the open wound, which has since closed, and the skin looks intact. Did you know that it still takes at least six months for the collagen within the dermis to be fully healed? Now is the time to take steps to help normalize the healing process. The topical over-the-counter gel Mederma shows excellent results in helping prevent freshly healed wounds from scarring badly. The wound must be healed, without raw, open areas, before Mederma is started. As Mederma is derived from onions, it is safe to use even if you're pregnant or nursing and is okay for young children. Mederma is usually applied three to four times a day, for anywhere from eight to twelve weeks.

---

mal defect. While none of these methods is permanent, results tend to last between three and six months.

Punch Excision

Ice-pick acne scars have hard, irregular, jagged borders, and often the depth is irregular as well. Simple excision of these scars with a sutured closure allows the dermatologist to bring the dermis back together, remove ragged margins, and close the area with a fine, uniform line.

The tiny linear scar may be allowed to fade on its own. Or the procedure may be followed by a more generalized resurfacing, like dermabrasion, microdermabrasion, a chemical peel, or laser resurfacing.

Subcision

In this procedure, the dermatologist undermines the acne scar with a sharp instrument like a tiny scalpel or needle. Subcision helps break fibrous bands of scar tissue that create tension between the epidermis and deeper structures, and also helps induce new collagen formation.

Dermabrasion

Dermatologists have been performing dermabrasion for decades. With the availability of newer, easier-to-use techniques, this procedure has fallen somewhat out of favor. In dermabrasion, the skin is anesthetized and frozen and an extremely sharp, rapidly rotating blade shears away damaged tissue. The ultimate result is similar to laser resurfacing.

Microdermabrasion

Microdermabrasion is not a substitute for traditional dermabrasion, which may still be required for advanced cases of ice-pick acne scarring. However, recent microscopic studies of treated tissue show that microdermabrasion leads to significant improvement.

A series of microdermabrasions is performed in an outpatient setting, usually the physician's office or even a day spa. A combination of topical products can help expedite this procedure. (See "Topicals for Atrophic Scars," below.)

The addition of exfoliating home microdermabrasion creams can help with minor acne scars. However, I prefer to use it chiefly to treat postinflamatory hyperpigmentation.

Chemical Peels

A chemical peel involves the application of a high-potency acid to the skin—the more potent the acid, the deeper the penetration. Personally, I like to restrict this treatment to postinflammatory skin color changes and the most minor acne scars.

Ultra-aggressive phenol peels, which reach the deeper dermis, must be approached with great care and administered in a hospital-like, monitored setting; they have been associated with heart arrhythmias.

Topicals for Atrophic Scars

Everyone always wants to know what topicals can help acne scars. I have many clients who swear by Mederma for helping improve saucer-shaped, depressed acne scars (usually newer ones).

Certainly anything that has been shown to help stimulate collagen bundle formation, like products containing L-ascorbic acid (a form of vitamin C) or amino acid peptides may be beneficial.

I encourage those with acne scars to explore these options. Also keep in mind that a procedure is going to maximize your results, whether done alone or incorporated with a topical regimen.

FINAL THOUGHTS

Acne scarring is no longer a problem without a solution. All of the techniques I have described have become invaluable treatments for patients seeking to eradicate acne scarring. But never forget that scarring is preventable. Don't put off acne therapy. The earlier acne is dealt with, the less likely you are to suffer acne scars. Prevention is the best and most effective form of treatment.

Ask the DERMAdoctor

Question:

I have just finished a course of Accutane and have heard that there are many products I can't use, including hydroquinone bleaching cream to deal with discolored areas. I've also heard that Accutane-induced acne scars are more likely! Can you tell me which procedures and treatments are safe and which aren't, and what to expect in the way of skin changes?

The DERMAdoctor:

Accutane use increases the potential for severe keloidal scar formation in response to skin procedures (not the acne itself) for three years following therapy. That vulnerability precludes the use of dermabrasion and laser resurfacing during this time. There are no firm guidelines regarding less invasive procedures like microdermabrasion, nonablative lasers, or chemical peels, although it is recommended that you wait at least six months after discontinuing Accutane before considering having any of these procedures performed; I would add filler agents to that list. As for topicals for discoloration, there is no waiting time for treatment of PIH. Nor do you have to postpone using products like Mederma, vitamin C, or amino acid peptide therapies.

AGE SPOTS

It's Never Too Late to Look Younger

The term "age spots" is used so loosely that it's often unclear just what is being discussed. And if you aren't certain what your problem is, it's unlikely that you're going to find the right therapy.

There are three conditions that people tend to call age spots:

- Liver spots, or age-related freckles. Dermatologists call these *solar lentigos*.
- Seborrheic keratoses, thick, waxy, wartlike growths also commonly called "barnacles of life."
- Actinic keratosis (by far the most serious of the three conditions), a scaly spot that can be a precursor to skin cancer.

Each of these "age spots" is distinct from the others and responds to a different type of treatment.

LIVER SPOTS: FRECKLES THAT AREN'T SO CUTE

Despite the name, these flat brown or black spots have nothing to do with the liver. But they have everything to do with the sun.

Years of direct exposure to the sun's ultraviolet radiation damage the color-producing cells of the skin; they become hyperactive, depositing more pigment. That's why the spots become more numerous as you age—you've logged more time in sunlight—and why they occur on the areas of the body most frequently exposed to the sun, like the back of the hands and the face.

The good news: liver spots are harmless. You don't *have* to treat them. But many women want to.

Rarely, a spot will develop a melanoma within it. If you have a spot that seems to be growing rapidly and has irregular pigmentation or develops a sore, see your dermatologist.

Spotless Skin

Cryotherapy—freezing the darker area—is sometimes used by doctors to treat liver spots. Personally, I've seen more spots worsened than helped by freezing; the freezing inflames the skin and further darkens the problematic area.

You can also choose laser treatment. But, as with freezing, postinflammatory hyperpigmentation is a possibility.

I think the safest, most reliable treatment for liver spots is bleaching. And the newest FDA-approved prescription treatment for bleaching liver spots is Solagé.

This prescription topical treatment—a liquid with an applicator—is a combination of 0.01% tretinoin (a vitamin A derivative) and 2% mequinol (a derivative of hydroquinone, one of the most effective and popular prescription bleaching ingredients). Solagé is applied to the age spot twice a day. You may see lightening in four to six months, though results can take up to a year.

Using an SPF 30 sunscreen is a must to protect the area while you use Solagé (or any other bleaching treatments) and to help keep spots from returning.

Solagé shouldn't be used by those taking drugs that increase their sensitivity to the sun, who have a family history of vitiligo (a pigmentation condition), or who are pregnant or nursing.

DERMAdoctor Immaculate Correction provides effective skin lightening for liver spots in a two-part process. It uses botanically derived skin brighteners that are related to hydroquinone but don't have its potential side effects (like increasing the darkness or irritation), and that also hasten cellular turnover rate. This eliminates pools of pigment already in the epidermis *and* stops pigment from forming and worsening discoloration.

(For self-care advice on how to reduce skin discoloration with bleaching, please read the chapter "Melasma" (Mask of Pregnancy) on page 158. For more tips on preventing liver spots and other types of sun damage to the skin, please refer to the chapter "Sunscreens and Sun Protection" on page 359.)

SEBORRHEIC KERATOSES: BARNACLES OF LIFE

Often referred to as "barnacles of life," "wisdom spots," "age spots," or even (mistakenly) "senile warts," seborrheic keratoses (SKs) are the most common noncancerous growth associated with aging skin. SKs form within the epidermis, the outermost layer of the skin. And while considered annoying and unsightly, SKs may not be so "senile" after all. A study of Australians showed that a surprising 23.5 percent of those between the ages of fifteen and thirty had at least one SK. But, overall, statistics do support the concept that SKs are more common among the older set. Another study of Australians revealed that by age seventy-five, 100 percent of those examined sported at least one SK.

Seborrheic keratoses certainly aren't limited to those living Down Under. Similar U.S. studies suggest that, given enough time, everyone will find an SK lurking on their skin. And gender plays no favorites: men and women are equally affected.

The Superficial Skin Growth

Seborrheic keratoses can develop anywhere on the body, but the upper chest, back, neckline, and forehead frequently grow a barnacle or two. SKs are often thick, bulky, and waxy. They're also incredibly superficial—they look as if you could slip a fingernail beneath one and pull it off. (You can, but you shouldn't—you could bleed and create a scar.) Other than those characteristics, their appearance varies widely. They can be large (about the size of a quarter) or small (a couple of millimeters in diameter), single or multiple, and they come in a multitude of hues, from golden brown to black.

Because of this wide color palette, diagnosis can sometimes be tricky. It is not uncommon for a dermatologist to biopsy a dark growth for melanoma—and later hear the good news that it was really an SK in disguise.

Seborrheic keratoses are usually symptom-free. But because they rise above the skin's surface, they can become irritated, resulting in redness, tenderness, itching, or infection.

Variations on a Theme

There are two common subtypes of seborrheic keratoses.

Stucco Keratoses. These are barely raised SKs of the lower legs, often multiple and randomly arrayed, like paint splatters on the skin. They are commonly pale brown, grayish, or flesh toned. Stucco keratoses most commonly plague seniors. Are these actually warts in sheep's clothing? While it is not thought that HPV (human papillomavirus, the cause of warts) has anything to do with the formation of "normal" seborrheic keratoses, in at least a few instances HPV has been identified in stucco keratoses. In a study reported in the *British Journal of Dermatology*, several variants of HPV were detected in the stucco keratoses of a seventy-five-year-old man. His skin was fully cleared by the use of an antiwart medication: 5% Imiquimod cream, applied overnight three times a week for five weeks. This is certainly an "off-label" treatment worth talking to your dermatologist about if you have a recalcitrant form of this condition.

Dermatosis Papulosa Nigra (DPN). African-Americans tend to develop a variant of seborrheic keratosis called dermatosis papulosa nigra. DPNs are small and dark and often hang by a stalk. Most DPNs are found on the upper face, particularly the apples of the cheeks and the temples. Like other SKs, there can be a few small growths or multiple large lesions. DPNs tend to form earlier in life than other types of SKs.

DPNs respond nicely to a very light electrodesiccation and curettage (burning and scraping). However, I highly recommend that a small procedure be performed in a test area before widespread treatment is attempted, and that the test area be as far from the middle of the face as possible. Skin discoloration is a risk associated with this procedure, and it's more likely to develop on darker skin. This postinflammatory color change can be lighter or darker than the natural skin tone. Performing a preliminary trial in a hidden area helps you avoid unsightly results if the worst should happen.

Trigger Factors

Medical science hasn't discovered the reason why seborrheic keratoses develop, but research has provided insight into potential triggers.

Sunlight. There is no question that SKs develop more commonly on skin exposed to the sun. And SKs that form in sun-drenched areas tend to be larger and more numerous than those that arise in zones hidden from the light of day. Even more fascinating, we're now seeing an increased rate of SK formation that parallels the increase in the rate of skin cancer. So it seems that sunlight may indeed play some as yet unknown role in anyone genetically predisposed to the formation of SKs.

Genetics. Genetics definitely plays a role for those who grow more than their fair share of seborrheic keratoses. While some of us worry that we've inherited our mother's thighs, our father's nose, or our grandmother's thin hair, I have often wondered if SKs would be the bane of my skin's existence. Let's just say that the maternal side of my family leaves much to be desired in this realm. So far so good. But I'm just biding my time waiting for my share to show up.

Hormones. It's long been recognized that hormones play some role in stimulating the growth and development of SKs. Any woman who's been pregnant knows that this is a time when any of a number of unwanted skin growths may suddenly sprout, whether it's a skin tag, a cherry angioma, or an SK. There are many theories as to the link between hormones and SKs. For example, a genetically higher number of hormone receptors may exist on some people's epidermal cells.

Getting Rid of SKs

Unfortunately, there is no preventive therapy for seborrheic keratoses. No cream or pill exists that will keep SKs from forming.

Understandably, most people dislike the look of these waxy plaques and want them removed. The standard and most effective treatments are somewhat limited: they are aimed at peeling off the growths. (Cutting and stitching is reserved for biopsies, when the clinical diagnosis is unclear.)

Liquid Nitrogen. The most common method of eradicating SKs is liquid nitrogen. This is nitrogen gas that has been condensed under pressure to an extremely low temperature of approximately −196°C. It used to be that dermatologists applied liquid nitrogen with a thick cotton swab. I like applying it with the Cry-Ac, which is an insulated thermos with a power spray attachment—in other words, a spray gun. When sprayed on, the liquid nitrogen penetrates more deeply and gives a more thorough freeze. And when there are many SKs, the spray gun helps treat the growths more quickly. When dealing with a large or especially thick SK, a second treatment may be necessary.

Liquid nitrogen can produce a stinging, somewhat burning sensation. The treated area will be pink and puffy for a few days. Sometimes a blister or a scab will develop. The treated SK typically falls off within two to four weeks.

Many people ask me whether they can buy liquid nitrogen for home use. The answer is no. Liquid nitrogen is not readily available for purchase, which is just as well. This treatment needs to be handled very carefully by a physician trained in its proper use; improper use can lead to frostbite, injury to the tissue, or scar formation.

Once a seborrheic keratosis is gone, it usually doesn't grow back, but there's certainly no guarantee. And don't forget that if you're prone to forming SKs, it's more than likely that others (perhaps in another area) will spring up from time to time.

Curettage. This procedure literally scrapes off the seborrheic keratosis. The area is locally anesthetized and the SK is pulled off the skin, often with the use of electrocautery (burning the base of the growth). As this method is somewhat more invasive, I usually reserve it for very large, thick, isolated lesions. This also isn't a method that lends itself easily to the rapid removal of multiple SKs.

After the Treatment

Both liquid nitrogen and curettage can result in some remnant skin discoloration and, if the freezing is too deep or scraping is performed, a scar as well. Proper treatment with liquid nitrogen is usually well tolerated and leaves minimal surface skin changes. Residual color from the SK (often light brown) may remain after the growth has come off. After either procedure, no maintenance therapy is required, aside from commonsense wound care with hydrogen peroxide and an antibiotic ointment.

Charge It

Your medical plan may not cover the removal of seborrheic keratoses. Certainly, if there is any question regarding the true diagnosis of the growth, a biopsy should be a covered benefit, provided you've met all the requirements of your particular plan. But when it comes to anything even remotely considered "cosmetic," most medical insurance companies have drastically reduced their coverage.

They followed the lead of Medicare, which declared the removal of most benign growths "nonessential" (cosmetic), and thus a noncovered benefit. A few stray plans still offer coverage. Check with your particular insurance company. If you find yourself footing the bill, the cost shouldn't be overwhelmingly high. Removal of multiple SKs in a single session should fall somewhere between $150 and $200. Don't be shy: ask your dermatologist the price before the spraying (or other treatment) begins.

ACTINIC KERATOSES: THE MOST DANGEROUS AGE SPOTS

Actinic keratoses (AKs) are the potential precursors of squamous cell carcinoma, a type of skin cancer that originates in the epidermis. It is estimated that in at least half of the five million cases of non-melanoma skin cancer diagnosed each year, either the cancer developed from an AK or the patients had AKs. The chance of an actinic keratosis developing into a skin cancer is estimated at between 10 and 25 percent. And the growth is very common: approximately 50 percent of Americans over the age of fifty have AKs.

AKs are very slow growing; they develop from prolonged, cumulative sun damage over the course of a lifetime. They typically start appearing during one's late forties, becoming increasingly more common with each decade. However, with the advent of tanning beds and increased sun worshiping, I have seen AKs develop on young adults in their early twenties. The actinic keratosis is often felt before it's seen, first appearing as an area with a persistent rough texture and eventually becoming a visible, reddish-brown, scaly patch.

Easy Come, Not So Easy Go

AKs come and AKs seem to go, in a normal cycle of periodic flaking, but they always end up returning if you haven't had them treated. So don't put off your trip to the dermatologist simply because that area of roughness (present for three months or more) suddenly seems smooth. The precancerous damage is deep within the epidermis, in what is called the basal layer. The superficial scaling is simply a symptom of the damage that must be dealt with. Without treatment, the scale will return over a period of days to weeks, and the precancer may ultimately change into skin cancer.

Who's at Risk?

Sunburns lead to cellular DNA damage, setting the stage for an AK to appear. Our skin has a repair system to literally cut out the damaged

DNA and replace it with new, healthy code. But too much damage overwhelms the system.

Obviously, the lighter your skin tone, the more likely you are to sunburn and develop AKs. Redheads and fair blonds with blue eyes are notorious for developing precancerous sun damage. But anyone's skin can be damaged by the sun, regardless of their race or skin tone.

A lifelong history of exposure to the sun increases one's risk of developing an AK. This category encompasses people raised on farms, construction workers, and basically anyone who has spent a lot of time outdoors. Truck drivers, for example, are prone to AKs on the left arm and the left side of the face.

And anyone with a suppressed immune system (especially a transplant patient) is likely to see the rapid and early development of actinic damage.

The Best Treatments

Several fascinating treatments have been added to the already respectable options for eliminating actinic keratoses. Here, I'll discuss the therapy against which all other therapies are judged for effectiveness, as well as other promising treatments.

Liquid Nitrogen. Liquid nitrogen is the standard treatment for actinic keratosis. As with treating SKs, I prefer applying the liquid nitrogen with a spray gun rather than a cotton swab. A spray rapidly targets multiple spots. Treating AKs with liquid nitrogen takes some practice; if misused, the incredibly cold temperature of the liquid can cause severe dermal damage and scarring. A trained dermatologist best understands how to handle this form of therapy and is less likely to make mistakes. If you are unable to see a specialist and your primary care physician is going to use liquid nitrogen, you may want to ask how often they've performed the procedure.

The AK is sprayed lightly with the liquid nitrogen until a very slight pinkness develops around the edge. The treatment is cold and stings, but it is over quickly. After the treatment the area may be somewhat pink and puffy. Blistering or weeping of the treated site can also occur. If you absolutely have to, you can deflate the blister at the edges with a sterile needle, but don't pull off the top. Let the area dry up and heal. Keep makeup off all blisters and open wounds. Keep any open areas clean with Polysporin ointment. You may see a scab form. An AK treated with liquid nitrogen is often fully healed within two weeks.

For those with a plethora of AKs, treatment is done in sessions. It's very uncomfortable for a patient to have hundreds of AKs sprayed at once!

5-Fluorouracil. 5-fluorouracil (5-FU) is a form of chemotherapy used to fight certain cancers. It is known by a variety of names, including Efudex and Fluoroplex. Applied topically, it destroys AKs. It works by selectively inhibiting the reproduction of cancer cells in the epidermis. 5-FU is one of those therapies I keep on hand for anyone literally covered with AKs. While effective, it's not an easy treatment to tolerate. However, if an affected area has more damaged skin than normal skin showing, this type of therapy may be appropriate for you.

5-FU is available as a cream or a liquid and in a variety of strengths. It is applied by the patient, at home, twice a day for four to six weeks. When the cream is applied, protective gloves should be worn, or an applicator should be used. Since 5-FU is a chemotherapy drug, pregnant women should avoid exposure to it.

5-FU causes only the sun-damaged areas of the skin to become swollen, red, and weepy. This can be uncomfortable. It can also be quite surprising to see how much invisible sun damage is really present!

After completing your four to six weeks of therapy, use a steroid cream to quickly resolve the inflammation. (Don't use the cream during therapy; if you do, you'll reduce the effectiveness of the 5-FU.) The inflammation should go away in about two weeks. At this point, check in with your doctor to determine how well the 5-FU worked. (It's difficult to determine how thoroughly the AKs have been destroyed when the skin is red, weepy, and swollen.)

The inflammation caused by 5-FU has inspired the development of other, less irritating treatment options to deal with widespread AKs.

Levulan Kerastick. Newer therapies like the Levulan Kerastick—the culmination of years of rigorous research—are always exciting. This is a two-day, two-step photodynamic therapy for treating AKs on the face and scalp.

The first day, a chemical solution is applied to the visible AKs. The chemical—aminolevulinic acid HC (20% strength)—binds with abnormal cellular DNA, making the abnormal cells light sensitive. On the second day (ideally, about fourteen to eighteen hours after the chemical solution is applied), the treated areas are exposed to a special light for about sixteen minutes. During this photodynamic portion of the therapy, your skin may sting or burn.

Over the next few days, the AKs become dark and dry up and, ultimately, peel off. It takes four weeks for full resolution of the AKs— studies show that the treatment eliminates on average 75 percent of the growths—and full healing of the skin.

People with light sensitivity, such as those with lupus or porphyria, are not candidates for this therapy.

Solaraze. Most people are familiar with nonsteroidal anti-inflammatory drugs, or NSAIDS, like Advil, Motrin, and Naprosyn. Solaraze gel (diclofenac sodium) is the first prescription *topical* NSAID approved by the FDA for the treatment of actinic keratoses. This is an entirely new class of therapy.

Exposure to ultraviolet light increases the production of prostaglandins in the skin, which contribute to the development of actinic keratosis. Like any other NSAID, diclofenac sodium inhibits prostaglandin synthesis.

The nongreasy gel is applied twice daily for two to three months. Some of the most commonly reported side effects include peeling, dryness, irritation, and contact dermatitis. Anyone with a known allergy to NSAIDs or aspirin should not undergo this therapy.

Aldara. Aldara (imiquimod) is an immune-response modifier. Originally developed as a prescription therapy for genital warts, it has been approved by the FDA to treat AKs. The cream should be applied twice a week for sixteen weeks.

It may cause redness, itching, inflammation, blisters, scabbing, flaking, and sores. It should not be used by pregnant or nursing women.

Future Treatments
Another being evaluated for treatment of actinic keratoses is PEP005.

PEP005 modulates the levels of protein kinase C, which plays a role in cell development. It is hoped that PEP005 will thwart the formation of skin tumors. It is also being investigated as a treatment for basal cell and squamous cell carcinomas.

Celecoxib is a Cox-2 inhibitor used to treat arthritis. The Cox-2 enzyme is produced by inflammation and precancerous tissue, and researchers hope that by blocking it they will be able to stop further progression of precancerous growths or treat those already present.

FINAL THOUGHTS

If an AK is beginning to itch or bleed, it's possible that a squamous cell carcinoma is beginning to form. Another telltale sign is marked thickening of the AK, known as hyperkeratosis. And I often consider the possibility of a malignancy if the AK remains resistant to aggressive treatment. At any of these points, it's time to perform a biopsy.

Depending on the extent of actinic damage, I will recheck these patients anywhere from every eight to twelve weeks to one or two times a year.

And for all AK patients, I stress the importance of having a complete skin exam by your dermatologist. Where there's enough sun damage to create actinic damage, other potential skin cancers and abnormal moles may arise. I usually recommend that this be done once a year or more, depending on the type of changes the patients is experiencing.

Ask the DERMAdoctor

QUESTION:

I have actinic keratosis on my face and hands. I have tried liquid nitrogen treatments and 5-fluorouracil to combat the problem. Are there other options?

The DERMAdoctor:

A technique called the fluorhydroxyacid peel has been shown to be very helpful in the treatment of diffuse actinic damage. It uses a glycolic acid peel, such as M.D. Forté, along with 5-FU (discussed earlier in this chapter). The peel is performed as a series of six to twelve treatments in the physician's office. First, a 70% glycolic acid peel is left on the skin for six minutes. After it is neutralized with water, a single application of 5% 5-FU cream is applied. I will advance to a 99% concentration of glycolic acid compound peel if the first six sessions do not give adequate results and, if needed, will sometimes extend the length of time the glycolic acid is left on.

The beauty of this procedure is that the patient experiences almost no irritation, and studies show that the results are better than when using the 5-FU alone. The procedure is so well tolerated and the patient's skin looks so normal afterward that no one can tell you just had the peel done until the positive results begin to show. Unfortunately, if your medical insurance doesn't cover liquid nitrogen treatments for AKs, it probably won't cover this peel. I have, however, fought with insurance companies and won when it came to treating certain high-risk patients.

CELLULITE

Are There Really Any Cures?

It's hardly fair. Between 80 and 90 percent of women will develop cellulite after the age of eighteen. Few men will. Why isn't Mother Nature on *our* side?

Cellulite is caused by a variety of factors. Some of them are particular to women, like female hormones, and possibly a different structure in the architecture of our fat layer. Add genetics and aging, and you've got an incurable situation. You can't *cure* cellulite, no matter what you've read, seen on TV, or purchased. But you can *improve* that unsightly puckering—by understanding what causes cellulite and influencing the factors that are under your control.

SHEDDING LIGHT ON CELLULITE

Cellulite is an unattractive dimpling and puckering of the skin, usually on the thighs and buttocks. While most women carry their weight gain in these areas, you don't have to be overweight to have cellulite; you just have to age.

Collagen and elastin—bundles of protein that maintain the skin's structure—break down as we age, weakening the dermis, the deepest layer of the skin. We're all familiar with what this process does to our faces: wrinkles. On the legs and buttocks, this loss of dermal elasticity allows sections of fat to move into the lower dermis, where it doesn't belong. There, fibrous bands that tether the skin to the fascia surrounding the muscle trap the displaced fat, creating the lumps and bumps we know as cellulite.

CELLULITE TREATMENTS: WHAT WORKS, WHAT DOESN'T

So how do you reduce or get rid of all that unsightly cottage cheese sitting on your thighs? Does anything *really* work to change the appearance of cellulite? Happily, the answer is yes.

Endermologie

So far, the government's Food and Drug Administration has approved only one treatment for cellulite: a form of machine-assisted deep massage called Endermologie, which provides a temporary improvement in its appearance. Endermologie came to the United States from France, where it has been used since the 1980s. In 1999, in a study that was widely publicized, researchers at Vanderbilt University reported that this procedure dispersed trapped fat and helped improve the structure of the skin.

An Endermologie machine rolls and sucks the skin in a vacuum-like manner. This loosens or breaks down some of the fibrous bands and disperses the lumps of fat into a smooth layer.

Typically, anywhere from fifteen to twenty forty-five-minute treatments are needed to achieve whatever the maximum effects will be; then you undergo periodic maintenance therapy every four to six weeks. (Unfortunately a single "emergency" treatment for a special occasion is unlikely to do much for your cellulite.) The cost for a full series of treatments is well over $1,000; maintenance treatments are about $100 each.

No treatment is guaranteed, of course—especially when it comes to cellulite. But Endermologie, combined with a good diet and regular exercise (which keeps your body trimmer and the cellulite less visible) and adequate daily water intake (which also diminishes dimpling) can help many women improve the look of their cellulite.

Home Massage

Another study from researchers at Vanderbilt, published in the *Journal of Plastic and Reconstructive Surgery,* showed that deep massage with handheld mechanical devices (not endermologie) can help improve the appearance of cellulite. Although the results were highly dependent upon the skill of the masseuse, this sparked a huge interest in home massage techniques for eliminating cellulite.

A variety of massage tools—devices with rubber tips, wooden balls, and motorized massagers—are sold with the claim that they can help improve the appearance of cellulite. They tend to be inexpensive; less than ten dollars for the wooden balls, for example.

I take a realistic view of these devices. While I don't think they will harm you (provided you're not applying pressure to the point of bruising), it's unlikely that they will provide more than limited improvement. Still, a modicum of improvement, if it happens, is better than none at all. From a practical standpoint, I think you may increase your chances of success by having someone else administer the home massage; another person can apply more direct pressure on the skin.

Body Brushing

Spas have taken the idea of deep massage for cellulite in a slightly different direction, offering a Japanese treatment known as body brushing. In this technique, a plant-based (usually coconut-husk) bristle brush is roughly moved across the skin's surface, in an attempt to exfoliate the outermost portions of the epidermis. The theory: increase blood flow and lymphatic drainage, thus removing toxins from the skin and improving the appearance of cellulite. The reality: this makes absolutely no physiological sense.

While you may find that your skin takes on a nice glowing appearance (similar to what you'd see after a microdermabrasion treatment), neither increased blood flow nor lymphatic drainage has any bearing whatsoever upon the causes of cellulite. Enjoy the treatment for what it is, but don't expect to transform those lumpy legs.

Cellulite Creams and Pills

There are many cellulite creams out there; most of them contain the active ingredient theophylline, which is best known as an asthma medication. The topical application of theophylline doesn't cure cellulite, but it does temporarily plump up the skin for a few hours, creating a smoother texture.

As for pills: the Federal Trade Commission charged that the maker of Cellasene (the most widely promoted anticellulite pill) made unsubstantiated claims about the product's ability to eliminate or reduce cellulite.

Topical Vitamin C

The dermis thins with age, contributing to the formation of cellulite. Theoretically, strengthening it should prevent or improve the problem.

Studies show that topical L-ascorbic acid (vitamin C) stimulates fibroblasts, cells in the dermis, to produce collagen. Cellex-C Body Smoothing Lotion is one vitamin C–containing product that can help rejuvenate the skin and may help improve the appearance of cellulite.

You shouldn't think of this or any product as "the cure" for cellulite. But used in combination with other treatments—deep massage or endermologie; a well-rounded diet; plenty of water; regular exercise (including weight training for toning)—it might at least help make your skin look smoother and more supple, the same way that L-ascorbic acid helps with puffiness and fine lines on the face and neck.

FINAL THOUGHTS

In a way, it's comforting to know that almost all women get cellulite to some degree. It seems to be one of those sisterhood things. It's equally comforting to know that there are some steps we can all take to help improve its appearance.

Ask the DERMAdoctor

QUESTION:

I have seen a new product advertised for cellulite that contains caffeine, along with retinol and seaweed extract. Do you think this would cure cellulite?

The DERMAdoctor:

Caffeine is often incorporated into skin care products to help temporarily reduce the swelling of the skin. Retinol, a vitamin A derivative, helps soften and smooth the skin. (Be aware that it can increase your risk of sunburn, so wear a sunscreen with SPF 30 or greater when out in the sun.) Will such a product cure you of cellulite? Probably not, in my opinion. Will it temporarily help improve the appearance of your skin? Possibly.

CHAPPED LIPS

Restore the Moisture, Discover the Cause

A dermatologist knows it's officially winter when everyone starts complaining about cheilitis (a.k.a. chapped lips). But while there is no question that cold weather and windy conditions play a big role in chapping, you might be surprised to learn that numerous everyday products (like toothpaste) and various medical conditions (like a yeast infection) can also be to blame.

So if you find yourself in a never-ending battle with chapping, before you simply open up a fresh Chap Stick, take a closer look at *why* you have chapped lips in the first place.

BABY, IT'S COLD OUTSIDE

Cold weather chapping is caused by environmental conditions that result in dehydration. When lips are too dry, the painful cracking and peeling begin. So the first brisk day should act as the perfect reminder that reasonable, consistent use of a protective balm can prevent your lips from drying out in the first place.

That's right: your Chap Stick or other wax-based lip balm is something you should apply *before* you've got problems. Think about it. How much moisture does a tube of wax give your lips? Very little. Wax is a protective barrier, not a healing agent.

If you start the winter with healthy lips, a wax-based balm can keep them that way. So can a moisture-rich lipstick, ointment, or gloss that is applied several times a day.

DERMAdoctor Poutlandish Hyper Moisturizing Lip Paint &

Treatment SPF with Nanotechnology is such a product. It can protect your lips. But, more important, it can also rapidly heal lips that have already become dry, cracked, and chapped—even lips that are scaly because of Accutane use.

EMOLLIENTS TO THE RESCUE

Emollients—like Vaseline, Aquaphor Healing Ointment, and English Ideas Lip Solution Hydrating Lip Gel—are an option for restoring moisture to parched areas of dried-out lips. But in order for them to work, you need to apply them obsessively. And I do mean *obsessively*. The more frequent the application of the emollient, the faster your results.

BEYOND OTC

For resistant cases of dehydrated lips, I like to prescribe 2.5% hydrocortisone ointment, which can be applied as often as three or four times a day, if needed. It's amazing how adding a low-potency steroid ointment can make such a big difference in a lip-healing regimen.

In an extreme case, I will prescribe higher-potency topical steroid ointments, but never for more than a week or two. Steroid ointments don't taste good, but a little won't harm you. However, common sense tells us that consuming large quantities of hydrocortisone ointment—something that might happen were you to use the ointment year-round—isn't appropriate. When it comes to chapping, topical steroids are a short-term fix, not meant for continuous use.

DERMADOCTOR, P.I.

There are many (many!) possible causes of chronically chapped lips. Medical sleuthing is never easy, but the ideas in this chapter may help you discover the culprit. (In fact, after reading the chapter you may know more than your doctor when it comes to pinpointing possible causes of chronic cheilitis!)

Here's a very important point to remember when figuring out the cause of cheilitis: a substance that produces a red, blistery, itchy rash on your skin may simply cause routine chapping and cracking on your lips. This is certainly true with a contact allergy (an allergy to something that touches the skin) and phototoxicity (a skin reaction to an ingredient that occurs only when skin is exposed to sunlight).

Your Cheilitis Checklist

Lipstick. The ingredient propyl gallate in lipstick can cause a contact allergy.

Other Lip Care Products. Phenylsalicylate (salol), an ingredient in lip-care products, can be the culprit.

Toothpaste. Your toothpaste may be to blame if it contains guaiazulene, which can cause a contact allergy.

Also check the ingredient label on your toothpaste for sodium lauryl sulfate (SLS). This substance has been blamed for chapped lips, as well as skin irritation and even perioral dermatitis (a rash around the mouth). Avoiding sodium lauryl sulfate can often help clear up a case of chapped lips. Squigle Enamel Saver Toothpaste is SLS-free.

Red Dye. An allergy to the red dyes used in candy, mouthwash, toothpaste, and other substances can be the cause.

Cinnamon Flavoring. On the same note, cinnamates (for cinnamon flavor) used in candy, lozenges, gum, mouthwash, and toothpaste can cause chapping.

Gums. Check for periodontal disease or abscesses. There are scientific reports that deep cleansing of the mouth performed by the dentist (possibly under anesthesia) may help solve the problem.

Orange Juice. The juice from citrus fruits can irritate your lips and cause a phototoxic reaction that looks like chapped lips.

Figs. Eating this fruit can sometimes result in phototoxicity.

Medications. The blood pressure medication Inderal (propranolol) can cause cheilitis as a side effect, as can Stemetil (prochlorperazine), a medication for vertigo.

Vitamin A. Too much vitamin A, whether from nutritional supplements, prescription medications like Accutane or Soriatane, or foods (like carrot juice), can lead to peeling lips. Check the label on your supplement. If you're taking more than 25,000 I.U. a day, you may have found your cause.

Vitamin B$_{12}$ Supplements. You can develop an allergy to cobalt from taking vitamin B$_{12}$ supplements. It usually shows itself as unexplained episodes of recurrent swelling and crusting of the lips, made worse by wind and sun exposure. *Important:* you can have a negative patch test to vitamin B$_{12}$ even if you have a cobalt allergy.

Paper Clips. An allergy to nickel can show itself on the lips, too. (For more information on this allergy, please see the chapter "Contact Allergies" on page 53.) Remember, don't put metallic items like paper clips in your mouth!

Clarinet. Clarinet players can develop chapping at the spot where the lip contacts the reed.

Medical Conditions That Can Cause Chapping

Actinic Cheilitis. Years in the sun can cause this type of precancerous change in the lips. Treatment with Efudex, a topical chemotherapy medication, can clear it up.

Candida Infection (Yeast). Is there scaling and cracking at the angles of your mouth? This is known as perlèche and may be due to a candida infection (yeast), which could involve the rest of the lips as well. Treatment with Nystatin Oral Suspension, an oral antiyeast preparation, can solve the problem. Diabetics are particularly prone to this condition, which may be recurrent.

Cheilitis Granulomatosa. This rare chapping condition may require a biopsy for diagnosis.

Down Syndrome. These patients have a genetic predisposition to chapped lips. Treatment with a thyroid supplement and potent topical steroid ointments can clear the condition.

Lupus (and Other Autoimmune Diseases). Do you have lupus or a history of autoimmune disease? Photosensitivity may present itself on your lips. Use a lip treatment that includes an SPF of at least 15, such as DERMAdoctor Poutlandish SPF 15.

Psoriasis or Lichen Planus. Very rarely, either of these two skin conditions can involve the lips. If the scale and crusting are particularly thick, one of these conditions could be the culprit.

Sjögren's Syndrome. Are your eyes and mouth dry? You may have an autoimmune condition known as Sjögren's syndrome, which can also cause dry lips.

Snoring. Do you snore? That continuous flow of breath across your lips all night long—caused by enlarged tonsils, adenoids, or sleep apnea—can grossly dehydrate your lips. If you don't know if you snore, it may be worthwhile to have someone check on you periodically during the night to find out. Come bedtime, consider applying a protective barrier like SBR-Lipocream Skin Barrier Repair Cream to your lips, and station a humidifier in your bedroom.

Stress. Do you respond to stress by habitually licking or chewing your lips? Continuous contact with saliva—which is chemically constituted to help break down and digest food—can dehydrate and irritate the lips. Many people are totally unaware of this habit; sometimes it even occurs during sleep. If you're uncertain, be candid with family and friends and ask them if you lick or chew your lips constantly. Have a family member check you periodically when you sleep, too. Sometimes antidepressants or relaxing medications can help solve the problem. Often, simple awareness of the situation will go a long way to helping someone kick the habit.

Thyroid Disease. Do you have a history of thyroid disease? Hypothyroidism can cause dry skin and lips.

AT THE DOCTOR'S

Still haven't discovered the cause? It's time to make an appointment with your dermatologist for further workup. In the interim, follow this list of don'ts:

Don't hold metal objects (such as paper clips) in your mouth.

Don't lick envelopes.

Don't suck on orange peels or other citrus-fruit rinds.

Don't kiss someone on the lips who is wearing lipstick.

And, finally, don't lose hope!

Once you're at the doctor's, make sure that you give your physician a good, thorough history and that you get a full examination of the mouth, lips, tongue, tonsils, and even elbows, knees, scalp, and nails (to see if you have psoriasis). You should also see that your lab workup includes the following tests:

- KOH for yeast
- Patch testing, to rule out contact allergies
- Blood testing, to rule out lupus
- Vitamin A level
- Thyroid test
- Lupus test (photosensitivity reaction)
- Throat culture, for strep

If nothing surfaces in your workup, be prepared—your doctor may put you through the paces of eliminating foods and personal care products from your routine to see if any of them is the cause of the chapping.

When all else fails, an excisional wedge biopsy may be required to diagnose the condition. Make sure your doctor is experienced at this procedure. You want to make sure that the lip gets put back together perfectly, without a notch left in the vermilion border (red edge) of the juncture between the lip and the skin.

FINAL THOUGHTS
Chapped lips can be a challenge. But again, don't lose hope. The reward for your patience and persistence can be moist, smooth lips.

Ask the DERMAdoctor

QUESTION:

I stopped taking the antiacne medication Accutane more than seven months ago, but I still suffer constantly from very dry, chapped lips. What can I do?

The DERMAdoctor:

It is unlikely that Accutane could permanently damage your lips. It is much more likely that your lips got out of control while you were on Accutane, which is very drying, and have not been given enough help to heal. (Or, although it's improbable, another drying condition may have occurred during this time.) Ask your dermatologist if it is appropriate for you to use prescription strength 2.5% hydrocortisone ointment several times a day for a few weeks. This should help solve the problem. In addition, use emollients like DERMAdoctor Poutlandish clear or Aquaphor Healing Ointment.

COLD SORES

Stop or Shorten the Outbreak

Who can forget their first bout of cold sores—those swollen, painful, oozing blisters that popped up on your lip during childhood. (And seemed to reappear during your teen years before just about every big date!)

Cold sores, also known as fever blisters, are caused by an infection by the herpes simplex virus (HSV). Patients often want to know whether they're infected with HSV-1 (the viral subtype usually associated with cold sores on the lip) or HSV-2 (the subtype linked to genital herpes). But with today's sexual mores and the fact that the virus can be transmitted by any skin-to-skin contact—a kiss on the cheek or a kiss in the bedroom—you're just as likely to be infected with HSV-2 as with HSV-1. Since the treatment is the same for both subtypes, it isn't worth dwelling on which you have. Instead, concern yourself with your primary goal: getting rid of the cold sore as quickly as possible and preventing new outbreaks.

You can never be completely cured of cold sores; once infected with herpes, you stay infected for life. The viral particles remain within the nerve endings that supply the infected location, which is why the sore always recurs in the same place. Whenever a patient says that the sore comes up in different locations each time, it tells me one of two things: either she is dealing with more than one infected site, or she doesn't have herpes.

THE FIRST IS THE WORST
The first eruption of a herpes blister (or blisters) can be quite swollen and painful. And it's sometimes accompanied by other symptoms, like

swollen lymph nodes, a low-grade fever, or a general feeling of illness. Fortunately, these symptoms—including the degree of swelling and pain in and around the blisters themselves—don't typically occur with subsequent eruptions.

A TYPICAL OUTBREAK

After the first eruption, subsequent outbreaks are usually triggered by a cold (hence the term "cold sore"), sunlight, stress, or hormonal changes, like your period. If you can control these trigger factors, you can limit outbreaks. Colds, stress, and fluctuating hormones are next to impossible to prevent. But you can control sunlight exposure—and minimize sunlight-induced cold sores—by using sun-protective lip products, like DERMAdoctor Poutlandish, or your favorite wax-based lip balm with SPF 15.

If, in spite of your best efforts, you get an outbreak, one or more blisters will usually form on the outer edge of the lip, an area dermatologists call the vermilion border. Or they can occur nearby. (An ulceration inside the mouth—on the gums, the tongue, or the inner mucosal lining of the lip—is not a cold sore. It is usually an aphthous ulcer, or canker sore, which is caused by stress.)

Many people notice an itching, tingling, or burning sensation that precedes the herpes blister by a few hours or days. This is called a *prodrome*. Recognizing the unique symptoms of your prodrome can cue you to start HSV medication even before a blister erupts. For most people, starting medication early can completely block an outbreak. (More about those medications in a minute.)

Once the prodrome is over, a blister arises, usually on a red base and filled with clear fluid. Or there can be a cluster of blisters. The fluid in the blister can ooze, and the blister can pop before the last phase begins, when the blister dries, crusts, and forms a scab. Eventually, the scab falls off. From blister to complete clearing, an outbreak can last up to three weeks.

ARE YOU INFECTIOUS?

Herpes simplex on the skin or mouth doesn't shed viral particles without the presence of a blister, so when you don't have a cold sore you're not contagious. When you *do* have a cold sore, you're contagious until the blister is completely dried out. To prevent infecting others, wash your hands frequently, avoid kissing, and don't share drinking cups.

Frequent washing of your hands will also minimize the risk of autoinoculation—spreading the infection to other parts of your body. Autoinoculation of the eyes is extremely serious, as it can lead to blindness. If you think HSV is affecting your eyes, contact a doctor immediately, preferably an ophthalmologist.

THE BEST ORAL MEDICATIONS

The standard medical treatment for a cold sore is a pill called Zovirax (acyclovir). You take the drug at the first sign of a cold sore—either a prodrome or that cold sore you found sitting on your lip when you woke up. The typical dose is 200 milligrams five times a day, for five days. For a first outbreak, which is frequently more symptomatic and difficult to control, the medication is taken for ten days.

Zovirax doesn't usually cause any side effects in healthy people. However, I always recommend that eight ounces of water be taken along with each pill, to wash it through the kidneys. And anyone prone to kidney dysfunction should take a lower dose. As with most medications, don't take Zovirax during pregnancy.

Zovirax is available topically, but I've never found it to be very effective; I recommend going straight to the pill. It is also available intravenously for serious, systemic infections of herpes, and as a syrup for children.

Other medications for the treatment of HSV include Famvir (famciclovir) and Valtrex (valacyclovir). Both of these medications are metabolized to acyclovir during the absorption process, but they have an advantage over acyclovir: they're better absorbed. That means you don't need to take them as frequently.

You and your doctor will need to determine which of these medications is best for you. A patient may discover that one drug works better than another; some options are contraindicated for people with certain diseases; and insurance may cover one but not another.

TOPICAL TREATMENTS THAT WORK

Denavir (penciclovir cream) is a prescription antiviral cream approved by the FDA for the treatment of cold sores. It can speed the healing of cold sores by about a day. It also stops viral shedding and reduces pain.

Start the cream within one hour of noticing symptoms—whether the prodrome or the sore itself—and continue using it for four days, applying it every two hours while awake.

Denavir is a good option if for some reason you can't take Zovi-rax, Famvir, or Valtrex. However, many of my patients find it difficult to stick with the every-two-hour regimen.

A Nonprescription Option

Maybe you're getting a cold sore—you've got a prodrome, or a sore popped up before you had a chance to treat it—and you don't have a prescription medication on hand or time to get to a doctor. Then get to a drugstore.

An over-the-counter topical medication called Abreva can help get rid of a cold sore. It contains docosanol, an ingredient that helps stop the spread of the herpes infection from cell to cell. Use it at the first sign of tingling, itching, or burning, or to help heal a cold sore that's already there. Apply Abreva five times a day, either until the pro-drome is gone or the cold sore dries and crusts and the scab falls off.

While using Abreva or any cold sore medication, using Domeboro Astringent Solution helps the blistered area dry out rapidly. I also rec-ommend applying a topical antibiotic ointment like Polysporin oint-ment, which helps prevent secondary bacterial infection of the sore. (Many people carry *Staphylococcus aureus* bacteria in their nasal pas-sages, which can contaminate an open sore.)

HELP FOR CHRONIC COLD SORES

A cold sore every once in a while is a nuisance. A cold sore every month (or more) is a nightmare. It's amazing how much these fre-quent outbreaks can affect your lifestyle, creating social unease, pre-venting intimacy, and wearing you out with physical discomfort.

If you have one or more outbreaks a month, consider mainte-nance therapy—taking a low daily dose of acyclovir or a similar antiviral drug to prevent cold sores.

For some people, cold sores trigger other skin problems, like ery-thema nodosum (red lumps), erythema multiforme (a targetlike skin rash), or hives. Maintenance therapy is a great way to stop these sec-ondary (but extremely bothersome) skin problems.

FINAL THOUGHTS

Your cold isn't the real reason for that cold sore; the herpes simplex virus is. Medical science now offers several effective therapies to keep cold sores away and your lips looking their most kissable.

Ask the DERMAdoctor

QUESTION:

I've read that taking a supplement of the amino acid L-lysine might stop my cold sores from coming back. Is that true?

The DERMAdoctor:

There have been few rigorous studies to determine the actual effectiveness of this popular natural approach to preventing or treating cold sores. However, it's unlikely that you'll hurt yourself by taking the nutrient, following the dosage recommendations on the supplement label. But use a well-known national brand. About a decade ago a bad batch of L-tryptophan (an amino acid used for mood disorders) caused several deaths in the Michigan area.

QUESTION:

I think I get cold sores on my lips, but my boyfriend says he's seen cold sores before and I don't have them. Is there a test that a doctor can do to tell if what I've got is really a cold sore or not?

The DERMAdoctor:

The Tzanck prep is a microscopic test done by a dermatologist right in the office. It is simple to perform, easily tolerated by the patient, and the results are immediate. A blister is opened, the base is gently scraped, and the fluid is applied to a glass slide. The slide is stained and examined for the presence of multinucleated giant cells, the hallmark of a HSV infection. Unfortunately, the government now requires doctors to complete costly licensing and labor-intensive paperwork in order to perform this simple test. So fewer dermatologists are willing to offer the test in their offices. A viral culture can be done instead to verify the diagnosis, but results can take a few weeks.

CONTACT ALLERGIES

Patch Testing: The Key to Control

You no doubt know somebody who is allergic to a common allergen like pollen, mold, or grass. But do you know someone who is allergic to their wedding ring, a yellow marking pen, or cement?

Well, those objects (and many more) can be responsible for a case of *contact allergy*—an allergic reaction to a substance that comes in contact with the skin. The condition is also called *contact dermatitis*. (*Dermatitis* is a term dermatologists use for inflamed skin.) In contact dermatitis, the skin becomes red and rough, possibly with scaling, cracking, and weeping. Sometimes there are tiny, fluid-containing blisters. And it's likely to itch.

A seemingly endless variety of substances can cause contact dermatitis. Patch testing is one of the most effective techniques a dermatologist can use to determine what's really happening to a patient with a chronic skin eruption that resembles contact dermatitis.

Patch testing helps a dermatologist diagnose whether you really have contact dermatitis. (Sometimes it's difficult to distinguish between contact dermatitis and other types of skin inflammation, like eczema and psoriasis.) Patch testing also helps the doctor figure out exactly what you're allergic to.

THE T.R.U.E. TEST PATCH TEST
Patch testing used to be a time-consuming and cumbersome process, and many dermatologists had stopped performing it—until the T.R.U.E. Test Patch Test kit became available. This type of patch test is easy for a doctor to give and a patient to take.

Twenty-three of the most common chemicals that cause contact dermatitis are contained in individual wells imbedded on two pieces of tape. The tapes are applied to the upper back and left in place. Typically, patches are applied on a Monday, removed and read for the first time on Wednesday (forty-eight hours after the initial application), then reapplied; a final reading is performed on Friday (ninety-six hours after the initial application). Redness, puffiness, and occasional blistering, when found in alignment with the location of a specific allergen, signal a positive reaction.

(Remember: patch testing is *not* the scratch testing usually performed in an allergist's office. Patch testing searches for an allergic reaction that is limited to the skin; scratch testing looks for the source of a systemic allergic reaction, to substances such as grass, molds, pollen or penicillin.)

A STRATEGY FOR BEST RESULTS

To obtain the best results from a patch test, follow these guidelines:

The area of the back where the patches will be applied must stay dry for the four days (that's ninety-six hours) during the test. You can wash around the areas. So plan your hygiene ahead: shower before you're scheduled to see the doctor for the patch test. And no swimming!

Avoid the use of systemic steroids within six weeks of patch testing—no prednisone, Medrol dose packs, or steroid shots. And don't apply any topical steroid to the patch-test area during the duration of the test. Steroids reduce inflammation, so you're less likely to react to a chemical, even if you're allergic to it.

Don't take oral antihistamines (Benadryl, Claritin, Atarax, etc.) during patch testing. They, too, will decrease your likelihood of a positive reaction to a chemical in the test. Ideally, you should also minimize their use for at least a week preceding the test.

THE 23 LEAST WANTED

Below is a list of the twenty-three ingredients found in the T.R.U.E. Test patches. They account for approximately 70 percent of all cases of contact dermatitis.

nickel sulfate	epoxy resin
wool alcohols	carba mix

neomycin sulfate	black rubber mix
potassium dichromate	Cl+Me–isothiazolinone
caine mix	quaternium-15
fragrance mix	mercaptobenzothiazole
colophony	*p*-phenylenediamine
paraben mix	formaldehyde
cobalt dichloride	mercapto mix
balsam of Peru	thimerosal
ethylenediamine dihydrochloride	thiuram mix
p-tert-butylphenol formaldehyde resin	

If the test fails to reveal a contact dermatitis to any of those twenty-three chemicals, a more involved workup is the likely next step. For example, I had a patient who didn't respond to any of the chemicals used in the patch test—but more extensive testing revealed that she was allergic to the cayenne pepper in the spicy fried chicken batter used at the restaurant where she worked. Another woman was allergic to the yellow fluorescent Magic Marker used in the patch testing. (This was a crucial discovery, because it turned out that her boss used a yellow highlighter on every piece of paper in the office.) Other patients have had allergies to various components of cement.

I was able to help these patients figure out what their allergen was; others required a referral to a specialist in contact dermatitis.

AVOIDING YOUR ALLERGENS

Avoidance is the best way to treat a contact allergy. In other words, stay away from what you're allergic to! That's easier said than done, however. If you are allergic to one or more of the chemicals in the patch test, how do you know *exactly* which objects and substances to avoid? It is amazing how many different names a single chemical can go by and the wide array of different products that can contain it.

These issues are why I am a strong proponent of the T.R.U.E. Test. For every allergen in the test, the manufacturer has prepared an information sheet that discusses the various names the chemical may

NICKEL ALLERGY: RING AROUND THE FINGER

Have you ever worn a new pair of earrings and found that, after a week, your earlobes itched endlessly? What about your gold wedding ring? After years of wedded bliss, has the skin in contact with the ring suddenly developed redness, scaling, weeping, and itching? Perhaps an allergy to nickel is to blame.

Nickel allergy—a form of contact dermatitis—is a common reaction to minute amounts of nickel particles coming into direct contact with the skin. Culprits may include jewelry, watches, zippers, snaps, and eyeglasses. Even "good" gold or silver jewelry can be to blame; *all* metallic jewelry contains some small percentage of nickel. And the longer you wear a good piece of jewelry, the more the microscopic "good" metal molecules are worn away, exposing the nickel molecules to the skin. This is how you can suddenly become allergic to an object you've worn "forever."

Because women tend to wear more jewelry, particularly costume jewelry, which has a high nickel contact, the fairer sex is more frequently affected. When men experience nickel dermatitis, it is often through occupational exposure.

YOUR OPTIONS

Nail Polish. Apply a coat of clear nail polish to the contact surface of the ring. Nail polish periodically flakes off, so perform maintenance touch-ups. Use a formaldehyde-free polish. (You could develop a contact allergy to formaldehyde. If the rash worsens, discontinue use.)

Dry Skin. Keep your skin dry where metal contacts you. Placing your hands into a sink full of water, for example, allows the metal ions to penetrate more deeply into the skin. And perspiration hastens the rate at which "good" metal particles of gold and silver wear away, exposing the nickel.

Moisturizing Cream. Wear a good layer of protective, bland moisturizing cream, like Triceram, Nouriva Repair moisturizing cream, or TheraSeal Hand Protection. The better the barrier between you and the metal, the less likely it is that the reaction will occur.

Steroid Cream. Try a mild over-the-counter 1% hydrocortisone cream under the metal, when needed. Steroids that are applied beneath jewelry may be driven more deeply into the skin, posing the risk of undesirable skin atrophy. If you plan to wear that ring or bracelet or earrings, don't apply a more potent prescription-strength steroid first. Use it later.

Electroplating. Take the offending piece back to the jeweler and see if a new layer of "good" metal can be electroplated to the contact surface. This prevents leaching of the nickel particles onto your skin, at least for a while.

Minimize Use. Take your jewelry off when you don't absolutely need to wear it. Diminished contact with the skin decreases the amount of allergen you're exposed to.

Piercing Precautions. Nickel coming in contact with an open wound is a source of sensitization. Ear piercing, for example, can act as a major form of nickel sensitization. Use of stainless steel or medical-grade titanium earrings are vital during the ear-piercing process to reduce this risk.

Nickel-Free Earrings. Blomdahl offers earrings in both medical-grade titanium and plastic that are safe for those with a nickel dermatitis. Titanium has the smallest amount of nickel of any metal, and the titanium particles bond around any residual nickel molecules, making for a virtually nickel-free experience. Natural titanium looks much like platinum. For anyone exquisitely sensitive to nickel, Blomdahl also makes medical plastic earrings, which are entirely metal- and nickel-free. Twenty-four-karat gold plate offers another option.

Use a Home Nickel-Testing Kit. The Allertest Ni nickel-detection kit helps you avoid unnecessary, repeated exposures to nickel. The basis of the test is a chemical reaction that produces a color change in the presence of nickel. You simply apply two drops of Solution A and one drop of solution B to a cotton swab, then rub the object in question. The appearance of a strawberry-red color indicates the presence of nickel. The test is highly sensitive, detecting a concentration of only one ten-thousandth of the amount of nickel necessary to cause an allergic reaction. The Allertest Ni nickel-detection kit is an indispensable tool to keep on hand in managing nickel dermatitis.

go by; the names and types of products it is commonly found in; ingredients and compounds that may cause a cross-reaction; and product substitutes that offer a safe alternative.

You must have this information. Even the most knowledgeable dermatologist can't always remember every one of the chemical's names and all the intricacies of avoiding the products that contain it.

REDUCING THE RASH
You've discovered and are avoiding your allergen(s)—but there still may be times when you need to treat the dermatitis itself. Treatment options include topical steroids and antihistamines. An over-the-counter 1% hydrocortisone cream, like Cortaid Steroid Cream, is useful in reducing inflammation when a rash flare-up catches you unprepared.

FINAL THOUGHTS
Working up a contact dermatitis case involves some sleuthing on the part of both the patient and the dermatologist. For those inexplicable, chronic rashes, particularly when the hands are involved, ask your doctor about patch testing—it may just help solve the mystery.

Ask the DERMAdoctor

QUESTION:

I am a longtime user of brown Vaseline but can't find it anywhere. Can you tell me where to locate it?

The DERMAdoctor:

Brown, or carbolated, Vaseline was a popular product in the South, especially in the African-American community. Long used as a "medicated" form of petroleum jelly, this product contained phenol and parachlorometaxylenol (PCMX) in a petroleum base. Unfortunately, carbolated Vaseline was reported to have caused cases of contact dermatitis, presumably a reaction to the PCMX. A study by researchers at the University of Pennsylvania showed that patients who had sensitivity to carbolated Vaseline could also experience skin irritation from the phenol (carbolic acid) contained in the product. Carbolated Vaseline has since been discontinued by the manufacturer.

DANDRUFF

Don't Be Snowed

Oh, the joys of dandruff. The tiny flakes dusting your favorite sweater. The constant itching and uncontrollable scratching.

But do not fear: you can keep unwanted flaking at bay and have a beautiful, healthy scalp (and hair)—if you understand that there *is* a method to the apparent madness of keeping dandruff under control.

WHAT'S IT ALL ABOUT?

Dandruff is a lay term referring to all the flaking that takes place on the scalp (or face). The majority of patients mistake dandruff for a bad case of dry skin. Most dandruff, however, is due to a genetic condition known as *seborrheic dermatitis,* or simply *seborrhea.* In this hereditary problem, there's a kind of "short circuit" in the way the skin is made. Periodically, and often unpredictably, the skin cells in the affected areas start reproducing faster than normal. Typically, skin cells are shed in small, unnoticeable amounts; in seborrhea, so much extra skin is shed that flakes start to appear.

Seborrhea can develop any time after puberty begins. That's because the sebaceous glands are involved, and they don't start functioning until puberty. But those glands don't merely *function* in seborrhea—they go into *overdrive,* producing the sebum that contributes to the "greasy" texture of dandruff. And where there's a sebaceous gland, there's a hair follicle; hence, the connection between dandruff and hair.

The length of time that the dandruff is active and the rate of recurrence vary for each individual. Most people find the sheer unpredictability maddening. Not to mention the inflammation that often accompanies dandruff, leading to itching.

Seborrhea definitely has trigger factors. Seasonal changes (especially winter weather) are a common stimulus. So, too, are illness, stress, infections, hormonal imbalances, and neurological conditions (like Alzheimer's, stroke, and paralysis).

Unfortunately, you can't control these life events. And since seborrhea is genetically programmed, there is nothing you can do to permanently rid yourself of the condition. Consider dandruff to be highly controllable, rather than curable.

ONE SHAMPOO WON'T DO

All that flaking is the result of several biological missteps. That's why dandruff doesn't respond well to a single therapy; if you want flake-free hair, you have to disrupt the dandruff pathway at several points, using products that work synergistically. Here's what to do.

Kill the Bacteria and Yeast That Drive Seborrheic Dermatitis

What's bugging your scalp?

Normal flora (the natural yeast and bacteria that reside on the skin and scalp) are an important trigger for both seborrhea and psoriasis.

Ketoconazole is an effective antiyeast ingredient, available in two shampoos (prescription-strength Nizoral 2% and over-the-counter Nizoral A-D 1%) and in a cream form that can help treat both scalp and facial seborrheic dermatitis.

Carmol Deep Cleansing Antibacterial Shampoo takes aim at bacteria and also smoothes away flaking with urea, a potent humectant.

Loprox shampoo is the newest prescription antiyeast dandruff treatment. Its active ingredient is ciclopirox.

Zinc pyrithione kills bacteria and yeast, making the environment inhospitable to their growth. DHS Zinc Shampoo is my favorite. DermaZinc makes a zinc pyrithione liquid for the scalp that may be applied twice a day. It's a great option for anyone who can't wash their hair daily or is looking for an added, nonsteroid treatment.

Chemically Exfoliate Cellular Buildup (Get Rid of Those Flakes)

All that scale builds up with nowhere to go (except your shoulders). Salicylic (BHA) and glycolic (AHA) acids debride it away, leaving your scalp flake-free and your hair luxurious. Look to Meted, Ionil Plus Conditioning Shampoo Salicylic Acid Formula, and P&S shampoo for your BHA dandruff-fighting shampoo solutions. Aqua Glycolic

Shampoo is a glycolic acid alternative for removing scales and crusts.

Both salicylic- and glycolic-acid-based shampoos also help remove oil buildup, an important goal.

Reduce Inflammation—the Source of Redness and Itching

If you've ever had a bad case of dandruff, you know that itching and scratching are an unavoidable part of the process. At the height of the flare-up, when shampoos aren't enough to control the situation, topical steroid solutions are necessary. These are packaged in the same type of bottles as over-the-counter eyedrops; five to eight drops are randomly scattered onto the scalp, twice a day. When dandruff subsides, the drops should be shelved until the next bout. Steroid solutions vary widely in strength; I base my selection on the severity of the condition.

Topical steroid solutions (both over the counter and prescription) may be applied once or twice daily during intolerable flare-ups. They are a short-term fix to get you through the rough times. Don't rely on them indefinitely; make two weeks your cutoff, unless directed otherwise by your physician.

Capex is a steroid shampoo that works quickly to regain control of a nasty problem. Use daily for a week, then weekly as needed.

DermaSmoothe F/S Liquid is a potent steroid mask for your scalp. It is more commonly used for dandruff due to psoriasis, when powerful therapy is needed to cut through thick crusts. DermaSmoothe F/S is applied at bedtime, usually two or three nights in a row, and a shower cap worn overnight. Then the lotion is shampooed out each morning. Both Capex and DermaSmoothe F/S are available by prescription.

Retard the Rate of New Skin Cell Formation

Somehow, that "short circuit" flips the "on" switch for epidermal skin cells, increasing the rate of cell development to twice the norm. Tar helps slow the process, by interfering with cellular reproduction. Many tar shampoos are available. (Look for a "T" in the name.) Pentrax is a DERMAdoctor favorite. Remember: if you have blond or gray hair, tar shampoos may cause some discoloration.

Strategic Shampooing

The best long-term strategy is to buy three or four shampoos: one with an antifungal ingredient (like Carmol or Nizoral A-D); one with zinc pyrithione (like DHS Zinc Shampoo); and one with either salicylic acid or glycolic acid. Don't worry about being precise with your regimen—just use one shampoo for a few days and then switch to another. If you're a brunette, or you simply need additional help, add a tar shampoo to the mix.

Restore the Moisture

There's no question that dandruff shampoos can be somewhat harsh on your hair. I have found that Ionil Rinse is a very good choice for helping restore moisture. I was diagnosed with seborrhea while in college, and have personally gone through countless bottles of DHS Zinc Shampoo and Ionil Rinse.

If this round robin of shampoo therapy doesn't work, you'll need to talk with your doctor about incorporating prescription liquid drops, steroid-based shampoos, like Capex, or prescription-level Nizoral or Loprox shampoo.

P&S Liquid

A special mention goes to P&S Liquid. Think of it as a mask for your scalp. While it doesn't peel off the way a facial mask does, applying P&S Liquid to the scalp at night and washing it out in the morning is a heaven-sent treatment for anyone with severe scaling of the scalp. You'll only need to use it nightly for about three nights. After that, use it periodically, when recurrences aren't responsive to other treatments.

ADVICE FOR AFRICAN-AMERICANS

African-Americans who suffer from seborrhea are often in a quandary about how to handle their scalp care because of styling concerns. Shampooing daily is out of the question for all but the worst cases. I advise my African-American patients to shampoo weekly with whichever dandruff shampoo we have agreed upon. For daily dandruff care and control, they rely upon daily applications of medicated solutions (steroidal or zinc-based DermaZinc or both) and oils. And since oils are often used for styling purposes, a prescription steroid-based oil, DermaSmoothe F/S Topical oil, is often an excellent temporary substitute for a styling oil.

DANDRUFF . . . ON MY FACE?!

Although most people are familiar with dandruff, they are usually unaware that it may appear on the face, including the eyebrows, the area between the brows, the nasolabial folds (the creases that extend from the nose to the angles of the mouth), and, for men, the beard area as well. Only in extremely ill individuals have I seen seborrhea elsewhere on the body, but honestly, any hair-bearing area, such as the torso and even the legs, has the potential to develop seborrhea.

Remember that dandruff is unpredictable. This year's scalp condition may be next year's facial concern. This is definitely a "go with the flow" type of skin disorder. If you take a more relaxed approach, not only will you be happier but the reduced stress will be good for your dandruff, too.

For the face, I will usually prescribe a low-potency steroid lotion, such as DesOwen Lotion, to be used twice daily. At times, I will also have the patient simultaneously apply prescription-strength Nizoral cream. Mixing them makes for easier application. Of course, all of these products need to be kept out of the eyes.

Sulfur has long been used for its antibacterial and exfoliating properties. One of my favorite "old-fashioned" prescription formulations includes 3% precipitated sulfur mixed with a mild topical steroid cream. It does seem to work well for seborrhea on the face or chest that has not responded to other treatment options.

Ovace, a prescription cleanser for the treatment of facial seborrheic dermatitis, is a sulfa-based wash that contains 10% sodium sulfacetamide combined with sulfur. It is used once a day.

Home Solutions for Clearing Facial Dandruff
Wash your face once daily with DERMAdoctor Born to Be Mild Medicated Cleanser or ZNP Bar. Both contain 2% zinc pyrithione. The cleanser is hydrating and calming and is unlikely to cause dryness or irritation. The bar works very well but patients at times complain of drying, particularly during the dry winter months, when you are most likely to develop facial dandruff. Just don't overdo it.

A Dermatologist's "Off-Label" Trick. Cortaid layered with equal parts DERMAdoctor Feet Accompli or Lamisil AT Cream for athlete's foot is an effective treatment. Apply to the affected area twice daily. Once you are clear, try weaning your skin off the steroid over a week or two and relying only on the antifungal treatment. If you stay clear, then slowly, over another week or two, try to stop treatment altogether.

If you want to try to re-create the concept of using sulfur mixed with steroid cream, consider layering equal parts of Cortaid with Rezamid. Start out just once daily; if you do not experience unwanted dryness, advance to twice daily. Rezamid Acne Treatment Lotion contains resorcinol, a drying agent, so you want to be careful not to parch your skin.

FINAL THOUGHTS

It is important to remember that seborrhea is controllable, not curable. Everyone experiences their own pattern (or lack thereof) of dandruff recurrences. Your best strategy for managing dandruff is to stay away from steroid-based treatments whenever possible. Simply shelve them when your condition is clear and see how your other medicated products handle the situation.

It is always fine to stop your seborrhea products when you are fully clear and take a wait-and-see approach. You can always restart them when the time is right.

Ask the DERMAdoctor

QUESTION:

I have an itchy, dry, flaky scalp that responds well to Nizoral shampoo. However, now that I've begun covering those gray hairs with permanent hair color, I've noticed that Nizoral removes some of the hair dye, shortening the time between color treatments. Is there a shampoo or other product that will help control dandruff without pulling out the hair color?

The DERMAdoctor:

To be honest, I think most dandruff shampoos strip away hair color a bit faster than desirable. (Suffering from this situation myself, I speak from experience.) Try to use a good conditioner after shampooing, make sure you are using a pH-balanced salon-quality shampoo on the off days, and apply a deep conditioner once a week to help prevent chemically treated hair from getting too dry and fragile. You may also want to consult your hair colorist, as there are some shampoos and conditioners that help put some of the hair color back while you shampoo with them. Fortunately, most dandruff patients need to use their medicated shampoos only a few times a week in order to control the problem.

DARK CIRCLES

Lighten Up

No facial flaw is more noticeable than dark circles under the eyes. They age the face and create a tired, haggard appearance and a deceptively uninterested expression. Don't tolerate dark circles one minute more! Neutralize them—and reclaim the wide-eyed, dazzling look you deserve.

WHAT'S TO BLAME?

A combination of different factors can conspire to form dark circles: aging, sun damage, heredity, allergies, and even poor lighting!

Fat You Don't Want to Lose

Perhaps the only layer of fat you'll ever really yearn for lies just below the eye and above the cheekbone, called the *infraorbital fat pad*. It thins with age, producing a sunken appearance. Light reflects off this recessed area, creating the illusion of shadowy circles. (Contrary to popular belief, most dark circles have nothing to do with actual changes in skin color.)

So while boomers struggle with fat accumulating around their hips, tummy, and jawline, the opposite problem is also happening—right under their eyes!

You're So Vein

Because of aging and years of sun damage (with perhaps a genetic tendency thrown in for good measure), microscopic blood vessels under the eyes can lose their stability and strength. The body compensates by forming lots of tiny new veins. A thinner fat pad means those veins are closer to the skin's surface. The result: darker dark circles.

Excess Baggage

What could be worse than dark circles? Try dark circles *and* bags under your eyes—the bags exaggerate the circles and intensify that tired-looking appearance.

Aging is usually the culprit. The dermis weakens, gravity tugs, years of sun damage inflame the area, microscopic blood vessels called capillaries start to leak, drainage of waste-disposing lymph is impaired—and all of that (along with hormone-caused skin changes) leads to pooling of excess fluids in the tissues under the eye.

MELLOW WITH YELLOW

There are products that can help rejuvenate aging skin around your eyes, but they take time to work. If you want to look your best *today,* you need a quick fix. Start with a concealer. Hiding dark circles provides immediate gratification and restores radiance to the eye area. Yellow neutralizes blues, purples, and dusky hues on the skin.

A simple, effective concealer (and treatment) is DERMAdoctor Eye Spy Dark Circle Disguise & Neutralizing Agent. You can read more about it below. T. LeClerc makes a lovely cosmetic concealer in banane (yellow). Together, they'll reduce more shadows than the neutral used alone.

Finally, don't hesitate to apply a neutral concealer in a color close to your skin tone on top of the yellow concealer to hide a horrid case of dark circles.

QUICK FIXES FROM THE KITCHEN

Applying moist, cool tea bags (caffeinated, like Earl Grey or English breakfast) is a quick fix for puffiness. The tannins in the tea decrease inflammation, reducing swelling. The caffeine draws water from the skin, deflating puffiness.

You can find another quick fix in the vegetable crisper: cool cucumbers. Enzymes in cucumber slices reduce tissue inflammation, shrinking bags and helping erase unbecoming shadows.

Keep teabags and cucumbers on hand for those little eye-wearying emergencies, like when your kids have kept you up all night. They're also a wonderful appearance enhancer for special events and for other times when you need to look your best. They're temporary solutions—but they work!

ANTIOXIDANTS ARE ANTIBAG

Antioxidant treatments help shrink bags by reducing fluid buildup, making the face look fresher, more rested, and youthful. The best of the antioxidants also stimulate the activity of fibroblasts, cells in the dermis that help create skin-strengthening collagen. This firms and tones the area.

The best fibroblast-stimulating antioxidants include vitamin C (like Cellex-C Eye Contour Cream and SkinCeuticals Eye Gel) and GHK copper peptides (like Neova Eye Therapy).

TREATING BLOOD VESSELS

Topical vitamin K products restore stability and strength to the tiny blood vessels under the eyes, reducing their proliferation. A study in the *Journal of Cosmetic Dermatology* demonstrated that the use of topical vitamin K *and* a topical vitamin A derivative (like retinol, whether over the counter or prescription) was even more beneficial than vitamin K alone. I must point out that both vitamin K and retinols can be irritating when used on the delicate skin around the eyes. Consider a daily routine that uses vitamin K–containing products—like Peter Thomas Roth Power K Eye Rescue or K-Derm Gel—along with a vitamin A–containing treatment, like Afirm 2X.

Use the retinol product by itself, every other night. On nonretinol days, use the vitamin K treatment, once or twice a day.

EYE SPY: CONCEAL *AND* TREAT

I've always been struck by the fact that the approach to handling dark circles seems so scattered. Why conceal without treating? Why treat for six months without concealing?

In response to this dilemma, and wanting to simplify the process, I created DERMAdoctor Eye Spy Dark Circle Disguise & Neutralizing Agent. A universal yellow concealer helps hide the dark circles—and also contains every ingredient necessary to eliminate them, including caffeine, to shrink the bags and reduce inflammation; white tea, a potent antioxidant; palmitoyl tetrapeptide, to diminish visible puffiness and improve skin firmness and elasticity; retinol, to help reduce fine lines and puffiness; and hesperidin methyl chalcone (a nonirritating alternative to vitamin K) to decrease capillary permeability and prevent fluid buildup within the skin.

FAT TRANSPLANTATION

Sometimes treating the problem with skin care products isn't enough. Sometimes, in order to eliminate the problem, you need to fill the deep hollows that create the dark circles. Fat transplantation is one way to do that—it has become a popular method of dealing with recalcitrant dark circles due to loss of tissue.

In this procedure—which is typically performed by a plastic surgeon—fat is removed from a locally anesthetized hip, thigh, or buttock through a syringe or liposuction tube. The fat is rinsed and injected under the skin, into the hollow. The added fat instantly plumps up the skin, preventing the reflection of light that was creating the dark circle.

Fat transplantation isn't a permanent solution. And you may need to undergo more than one treatment in order to see results. But it can be worthwhile.

SCULPTRA

Sculptra has recently been FDA-approved to fill hollows in HIV patients who are losing facial fat. Some plastic surgeons are using it "off label" to treat facial hollows in otherwise healthy individuals, including areas of fat loss under the eyes.

VEIN STRIPPING

Rarely, large blood vessels—perceivable, not microscopic—will cause the dark circles. To treat this problem, consult with a plastic surgeon who specializes in facial surgery or with an ophthalmologist who specializes in plastic surgery. The surgeon may need to perform fat transplantation *and* vein stripping. This is a major procedure and shouldn't be done by just anyone.

BLEACH RELIEF: FOR ALLERGY SUFFERERS ONLY

Sometimes allergy sufferers react to itchy, watery eyes with chronic rubbing; this can lead to darkening of the skin under the eyes. The more rubbing, the darker the skin gets.

A bleaching agent is the best way to solve the problem—in fact, it's the *only* situation where bleach is the right response to dark circles under the eyes.

But don't start with bleach. First, control the allergic symptoms with an oral antihistamine like Benadryl or Claritin. That will stop your eyes from itching and watering, eliminating the urge to rub. If those medications don't work, ask your physician if a prescription antihistamine might help. Another possible source of prescription relief: brief, intermittent use of low-potency topical steroids, like Protopic (tacrolimus) or Elidel (pimecrolimus). *Caution*: Be sure to keep these ointments out of your eyes.

As you're getting your symptoms under control, you can also try bleaching this delicate area. It's a bit tricky, but not impossible. During the daytime, apply Peter Thomas Roth AHA/Kojic Acid Under Eye Brightener or DERMAdoctor Immaculate Correction, followed by a broad-spectrum sunscreen, like DERMAdoctor Body Guard Exquisitely Light SPF 30 or Vanicream Sunscreen SPF 35. You'll brighten your skin—and your appearance.

FINAL THOUGHTS

Eradicating dark circles isn't easy. But through perseverance (and a little makeup magic) you can improve the overall health and look of the skin around your eyes.

Ask the DERMAdoctor

QUESTION:

I not only suffer from dark circles under my eyes, but the area is always very dry and flaky. What can I do?

The DERMAdoctor:

Under-eye dryness is a major contributor to exaggerating the appearance of wrinkle lines around the eyes. A moisturizer won't eliminate the wrinkles, but it sure can soften their appearance. That's why night creams have become the staple of the cosmetic counter in a skin rejuvenation routine. Just don't forget: keep it light, and keep it in perspective. Instead of a straight moisturizer, you can try an ultrahydrating treatment like DERMAdoctor Wrinkle Revenge Eye Balm. It restores the protective ceramide barrier, which is breached by relentless aging, possibly causing your eye area to become dry and flaky.

DISEASE SYMPTOMS

Early Warning Signs from Your Skin

Maybe you're not a doctor; your skin, however, is a diagnostician. As the largest and most expressive organ of the body, it can reveal an internal disorder, like diabetes or even cancer. And that's a tip-off you don't want to ignore, because the sooner you and your doctor attend to a health problem, the better off you'll be.

And if you already know you have a disease, your condition may have a skin manifestation that you and a doctor will need to deal with effectively.

Here's a guide to what your skin may be trying to tell you, along with some treatment information about disease-caused skin concerns.

DIABETES

Eighteen million Americans suffer from diabetes, a disease of uncontrolled blood sugar (glucose)—the incidence of which has increased by 50 percent in the past decade!

There are three types of diabetes. Type I, juvenile diabetes, is caused by a failure of the pancreas to produce insulin, a hormone that ushers blood sugar into the cells. Type II is due to insulin resistance: the body can't properly utilize the hormone. Ninety to 95 percent of people with diabetes have type II, and scientists think that in most cases it's a lifestyle disease caused by factors like being overweight, a diet high in sugars and fats, and lack of exercise. A third type of diabetes, gestational, affects 4 percent of pregnant women and is a risk factor for developing type II later in life.

Skin Symptoms of Diabetes

Dehydration. High levels of blood sugar cause the kidneys to draw water from the bloodstream, increasing urination. As a result, the skin becomes extremely dehydrated, inflamed, and cracked. Dehydrated skin is further worsened and complicated as poor nerve function (diabetic neuropathy) diminishes the production of sweat. While excessive sweating is undesirable, a normal level of sweating helps keep the skin moist.

Infection. Broken skin creates a portal of entry for infection-causing bacteria, fungi, and yeast, while uncontrolled blood sugars increase susceptibility to those infections. Diabetic patients are far more prone to developing many skin infections, including cellulitis (bacterial skin infections), athlete's foot (a fungal infection), nail fungus, perlèche (a yeast infection affecting the corners of the mouth), and intertrigo (a yeast infection arising within the skin folds).

Sensation. High blood sugar and reduced blood flow (a common problem caused by diabetes) affect the nerves of the skin, and one's sensation becomes altered. Diabetic patients become unable to sense trauma, and injuries can go unnoticed. Daily monitoring of the skin— particularly on the hands and feet—helps the diabetic patient find and care for small nicks and sores before they get out of control.

Diabetic Ulcers

Fifteen percent of all diabetics will eventually form a painful, often debilitating ulceration—and no skin condition is more feared. That's because 70 to 90 percent of diabetics who face lower-leg amputation first dealt with an ulcer of the leg or foot, where the problem typically begins. These ulcers have two main causes: poor circulation; and trauma (due to diabetic neuropathy) combined with faulty wound healing.

Understanding one's options in ulcer care is extremely important. Effective treatment can help hasten healing, reduce discomfort, improve the prognosis, and in many cases help prevent future ulcers. Initial treatment for new, small ulcerations focuses on localized wound care, infection control, and maximizing blood flow to the skin. If your physician seems unfamiliar with diabetic wound care, there is often a wound care nurse or department affiliated with the local hospital.

Moist Dressings. The use of antibiotic ointments and moist (hydrophilic) dressings is the first step. Lifting off a dry dressing can do more harm than good.

GHK Copper Peptides. GHK copper peptides—commonly used for skin rejuvenation but initially developed to help in wound care—improve fibroblast activity and collagen formation, and can help strengthen healing skin. Iamin gel consists of a patented hydrogel and GHK-copper-peptide formulation for the dressing and management of diabetic ulcers, as well as other types of wounds.

Growth Factors. Growth factors are essential for maximum wound healing, but there is a decrease in or absence of growth factors in diabetic ulcerations. Currently, the only growth factor–based therapy approved by the FDA for healing diabetic foot ulcerations is Regranex (becaplermin) gel, which aids wound closure and speeds wound healing.

Improving Circulation. Narrowing of major blood vessels in the legs needs to be addressed. Initial studies may include ultrasonography. Depending on the findings, angiography accompanied by angioplasty may help pop stenosed (blocked) vessels open.

The prescription medication Trental (pentoxifylline) helps improve blood flow through narrowed blood vessels and restores oxygenation, vital for healing as well as for preventing ulcerations.

Compression with medical hosiery helps reduce blood pooling in the lower legs due to vascular insufficiency. The swelling of the tissues surrounding tiny, already compromised blood vessels is minimized, which helps prevent them from being choked closed. This can improve overall oxygen levels and allow for elimination of toxins.

Other Treatments. Other treatments being investigated for the prevention and resolution of diabetic ulcer formation include topical bFGF (basic fibroblast growth factor), VEGF (vascular endothelial growth factor), and nitrous oxide.

Necrobiosis Lipoidica Diabeticorum

Necrobiosis lipoidica diabeticorum (NLD) is considered one of the quintessential eruptions associated with diabetes, but fewer than 1 percent of diabetics ever develop it.

NLD is a disorder of collagen degeneration. The precise cause is unknown, but a narrowing of the blood vessels is highly suspect. Microscopic vascular changes that affect the eyes and kidneys in diabetics resemble those seen in NLD.

NLD consists of slow-growing, yellowish, shiny, waxy-looking plaques that develop depressed (atrophic) centers. It appears primarily on the shins. (When it develops elsewhere, it is less likely to be associated with diabetes.) In 75 percent of cases, the areas may become numb, due to dermal nerve damage. In 25 percent of cases, the plaques can become painful.

The average age of onset is thirty, although NLD may affect children and seniors. It strikes three times as many women as men.

Fifteen percent of those with NLD develop it before a diagnosis of diabetes is made. Sixty percent already have been diagnosed with the disease. Necrobiosis lipoidica diabeticorum has no correlation to the severity or control of ongoing diabetes.

Treatment. NLD is difficult, if not impossible, to control. There are random reports of limited benefit from oral ticlopidine, nicotinic acid, clofazimine, dipyridamole, and aspirin, as well as intralesional heparin injections. For those cases of NLD that progress into significant atrophy, topical tretinoin has had some reported benefit.

The use of topical steroids, intralesional steroid injections, and/or steroid tapes can calm associated inflammation early on, as well as reduce the height of the raised border. However, steroids can contribute or hasten skin thinning and should be discontinued if signs of worsening atrophy are seen.

Protection of the legs with elastic support stockings (such as those made by Jobst) can help reduce trauma-induced ulceration, which forms in up to one-third of NLD lesions.

Infection prevention is critical in avoiding cellulitis (a bacterial infection of the skin, often requiring antibiotic treatment). Bovine collagen dressings may be beneficial in healing open wounds. Ulcerations may heal with scarring or discoloration.

HIGH BLOOD FATS
High levels of the blood fats cholesterol and triglycerides don't just clog your arteries—they may also clog your skin.

Eruptive Xanthomatosis
A hailstorm of yellow bumps, eruptive xanthomas result from high triglyceride levels. Scavenger cells clean up the fatty debris and settle out in visible clusters beneath the surface of the skin.

A low-fat diet, cholesterol-lowering medication, and blood-sugar control are essential steps. Once blood fats are lowered, eruptive xanthomas typically resolve.

Xanthelasma
Ever notice someone with thin yellow plaques wedged between the inner eyebrows and the nose? The most common skin finding associated with high blood fats, xanthelasmas are frequently accompanied by elevated blood fat levels, low levels of HDL (good cholesterol), and (sometimes) poorly controlled diabetes.

Without treatment, xanthelasmas remain on the skin permanently, at times increasing in size. Most patients are distressed by their appearance and will visit a dermatologist for treatment. Because an estimated 50 percent of affected patients suffer from lipid disorders, a complete fasting lipid panel, checking for cholesterol, triglycerides, HDL, and LDL levels, should be performed. Removal or destruction remains the sole therapeutic option for xanthelasmas. Surgical excision, chemical destruction with trichloracetic acid, laser removal, and electrodesiccation and curettage give the best results.

THYROID DISEASE
The thyroid is a vital gland, producing a hormone that maintains the body's metabolism and is critical for proper organ function. Disruptions in thyroid function wreak havoc throughout the body.

Workup of a suspected thyroid disorder should be done as soon as possible with a full panel of thyroid-function blood tests. This can help pinpoint the diagnosis. Whether overfunctioning (hyperthyroidism) or glandular failure (hypothyroidism) are to blame, the problem must be corrected as quickly as possible.

Hyperthyroidism

While many of us with a few pounds to shed might wish our thyroid were hyperactive, those with true hyperthyroidism—when the gland frenetically overproduces or overreleases thyroid hormone, increasing the metabolism—know that it's no bed of roses. In fact, it's more like a bed of nails. Skin changes seen in hyperthyroidism include:

* Increased sweating
* Redness of face and palms
* Pretibial myxedema (PTM)
* Thickening of the epidermis
* Faster nail growth
* Smooth skin texture
* Increased pigmentation
* Thinning hair on scalp
* Thickening of fingers and toes
* Prematurely gray hair
* Skin color changes—vitiligo or hyperpigmentation

Pretibial Myxedema (PTM). Thyroid hormone is thought to stimulate dermal fibroblasts to form excessive amounts of hyaluronic acid, a substance that plays a role in the structure of the skin. This may explain the development of thickened skin and digits—and the formation of pretibial myxedema, which afflicts three times as many women as men.

In this disorder, dusky pink, firm plaques and nodules begin to develop on the shins. The hair follicles get very visible, as they become distorted from the deposition of the hyaluronic acid within the dermal tissues, resulting in the classic "peau d'orange" (orange peel) appearance. Occasionally, PTM may occur on other areas of the body.

Therapy for PTM is limited. Potent topical steroids help thin the affected areas. Fortunately, the condition often resolves spontaneously.

Treatment of hyperthyroidism consists of surgical removal and/or destruction of the tissue with radioactive iodine therapy.

Hypothyroidism

Hypothypoidism is, of course, the opposite of hyperthyroidism: a lack of thyroid hormone slows down the body's metabolic rate. It is the second most common metabolic disorder in the United States. And women again far outnumber men—an astounding 2 to 3 percent of all women over age fifty will develop hypothyroidism. Patients become tired, listless, and depressed and gain weight.

No single cause can be blamed. Hashimoto's thyroiditis, an autoimmune disorder in which the body attacks and destroys thyroid tissue, is the most common cause. Other possible causes include trauma; such invasive tissue diseases as sarcoid (a systemic disease characterized by the formation of granulomas in the skin, lungs, and other organs); and medications, including lithium, used to treat depression, and interferon, used to treat viral infections.

The skin becomes swollen (edematous) from acellular mucopolysaccharides being deposited in the dermis. This is the classic hypothyroid myxedema. Skin changes seen in hypothyroidism include:

- Skin feels cold
- Skin becomes pale
- Changes in vitamin A metabolism may cause skin to yellow (carotenemia)
- Skin becomes dry
- Palms and soles become very thick
- Hair becomes dry and coarse
- Absence of sweating
- Hair loss may develop, including on the outer eyebrows, scalp, and vulva
- Puffiness of face, eyelids, and hands
- Nails become thick and brittle
- Eczema craquelé
- Increased bruising
- Poor wound healing

A gentle skin regimen and lots of tender care with emollients will help hydrate the skin. Hypothyroidism itself is treated with thyroid hormone supplementation.

LIVER DISEASE

We all know we can't live without a liver, but exactly what does it do? This organ produces many essential proteins, manufactures hormones, essential blood fats, and vitamins (especially vitamin K), and makes clotting factors to prevent excessive bleeding. It also cleanses medications and toxins from our bloodstream and helps in fluid balance. And the liver destroys approximately 1 percent of our red blood cells daily, making way for younger, healthier ones. (As red blood cells are broken down, bilirubin is released into the bloodstream to be eliminated in the stool. Bilirubin is yellow.)

Drugs (excessive consumption of aspirin, Tylenol, and NSAIDs, to name just a few) and alcohol can cause liver damage. Infections, including hepatitis B and C, can also result in liver dysfunction. As liver function is lost, bilirubin levels rise and diffuse into the tissues, and jaundice—a yellowing of the skin, eyes, and mucous membranes—develops.

Itching is a common problem faced by a patient with liver disease. It is believed to be due to an increase in bile salts within the blood.

Skin signs of liver disease include:

- Jaundice
- Generalized itching
- Widespread spider vein formation
- Bruising (from a lack of vitamin K, which is an essential component of blood clotting)
- Androgen levels drop, so hair becomes finer in texture and diameter
- Seborrhea flare-ups
- Acnelike eruption on upper torso

Questran (cholestyramine) increases fecal elimination of bile salts and can relieve itching. Itching is also controlled both topically (preferred) and orally with Benadryl and, if necessary, with medical ultraviolet light therapy.

Vitamin K injections can be used in cases of excessive bleeding or bruising.

Spider veins can be destroyed with electrodesiccation (electrical cauterization).

Seborrheic dermatitis is controlled topically. Please see the chapter "Dandruff" on page 59.

Overall treatment is targeted at correcting the underlying causes of liver disease and providing support to the organ.

KIDNEY DISEASE

Patients with end-stage renal disease (ESRD) almost always have some skin manifestation of their condition. By far the most common (albeit nonspecific) complaints are dry skin and itching.

Fifty to 75 percent of those being treated for kidney failure with dialysis experience an overall decrease in sweat volume, as well as the atrophy of their sebaceous glands.

Skin signs of renal disease include:

- Dry skin
- Itching
- Acquired perforating disorder (Kyrle disease)
- Hair loss
- Skin discoloration
- Blistering disease of dialysis
- Calcinosis cutis (calcium deposits form in the skin)
- Calciphylaxis (calcium deposits and narrowing of blood vessels, resulting in skin ulcerations)
- Half-and-half nails
- Lichen simplex chronicus (thickened leathery skin due to scratching)
- Prurigo nodularis (skin nodules formed in response to chronic scratching)
- Uremic frost (urea content in sweat increases and crystallizes on skin)

Itching may respond to moisturizers, topical analgesics, topical steroid creams, and ultraviolet B (UVB) light therapy.

Forty percent of dialysis patients develop half-and-half nails. The outer half of the nail turns dark brown; the inner portion of the nail appears white. The fingernails are more commonly affected than the toenails. It disappears spontaneously several months after a successful kidney transplant.

Various events in renal disease affect skin color. ESRD is typically associated with anemia, hence a pale skin tone. At the same time, the kidney is a major location for the production of melanocyte stimulating hormone (MSH). Chronic renal failure increases the levels of MSH, which in turn leads to patchy hyperpigmentation in areas of the skin exposed to the sun. And, finally, iron overload from blood transfusion may cause the skin to turn slate gray.

Although uncommon, Kyrle disease is characteristic of ESRD (it may also be seen in diabetes). Large bumps form about the hair folli-cles, with a hard central keratin plug that may ultimately break down and form a sore. Treatment is challenging and not often successful. Topical and systemic retinoids, steroids, methotrexate and 5-fluo-rouracil may be considered.

CANCER

Cancer may grow slowly, at times taking years before making its presence known. Yet sometimes the body may recognize the malignancy, setting up a response that sends out clues upon the skin. Or growth factors that nurture the tumor may trigger an unusual cutaneous response.

Acanthosis Nigricans

Acanthosis nigricans is an instantly identifiable skin change in which thickened patches of velvety brown skin form under the arms, about the neck, and in the creases of the arms.

Acanthosis nigricans can develop without reason or may be linked with diabetes or polycystic ovary syndrome. (Both are disor-ders involving insulin, which is a suspected trigger of this epidermal skin-cell growth.)

Treatment isn't simple, but a combination of weight loss, a low-carbohydrate diet (which helps control insulin levels), topical retinoids, and bleaching agents can be effective.

A gentle nonirritating antiperspirant is critical; inflammation will only increase skin discoloration. DERMAdoctor Total NonScents Ultra-Gentle Brightening Antiperspirant provides an effective two-in-one approach.

Malignant acanthosis nigricans is most commonly associated with a form of colon cancer. What distinguishes this from other forms of acanthosis nigricans is a more rapid onset with a more widespread distribution. Some lesions even develop on the face and hands.

Paraneoplastic Syndromes

Paraneoplastic syndromes are an unusual group of skin eruptions that form in response to an underlying, often aggressive malignancy. Malignant acanthosis nigricans is one. Others include:

The Sign of Leser-Trelat. A sudden onset of numerous seborrheic ker-atoses, with red inflammation and itching of the skin. Associated with stomach, colon, and squamous cell carcinomas, lymphoma, and leukemia. Often coincides with malignant acanthosis nigricans.

Hypertrichosis Lanuginosa Acquisita. An excessive growth of fine facial hair. May be seen in other disorders, but when it abruptly appears without a history of other disorders or medication, it is likely in response to a malignancy.

Erythema Gyratum Repens. Seen with cancers of the cervix, breast, stomach, bladder, and prostate. Slow-moving, wavy, red, raised, scaling bands migrate in a "wood grain" pattern across the body.

Necrolytic Migratory Erythema. Associated with a tumor of the pancreas. Patchy red areas covered with blisters develop on the abdomen, buttocks, and legs.

Pancreatic Panniculitis. A sign of pancreatitis or pancreatic cancer. High levels of pancreatic enzymes (lipase and amylase) lead to inflammation and liquefaction of fat. Appears as red nodules of the skin, accompanied by fever and joint pain.

Paraneoplastic Pemphigus. A life-threatening, blistering disorder most commonly seen with non-Hodgkin's lymphoma.

VITAMIN DEFICIENCIES

We are fortunate that malnutrition and vitamin deficiencies are now uncommon in the United States. Vitamin-enriched foods, daily supplements, and an abundance of fresh produce supply the vital nutrients we need to stay healthy. But a paucity of vitamins can put on a show upon the skin. Just look.

Vitamin B_3 (niacin) deficiency results in pellagra. The mucous membranes inside the mouth become smooth and bright red; an eczematous "necklace" develops around the neck and upper chest; patients can also develop diarrhea and delirium.

Biotin deficiency affects hair and nail health. Hair becomes fragile and may fall out, while nails become brittle.

Vitamin C deficiency causes scurvy. Patients bruise more easily, their gums bleed, and telltale bruising develops around the hair follicles, with "corkscrew" hairs.

Vitamin K deficiency leads to increased bruising.

Iron deficiency leads to anemia. Lack of iron makes nails fragile, and plate deformities develop, including ridging and a spoonlike depression. The nail beds become pale. Hair develops splits, becomes dry and lifeless, and begins to shed. Changes of the mucous membrane inside the mouth develop.

Zinc deficiency leads to nail loss and to small blisters, pustules, crusting, and flaking lesions on the scalp, genitalia, and about the mouth.

Vitamin Excess

How many times have you heard about someone's skin turning orange from eating too many carrots? It's true! Vitamin A and beta-carotene are notorious for causing skin problems when taken in excess.

Vitamin A overdose causes the skin to become dry, the lips to chap and crack, and the hair to fall out. Not to mention all the internal problems it can lead to, such as increased triglyceride levels, disruption of liver function, and depression of blood counts.

Beta-carotene overdose can cause the skin and nails to turn orange.

Vitamin B_6 (pyridoxine) overdose can lead to numbness, bloating, nerve damage, and fatigue.

Vitamin D overdose can cause calcium deposits to form within soft tissues.

Folic acid overdose leads to skin hypersensitivity, smooth tongue, fatigue, and peripheral nerve damage.

Vitamin C overdose causes hot flashes and skin rashes.

Vitamin B_3 (niacin) overdose is known to cause flushing and rashes.

FINAL THOUGHTS

Internal disease often is accompanied by dermatological manifestations. These signs may precede other symptoms and prompt an earlier diagnosis. Pay attention to what your skin is telling you. It may save your life.

Ask the DERMAdoctor

QUESTION:

My boyfriend was just diagnosed with ulcerative colitis, a type of inflammatory bowel disease, and we found out that his mouth ulcers and skin rash are all connected. What is the best treatment for the skin rash?

The DERMAdoctor:

There are several possible causes for a skin rash that occurs in association with ulcerative colitis: a drug rash in response to the sulfa in the medication he is taking; erythema nodosum, which produces reactive painful nodules upon the shins; pyoderma gangrenosum, marked by deep, painful pustular eruptions and ulcers of the skin; a zinc deficiency known as acrodermatitis enteropathica; pyoderma vegetans or vasculitis, due to inflammation and destruction of the blood vessels of the skin; and, finally, epidermolysis bullosa acquisita, a blistering disorder often seen with a variety of immunological disorders. The treatment will depend on the cause of the rash. I would advise him to see a dermatologist for evaluation, diagnosis, and treatment of his skin concern.

DRUG RASHES

What You Need To Know

My babysitter counts herself lucky that she works for a dermatologist.

One Sunday morning, she awoke to find herself covered from head to toe with a mysterious, overwhelmingly itchy rash. What was it from? Was it the symptom of a serious disease? Of course, she was able to drop in and see me that morning. (Her primary care physician later asked in awe, "Are you *sure* it was a dermatologist you saw on a Sunday?") Together, my sitter and I figured out that the rash was a reaction to a medication she had started two weeks previously.

The good news is that the rash disappeared and she's feeling better. But for those of you who don't have a dermatologist at your beck and call, I want you to understand the implications of a drug rash and be able to handle this serious (and potentially life-threatening) medical situation.

WHAT IS A DRUG RASH?

Simply stated, it's a rash caused by an allergic reaction to a medication. Your immune system mistakes the drug for a foreign invader and stages a counterattack, which triggers the release of histamine and immunoglobulins (proteins that fight the allergen). These create the itching, swelling, redness, spots, and other symptoms that characterize an allergic reaction.

The Top Offenders

Any medication—over the counter or prescription—can cause an allergic reaction. The top offenders include antibiotics; heart and blood-pressure medicines (like ACE inhibitors); muscle relaxants, anticonvulsants, morphine derivatives (like codeine), and anesthetics; some nonsteroidal anti-inflammatory drugs (like ibuprofen and aspirin); chemotherapy drugs for cancer; some vaccines; and certain preservatives in drugs.

Timing Is Everything

If you've never been exposed to the offending drug, it takes the body between ten and fourteen days to form an allergic reaction. If you've previously taken the drug, it's possible to break out within a few hours, although it usually takes a few days. However, seven to ten days is typical.

Drug rashes may wax and wane for up to six weeks once the drug use is discontinued. So if you continue to see faint pink or red blotches or bumps without more serious warning signs (discussed below), don't panic. Tell your doctor what's happening, but realize that the situation is not unexpected.

What It Looks Like

Drug rashes can look very different from one another. They can mimic lichen planus or pityriasis rosea. They can form sores or blisters or cause joints to swell. But the majority of drug eruptions are an amorphous blend of blotchy red bumps and patches (maculopapular). Others look more like measles.

These different manifestations can help dermatologists pin down the problematic drug, particularly in cases where the patient is taking two or more medications. This doesn't always work, but when it does, it sure makes life a lot easier for both doctor and patient.

A "classic" drug rash most commonly presents on the head and upper torso and, over the next day or two, progresses down the body. Similarly, improvement begins at the head, with the lower extremities being the last to clear.

WARNING SIGNS OF A VERY SERIOUS PROBLEM

Most drug rashes are annoying, and a sign that you should avoid the medication in the future. Usually that's where it ends. But some drug rashes are medically worrisome, and one type is unquestionably life threatening. In order of their progression from bad to worst, they are:

- Erythema multiforme (EM)
- Stevens-Johnson syndrome
- Toxic epidermal necrosis (TEN)

How do you know when a drug rash has progressed to a serious medical situation? Here are the warning signs:

Your skin looks like it's been used for target practice. This can indicate erythema multiforme (EM). Individual "spots" resemble targets (a red circle surrounded by a white circle, surrounded by a red circle, etc.).

Development of the rash on your palms and soles. This is also suggestive of EM.

Mucosal sores. Sores or erosions developing within the mouth (any mucosal surface, including the gums, tongue, and palate), on the conjunctivas of the eyes, or on the musoca of the genital region. This indicates the involvement of deeper tissues and elevates the rash of EM into the more serious category of Stevens-Johnson syndrome.

Blisters on nonmucosal skin.

Pain with urination. This may indicate that erosions have developed within the urethra.

Widespread, sunburnlike redness (erythroderma).

Purplish duskiness developing within the sunburnlike redness. This indicates that the allergic reaction is involving deeper layers of the epidermis.

Fevers and chills. This is often due to massively increased blood flow to the skin, with generalized erythroderma or Stevens-Johnson syndrome.

Sloughing or crinkling of the skin due to simple light touch. Similar to the look of plastic wrap, this symptom is called a "positive Niolsky sign" and signals that the reaction has moved into the most serious and potentially fatal form, toxic epidermal necrolysis (TEN). At this point, the destruction caused by the reaction is similar to that of a deep burn.

IF YOU SUSPECT A DRUG RASH

Take action right away. You should:

Call Your Doctor Immediately

It is important that the drug you are allergic to be stopped as soon as possible, so make sure you call your doctor. (If you're on multiple medications prescribed by different doctors, call your primary care physician.) But don't stop taking the drug without a doctor's okay.

For instance, what if you have out-of-control high blood pressure, were placed on a calcium channel blocker, and then broke out in a rash? If you stop the medication, you might endanger your health even further. Most likely, your doctor will switch you to another category of medication at the same time that you stop taking the suspect drug.

Try to See or Talk with Your Dermatologist—Immediately

No one is better qualified to identify and handle a drug rash. Also, many nondermatologists are inexperienced regarding the best management for drug rashes. (See "Treating the Rash," below.)

FIGURING OUT THE CAUSE

Are you having an allergic reaction to a drug—or does the rash have another cause? It's not always obvious.

In a questionable situation (especially when several new drugs were begun at the same time), testing may be able to identify the culprit. Your doctor may order one or more of the following: RAST (radioallergosorbent) testing; an absolute eosinophil count (a test for a type of blood cell often produced in elevated quantities during an allergic reaction); and scratch testing (performed after the rash has gone away). My son underwent these, and while they were unpleasant for a small child, it was well worth it to know he could safely take penicillins. Most adults find the testing annoying and uncomfortable but tolerable.

TREATING THE RASH

Two classes of drugs—antihistamines and steroids—are the best therapies for a drug rash. And there are a number of other products you can use to reduce the discomfort of symptoms.

Antihistamines: Stay in the Comfort Zone

Antihistamines are the treatment of choice for a drug rash. As their name implies, they help reduce or eliminate the release of histamine, which, as I explained earlier, is an important factor in the allergic process.

When a drug rash catches you by surprise, try Benadryl Allergy Liquid (diphenhydramine). This will allow you to achieve relief, in dosing you can control. But to effectively shut down a drug eruption, you need to take the antihistamine (as tolerated) around the clock, not just when you are itching.

Topical Anesthetics: Stop the Scratching

PrameGel, Caladryl Clear Lotion, and Aveeno Anti-Itch lotion will let you treat rather than scratch. And never overlook the soothing benefits of Aveeno Oatmeal or baking soda baths.

Steroids: Reduce Inflammation

In addition to round-the-clock treatment with antihistamines, it is also important to use inflammation-reducing steroids—topical and, in some cases, systemic. In fact, twice-a-day application of a mild prescription topical steroid cream, like triamcinolone, is standard medical practice in treating a drug rash. For more serious drug rashes (like EM) or one that continues to worsen despite antihistamines and topical steroids, a doctor also can prescribe prednisone, a systemic steroid.

It is very important that you understand systemic steroids—because your doctor might not! Most nondermatologists don't understand the repercussions of improper use. Here's what can happen.

Very often, steroid shots or a five-day "tapered" course (the dosage is reduced each day) of steroid pills will be offered to patients who go to the emergency room or their primary care physician with a drug rash. The problem with this approach is that a significant number of drug rashes *return* as the medication is being eliminated from the system or afterward. This is known as a rebound phenomenon. It is the dermatologist who often ends up seeing a rash-plagued patient after two or three rounds of steroid injections or a quickie taper—and who has to undo the damage. (I know, because that dermatologist has often been me.)

If systemic steroids are required for a drug rash (assuming the patient is an otherwise healthy adult who can take steroids), the use of a high-dose, prolonged taper almost always stops the reaction *without* a rebound flare. My recommended prednisone taper employs 10-milligram tablets in the following daily format of number of pills per day:

Day 1:	6	Day 9:	2
Day 2:	6	Day 10:	2
Day 3:	5	Day 11:	1
Day 4:	5	Day 12:	1
Day 5:	4	Day 13:	½
Day 6:	4	Day 14:	½
Day 7:	3	Day 15:	Done
Day 8:	3		

If you develop a drug rash, you want to receive the right treatment right away. This is why you should contact your dermatologist first, or request that your doctor get you in to see one immediately. If you can't see a dermatologist, talk with your doctor about the proper use of prednisone for a serious skin rash.

In dire cases, hospitalization and intravenous steroids may be required. Fortunately, this is the exception to the rule.

LABEL YOUR MEDICAL RECORDS (AND YOURSELF)

The worst thing you can do to yourself after you get better is to once again take the rash-causing drug (or a chemical cousin). That's because a second allergic reaction to the drug is likely to be far more severe—and even life threatening.

During my dermatology residency, I saw several patients succumb to their drug rashes. Almost all of them had retaken a medicine they were allergic to.

The two best ways to prevent a second bout with the drug are: 1) Make sure your medical records at the doctor's office are labeled with the drug allergy; and 2) Buy a Medic Alert bracelet or dog tag that says you're allergic to the drug.

Whenever I see a patient with a drug allergy, I always send a letter to their primary care physician and request that the patient's chart be labeled; I also update the doctor as to the patient's progress. However, don't assume that this will be done. Follow up on your own to make certain your records are labeled.

The second recommendation is very important. If you happen to see a new doctor or go to the emergency room, you may forget or be unable to mention that you have a drug allergy—so your Medic Alert bracelet had better say so for you.

If you don't want to wear a Medic Alert tag or bracelet, at least carry a medical card in your wallet that lists all the medications you take and any allergies you have. If you are found unconscious and can't relay information about your drug allergies, you'll be protected from additional harm. Medics and emergency room personnel always check a patient's wallet for this type of vital information.

FINAL THOUGHTS

I hope you won't ever wake up to find yourself covered with a drug rash. But if you do, now you'll be able to take control—even if you can't see a dermatologist on a Sunday!

Ask the DERMAdoctor

QUESTION:

I started taking birth control pills and after a week or so broke out in a very unusual skin rash, with little, dark, itchy bumps. What's happening?

The DERMAdoctor:

Any medication is capable of causing an allergic reaction; oral contraceptives are no exception. Many drugs cause their own unique type of rash. Birth control pills may cause a lichenoid drug eruption (meaning it looks similar to lichen planus, a rash that consists of small lavender to dark purple angular bumps that appear out of nowhere and itch like crazy). Stopping the Pill should resolve the rash—not immediately, but certainly within four to six weeks. Ask your doctor about another contraceptive choice.

DRY SKIN

It's No Surprise: You Should Moisturize

Realtors have a favorite line: "Location, location, location." When it comes to treating dry skin, dermatologists also have a standard mantra: "Moisturize, moisturize, moisturize."

That's particularly true in the fall, after summer sun and water exposure have depleted your skin of precious moisture and nutrients. And it's also true in the winter, when cold and wind (and dry indoor air) can make your skin look like it's a matching accessory for an alligator purse.

Here are helpful tips to keep your skin soft and moisturized.

BATHING BEAUTY

Dermatologists used to tell those prone to horribly dry skin to bathe just once a week. Can you imagine? But this incredibly wrong-minded advice does have a kernel of truth in it.

After a bath or shower, the water evaporates from your skin, taking valuable moisture with it and leaving you vulnerable to dryness. So, yes, if you've got dry skin and you bathe more than once a day—perhaps because of personal preference, perhaps because you've got a grimy job—cut down on the frequency. And no matter how often you bathe, heed the following advice.

Towel Dry Well

Dry off thoroughly and you'll help stop evaporation from drying you out. Also, consider using a product like the Aquis bath towel, which looks like a towel but works like a sponge. It quickly removes water from your skin before evaporation has an opportunity to dehydrate it.

Moisturize Immediately After Washing

After you towel dry, increase the moisture content in your skin by applying a hydrating body cream. Particularly dry skin may savor an extra-emollient base, like SBR-Lipocream Skin Barrier Repair Cream.

Add Bath Oil

If you prefer taking baths, a great way to help hydrate your skin is to add bath oil to the water. It's luxurious and leaves the skin feeling smooth. Some bath oils also contain aromatherapy ingredients that help create a relaxing mood (something we can never get enough of).

Robathol Bath Oil and Neutrogena Body Oil are great options.

Bath oils also come in therapeutic formulations intended for specific skin problems. If you're prone to psoriasis, for example, Balnetar Therapeutic Tar Bath is one of those can't-live-without items from September through May. The tar helps alleviate the itching and flaking, while the oil base helps hydrate dry, cracking skin.

A note of caution when using any bath oil: they make your tub slippery! Watch your step.

And for those of you who would rather shower than take a bath: nothing says you can't splash some bath oil onto your skin while you shower.

Bubble Trouble

Bubble bath is often just detergent added to water. If you're looking for something to create ambience, try an herbal bubble bath that contains hydrating essential oils, like California Baby. It will hydrate your skin and is less likely to cause dryness or irritation.

MOISTURIZE MORE THAN ONCE DAILY

Who says that a moisturizer should be applied only in the morning?

Multiple applications of moisturizer help speed up hydration and skin healing for anyone whose dry skin has gotten out of control.

It is not uncommon for me to tell patients with parched, cracked, rough skin to apply their moisturizer four or five times a day for a

HAND AND FINGER SKIN PROBLEMS

Hand and finger care is very important and yet often neglected, leading to dry, cracked, painful skin. Fortunately, a little prevention and some smart treatment regimens can help keep hands and fingers supple year round.

The H_2O has got to go. As water evaporates, it dehydrates the skin. Cut down on exposure. Ask your husband or kids to do the dishes. When you wash your hands, use a mild soap like Vanicream Cleansing Bar or Oilatum Cleansing Bar, unscented.

Use a "passive protectant" in a crisis period. Heavy, bland emollient creams—passive protectants—keep the skin hydrated and sealed and are essential for placing a barrier between you and the environment. No barrier, no healing. Lotions won't do; they're incapable of healing thickened, dry skin splits.

Apply a passive moisturizer as frequently as possible—every time you wash your hands, do the dishes, and so on. Keep a second moisturizer at work or in your purse. Some passive moisturizers are:

- TheraSeal Hand Protection
- Vanicream Moisturizing Skin Care Cream
- SBR-Lipocream Skin Barrier Repair Cream
- Eucerin Cream
- Triceram

Use an "active" moisturizer in a quiet period. Active hand care products contain ingredients that soften and exfoliate skin. Adding them to your routine when hands and fingers are in a quiet phase can help prevent flare-ups. If you have thickened, rough skin or are prone to finger splits, these are the types of products you want to include for preventive purposes. Alternate various active hand creams, or combine them in a regimen with passive hand care emollients. Some active hand creams include:

- DERMAdoctor KP Duty
- AmLactin 12% Moisturizing Cream
- M.D. Forté Hand & Body Cream
- Carmol 10 or Carmol 20

First aid for finger splits. Most people don't think about hand and finger care until they're plagued by split fingertips, which can be exquisitely painful. You can nurse splits back to health with the following routine:

- Apply Polysporin ointment to the splits twice a day. Don't use a topical antibiotic ointment that contains neomycin, which is a notorious skin sensitizer and frequent cause of contact dermatitis.
- Use DERMAdoctor Handy Manum or an over-the-counter medicated dry oil containing 1 percent hydrocortisone at least once or twice daily.
- Apply your passive barrier cream obsessively.

---

week. When they do, they often see a significant and rapid improvement in symptoms.

If Necessary, Use an Active Ingredient

An active ingredient in a moisturizer is one that helps do more than protect the skin—it also helps dissolve the "glue" between dead skin cells, effectively exfoliating and softening parched skin. Glycolic acid (AHA), salicylic acid (BHA), lactic acid, and urea are all helper ingredients.

While you don't want to rub one of these gentle acids into an open fissure, their use can help promote softer, supple skin that is less likely to crack during the depths of winter.

You may find that you want to mix and match these various active agents, alternating products like DERMAdoctor KP Duty, M.D. Forté Hand & Body Cream, AmLactin 12% Moisturizing Cream, and Carmol 20.

Or use one periodically, along with a standard moisturizing cream. AHAs increase the skin's sensitivity to the sun. While a broad-spectrum SPF 15 should be worn daily, it's especially important that AHA use always be accompanied by sunscreen use.

Carry Extra Hand Cream with You

Have you ever thought about how many times you wash your hands a day? While I've never stopped to count, it has to be at least ten, if not significantly more.

Constant contact with water—not to mention harsh soaps—can

cause dry cuticles, fragile nails, and painful finger splits. To prevent this, carry extra hand cream with you and apply it after every hand washing.

If you have a job that requires lots of hand washing (like bartending, hair styling or health care work), keep an extra container of hand cream by the sink or in your desk drawer or locker.

EVALUATE YOUR OTHER SKIN CARE PRODUCTS

You will create a better barrier between you and the environment if you use a cream-based rather than a lotion- or serum-based product. Rethink your product base, particularly during the fall and winter. If you are fighting dry skin and your particular skin care product (for skin rejuvenation, acne, etc.) has a hydrating option, switch to it.

Be Wary of Vitamin A in the Winter

Vitamin A has a variety of molecular cousins used in the topical treatment of acne, psoriasis, and skin rejuvenation: tretinoin (Retin-A, Renova, Avita), tazarotene (Tazorac), adapalene (Differin), and retinols (Afirm). All of these are likely to cause exaggerated dryness, irritation, flaking, or redness during cold weather.

You may find that your skin is better off when you use the product less often. Or you may want to continue using the product, as well as a moisturizer specifically formulated to heal dry skin caused by the use of vitamin A–containing agents, like M.D. Forté Replenish Hydrating Cream.

Kinerase Cream and DERMAdoctor Wrinkle Revenge are popular skin rejuvenation treatments for those who can't tolerate the use of vitamin A–based products during the winter.

HUMIDIFY YOUR ENVIRONMENT

If you don't have a humidifier on your furnace, once you turn on the heat the air in your environment becomes very dry. And outside isn't much better—fall and winter air lacks the humidity Mother Nature provides the rest of the year.

The best solution: install a humidifier on your furnace, or use individual humidifiers in each room. If you humidify your environment, your skin will thank you for it.

NIP ITCHING IN THE BUD

Dry skin is usually itchy skin. And itchy skin tends to stay itchy—no vicious cycle is harder to stop than the itch-scratch cycle. The more you scratch, the more the inflamed skin itches, and the harder it is to heal the affected area.

Preventing dry skin is your best option for staying off this maddening treadmill. But if the cycle has started, make sure you treat the dry skin *and* the symptoms of itching.

Oral antihistamines like over-the-counter Benadryl and topical anesthetics like PrameGel, L.M.X.4, or Prax Lotion can help keep you from scratching your skin raw. Prescription options, including pills like oral hydroxyzine or doxepin or Zonalon cream, can also help.

I have found that nonsedating oral histamines used to control the symptoms associated with hay fever rarely help stop itching.

FINAL THOUGHTS

You can avoid rough, dry skin in the fall and winter by planning ahead—buying the products you need and using them. And don't forget: moisturize, moisturize, moisturize.

Ask the DERMAdoctor

QUESTION:

I am forty-five, with fair, very dry skin *and* acne. Most of the treatments for dry skin make my acne worse, and most of the treatments for acne make my dry skin worse. Any suggestions?

The DERMAdoctor:

The combination of very dry skin and acne can be a challenge in both skin care and therapy. I tend to concentrate on giving the acne treatment precedence while letting the routine daily skin care products be gentle rather than therapeutic. This approach helps baby delicate, dry skin while also treating it.

Apply your topical acne therapy only to problematic areas. Ask your dermatologist if the medication prescribed is available in a more gentle, hydrating base.

In certain cases, skin may be so incredibly sensitive that prescription oral acne therapy is substituted for all topical blemish medications.

Wash with a gentle cleanser, such as Cetaphil Gentle Skin Cleanser or M.D. Forté Replenish Hydrating Cleanser.

Noncomedogenic moisturizers help hydrate the skin, and also protect and restore hydration lost from use of acne treatments. Try M.D. Forté Replenish Hydrating Cream or Moisturel Therapeutic Cream.

Sunscreen is a daily necessity. Use one with an SPF of at least 15, preferably 30. DERMAdoctor Body Guard is not only oil-free and non-comedogenic but also helps restore moisture and the barrier necessary to protect against the elements.

ECZEMA

Protect Your Skin, Reclaim Control

Eczema sends a lot of people to the dermatologist; from newborns to the elderly, no one is immune. But your dermatologist might call the problem *atopic dermatitis, nummular eczema,* or *dyshidrotic eczema*—there are many different names for the various forms of the disease. Still, eczema is eczema: rough, itchy, scaly skin that often cracks in areas subject to motion. So even though medical science has different labels for different forms, the understanding and treatment of this troubling skin problem—which is not life threatening but can be lifelong—are the same.

THE MANY FACES OF ECZEMA
Sometimes it's in patches. Sometimes it's just on the hands. Sometimes it has blisters. Sometimes it doesn't. But it's always eczema.

Atopic Dermatitis
Eczema is often hereditary; medical texts call this common form *atopic dermatitis*. The tendency to develop atopic dermatitis is located on the same gene as the tendency for asthma and hay fever. Some unfortunate patients suffer from all three.

Atopic dermatitis usually surfaces during early childhood, though I have seen more than a few adults who, surprisingly, developed it later in life. Most (but not all) children outgrow their symptoms.

The most common locations are the skin folds, like the neckline, where the arm bends, and behind the knees. Other common spots are the palms and the soles of the feet. However, any area can develop eczema.

Eczema is worsened by stress, illness, infections, and, sometimes, hormonal changes. The change of seasons can also cause it to flare up. The worst weather for eczema is anything with extremes in temperature and humidity, like the coldest, driest days of winter and the most humid days of summer.

A common cause of chronic flare-ups among children is the bacterium *Staphylococcus aureus*. Kids often carry this bacterium in their nose, and it finds its way via their fingernails onto the skin. Applying a tiny swab of Polysporin ointment just inside the inner rim of the nostrils can help control the problem.

Pityriasis Alba

Pityriasis alba (PA) is the common childhood condition in which light or white patches remain (usually on the face) after eczema has resolved. The discoloration is a response to inflammation and almost always goes away by itself. Keeping eczema under control and skin well hydrated helps prevent PA.

Dyshidrotic Eczema

Dyshidrotic eczema affects the hands and feet, where tiny, fluid-filled blisters form just below the skin's surface. The blisters signal an acute flare-up, as serum pools just beneath the surface of the skin, usually accompanied by intense itching, deep and painful cracks, and scaling. Dyshidrotic eczema is often a chronic condition, appearing periodically throughout adulthood.

This form of eczema resembles a skin allergy (allergic contact dermatitis), and sometimes a skin allergy may trigger the problem. Chronic, inexplicable hand dermatitis deserves patch testing to help sort out the situation.

Nummular Eczema

Nummular eczema presents as round, coinlike patches of eczema. While the location and appearance differ from eczema in skin folds, the treatment remains the same.

Skin Changes

Eczema itches—and chronic scratching can cause temporary or permanent skin changes.

You can develop dark or light patches of skin. You can have textural changes, like leathery thickening (lichen simplex chronicus, or LSC) or thickened "knots" (prurigo nodules, or PN). Thickened areas can take on a life of their own and chronically itch, whether or not the eczema is active.

These skin changes are one reason why it's so important to learn how to protect your skin when eczema is quiet and how to rapidly reclaim control when it flares up.

THERAPY FOR ECZEMA

For many years, therapy for out-of-control eczema was limited to steroids, usually topical or systemic (pills or shots). But long-term use of topical steroids can thin the skin, causing bruising, increased skin fragility, and tearing, as well as the formation of tiny, visible blood-vessels. And systemic steroids can trigger weight gain, increase blood sugar levels (a risk for diabetes), boost blood pressure (a risk for heart disease and stroke), and cause ulcers (to highlight just a few of the biggest concerns).

That's why when cortisone is necessary, your doctor will likely opt for a cream, ointment, or lotion.

Obviously you should try to minimize the length of time systemic steroids are used. But should you require them for a severe flare-up, it's equally important to do it right. Short pulses of steroids (in the form of injections or five-day dose packs) may cause the rebound phenomenon. The dosing is just enough to begin to make the patient feel good and the rash improve but may not be enough to regain control of the eczema. Once the steroids have been eliminated from your system, it's common for the eczema to return worse than ever!

It's no wonder dermatologists have looked for nonsteroidal treatments to control itching and protect sensitive skin. Over the past few years, several new and unique treatment options have become available—and they've been wonderful for patients and doctors alike.

Topical Immunomodulators

These steroid-free, topical prescription therapies include Protopic (tacrolimus) and Elidel (pimecrolimus). They are TIMs, or topical immunomodulators. In a person with eczema, the skin's immune cells react to irritants, such as dust, producing chemical messengers that cause a flare-up. TIMs stop the immune cells from creating these chemical messages, slowing or halting eczema.

Protopic and Elidel are typically prescribed for eczema that is unresponsive to topical steroids and antihistamines. Side effects include itching, stinging, and burning, but they're usually mild and brief. However, neither should be used on an area with an active herpes simplex infection, as it can prevent healing or cause a flare-up.

Triceram

Eczema disrupts the barrier function of the epidermis, the top layer of skin.

Scientists at the University of California at San Francisco have discovered the exact molecular ratio of three epidermal fats (ceramides, fatty acids, and cholesterol) that is necessary to repair and restore the barrier function.

Triceram and Nouriva Repair are moisturizers that help restore and repair this barrier.

These creams are nonsteroidal, noncomedogenic, hypoallergenic, and fragrance-free. They are safe for long-term use by both adults and children.

Light Therapy

In eczema resistant to other forms of treatment, a dermatologist may prescribe PUVA, a combination of the topical or oral drug psoralen (P) and treatment with medical-strength ultraviolet radiation (UVA). Psoralen sensitizes the skin, allowing the light waves to decrease the activity of the white blood cells responsible for inflammation.

Light therapy isn't without drawbacks; it can have short-term side effects, like burns, and long-term risks, like skin cancer.

Tar

It may not be aesthetically pleasing, but tar can help control itching, redness, and scaling when all else fails. An old-time concoction prepared by dermatologists includes 10% liquid coal tar distillate, 5% salicylic acid, and 3% lactic acid in an ointment base. It smells bad and stains the skin, but old-time southern dermatologists swear by it.

More Topical Options for Itch Control

Zonalon cream is a topical antihistamine cream that helps resolve some of the worst itching associated with eczema. It's intended for short-term use.

Pramoxine is a very helpful ingredient whenever you want to deaden that dreadful itching. Applying it instead of scratching helps cut down inflammation, allowing the skin to heal more rapidly, diminishing the risk of skin infection, and helping prevent unsightly thickening. You can find pramoxine combined with a hydrating base for sensitive skin (Prax Lotion) or with menthol (PrameGel).

Oral antihistamines such as nonprescription Benadryl and prescription Atarax (hydroxyzine) are lifesavers when treating highly itchy skin. These antihistamines make you drowsy; watch your dosing. In my opinion, nonsedating antihistamines don't adequately control eczema-induced itching.

Avoid applying over-the-counter products that contain a topical anesthetic like lidocaine to active eczema—they can cause allergic contact dermatitis.

Natural Treatments

Evening primrose oil, black currant–seed oil, and borage-seed oil all contain high levels of gamma linoleic acid (GLA), an essential fatty acid that may help control eczema. GLA promotes the production of prostaglandin E_1 (PGE 1), an anti-inflammatory biochemical. And GLA helps protect and repair the epidermal barrier. Research shows that people with eczema may have an abnormality in their ability to process fatty acids, resulting in a deficiency of GLA. These oils are often incorporated into supplements and topical skin care, to help restore the disrupted barrier. Foods that deliver linolenic acid—which, theoretically, can be converted into PGE 1—include nuts, seeds, and vegetable oils.

On the downside of natural treatments: two eczema patients developed kidney failure after ingesting a Chinese herbal remedy for eczema that contained aristocholic acid. One of these patients subsequently developed kidney cancer. Needless to say, I strongly caution you against using any herbal remedy containing this ingredient.

SKIN CARE FOR ECZEMA PATIENTS

Successful treatment of severely dry or cracked and split (fissured) skin is highly dependent upon the choice of moisturizers. Using a light hand lotion will *not* hydrate dried, fissured areas, allowing cracks to heal. You can nurse fissures back to health by following a three-step healing routine.

Cracks? Fight Back

Twice a day, apply antibacterial Polysporin ointment into the splits. Do not use a topical antibiotic ointment containing neomycin, which is a notorious cause of contact dermatitis.

At least nightly, use DERMAdoctor Handy Manum. It contains 1% hydrocortisone in a base that will soften splits and restore a protective skin barrier.

As often as you think of it, apply your moisturizing cream. Consider Vanicream Moisturizing Skin Care Cream, Triceram, Moisturel, or TheraSeal. Often means *often:* apply the moisturizer every time you wash your hands or do the dishes. Keep a second container of the product in your purse or glove compartment so you always have it available.

Don't use cyanoacrylate super glue. It doesn't help heal fissures and can lead to allergic contact dermatitis.

Beating a Bacterial Infection

Many patients scratch themselves to the point of developing a bacterial infection of the skin, indicated by weepy skin or golden-colored crusting.

Domeboro, a topical astringent, helps resolve the weeping and eliminate early infection. Mix the Domeboro according to the directions on the package and apply it with a moist compress.

I also ask patients to apply Polysporin, Bacitracin, or prescription Bactroban ointment to the area. I avoid topical neomycin-containing antibacterial products, as many eczema patients are allergic to these. Oral antibiotics are sometimes required for more advanced cases of skin infection or for areas that simply won't heal.

Picking the Right Products

The skin of eczema patients is very sensitive to ingredients found in skin care products—which is why these products are often the cause of their excessive itching. Avoiding products containing fragrance and color is crucial in reducing skin irritation. Products by Vanicream and Free & Clear are ideal if you have eczema. Created by a former Mayo Clinic pharmacist, they are free of just about everything in a skin care product that can cause skin irritation.

Avoid household items that are notorious for aggravating eczema.

They include: fabric softener dryer sheets (unless you've found a brand that is fragrance- and color-free); traditional detergents; soap (containing lye, which is quite caustic); and ordinary antibacterial soaps. (If you want to use an antibacterial soap, Lever 2000 has a mild base less likely to cause skin irritation.)

Here is a short list of some of my other favorite easy-to-find products that are ideal for eczema patients:

Soaps: Cetaphil Gentle Skin Cleanser, Vanicream Cleansing Bar, Aveeno Moisturizing Bar for Dry Skin, Oilatum Cleansing Bar, Unscented.

Moisturizers: Vanicream Moisturizing Skin Care Cream, Eucerin Cream, TheraSeal, Triceram, Nouriva Repair, and SBR-Lipocream Skin Barrier Repair Cream.

Detergents: Cheer Free, All Free, Dreft, Woolite.

FINAL THOUGHTS

Don't forget to moisturize immediately after bathing. Moisturize again at least once more during the day, especially during the fall and winter. Keeping the skin hydrated and maintaining a good barrier between you and the environment can go a long way to preventing significant flare-ups. (And I can't overstress the importance of frequent use of hand moisturizing creams for those prone to dyshidrotic eczema.)

Anyone with eczema should have regular follow-up appointments with her dermatologist, keeping prescriptions up to date, to nip flare-ups in the bud.

Ask the DERMAdoctor

QUESTION:

Can you please tell me which laundry detergents are best for someone with eczema?

The DERMAdoctor:

I suggest selecting laundry detergents that are free of both fragrance and color. Many brands have added these as options to their lines. Tide used to be a notorious problem for those with eczema, but they now have a product that is both color- and fragrance-free. Cheer also makes one. I have traditionally suggested either Dreft or Woolite. Remember, if a product says it is "free," make sure it means free of color and fragrance, not just a harsh chemical or phosphates.

Avoid fabric softener dryer sheets. The reason they leave clothing smelling so nice is that they deposit a heavy residue of fragrance, a notorious flare factor for eczema.

ENLARGED PORES AND BLACKHEADS

The Theory and Practice of Porefection

Concern with pore size is practically a national obsession, no doubt provoked by the inescapable media images of glamorous faces air-brushed to an impossibly unattainable perfection. This skewed perception of how skin should look is about as realistic as thinking a Barbie doll's shape is similar to true female anatomy. The truth is: pores are a fact of life. They aren't invisible, and everyone has them. But not everyone knows the best way to minimize their appearance.

THE PURPOSE OF PORES

A pore is really nothing more than the opening of the hair follicle onto the surface of the skin; wherever there is a hair, there is a pore. But that opening plays a vital role in normal skin function. Without pores, there'd be nowhere for hair to grow out of, and no method for skin oils to reach the surface, protecting skin from environmental dehydration.

The source of the hair follicle lies within the dermis, the deepest layer of skin. Midway up the dermal layer, the sebaceous oil gland empties into the hair follicle. And both skin oil (sebum) and hair breach the surface through the tiny aperture of the pore.

Why do pores appear larger than life?

Anything that attracts attention to pores or expands their natural architecture magnifies their appearance. You can deal with these factors. However, the closer you look in the mirror, the larger your pores will appear. If you habitually examine your skin in the magnifying side of your beauty mirror, maybe that mirror isn't really your best friend. So put it aside and address the factors that really *do* wreak havoc with your pores.

PORELY DESIGNED

Genetics may be to blame. Pores are barely visible on those prone to drier skin, while individuals with oily, thicker skin tend to have larger-looking, more noticeable pores. Skin type is hereditary.

Sun damage is another cause. Sun damage and aging cause the epidermis to thicken, making it more likely that a rim of cells will collect around the edges of individual pores. While microscopic, these added rings exaggerate pore diameter.

Pores can become more visible due to lack of good skin grooming and poor exfoliation. Too much surface oil and the remnants of naturally shed skin cells can collect within and around the pores, exaggerating pore size.

Blackheads and enlarged pores often go hand in hand. Blackheads can either expand pores or simply focus attention on them.

FILMY NOIR

Pores are a natural part of the skin; blackheads are the superficial plugs that can form within them. Why does anyone get blackheads?

The process starts in the interior of the gland, where sticky cells aren't properly shed and form a microscopic plug. Sebaceous glands continue to produce sebum, which accumulates behind the plug. The excess oil nourishes bacteria (like *Proprionibacterium acnes* and *Staphylococcus epidermidis*). Oils, bacteria, and dead skin cells form a larger plug, which chokes the opening of the hair follicle and expands the diameter of the pore. Contact with air allows oxygenation to take place, turning the plug black and making the plug—and the pore—even more visible.

IN SEARCH OF POREFECTION

You can't change the physical diameter of a pore; it's determined by nature and genetics. But you can successfully mask the visibility of a pore.

However, the best way to do that is *not* necessarily with facials and extractions. Yes, a well-performed manual exfoliation can cleanse cellular matter that has been caught beneath the surface. But a poorly performed facial or extraction can rupture oil glands, contributing to sudden acne flare-ups. And neither a facial nor an extraction tackles other factors that contribute to large-looking pores.

A strategic combination of skin care products can often solve the *multiple* issues that contribute to larger-looking pores, producing the best results. By targeting the seven key factors that cause exaggerated pore diameter, you can quickly minimize visibility. You want to:

- Unplug debris
- Eliminate bacteria
- Reduce excessive oiliness
- Remove blackheads
- Reduce sun damage
- Smooth out edges of pores
- Draw the pores closed

GREAT SKIN CARE FOR PORES

So you know what needs to be done, but how do you accomplish these goals? By knowing the hows and whys of the following pore-minimizing performers.

Topical Vitamin A Treatments

Topical vitamin A treatments work by normalizing the keratinization process. This helps prevent the cells that line the gland from sticking together and thereby promotes more effective exfoliation. Used on blackheads, they loosen the plug and chemically "peel" the rim of the pore. However, they can cause the skin to flake and become red and irritated.

There are many different prescription medications in this category: Retin-A, Retin-A Micro gel, Tazorac, Avita, and Differin. Renova and Avage are prescription topical retinoids targeted at skin rejuvenation, but they also work as potent pore minimizers.

Retinol is an over-the-counter form of vitamin A. While not as potent as its prescription counterpart, it still offers help in reducing pore visibility and improving skin texture. Afirm 3X contains 0.6% retinol and SkinCeuticals contains up to 1% retinol; both are highly concentrated.

Don't let retinol fool you; it's still as potentially irritating as the prescription options. Use prescription and over-the-counter topical vitamin A treatments sparingly: every other night, waiting thirty minutes after washing before application.

All topical retinoids increase one's sensitivity to the sun, so don't forget your SPF 30 during the day. Vitamin A products should never be used while pregnant or nursing.

Retinyl palmitate is another over-the-counter form of topical vitamin A; it is less potent than retinol. Nevertheless, follow the advice above when you use it.

AHAs and BHA

As far back as Cleopatra, alpha hydroxy acids have been used in skin care.

Alpha hydroxy acid (AHA) is a blanket term for a variety of fruit- and milk-derived acids, including glycolic, citric, lactic, malic, and tartaric. AHAs help disintegrate the "glue" that holds dead, dry skin cells to the surface of the skin. The epidermis is thus exfoliated, leaving a silky texture. And removal of this external barrier enables easier, deeper penetration of other skin treatments.

BHA (beta hydroxy acid) is the trendy term for salicylic acid, a natural acid derived from willow bark, wintergreen leaves, and sweet birch bark. It also works to exfoliate cellular debris and unplug pores. It's a "golden oldie" and a very effective ingredient, long used in dermatology for acne therapy. Many skin care products blend AHA and BHA to help amplify chemical exfoliation—try, for example, M.D. Forté Glycare Perfection Gel.

Azelaic Acid

Azelaic acid is a naturally occurring acid found in grains like wheat, rye, and barley. In lab studies, it's been shown to possess antibacterial activity against the common skin bacteria *Proprionibacterium acnes* and *Staphylococcus epidermidis*.

And as shown by electron microscopic and routine microscopic evidence of patients enrolled in Azelex Cream studies, azelaic acid appears to be an effective means of reducing microcomedones, or early blackhead and whitehead formation.

Azelaic acid can be found in prescription Azelex Cream and Finacea.

Oil Reduction

Granted, not everyone looking to minimize the appearance of their pores has an issue with oiliness. But if you do, or if blackheads are an issue, reducing excess oil on the surface of the skin will make it less likely that your pores will develop the plugs that contribute to more visible pores.

DERMAdoctor Tease Zone Oil Control Gel helps absorb oils and gives the skin a matte appearance without drying it out.

Those plagued by extreme oiliness may find it highly beneficial to wash with M.D. Forté Glycare Cleansing Gel once or twice a day, followed by the application of M.D. Forté Glycare I and then DERMAdoctor Tease Zone Oil Control Gel.

Using a topical vitamin A therapy, solo, every other night, such as Tazorac Gel, rapidly controls severe oiliness.

Physical Exfoliation

Whether you are looking to use an exfoliating cleanser like Peter Thomas Roth AHA/BHA Face & Body Polish, home microdermabrasion creams, or the DermaNew Microdermabrasion Facial Rejuvenation System, or simply trying to extract that stubborn blackhead with a Tweezerman Comedone Extractor, remember: gently does it! Physical exfoliation has its place in minimizing the appearance of pores. But don't scrub until your skin bleeds! If aggressive exfoliation is your passion, consider investing in a series of medical microdermabrasions or medically performed chemical peels.

Picture Porefect

DERMAdoctor Picture Porefect works on multiple levels to reduce the visibility of pores. It effectively targets blackheads, past sun damage, excess oil buildup, bacterial proliferation, and poor exfoliation. It accomplishes all this by a unique blend of ingredients, including an active astringent that draws closed freshly cleansed pores. Essentially, Picture Porefect is everything you need for smaller-looking pores in a single product, keeping your regimen simple and highly effective. Apply it once or twice a day to keep your skin looking radiant and flawless.

FINAL THOUGHTS

If you're thinking about trying to get skin like that of the model on the cover of the latest beauty magazine, forget it—she doesn't have skin like that either! But that doesn't mean you have to let nature and genetics dictate how your pores look. Follow the guidelines in this chapter, and you'll be as "porefect" as can be.

Ask the DERMAdoctor

QUESTION:

One large blackhead keeps appearing along my underwear line, in the crease of my inner thigh. I have tried exfoliating, and I keep the area really clean, but it won't go away. Is there a product especially for this area, or should I treat it the same way I would the blackheads on my face?

The DERMAdoctor:

A large single blackhead is not an uncommon condition: I also have one on my hip. These giant dilated pores of Winer (as dermatologists call them) are isolated, physical pore enlargements, and short of having yours surgically removed (a simple enough procedure), it is there to stay. Periodically, you can express the debris with a comedone extractor, but it will most certainly fill up again over time.

The presence of a large "blackhead" can also be the first sign of a sebaceous cyst. Envision a water balloon filled with cottage cheese that continues to expand until it ultimately bursts; that's the life cycle of a sebaceous cyst. A firm nodule beneath the surface of the skin, a foul smell, or cottage cheese–like material emanating from the opening are all clues that there's more to the blackhead than a simple plugged pore. Surgical excision is recommended to remove this type of cyst.

FEMININE DERMATOLOGY

Delicate Subjects, Delicate Skin

Equality of the sexes doesn't always apply in dermatology; certain skin conditions or disease manifestations have symptoms unique to women. These "feminine" skin concerns deserve to be discussed.

LICHEN SCLEROSIS ET ATROPHICUS

Lichen sclerosus et atrophicus (LS et A) is a chronic inflammatory disorder that results in thinning (atrophy) of the skin. This atrophy is much like that seen with excessive steroid use: the skin becomes thin and white, and small, wispy spider veins may become visible. Genital lesions outnumber lesions that may arise elsewhere by five to one. LS et A can cause discomfort. Burning and/or itching may develop, and sexual intercourse may be painful.

No cause has been discovered. Biopsy with DIF (direct immuno-fluorescence, a stain that helps detect autoimmune and blistering disorders) confirms the diagnosis.

Treatments for genital LS et A include topical steroids, topical testosterone, and systemic retinoids (Soriatane, Accutane). Other treatments that have been tried include penicillamine and systemic steroids. Theories involving infection with *Borrelia*, the spirochetal bacteria that causes Lyme disease, have also led to physicians prescribing antibiotic therapy.

LICHEN PLANUS

LP can cause lacy, white streaks and erosions of the genital mucosa. Genital LP can be present with or without extragenital involvement. Symptoms include painful intercourse, burning, and/or itching. Biopsy with DIF confirms the diagnosis. Treatment may include systemic retinoids (Accutane, Soriatane), cyclosporine, Lovenox, or steroids.

For more information, please see the chapter "Lichen Planus" on page 148.

FEMININE ITCHING

Vaginal itching is uncomfortable and embarrassing. It can be a laborious task to determine the source, given the seemingly endless list of possible causes. Here are just some of the many issues to consider.

Is it a contact dermatitis, a latex allergy, a chemical irritant, or friction and dryness?

Fragrance, detergents, and chemical irritants can all potentially cause a problem. Possibilities range from fabric softener dryer sheets, Clorox, and laundry detergent to spermicides, condoms, douches, and feminine sprays. Avoid applying perfume in this area, use fragrance- and dye-free detergent, and skip the fabric softener dryer sheets. Switch to white, unscented toilet tissue.

Condom Conundrums

Could you be allergic to condoms? If you have a latex allergy, you're undoubtedly already avoiding the "common" type of latex condom. But if you don't have this diagnosis and you suspect that your vaginal or vulvar rash, itching, and pain, or even systemic symptoms like hives or wheezing, are due to latex, there are steps you can take.

First, substitute condoms made of polyurethane for the latex versions. The female condom is also made of polyurethane.

Ask your doctor about testing to confirm (or disprove) your suspicions. A blood test called a latex-specific IgE and patch testing provide invaluable information.

If it's not the latex, could the problem still involve the condom? Some condoms contain a simple lubricant; in others, the lubricant is combined with a spermicide. Spermicidal jellies and other topical contraceptives (foams, creams, etc.) kill spermatozoa. But could they be causing irritation or allergy? Nonoxynol 9 and nonoxynol 11 are the spermicides more likely to cause irritation.

A Solution That May Be a Problem

Ironically, Vagisil, a product made to control itching, may on occasion be an irritant or cause allergic contact dermatitis. I once consulted on a patient who was literally addicted to Vagisil. Nothing could convince her to give it up, despite the evidence that she was experiencing a reaction to the product. Check the ingredients in your analgesic medication for feminine itching. If the product contains benzocaine, resorcinol, or fragrance, one of these could be the culprit.

YEAST INFECTIONS

Vaginal yeast infection (vaginitis) is due to the yeast *Candida albicans*. Symptoms include a thick, white, cottage cheese–like discharge, odor, irritation, and/or itching.

While most women won't make an appointment with their dermatologist to discuss a yeast infection, what will cause them to pick up the phone and call the dermatologist is a yeast infection triggered by an antibiotic, often an acne medication. Antibiotics upset the delicate balance within the vagina, killing the normal flora (bacteria) residing there. This allows overgrowth of "outside" microorganisms like *Candida* to flourish.

Vaginal yeast infections are not considered a sexually transmitted disease, although in some circumstances it is possible to pass the infection between partners.

Fortunately, up to 90 percent of cases rapidly respond to over-the-counter medications like Monistat.

I counsel patients who have begun antibiotics to try to remain on the medication while being treated for the yeast infection. Most patients will have a single bout of the yeast infection, after which their bodies will adjust to the antibiotic. For those who go on to experience chronic yeast infections, I either switch the type of systemic antibiotic or move to a nonantibiotic acne therapy.

MENOPAUSAL DRYNESS

The drop in estrogen as the body shifts into menopause can lead to new problems: vaginal dryness and the common complaint of feminine itching. Lubricants, topical estrogens, and hormone replacement therapy (when appropriate) can all help reverse this problem.

VULVODYNIA

Vulvodynia is characterized by burning, stinging pain of the vulva in the absence of any identifiable disorder or infection. For some patients, this pain is constant and disabling.

Treatment options include estrogen creams, calcium citrate supplements, biofeedback, and a low-oxalate diet. A combination of these approaches, rather than monotherapy, has shown the best results.

Oxalate is a chemical found in many foods (spinach, tea, chocolate, beets) that increases the formation of certain types of kidney stones. It is thought that reduced oxalate in the urine reduces irritation. Calcium supplements also reduce oxalates in the urine.

SEXUALLY TRANSMITTED DISEASES

Historically, dermatology was the field of dermatology and venereology. Dermatologists were the ones who diagnosed and treated (with the few therapies available at the time) sexually transmitted diseases. The reason: most STDs have some form of skin manifestation. So let's look at a few of these.

Syphilis

A rise in drug abuse (involving needle sharing) and unprotected sex has led to a surprising resurgence of syphilis. This infectious STD has significant, serious systemic implications. Caused by the microorganism *Treponema pallidum,* syphilis has a four-stage presentation: the chancre (sore), which forms at the site of inoculation; the rash of secondary syphilis; the latent period; and the late chronic tertiary period, presenting with neurological damage.

Unlike their male partners, most women never see the sore that develops at the site of infection, as it is typically obscured from view. This painless, firm, red, ulcerated nodule is likely to be accompanied by swelling of the lymph nodes in the groin. The chancre appears about three weeks after initial infection. Left untreated, it disappears by eight weeks. Six weeks later, the patient typically experiences low-grade fever and myalgias (muscle soreness)—typical symptoms associated with the onset of a flulike illness.

As the fever breaks, a characteristic rash develops, covering the body.

While syphilis has been called the "great imitator" and can have count-less forms, the rash most commonly resembles that of pityriasis rosea. Important differentiating signs that help make the diagnosis include: more widespread involvement than PR; involvement of the palms and soles; possible sores within the mouth; and "growths" called condyloma lata on the moist genital surfaces. This is the stage that will cause most syphilis patients to see a dermatologist. During my residency, I don't think a month went by that I didn't see one or more syphilis patients.

A positive blood test (RPR or VDRL) confirms the diagnosis. The patient and all known contacts are treated with antibiotics. Syphilis in the primary and secondary stages is easily treated with long-acting peni-cillin G benzathine. Untreated, it progresses to an asymptomatic (yet contagious) latent period and, ultimately, to its tertiary form, accompa-nied by serious cardiovascular and neurological complications.

Syphilis can also cause birth defects when passed by an infected mother to her unborn child. In a recent year, 1,049 cases of congenital syphilis were reported in the United States.

Genital Warts

Genital warts are one of the most common sexually transmitted dis-eases, with an estimated twenty million Americans infected. Genital warts are caused by HPV (human papillomavirus) and are passed by intimate contact.

There are over one hundred strains of HPV that cause warts. Most strains of HPV are annoying but not dangerous. Warts that infect the skin on the hands and elsewhere on the body do not cause genital warts, and vice versa.

Venereal warts form in the genital region in both men and women. Male patients can form warts on the penis, scrotum, and anus. Female patients may develop genital warts on the vulva, labia, vaginal opening, and anus. Growths are flesh-toned or pink soft, moist bumps; they can appear individually or in small to very large clusters.

Both the visible wart and the viral particles shed by invisibly infected cells are highly contagious. Two-thirds of individuals who have unprotected sexual contact with an infected partner will become infected with HPV. The virus can be spread through any form of sex-ual contact (vaginal, anal, or oral).

Incredibly, only 1 percent of patients infected with HPV have visi-ble growths. In men, genital warts are easily visible, making the diagnosis simple. In women, growths are much more difficult to find. They may be hidden in an area not easily seen, or the infection may be picked up only when a Pap smear result is abnormal.

HPV can cause cervical cells to change (become dysplastic). Ultimately, cervical cancer may develop. Fortunately, while evidence of HPV is found in all cervical cancer, most women with HPV do not go on to develop cervical cancer. Genetics and exposure to carcinogens (like cigarette smoke) may play a role.

You can destroy the warts, but you cannot eradicate the infection. Treatment is aimed at removing visible or symptomatic warts and improving the patient's health (and thus immune system) and requires vigilant monitoring. Therapy for removing warts includes:

- Podophyllin (stops cellular division; this treatment is washed off after forty-five minutes)
- Podophyllotoxin (stops cellular division; this is left on)
- Imiquimod cream (immunomodulator)
- TCA (trichloracetic acid)
- 5-fluorouracil (topical chemotherapy)
- Alpha interferon injections (antiviral medication)
- Liquid nitrogen (cryotherapy)
- CO_2 ablative laser
- Electrodesiccation and curettage (burning and scraping)

Pregnant or nursing patients should not use podophyllin, podophyllotoxin, or 5-fluorouracil.

An abnormal Pap smear, a history of HPV, or visible genital warts should prompt your gynecologist to perform a colposcopy. The mucosal genital surfaces are painted with vinegar; HPV-infected cells will turn white. The doctor can then look at them more closely with the colposcope, a tool that magnifies skin cells. If necessary, a biopsy (piece of tissue) will be taken for further in-depth microscopic evaluation.

In unusual cases, HPV can infect a newborn during delivery. A potentially life-threatening condition known as laryngeal papillomatosis may result—warts form in the baby's throat and may obstruct breathing.

Prevention is your best option. Although practicing safe sex with a condom does not prevent the spread of HPV 100 percent of the time, currently it is the best method. Any woman who learns that her partner has HPV should make certain that a barrier method (condom or female condom) is used. It is also important to see your physician regularly for an examination and Pap smear.

Research on HPV is focusing on a preventive vaccine.

Pubic Lice

Pubic lice are six-legged insects spread by sexual contact. Commonly called "crabs" because of their crablike body shape, *Phthirus pubis* invades areas of coarse body hair—primarily the pubic hair (hence the name), eyebrows, eyelashes, facial hair (including the beard and mustache), and underarm hair. Pubic lice are not head lice, nor do they infest pets. Sharing of recently used towels, bedding, and clothing also spreads pubic lice.

Itching in the genital area is usually what brings a patient to the doctor. The skin may be broken—evidence of avid scratching. Nits (eggs) are the most common finding. These eggs are tightly attached to the hair shaft. Rarely, live lice may also be found.

Treatment is similar to that for head lice. Permethrin-based lice shampoos, such as Rid or Nix, are beneficial. Lindane (Kwell) is a prescription lice-killing medication. It is potent and effective but potentially associated with neurotoxicity; it's definitely not for use by pregnant or nursing women. After the patient washes with the medicated shampoo, the nits should be combed out of the hair. Treatment should be repeated in ten days to kill any newly hatched lice that escaped nit removal. Sexual partners should be treated at the same time.

Wash all clothing and linens in hot water, followed by a hot dryer. Any bedding or other materials that cannot withstand the laundry should be placed in plastic bags for ten to fourteen days. This allows residual nits to hatch and young lice to die.

A tip for avoiding pubic lice: when shopping for bathing suits, don't try on that suit bottom without your underwear.

Genital Herpes

No discussion of STDs would be complete without mentioning genital herpes, a disorder that affects an estimated forty-five million Americans and is caused by the herpes simplex virus.

Genital herpes is spread by skin-to-skin contact with an active lesion, most commonly through sexual contact (vaginal, oral, or anal). HSV can spread from one area of the body to another through contact with an open blister, but it doesn't spread via inanimate objects like toilet seats.

Women are infected with genital herpes (HSV type 2) more often than men, perhaps because of lowered immunity during menstruation or the ability of the virus to penetrate vaginal muscosa. Women also tend to experience more discomfort during the first outbreak (headache, flulike symptoms) and subsequent outbreaks (including painful urination).

And it's more difficult for women to be diagnosed with HSV. Men typically form easily visible clusters of blisters on a red base; in women the lesions usually form inside the vagina, urethra, or cervix. Plus, many women may misinterpret the discomfort of an HSV infection, wrongly blaming a problem like a yeast, bladder, or urinary tract infection. If you have recurrent (once a month or more) bouts of what you suspect is one of those infections, check with your physician for medical confirmation. A viral culture can help identify the true culprit, allowing your doctor to recommend an effective treatment.

Some women with genital herpes don't experience symptoms but are contagious, actively shedding viral particles via their vaginal secretions. If left undiagnosed, a woman can unknowingly infect her sexual partner or her child at the time of delivery. Neonatal herpes can threaten the life of a newborn. If you are pregnant and know that you or your partner has genital herpes, check with your physician to learn how to prevent complications.

Whether HSV presents as genital herpes or cold sores, the treatments are the same. Please refer to the chapter "Cold Sores" on page 48 for more information about the treatment of HSV.

JOCK ITCH

A woman with jock itch? Surely there must be a more feminine phrase. Regardless of what it's called (tinea cruris is the appropriate medical term), this condition is due to overgrowth of a "true" fungus, unlike the yeast that causes vaginal infections. Often seen as red, scaly patches on the inner thighs and inguinal folds, the fungus may continue to grow in an outward expansion.

Topical antifungal creams rapidly nip this problem in the bud. Try Lamisil AT for jock itch. Keep the area dry and avoid tight clothing. Occasional resistant cases need some help from prescription antifungal therapy like griseofulvin (Gris-PEG) or terbinafine (oral Lamisil).

As with most infections, tinea cruris may be spread through skin-to-skin contact. It's not an STD, but you could catch it from your partner.

BARTHOLIN CYSTS

Bartholin glands secrete fluid to moisten the vagina. Situated on either side of the vaginal opening, these glands may become plugged, leading to the formation of a cyst. If the cyst gets inflamed or infected, it may become swollen, red, and painful. Treatment includes incision and drainage, performed by your physician. Antibiotic therapy may also be prescribed.

POLYCYSTIC OVARY SYNDROME

One in fifteen women suffers from polycystic ovary syndrome (PCOS), a condition in which the ovaries become studded with multiple cysts.

Patients struggle with irregular menstrual cycles (or amenorrhea), obesity, acne, hirsutism (excessive facial hair), acanthosis nigricans (darkened, velvety thickening of underarm skin), and infertility. Excessive androgens, such as testosterone, wreak havoc upon the skin, stimulating blemishes and excessive facial hair.

Therapy focuses on medications that interfere with the formation of DHT (the active metabolite of testosterone), including spironolactone, Yasmin, and Ortho Tri-Cyclen. By effectively reducing DHT levels, these medications can control undesirable masculine skin changes.

ALL ABOUT THE BREAST
Inflammatory Breast Cancer (IBC)

This form of breast cancer accounts for a small percentage (1 to 4 percent) of all breast cancer cases. But it represents the worst-case scenario whenever a dermatologist evaluates a rash of the breast.

Inflammatory breast cancer (IBC) presents with swelling of the affected breast tissue. The area is warm to the touch, red, may develop a peau d'orange (orange peel) texture and itch, and the nipple may become inverted. Lymph nodes may or may not be swollen.

IBC is a rapidly growing form of breast cancer, and timely diagnosis and treatment is your best way to beat this serious illness. IBC may be confused with an infection, contact dermatitis, eczema, or mastitis (if breast-feeding). Biopsy is the best method to accurately make the diagnosis.

Inflammatory breast cancer is aggressively treated with mastectomy, radiation, and chemotherapy.

If the texture of your breast becomes dimpled, the color changes, or it becomes red and swollen, contact your physician immediately.

Paget's Disease of the Breast

Paget's disease of the breast is almost always limited to women. An uncommon form of breast cancer (1 to 4 percent of cases), Paget's is an intraductal cancer that grows outwardly onto the skin.

Patients will typically come to see to the dermatologist with a prolonged history of an eczema patch on the nipple and/or areola. Additional symptoms may include drainage, bleeding, burning, redness, ulceration, breast mass, nodule, or scaling. Skin biopsy is essential for an accurate diagnosis. As with most forms of cancer, early detection is critical.

Radiation Therapy for Breast Cancer

Radiation takes a toll on the skin, and delicate breast tissue is no exception. While radiation therapy itself is painless, the potential side effects can cause discomfort. Some tender, loving care will go a long way to helping protect the skin.

Radiation can dry and irritate the skin. Avoid soap that contains fragrance and dye; choose a gentle cleanser instead. Apply a protective moisturizing cream. Vanicream, Triceram, and Nouriva Repair are all excellent options.

Radiation may darken the skin, increase the appearance of pore size, increase sweating and produce sunburnlike skin changes. Don't forget to wear a sunscreen of SPF 30 daily; it's important to protect the skin from further light exposure. Pore size and blotchy skin discoloration usually return to normal once radiation therapy is complete.

Breast Engorgement or Breast Infection?

Nursing can lead to skin changes that may seem similar yet have very different causes and treatments.

Breast engorgement is due to a slowing of blood flow and lymphatic drainage, which causes pooling of fluid. It is corrected by increasing milk production. The use of an electric pump may be desirable. Ice packs are useful. A doughnut-shaped gel pack that can be placed in the fridge, called Bustbuddies, is innovative and effective.

Mastitis is an infection of the breast that is seen in 1 percent of nursing women. Systemic symptoms of fever and fatigue and general flulike symptoms distinguish mastitis from breast engorgement. Antibiotics and warm compresses help treat mastitis.

Breast-Feeding and Thrush

Warm, moist conditions are the perfect breeding ground for thrush, a common yeast infection caused by *Candida albicans.* Both the nursing infant and the mother can develop symptoms. White patches develop on the tongue and palate; infected nipples may become red and sore. Treatment with antiyeast medications may be prescribed by your physician.

Concerns About Breast Implants

More than 1 percent of all American women have enhanced their appearance with breast implants. The primary problems associated with a breast augmentation include scar formation, capsular contraction, and rippling.

Scar Formation. Postsurgical scarring isn't minor, but it is fairly straightforward. Thick, raised keloid scars may be treated with steroid injections, silicone gels and tapes, and, sometimes, scar revision, a surgical process.

Capsular Contraction. As a part of the natural healing process, the body builds a wall around the implant; in other words, the area is encapsulated. Should the capsule contract, it will squeeze the fluid-filled sac, making the skin feel hard, causing pain, or dislodging the implant.

It is estimated that 5 to 10 percent of all breast-implant patients will experience capsular contraction, which can affect one or both breasts. Silicone-filled implants are more likely to cause capsular contraction; saline implants have less risk. Placement of the implant can also be a factor: implants placed beneath the muscle have a more favorable outcome than those placed above the muscle.

This problem is surgically correctable.

Rippling. Rippling refers to wrinkles that form on the skin surface in response to underfilled or leaking implants. Small implants placed beneath the muscle are least likely to cause rippling; implants significantly larger than the breast tissue and placed above the muscle are most likely to cause this problem.

FINAL THOUGHTS

Feminine skin concerns can be distressing, embarrassing, and at times very uncomfortable. Today, however, an atmosphere exists where health matters, no matter how personal, can be openly discussed. Don't let embarrassment prevent you from seeking the answers you deserve.

Ask the DERMAdoctor

QUESTION:

I'm twenty and I was told at sixteen that I have a mild form of polycystic ovary syndrome. I have had acne since I was eleven. I have tried many products, both prescription and over the counter. I was on a contraceptive for four years, hoping my acne would clear up, but to no avail. Do you have any recommendations?

The DERMAdoctor:

Polycystic ovary syndrome can result in facial acne due to hormonal variations. Oral contraceptives have been used for both acne and PCOS. You may want to discuss with your physician the possibility of trying oral spironolactone (Aldactone). This water pill (diuretic) interferes with DHT, the active metabolite of testosterone that increases male hormonal symptoms such as cystic acne of the face. The possible downsides: lower blood pressure and, for some women, irregular menstrual cycles.

Since polycystic ovary syndrome can put a patient at a slightly higher risk of developing insulin-resistant diabetes, one way to deal with both the acne and to reduce insulin resistance would be to reduce your carbohydrate intake. While it remains unclear whether what you eat causes acne, a recent study suggests that highly processed carbohydrates (white bread, pasta, pastries) can increase the potential for acne. Aerobic exercise is also helpful in treating insulin resistance.

QUESTION:

Which is more effective at treating recent post-breast-augmentation scars: Kelo-cote (silicone gel) or Mederma?

The DERMAdoctor:

The clinical appearance of the scar is going to have the biggest impact on how it is dealt with. If it is a simple, flat scar, then typically something simple like Mederma is appropriate. If the scar is raised, then silicone gel or sheeting and/or injection of a steroid solution, such as Kenalog, into the keloidal scar will be more effective. Check with your surgeon for his or her opinion.

HAIR LOSS

Stop the Thinning

Just *thinking* about hair loss can make you anxious. Suspecting that you're actually losing your hair is far worse.

You lose some hair every day, of course: about 150 to 200 strands, out a total of 100,000 to 150,000. It may take a loss of up to 80 percent of normal hair for even a medically trained eye to diagnose a true thinning condition.

HAIR GROWTH CYCLES

To better understand hair loss and its treatments, you need to understand the normal biology of hair. Hair follicles go through three stages of development: growth, resting, and shedding. But not all hairs are in the same stage at the same time. (If they were, we'd all go completely bald every so often!)

The *anagen* (growth) phase lasts anywhere from two to six years. For Caucasians, hair grows approximately one-half to one inch a month; for African-Americans, it's much slower. The hair shaft is thickest during the anagen phase.

The *catagen* (resting) phase lasts just a few weeks.

The *telogen* (shedding) phase usually lasts five to six weeks. New hair begins to grow, and the telogen hair is shed and replaced. Telogen hair is very fine.

THE FIRST STEP: SEE YOUR DERMATOLOGIST

You suspect your hair is thinning, you've talked to your doctor about your concern—and maybe you were told that it's just part of the aging process and nothing can be done. Don't allow yourself to be patronized! Maybe it is aging—but you should have a dermatologist rule out other, more serious (and potentially treatable) causes. The most common include:

- Female-pattern alopecia (yes, there is "female-pattern" hair loss, and it's the most common cause of thinning hair in women)
- Thyroid disease
- Severe anemia
- Protein deficiency (often associated with recent significant weight loss)
- Lupus (an autoimmune disease)
- Side effects from a prescription drug
- Hormonal imbalance
- Zinc deficiency
- Iron deficiency
- Biotin deficiency
- Syphilis
- Traction alopecia (physical trauma to the hair shaft)
- Telogen effluvium (intense stress like childbirth or surgery pushes hair into the telogen phase)

There are a lot of possibilities. The right tests can sort through them. When visiting your dermatologist, ask to have the following blood tests done:

- CBC (complete blood count), with platelet and differential (looks for anemia)
- Complete general chemistry (includes a check for protein deficiency, which can be a symptom of several serious diseases; includes serum protein and albumin)
- Thyroid panel (including TSH, thyroid stimulating hormone)
- Serum iron, biotin, zinc levels
- VDRL or RPR (checks for syphilis)
- Free and total testosterone and DHEAS (not DHEA, which I have seen erroneously ordered).
- ANA, antinuclear antibody (looks for initial signs of lupus)
- Further autoimmune blood work, if a subtype of lupus is suspected

Punch Biopsy

If the test results are normal or unclear but the clinical picture remains suspicious, the doctor may suggest a simple punch biopsy, which is performed under local anesthetic.

Possible causes of hair loss that are diagnosable through a biopsy include:

- Alopecia areata (an autoimmune disease in which the immune system attacks the hair)
- Traction alopecia
- Telogen effluvium
- Lupus erythematosus, discoid lupus (SLE, DLE)
- Syphilis
- Amyloidosis (a disease in which a type of protein is deposited in tissues)
- Seborrheic dermatitis (dandruff), lichen planopilaris, psoriasis (inflammatory skin conditions)

In addition to routine staining, make sure your doctor orders a special stain called DIF (direct immunofluorescence) to be performed on the biopsy specimen. Unless ordered, it's not routinely done, and it's the best test for diagnosing autoimmune and blistering disorders.

The vast majority of causes of hair loss are treatable. Work with your doctor to determine a diagnosis. Then you can eliminate all the guesswork and begin appropriate therapy.

Certain causes of hair loss are more common in women. They include alopecia areata, postpartum hair loss, traction alopecia, female-pattern alopecia (a.k.a. androgenic alopecia or androgenetic alopecia), and lupus (discoid and SLE).

ALOPECIA AREATA

Alopecia areata is an autoimmune disease; the body gets "confused," thinks the hair is foreign (like a germ), and sets out to destroy it. The immune system can target any hair on the body, but the condition most commonly affects the scalp. And, for unknown reasons, young women are the primary victims.

In the classic picture of alopecia areata, a few random bald patches develop periodically. Hair loss may be hidden beneath the rest of the hair or may be highly visible in severe cases. Extreme cases feature loss of all scalp, facial, and body hair. Fortunately, this is unusual; patients most likely to struggle with this form of the disease develop it in early childhood.

Treatment

Treatment is aimed at stopping localized inflammation. Swaths of hair located at the nape of the neck and behind the ears tend to be more resistant to therapy than scattered, coin-shaped patches.

My favorite therapy is to inject a dilute steroid solution directly into the affected area. Early hair regrowth will often occur within a few weeks. Unfortunately, many insurance companies no longer pay for this therapy, unfairly labeling this autoimmune disease a "cosmetic" condition.

Other therapy options include immunotherapy with topical Protopic (tacrolimus), Elidel (pimecrolimus), or cyclosporine. PUVA—light therapy with the use of the oral prescription medication Oxsoralen-Ultra (methoxsalen)—has also been tried. Therapy with topical anthralin, an irritant, has also been used with some success.

Recurrence

If there's one thing certain about alopecia areata, it's that it tends to recur. Most patients become very skilled at recognizing subtle changes that precede hair loss and quickly get back to their doctor for therapy.

While we still don't understand what triggers autoimmune disorders, we do know that stress depresses the immune system and is a frequently reported event prior to a recurrence of alopecia areata.

POSTPARTUM HAIR LOSS (TELOGEN EFFLUVIUM)

Telogen effluvium is a temporary shedding of hair caused by a transitional push of more anagen (growth-phase) hairs than usual into the telogen (shedding) phase. Major stress triggers the condition, and childbirth is most commonly the stress involved when a woman experiences telogen effluvium. Other such stressors can include major surgery, severe illness, and deep grief. It is unlikely that everyday stress from work, family, or life in general will cause telogen effluvium.

This form of hair loss appears anywhere from three to nine months after the insult to the system and can go on for several months, or up to a year at its worst. The hair usually grows back within months, and no treatment is required.

TRACTION ALOPECIA

Hair styling isn't always kind to hair. Traction alopecia is hair loss caused by unrelenting root damage from a tightly braided or pulled hairstyle. Children are especially prone to this condition.

Early signs of traction alopecia are broken hair around the forehead and what seems to be a receding hairline. So if you like to wear your hair in a tight style, make sure to loosen it a bit around the hairline.

If it appears that chronic trauma has caused extensive inflammation, your dermatologist may choose to treat the problem with an injectable steroid solution. This can help prevent permanent hair loss.

A WOMAN WITH MALE-PATTERN BALDNESS?!

Women are not immune to so-called male-pattern baldness (a.k.a. female-pattern alopecia, androgenic alopecia, or androgenetic alopecia).

In fact, the cause of this type of hair loss is the same for both men and women: hair follicles that are genetically predisposed to being sensitive to DHT (dihydrotestosterone), a metabolite of testosterone. (Biology 101 review: all women have some circulating testosterone, just as all men have some circulating estrogens.) These follicles shrink upon exposure to DHT until they are no longer capable of producing hair. At the same time the follicles are shrinking, the growth stage becomes shorter and the resting and shedding phases longer. Ultimately, this results in very thin, short hair . . . until growth stops altogether.

Timing: Men Sooner, Women Later

DHT can start to affect men early, sometimes in their late teens or early twenties. About 20 percent of men suffer from male-pattern baldness in their twenties, 30 percent in their thirties, and so on, until the figure is 80 percent in their eighties.

Women, on the other hand, usually begin to see DHT-caused hair loss somewhat later, beginning in their early thirties. About 20 to 30 percent of women experience female-pattern alopecia.

Pattern: Men Front, Temples, and Top; Women All Over

In men, the susceptible hairs tend to be at the front of the scalp, on the temples, and on the top of the head, leading to stereotypical male balding, with a remaining rim of hair surrounding the head.

In women vulnerable to the effects of DHT, *all* scalp hair is potentially at risk, leading to more generalized loss.

Do You Have It?

In men, the diagnosis of male-pattern baldness is usually straightforward. But, as I discussed earlier, figuring out the exact cause of a generalized pattern of hair loss in women can require tests to rule out an underlying internal cause. For example, increased levels of free testosterone and DHT in women are often due to polycystic ovary syndrome (PCOS).

In addition to female-pattern alopecia, most women's hairlines naturally tend to recede with age. If you've got any doubt, take a look at your picture in the high school yearbook. (I have read that thinning for women tends to stabilize by their fifties, but I would dispute this point. How many elderly women can you recall where you were able to see through their hairdo to their entire scalp? I'd venture to say quite a few.)

TREATMENTS FOR FEMALE-PATTERN ALOPECIA

Let's say the diagnosis has been confirmed—you've got female-pattern alopecia. Now it's time to figure out what to do. Here are your options.

Rogaine

Some perceptive soul noticed that a medication used to control high blood pressure was causing hair to sprout randomly—thus leading to the development of Rogaine (minoxidil). When used topically, minoxidil converts into minoxidil sulfate, which activates potassium-regulating mechanisms in the hair follicle, triggering growth. (It does *not* work by increasing blood flow—and the myriad products on the market that claim they increase hair growth by increasing blood flow don't have the science behind them.)

Rogaine is available over the counter and comes in two strengths, 2% and 5%. It is recommended that women stick with the 2% Rogaine for Women, to minimize the risk of growing hair elsewhere, like the face.

Rogaine is applied twice daily; women should use it all over the scalp. It has been shown to regrow hair, but I prefer to look at it as a way to *prevent* further hair loss. If you start using it as soon as you notice thinning, you are far more likely to slow down or stop the loss, but it's unlikely you'll regrow an entire head of hair. And, as with all hair-loss therapies, if you stop the treatment, the hair will begin to fall out again.

Propecia

Treatment for hair loss, which used to be limited to topical Rogaine, has become more promising since the advent of Propecia (finas-

teride), a once-a-day prescription medication that blocks the formation of DHT. It can help regrow recently lost hair and slow or stop
hair loss. As with all hair-loss therapies, the earlier the treatment is
started, the better. And you need to take it indefinitely.

One problem: finasteride may cause genital abnormalities in the
male fetus, and the FDA has approved it only for men because of concerns about birth defects if a women becomes pregnant while taking the
drug. Pregnant women who live in a home where finasteride is used—
whether as Propecia for hair loss or Proscar for prostate problems—are
urged not to handle the medication and to stay clear of its dust.

But for those women unable to conceive (because of tubal liga-
tion, hysterectomy, or menopause), Propecia has been used "off label"
with good results. However, I have had some female patients report
breast tenderness or discharge. One patient finally discontinued the
medication because of her discomfort, although she was loath to do
so, as her hair was growing back nicely.

Propecia takes approximately six months to work. You can expect
to pay about $50 per month for your prescription, which is usually not
covered by health insurance. Avodart (dutasteride) is also indicated for
benign prostatic hypertrophy. It inhibits both types of 5 alpha-reductase enzymes, versus Proscar, which blocks only a single form of the
enzyme. 5 alpha-reductase is responsible for converting testosterone
into DHT. I have been asked if this pill may be used for female-pattern
alopecia. At this time it is not FDA approved for this use, and the drug
has the same warnings for pregnant women as does Propecia.

FEMALE-PATTERN ALOPECIA AND TELOGEN EFFLUVIUM

Sometimes the natural onset of female-pattern alopecia occurs coinci-
dentally with telogen effluvium. This congruence can make workup,
diagnosis, and therapy decisions more complicated. There is no single,
best answer here, but if this seems to be happening, and the diagnosis is
not obvious, a temporary trial of Rogaine may be helpful—and reassur-
ing to the patient, who will appreciate the chance to try *something* to
improve her situation.

OTHER OPTIONS FOR FIGHTING HAIR LOSS

There are other options to choose from when fighting hair loss.

FNS Follicle Nutrient Serum. This product contains natural ingredients said to stimulate hair regrowth. Photos of hair regrowth from initial clinical studies look impressive.

Nizoral Shampoo. Preliminary research suggests that Nizoral A-D Shampoo may also provide some benefit to anyone struggling with androgenic alopecia.

Flutamide. This prescription medication blocks the effects of androgenic hormones like DHT. It is used to treat excessive facial hair growth in women, particularly those with PCOS. It can also reduce female-pattern alopecia. The use of Flutamide is not without concern. Cases of liver damage and death have been reported.

GHK Copper Peptides. Copper inhibits 5 alpha-reductase, enzymes necessary for the formation of DHT. As we age, the levels of copper within the skin begin to drop. You can apply Tricomin Follicle Therapy Spray twice daily to help restore copper levels.

Minimize Physical Trauma. Hair that is already vulnerable to loss doesn't need help in falling out. Eliminating practices notorious for traumatizing the hair shaft can help. Minimize your use of daily hot rollers, hair dryers, flat irons, and chemical therapies, including perms, dyes, and straightening agents.

To cut dryer time, wrap your hair in an Aquis Microfiber Hair Towel, which absorbs excess moisture.

I recommend dropping about four chemical sessions a year; it will save you some money—and your hair.

HAIR BREAKAGE OR HAIR LOSS?

Many people mistake breakage for hair loss, but there is a distinct difference. Hair loss is a medical condition; hair breakage is not (with the exception of a few rare diseases that can cause hair breakage). The average woman who discovers a new onset of hair breakage has typically and inadvertently done something that traumatized the hair shaft and damaged the hair. Follow these steps to keep your hair intact and looking healthy.

Shampoo Science

Shampooing is more than simply picking up a bottle of shampoo at your local grocery store and sudsing daily. There is an art and science to shampooing your hair. The first principle: make sure your routine shampoo says it is pH-balanced and avoid those that are alkaline.

Alkaline shampoos strip the hair's natural oils and disrupt the acid mantle, causing dehydration and leading to porous, fragile hair.

The protective cuticle of the hair shaft is composed of thousands of microscopic, keratinized cells that overlap, much like the shingles on a roof. Alkaline products will cause those shingles to separate.

Hot-Oil Treatments

Hot-oil treatments have become very popular. However, the very heat that causes them to penetrate the hair shaft can also lead to further damage of the hair. Over time, the continued, excessive heat exposure will cause the hair to become weaker. Stick with regular conditioners.

Use a Leave-in Conditioner

Consider the routine use of a leave-in conditioner or detangler. Typically applied after towel drying, these help reduce trauma and breakage when you comb through wet hair. This, in turn, helps reduce the formation of split ends, as well as fighting frizziness. Use it in addition to your regular conditioner.

FINAL THOUGHTS

Hair loss is scary. But don't feel that you have to sit at home and accept it without a fight. Make sure your primary care doctor understands that dermatologists have methods of diagnosis and therapy at their disposal and a working knowledge of the scalp. Seeing a dermatologist for hair loss can help increase your chances of putting a stop to the problem.

Ask the DERMAdoctor

QUESTION:
I've read a lot about special vitamins for stopping hair loss and even making your hair grow back. Do they work?

The DERMAdoctor:

Hair vitamins have received lots of attention, but they are often not well rounded. As a daily supplement for many patients who suffer from true hair loss, I recommend a well-rounded vitamin with some additional biotin, like DermaVite Dietary Supplement. Biotin is essential for healthy hair growth.

HIVES

Get the Red Out

Hives (in medical lingo, *urticaria*) are raised, itchy, red welts. They are the result of a visible allergic reaction. The mast cells of the immune system are triggered by an allergen to release histamine, which in turn causes hives and itching. And the allergens that can trigger hives seem just about endless: foods, medications, infections, even cold weather! Seemingly endless, too, are the number of Americans who get hives: fifty million a year, according to some estimates.

A lot of triggers, a lot of itchy sufferers; hives are hard to get under control. But there are effective therapies out there, and a call to your dermatologist can start you on the road to relief. Here's information that's important to know before you see your doctor.

IS IT REALLY A HIVE?
"Hive" and "welt" are two terms loosely used to describe a reddened area on the skin. But hives and welts aren't the same. Hives are red, raised, and often very firm. Their size and shape can vary. They last less than twelve hours. (This doesn't mean that you always suffer an outbreak of hives for twelve hours or less; it means that if you took a pen and circled a specific hive, there would be no sign of it twelve hours later.) And hives resolve without leaving any discoloration or scars. A welt is a raised, red area of skin that can arise in response to other triggers, such as a scratch or bug bite.

GETTING TO THE BOTTOM OF THE MYSTERY
There are three types of hives: acute, chronic, and physical. Let's look at the acute and chronic varieties before discussing the physical, which aren't really caused by an allergy.

Acute Urticaria. This is the most common of the three types—random hives that pop up anywhere and everywhere. Once the cause has been eliminated, the entire episode lasts no longer than six weeks.

Chronic Urticaria. A hive outbreak that continues for six weeks or more is called chronic urticaria.

Five Percent Satisfaction

Anyone with hives wants an answer to the big question: "Why me?" But, believe it or not, the cause of hives is never found in 95 percent of cases.

Hives are caused by allergens—the specific proteins you're allergic to. After a first exposure to an allergen, it can take ten to fourteen days to develop hives. But once the body has been repeatedly exposed to the allergen, hives can develop rapidly, within minutes or hours. Keep those facts in mind when considering what is new in your life—in your diet, in your medications, in your environment—that might be triggering hives. Top causes of hives include:

- Antibiotics
- Medication (look to drugs, vitamins, and herbal supplements you've started taking sometime in the last six weeks)
- Viral infection (particularly herpes simplex virus, or HSV)
- Bacterial infection (particularly strep)
- Intravenous X-ray contrast
- Nuts (peanuts, in particular)
- Seafood (shrimp, in particular)
- Tomatoes
- Citrus fruits
- Strawberries

If the cause of the hives isn't obvious and six weeks have passed, it's time for your doctor to do some sleuthing, performing a thorough workup that attempts to determine the exact cause and rule out possible serious internal causes. The skin is the largest organ, and it can provide surprising clues to the presence of internal disease; one of those clues can be hives. Fortunately, these tests usually reveal a perfectly healthy—but uncomfortable—patient.

Here are some of the tests you should discuss with your doctor if you have chronic hives:

TEST	PURPOSE
General blood chemistry	Checks liver and kidney function, etc.
CBC (complete blood count and differential)	Rules out leukemia and other blood abnormalities
Absolute eosinophil count	An indicator of parasitic infections, drug allergies, etc.
Hepatitis B and C panel	Checks for these viral diseases
ANA (antinuclear antibody test), Ro (formerly called SS-A), La (formerly called SS-B)	Rules out lupus, Sjögren's syndrome, and other autoimmune diseases
Thyroid panel	Rules out thyroid disorder
CH50 (total complement), C3, C4 (complement factors 3 and 4)	Rules out a complement-deficiency disorder
C1q esterase inhibitor level and function	Reveals hereditary or acquired angioedema
SED Rate	Usually elevated with hives, but especially with urticarial vasculitis
CEA (carcinoembryonic antigen)	General cancer screen
PSA (prostate-specific antigen)	Prostate cancer screen
PCR (polymerase chain reaction)	Checks for herpes simplex virus
Strep screen	Checks for infection with strep
HIV	Checks for infection with the HIV virus
Protein electrophoresis	Checks for multiple myeloma
Immunoelectrophoresis	Looks for certain abnormalities in the immune system
Chest X-ray	Checks for infection, cancer, lymphoma
Stool exam	Checks for parasites, colon cancer
Urine culture and sensitivity	Checks for bladder infection
IgE (immunoglobulin E)	Checks for reactions to specific allergens

If you're dealing with chronic hives, you'll also want to be up to date on your mammogram and pelvic exams and, if you're over fifty, have a baseline colonoscopy. Your dentist should check for hidden gum abscesses, which can cause the problem. And have your sinuses looked at, because ongoing sinus infections are a common cause of chronic hives.

Food Allergies

Food allergies add an extra twist to your sleuthing: hives can arise twelve to twenty-four hours after you've consumed the food you're allergic to, making it difficult to link any particular food to the outbreak.

And even once the problem-causing allergen is out of your diet, you can still have hives for up to six weeks, because the chemical reaction that was triggered within the body takes that long to stop. So if you think you're allergic to nuts and you stop eating them and continue to have hives, that doesn't mean you're not allergic to nuts. (No wonder hives can drive you nuts!)

The most common hive-causing food allergies are: peanuts; nut-containing products; strawberries; citrus fruits; tomatoes; seafood; shellfish; eggs; dairy products; yeast (including yeast-containing foods like fresh-baked breads, beer, blue cheese, and yogurt); and, if you have a latex allergy, bananas, kiwis, mangos, and chestnuts. (These foods are known to cause what is called a "cross-reaction" in people with a latex allergy.)

How do you figure out if any of these foods are triggering your hives? A girl's gotta live. First try a reasonable approach, eliminating the top food suspects and all vitamin pills and other supplements for six weeks. Then add them back one at a time, allowing at least four days (and preferably a week) after each addition. If you get hives when you add back the food or supplement, it's possible you've isolated the culprit.

Additives

Food additives like colorings and preservatives are also known to trigger hives (again, up to twelve to twenty-four hours later)—and are even harder than food to pin down as a cause. For example, it's possible that a brand-specific ingredient is responsible. I had a patient who got hives only when she ate a particular brand of chili powder; it turned out that she was allergic to a preservative found in just that brand. Other possible causes include flavored coffees and creams and herbal teas (due to hidden, allergy-causing extracts and colors). Read your labels!

The nitrates formerly used as preservatives in lunch meats and at salad bars are a common cause of hives. Fortunately, the FDA banned their use on fresh produce a few years back.

Sometimes the very industry responsible for creating skin-friendly products and treatments can make inexplicably unfriendly choices. One example is sodium metabisulfite, a nitrate, which can be hidden in skin care products and cosmetics. In susceptible individuals, it can cause serious allergic reactions, including hives, wheezing, severe asthmatic attacks, and anaphylaxis. Steer clear of skin care containing this highly allergenic preservative.

PHYSICAL URTICARIA

You can get a hive from the cold, from water, or from vibration. These so-called physical causes of hives (just a few among many) are not technically allergens, but they do trigger mast cells to release their histamine. Lifestyle changes, combined with medication, may help address the source and reduce flare-ups. Here are the two common types of physical hives:

Cholinergic Urticaria. If you're prone to this type of outbreak, your mast cells are releasing histamine in response to the presence of your own adrenalin (epinephrine). So any factor that causes the release of that hormone—stress, exercise, heat, hot showers, to name a few—can trigger the hives, which pop up quickly and last for thirty to sixty minutes. They look different from other types of hives, with characteristic multiple, tiny pink or red bumps that usually form in areas of higher blood flow and sweat formation, like the face. Treatment with an antihistamine like Zyrtec (cetirizine) can help control this condition.

Cold Urticaria. Some people get hives when they walk into an air-conditioned building in the summer or go near the freezer case in the grocery store! The antihistamine Periactin (cyproheptadine) is the therapy of choice, although it's not recommended for children, as it can slow growth.

TREATING HIVES

So now that you have hives, what are you going to do to feel more comfortable? Obviously, you want to avoid the allergen—if you're one of the lucky 5 percent who've been able to figure out what it is. For the other 95 percent, you need to stop hives from forming—and to do that, you need to stop the release of histamine from mast cells.

Treatment, no matter what the form or cause of the urticaria, is focused on controlling itching and stopping new hives from forming.

There are two types of histamine-releasing trigger points on the surface of the mast cells: H_1 and H_2. Block the receptors and you block histamine release; block histamine release and you control itching and hives.

H_1 Blockers

Antihistamines block the H_1 receptor, and Benadryl is the antihistamine most people are familiar with. A little too familiar, in some cases. I can't tell you how many times I've seen a patient—usually a small woman or an older person—who has been given large doses of sedating Benadryl (25 or 50 milligrams) every four to six hours. The person sleeps for hours every day! (I'm five foot one—I would too.)

But there's an upside to Benadryl. The manufacturer makes an over-the-counter fluid form, Benadryl Allergy Relief Liquid. Instead of trying to cut through a pill, you can easily cut the dose as much as you want by measuring out less of the suspension. You can feel better without getting too drowsy. Also, you can obtain the medication from an all-night pharmacy, so it's available even when a doctor isn't.

My prescription antihistamine of choice is Atarax (hydroxyzine). It comes in a 10-milligram tablet, taken every four to six hours. The dose can be increased as needed (and tolerated) to control hives. (I find that nonsedating antihistamines are relatively worthless for controlling itching related to hives.) Although it's only my impression, I feel that Atarax is somewhat more effective than Benadryl capsules, probably because it comes in smaller doses that patients can take more often, balancing effectiveness versus drowsiness, so that they actually use the drug.

Zyrtec (cetirizine hydrochloride), which has been found helpful in treating hives, is a less sedating, once-a-day alternative to Atarax.

HIVES PLUS

There are a few other types of hives (and hivelike conditions) than those discussed in the main text of this chapter. They are:

Angioedema. This problem is typically caused by an inherited deficiency or an acquired malfunction of an enzyme called C1q esterase inhibitor. It results in periodic, extreme swelling of the hands, feet, tongue, and eye areas, along with swelling of the throat—and hives. Treatment of this condition includes oral androgens (a type of hormone) like Danocrine (danazol), as well as antihistamines.

Urticarial Vasculitis. This condition appears to be hives but has an entirely different cause, in which blood vessels are attacked by the immune system. The individual hives last longer than twelve hours (even a few days) and, after they resolve, leave a bruise. Additional symptoms include aching joints, a low-grade fever, and fatigue. Diagnosis requires a skin biopsy with a test called DIF (direct immunofluorescence) in addition to the routine microscopic stains. Treatment often includes systemic steroids such as prednisone.

Dermatographism. The name of this conditions means "skin writing"— and it's not hives. Some people have more mast cells in their skin, which release histamine in response to scratching. Antihistamines may provide relief.

H_2 Blockers

When I see patients with hives, they're usually miserable—so I don't settle for just blocking the H_1 receptors. I also routinely prescribe a drug that blocks the H_2 receptors; they're a minor percentage of the overall number of receptors, but blocking them really makes a difference in whether or not a patient improves. You might be surprised to learn the class of medicines that block H_2 sites: heartburn medications like Zantac (ranitidine) and Tagamet (cimetidine). I usually prescribe a twice-daily dose of Zantac, which tends to be better tolerated than Tagamet.

If a patient's hives don't improve with H_1 and H_2 blockers, I sometimes prescribe doxepin, an antidepressant that has incredible H_1 and H_2 blocking ability.

Once a patient's hives are under control, I gradually reduce the daily dosages. Stopping a medication abruptly can sometimes trigger a recurrence.

Steroids? Not!

Systemic steroids are *not* a good option for hives. When a patient with hives gets a shot of steroids or a short-term pack of pills, her hives go away—and then usually get worse a few days later! This is called the rebound phenomenon, and it's the reason I almost never give systemic steroids for hives. Yes, if someone is in anaphylactic shock from hives, epinephrine *and* steroids *and* huge doses of antihistamines are appropriate. But, fortunately, most individuals with hives are nowhere near that sick. Don't take steroids if you have garden-variety hives!

Something to Get You Through the Night

Effective hive therapy will also include the use of topical treatments that hasten relief. It's always better to apply something to reduce itching than to scratch. Your topical emergency kit may include any of the following:

* Topical steroid creams (over-the-counter or prescription Cortaid)
* Topical anesthetics (PrameGel, Prax Lotion, Caladryl Clear, Aveeno Anti-Itch cream or lotion)
* Topical Zonalon (prescription topical antihistamine)
* Aveeno Oatmeal or baking soda baths

WHEN HIVES ARE AN EMERGENCY

A generalized release of histamine can lead to a major bout of hives, but it also can trigger a potentially fatal condition called anaphylactic shock. This includes a rapid drop of blood pressure and swelling of mucous membranes (like your tongue and throat), which can cause difficulty with swallowing and breathing. Anyone experiencing these symptoms should be taken immediately to the nearest hospital emergency room.

You can counter anaphylactic shock with the drug epinephrine, delivered by an EpiPen, which is available in prescription adult and child doses. If you have a past history of anaphylaxis, an allergy to peanuts, bee stings, latex, or other commonly encountered serious allergens, or suffer from cholinergic urticaria or angioedema, you're advised to learn how to use an EpiPen and to always carry it with you.

FINAL THOUGHTS

One in five Americans will develop hives at some point. Fortunately, most cases will be a onetime nuisance. And for those with a chronic case, it's good to know that there are tests to find out the cause, as well as treatments to keep them under control.

Ask the DERMAdoctor

QUESTION:

I am scheduled for an X-ray and a friend told me that she has read that X-rays can actually cause hives. That sounds silly to me. Is it true?

The DERMAdoctor:

X-rays won't cause hives. But some radiological studies require the use of an IV dye. This contrast solution can occasionally lead to an allergic reaction, most commonly hives. If you've had X-ray contrast before and you haven't had this problem, it's unlikely that it will develop. If a person knows she has this sensitivity and she needs to have an X-ray study, she should tell her radiologist. Often the radiologist can use something called low-osmolarity contrast instead. And if the study absolutely needs to use regular contrast, the patient can receive a dose of antihistamine and steroids to avoid the reaction.

KERATOSIS PILARIS

Say Good-bye to Chicken Skin

Chicken skin—it's such a simple yet instantly identifiable description of the skin concern doctors call keratosis pilaris. Can't you just visualize it?

Those tiny, rough bumps with their graterlike texture are most frequently scattered along the upper arms and thighs. However, the cheeks, back, and buttocks can all become involved. They're chronic, annoying, unsightly (though usually medically harmless)—and incredibly commonplace.

If you don't have this condition, odds are you know somebody who does. Whenever I talk about keratosis pilaris (more commonly called KP), inevitably the individual with whom I'm conversing pauses, gasps, then exclaims, "I didn't know *that's* what that was! My child [or husband or coworker—fill in the blank] has that!"

This reaction isn't surprising: keratosis pilaris affects 50 percent of the worldwide population. KP is somewhat more common in children and adolescents; 50 to 80 percent of children have it, compared to 40 percent of adults. Women are slightly more prone to developing it than men. And while it may become exaggerated at puberty, it frequently improves with age. Sometimes there are seasonal fluctuations, such as summertime improvement or wintertime flare-ups.

Keratosis pilaris is hereditary in the same way that eye color is hereditary—all it takes is a single gene from either parent to find oneself with less than perfectly smooth skin. But not everyone has a parent to blame; only 30 to 50 percent of KP patients have a positive family history.

KP often accompanies eczema and ichthyosis vulgaris (dry, scaly skin). So some patients find themselves dealing with KP *and* eczema *and* dry, scaly skin (and possibly even asthma and hay fever, which are genetically linked to eczema).

In spite of all these different possibilities, almost everyone with KP has two things in common: they're unaware that there is a designated medical term for the condition, and they don't know that treatment for KP exists.

THE CAUSE OF KP: SLO-MO SHEDDING

What causes the abrasive texture? Faulty keratinization, the process of forming epidermal skin.

Normally, old skin cells are sloughed off and discarded. In KP, that process is slower than normal, and surplus skin cells build up around individual hair follicles. Hair may become trapped beneath the debris and can't reach the surface. (During puberty, this is an ideal setup for triggering follicular acne.) Next, inflammation at the base of the follicle causes the formation of pinpoint red or brown polka dots beneath the miniature mounds of keratin. Multiply that process by the hundreds and the end result is a raised, rough, bumpy texture that gives your skin the embarrassing appearance of . . . chicken skin.

DON'T BE CHICKEN—TREAT KP

Keratosis pilaris is genetically programmed, so it's not curable. But it's definitely controllable. However, most people with KP—including those who are traumatized by the condition—don't realize that there really *is* something they can do about it. Additionally, there's no reason for teens to passively take a wait-and-see approach. After all, there's no guarantee that they'll grow out of it.

Most treatment is all about smoothing away the bumps. Chemical exfoliation can eliminate bumps and acne-causing plugs and improve the texture and overall appearance of the skin. And chemical exfoliation needn't be fraught with irritation, redness, or discomfort.

Glycolic Acid

In a dermatologist's quest to smooth out keratosis pilaris, an array of alpha hydroxy acids (AHAs) is utilized, including glycolic acid, a chemical exfoliating agent. M.D. Forté Hand & Body Cream is a buffered, 20% glycolic acid cream potent enough to help retexturize the skin.

Lactic Acid

Lactic acid is another AHA, and dermatologists often turn to over-the-counter and prescription lactic acid products to palliate KP. Low-potency LactiCare Lotion is appropriate for young children, particularly when treating areas of the face. The far more potent AmLactin 12% Moisturizing Cream, AmLactin AP Moisturizing Lotion, and prescription Lac-Hydrin work well for more stubborn, itchy flare-ups.

Urea

Urea is a powerful humectant, capable of extracting moisture from the air. It can soften the crustiest skin, making it a dermatological favorite. Urea-containing Carmol comes in two over-the-counter strengths: Carmol 10 and Carmol 20. Both are excellent in the fight against KP. For intractable KP, talk to your doctor about prescription Carmol 30 and Carmol 40.

KP Duty

KP is definitely one of those skin conditions that respond best to a multitherapeutic approach. In my experience, single-ingredient products or routines aren't nearly as effective as combination therapy. But all too often, my patients with KP had difficulty figuring out *when* to apply the combination of chemical exfoliation products that worked best. They also had trouble finding potent options that were also effective and well tolerated.

So I sat down and created a product for KP that combined the best active agents in a single cream. The result: DERMAdoctor KP Duty Dermatologist Moisturizing Therapy for Dry Skin. It combines dermatologist-strength glycolic acid and urea with green tea. The AHA and the urea work together as a team, eliminating bumps and softening the skin. Green tea contains epigallocatechin gallate (EGCG), which fights the inflammation responsible for postinflammatory skin discoloration so commonly seen in KP. Apply KP Duty once or twice a day and watch KP rapidly smooth away.

Therapeutic Dry Oil

For stubborn cases of KP (or if you're simply seeking more rapid improvement), consider including an additional treatment with the ability to reduce itching and inflammation. DERMAdoctor Handy Manum Anti-Itch Fissure Relief Serum is such a product, providing a protective barrier without leaving an unpleasant oily residue.

Try applying Handy Manum at bedtime to enhance your KP-clearing regimen. A tiny dab goes a very long way.

Retinoids

For recalcitrant cases, or when KP is complicated by acne, patients can turn to prescription vitamin A creams like Retin-A or Tazorac, which can help restore a smooth texture. (Afirm is a beneficial non-prescription option.)

However, overeager use of a vitamin A cream won't hasten the return of silky skin. Instead, it can leave skin parched, peeling, and painful. A tiny dab every other night is more than adequate when you're getting started. In a few weeks, or as tolerated, it may be used nightly. Always apply it solo.

Immunomodulators

KP is often thought of as a manifestation of eczema. So it stands to reason that the topical immunomodulators (TIMs)—new antieczema prescription medications like Protopic and Elidel, which work by suppressing immune cells thought to be responsible for inflammation—may play a role in treating KP.

I tend to reserve this medication for more complex cases of KP. But for the eczema patient who already has a tube at home, occasional use may be helpful.

Microdermabrasion

KP is a chronic condition. Committing yourself to never-ending, weekly sessions of medical microdermabrasion rapidly adds up to a big subtraction from your pocketbook. While effective at buffing skin to a healthy glow, medical microdermabrasion should be reserved for special occasions.

Instead, try less costly home microdermabrasion options, like DermaNew Microdermabrasion Total Body Experience, Neova Microdermabrasion Scrub, or even an exfoliating scrub like Peter Thomas Roth AHA/BHA Face & Body Polish.

FINAL THOUGHTS

When treatment for keratosis pilaris is discontinued, keratin again begins forming around hair follicles. So regular, ongoing maintenance is the best way to keep your skin silky smooth.

Keratosis pilaris is needlessly unsightly and so easy to control. Get ready for sleeveless fashions now and look your absolute best!

Ask the DERMAdoctor

QUESTION:

I have been diagnosed with keratosis pilaris, which covers my thighs, butt, breasts, the backs of my arms, and even appears high on my cheekbones. I am using AmLactin 12% Moisturizing Lotion, which is slowly giving me positive results. But what do I do about the hyperpigmentation that remains when the bumps have gone away?

The DERMAdoctor:

The cause of these polka dots is inflammation at the base of each hair follicle. Once you've successfully treated your KP, residual discoloration may remain. You can often see literally hundreds of tiny discolored spots, either pinkish purple if you're fair-complexioned, or brownish black if you have a darker skin tone. This discoloration can be more of a challenge to eradicate than the KP!

For all skin tones, the first step is wearing an SPF 30 sunblock that is oil-free and noncomedogenic (so you don't block the pores), like DERMAdoctor Body Guard.

Next, if your spots are more pinkish purple, the green tea in DERMAdoctor KP Duty will help improve the appearance of much of this redness. You can also consider using Mederma twice daily, a topical gel that can help reduce those types of spots without bleaching the skin or creating additional levels of skin discoloration.

It would be impossible to treat each and every discolored spot with a hydroquinone-based bleach—and you would undoubtedly end up with multiple hues. Instead, consider DERMAdoctor Immaculate Correction. This botanical brightening lotion helps reduce further discoloration formation, plus helps speed up the elimination of excess pigment pools found within the epidermis.

With these steps, you can expect spots to fade to some degree, and this will help reduce the obvious disparity of skin tones. I encourage you to be realistic. While one can hope for complete normalization of skin tone, try to look at any improvement with pleasure, even if you don't get 100% results.

QUESTION:

I have KP and have dark spots on my arms and legs. Since it is summer, can I use a self-tanner to hide the spots?

The DERMAdoctor:

A self-tanner will darken both normal and abnormal dark spots rather than evening out the color you wish to disguise. Controlling your KP and treating the discoloration are practical solutions.

Since any product used in KP treatment that contains an AHA (glycolic acid, lactic acid, etc.) or vitamin A (Tazorac, Retin-A, retinol, etc.) can speed up exfoliation, you may need to reapply the self-tanner a day or two earlier than normal.

Before applying the tanner, make sure your skin is exfoliated as much as possible. To do that, consider using Peter Thomas Roth AHA/BHA Face & Body Polish first. Use the scrub in the shower and then apply the self-tanner after toweling dry. Apply your self-tanner by itself rather than layering it with other products; this will produce a better, more even (less streaky) tan.

LICHEN PLANUS

Puzzling—but Treatable

Lichen planus is one skin disorder where the classic dermatological nickname—the Five P's—says it all. Lichen planus (LP) consists of pruritic, purple polygonal papules and plaques. Translation: small (often just two to three millimeters in diameter) lavender to dark purple angular bumps that appear out of nowhere and itch like crazy.

The cause of LP (which isn't contagious) is not known, though scientists suspect that the trigger might be an underlying viral, fungal, or yeast infection that provokes the immune system to react, resulting in a rash.

The average LP patient—an adult between the ages of thirty and seventy—intermittently experiences clusters of annoying purple bumps that appear without reason and last as long as eighteen months. I have seen patients who have gone twenty-five years or more without an outbreak, only to once again develop the rash!

The bumps often cluster on bendable areas, like the soft portion of the wrists and forearms and the backs of the knees. However, widespread involvement is not uncommon.

IT DOESN'T ALWAYS LOOK THE SAME

LP can have a variety of unusual appearances: it can form a ring or a line; develop blisters or thickened areas; resolve with depressed scars (atrophy); or develop only in areas exposed to the sun (actinic LP). Fortunately, LP has a characteristic pattern under the microscope, so no matter how the rash looks it's easily diagnosed with a skin biopsy.

OTHER AFFECTED AREAS

Lichen planus can also affect the hair and nails, as well as the inside of the mouth and the genital region.

The Mouth

More than 50 percent of LP patients have lacy white streaks within the mouth, most commonly located on the inner cheeks. A small number of these patients go on to develop painful sores (ulcerations) on the gums, palate, and tongue.

Avoiding foods that irritate ulcers—whether acidic foods like tomatoes or spicy foods like hot curry—helps relieve these symptoms. The application of a topical steroid, either alone or in a blend with a cream that helps bind the product to the sore, can also aid in healing these areas.

When these ulcerations are chronic and particularly severe, or if the area under the tongue is affected, patients run a higher risk of developing squamous cell carcinoma in these areas. If you suffer from these symptoms, have your dermatologist examine inside your mouth once or twice a year. You should also eliminate potential causes of oral cancer, like tobacco (cigarettes, cigars, chewing tobacco) and alcohol.

Nails

LP may cause ridging and thickening of the nails. Severe inflammation can lead to nail loss.

Vulva

Genital erosions can be difficult to differentiate from other serious conditions, particularly in women. For example, lichen sclerosus et atrophicus (LS et A) is often confused with LP, as both can cause painful sores in the vaginal area.

Hair

A form of LP known as lichen planopilaris causes inflammation within the hair follicle, leading to hair loss, most often on the scalp. Scarring of the follicle can make the loss permanent.

The nails and mucous membranes are often affected by this unusual form of LP, which strikes mostly women. Your doctor must also rule out other skin conditions, such as discoid lupus. A skin biopsy can help determine the correct diagnosis.

TREATING LP

If the cause of a problem isn't known, it's very difficult to treat—and LP is such a problem. So how do you treat a disease that has no known treatment? You try your best to find something that works.

Based on the theory that at least some LP patients develop their rash as a reaction to the presence of an infection, treatment with oral antifungal agents, antibiotics, and other similar therapies has been tried—unfortunately, with limited success.

Systemic steroids like prednisone can help alleviate itching and may help with blisters, but they rarely clear the rash.

Medications that help provide relief from nagging itching—prescription-strength topical steroid creams and oral antihistamines—should be incorporated into a treatment plan. (Though, like systemic steroids, these agents rarely resolve the rash.)

You can find itch relief in many nonprescription items, such as PrameGel, Caldryl Clear Lotion, Sarnol-HC, and Aveeno Oatmeal Bath Treatment.

A Blood Thinner for Severe LP?

Because treatment options are so limited for patients with debilitating LP, I have successfully tried a treatment that was reported in the *Journal of the American Academy of Dermatology* in 1998, the *British Journal of Dermatology* in 1999, and the *Journal of Dermatological Treatment* in 2001. Bear in mind that none of these small studies or my own experience with this therapy constitutes definitive scientific proof that the treatment works. The therapy is also considered "off label" because the medication has not received FDA approval for this use. However, I think it is an option worth discussing with your dermatologist.

It has been postulated that lichen planus is caused by the immune system's T cells, a type of white blood cell that enters an area of the skin and creates inflammation. If a medication could prevent these cells from traveling into that region, then perhaps it could resolve LP. The blood thinner Lovenox (low-molecular-weight heparin) has just this effect on T cells.

In 1998, Israeli doctors reported on ten patients with widespread, intensely itchy, and biopsy-proven LP. They gave the patients once-a-week injections of Lovenox (the U.S. equivalent is 30 mg per 0.3 ml in a prefilled syringe) for six weeks. The results were remarkable. In nine patients, the itch disappeared within two weeks. In four to ten weeks, eight patients had a complete regression of their rash, and one patient had marked improvement. One patient did not get better.

In a study reported in 1999, doctors in Greece treated eighteen patients with LP with weekly Lovenox injections. Eleven of the eighteen patients had complete remission, and two had marked improvement.

And in 2001, dermatologists at the University of Miami School of Medicine reported a study in which they treated seven LP patients with low-molecular-weight heparin; five experienced a marked improvement.

In 1998, when I read the first report, I found it so intriguing that I tried the treatment on three of my most severe LP patients. My results parallel the study's.

During a six- to ten-week course of treatment, itching resolved after two weeks, with regular skin lesions disappearing about six weeks after initiating the treatment. (For nail and hair lesions, I assume that effective therapy would need to be extended to account for the longer growth cycle of these tissues.)

Depending on the severity of your condition, your dermatologist can inject Lovenox once a week for six to ten weeks, just below the surface of the skin. From personal experience, I know that Lovenox can sting, so I recommend applying ice to the injection area for a few minutes before the shot, which should almost entirely eliminate the discomfort.

What about the "side effect" of blood thinning? The beauty of this treatment is that a once-a-week injection does *not* cause significant blood thinning.

Obviously, some people will not be able to use or tolerate this medication. However, if you suffer from severe LP, I strongly suggest that you discuss this therapeutic option with your doctor.

IS IT LP—OR A DRUG RASH?

It may look like LP, but are you actually experiencing a drug rash called a lichenoid drug eruption? It's likely your dermatologist has a book on hand with a long list of medications that can cause a lichen planus–like drug eruption, should this question ever arise. Below is a partial list of common medicines that can cause this drug rash.

Keep in mind that your medical history can play a role in determining if a drug has caused a rash. In most instances, drug rashes form only after ten days of therapy. And it's unusual to see a drug rash to a medication you've been taking for years.

DRUGS THAT CAN CAUSE A LICHEN PLANUS–LIKE RASH

- Phenytoin (Dilantin)
- Oral contraceptives
- Gold (auranofin, Ridaura)
- Isoniazid (Laniazid, Nydrazid)
- Hydrochlorothiazide (Hydrodiuril, Microzide, Oretic)
- Atabrine (quinacrine, mepacrine)
- Quinidine (Quinidex)
- Furosemide (Lasix)

FINAL THOUGHTS

Now you know about the Five *P*'s of dermatology. While lichen planus is an unusual skin condition, it does affect a surprising number of patients each year. Just remember: an ever-increasing group of medications is entering the market that may help you or someone you know who is affected by LP.

Ask the DERMAdoctor

QUESTION:

My son is eight years old and has had lichen planus for six months. I am very worried. I don't want to use steroid creams, but what else can I use?

The DERMAdoctor:

About 3 percent of all cases of lichen planus affect children. The use of a topical steroid cream will help control inflammation and itching. Since it's unlikely steroids will resolve the rash, you may wish to reduce their use by substituting topical analgesics containing pramoxine hydrochloride. I would probably skip the Lovenox therapy in a young child, unless it's absolutely necessary for other medical concerns.

QUESTION:

For about a year I have had a strange skin condition on my abdomen and the side of my face. A biopsy was done and I was diagnosed with lichen nitidus. What is the best way to treat this condition?

The DERMAdoctor:

Lichen nitidus is fairly uncommon but certainly not rare. We don't know why this condition occurs, but most scientists and doctors think it is a variation of lichen planus. While it may clear up spontaneously, it often remains unchanged for years. Many dermatologists are now trying Protopic and Elidel—immunomodulating ointments—for unresponsive skin conditions. You may want to talk to your dermatologist about this option.

LYME DISEASE

Don't Get Ticked

Lyme disease is an infectious illness that has gained nationwide recognition—and nationwide infamy. One reason for its scary reputation: you can be vulnerable in the seeming safety of your own backyard or neighborhood. You don't have to be deep in the woods or out camping to be at risk to this infection. You can be at risk wherever disease-carrying ticks infest a grassy or woody area.

Ixodes scapularis (also called the deer tick) is a prime carrier of the spirochete (an infectious particle) that causes Lyme disease, although at least one hundred species of ticks may actually transmit the infection. While not microscopic, these pinhead-sized ticks are a fraction of the size of the garden-variety tick most people are familiar with.

Deer within the northeastern and mid-Atlantic states commonly harbor *Ixodes* ticks. Over time, however, the endemic areas where people get the disease has expanded, as ticks were transmitted from animal to animal. The ticks fall off the deer and—given the opportunity—attach to human skin, transmitting the disease via a bite.

HOW TO AVOID GETTING LYME DISEASE

There are a number of steps you can take to avoid getting Lyme disease when you're outdoors in areas where ticks live.

Wear Protective Clothing. That means a long-sleeved shirt, long pants, and a hat. And gloves, too, if you're gardening. The less skin you expose, the harder it is for a tick to latch on.

Pick Pale Colors. Light-colored clothing lets you see ticks, which are black.

Tuck It In. Tuck pant legs into socks and shirtsleeves into gardening gloves.

Fight Back. Insecticide-containing repellents with DEET and permethrin kill ticks on contact. Use DEET on exposed areas of skin, avoiding the face and eyes; use lower levels on children. Permethrin is not indicated for tick prevention on skin, but you can apply it to blankets, clothing, and other materials.

Check It Out. After being outdoors, check yourself (and your pets) thoroughly for these tiny ticks.

Clear the Brush. If you live in an infested area, keep your yard clear of brush, as well as deer and other wildlife.

Vaccinate? Unfortunately, the LYMErix vaccine is no longer on the market.

HOW TO REMOVE A TICK

In spite of all your precautions, you can end up with a tick embedded in your skin. Here's what to do.

Using tweezers, gently pull the tick backward, straight out and away from the skin. Try to remove the entire tick, including the mouthparts. If you can't get the mouthparts out on the first or second try, don't keep digging; you need your doctor's help. Smashing the mouthparts can result in the release of infected tick saliva into the skin. And the remnants can act like a foreign body (like a splinter), causing the growth of a hard area called a granuloma. I've had to surgically cut out several granulomas from patients bitten by ticks.

As for folk remedies such as applying a hot match to the back of the tick or smothering it with nail polish—they don't work. This was actually a question on my dermatology board exam! (Yes, I knew the answer, having trained in an area where Lyme disease was endemic.)

If a tick bites you, call your doctor to find out if treatment is needed. And try to keep the tick! (Put it in a zip-top plastic bag.) You may have been bitten by a tick that doesn't carry Lyme disease.

ERYTHEMA CHRONICUM MIGRANS—WHEN YOU'RE THE TARGET OF LYME DISEASE

Erythema chronicum migrans (ECM) is the telltale dermatologic sign of the onset of Lyme disease, usually arising within a few weeks of the bite. Resembling a bull's-eye around the tick bite, this red, often raised ring continues to enlarge and extend outward from the bite. It can become as large as twenty or more centimeters in diameter, although it commonly grows to only a few centimeters. The development of ECM is always an indication to treat for Lyme disease.

ECM doesn't occur in every person who is bitten by an infected tick or who goes on to develop the disease. (However, the majority of people bitten by an infected tick do develop it.) There are even occasional patients who develop only a flulike syndrome when bitten by the tick, making diagnosis far more difficult. And sometimes the rash itself can have multiple rings, or even arise where the tick didn't bite.

If Lyme disease goes untreated, the patient can go on to develop full-blown systemic symptoms. This is due to the infecting agent, the spirochete *Borrelia burgdorferi*, spreading throughout the body from the site of the bite.

Lyme disease's most common symptoms include: an arthritis-like syndrome; neurological effects (facial nerve paralysis, encephalitis, balance disorders); and heart block, arrhythmias, and inflammation within the sac surrounding the heart. (Heart problems are among the most serious consequences of Lyme disease.)

Chronic Lyme disease can develop months or years later if the initial infection is left untreated. Symptoms typically affect the neurological and musculoskeletal systems, causing muscular aches or shooting pain, depression, difficulty concentrating, and even memory loss.

In tick-infested areas, therapy is often instituted at the first sign of Lyme disease. In other regions, a blood test called a Lyme titer is usually performed first, and treatment is started only if there is a positive result. If negative, the test is repeated again in six weeks. (It often takes this long after ECM appears for the test to show a positive result.) If positive, treatment is started, even in the absence of skin or systemic symptoms.

TREATING LYME DISEASE: IT'S EASY IF IT'S EARLY

Treatment is relatively easy if the disease is caught early. Oral antibiotics—doxycycline, 100 milligrams, twice a day—are taken for two to three weeks if the disease is caught early, and for three to four weeks for patients who have already progressed to systemic symptoms. Patients allergic to doxycycline or who are pregnant or nursing are typically treated with penicillin. If the disease has spread, long-term use of antibiotics is an option. If there is evidence of heart problems, baby aspirin and appropriate heart medications are also prescribed.

FINAL THOUGHTS
Enjoy your outdoor summer activities, but engage in them wisely. Don't forget to take protective measures that will help keep you and your family safe.

Ask the DERMAdoctor

QUESTION:
I'm going to a retreat center that is chemical-free. Is there a natural alternative to DEET-laden insecticides that I could use to prevent tick bites?

The DERMAdoctor:
Not that I know of. I know that neem oil (a natural ingredient) has been touted as helping prevent insect bites, but it doesn't have FDA approval for that purpose; nor am I aware of any medical evidence that it works to prevent tick bites. Other natural products that have been hyped as preventing insect bites (again, there are no medical studies to support their effectiveness) include cider vinegar, tea tree oil, eucalyptus oil, and lavender oil.

Make sure you wear protective clothing. Check yourself carefully after being outdoors. You may want to consider investing in a good pair of tweezers. Finally, should you experience any signs of Lyme disease in the weeks following your retreat, be sure to contact your physician.

MELASMA
(Mask of Pregnancy)

Defeat Discoloration, Resist Recurrences

Is your natural beauty hiding behind a mask of melasma?

This distressing cosmetic condition—commonly known as "the mask of pregnancy," since that's when it most often occurs—darkens facial skin, usually affecting the apples of the cheeks, the middle of the forehead, the jawline, and areas around the mouth. To blame are pigment-producing cells called melanocytes, which go into overdrive and produce extra, unwanted melanin, resulting in patchy discoloration. Triggers that can make for hyperactive melanocytes include pregnancy, oral estrogen (in the form of birth control pills or hormone replacement therapy), cellular hypersensitivity to normal estrogen levels, and exposure to the sun.

An estimated six million American women suffer from melasma. Needless to say, all of them want to get rid of it. In fact, I've had patients say they won't get pregnant again if it means they'll develop another bout of melasma! Well, this chapter offers the best defense against melasma: highly effective therapies that can erase the problem, and a smart maintenance plan to prevent recurrences.

JUST SAY NO—TO SUN

If you have melasma, the sun is your enemy. In fact, a year's worth of birth control pills won't make your melasma more noticeable *unless* you get sun exposure. Avoiding sun exposure is the first, crucial step in reducing melasma.

That means avoiding both UVA and UVB rays, the two types of ultraviolet light that can damage your skin. To do that, apply a broad-sunscreen spectrum of at least SPF 30 to your skin daily. Even better, apply Total Block Clear SPF 65, which blocks both ultraviolet and visible light. Also, put on a wide-brimmed hat or a sun-protective hat with an extra-long bill. And wear your favorite extra-large, glamorous sunglasses. (Think Garbo.) Then—even with all those precautions—reduce your sun exposure to the absolute minimum.

If you have melasma, you're probably using a skin-bleaching product; I'll talk more about those in a minute. But even if your bleach contains a sun protection factor (SPF), I strongly recommend that you use an *additional* sunscreen to both assist the lightening process and prevent the development of new dark areas not being treated with the bleach.

MEET YOUR MELANOCYTES

It may seem perplexing that something as minute as the microscopic melanocyte can wreak such havoc upon skin clarity—but it can! To eliminate unwanted skin discoloration, you need to understand how melanocytes produce melanin (pigment) and how to intervene at just the right point in the process. Consider this part of the chapter a user-friendly primer on pigmentation. Put your new knowledge into practice—and watch your skin glow.

Melanocytes are located along the bottom or basal layer of the epidermis, where they comprise about 10 percent of the cells. That percentage can differ over the body (and from person to person), accounting for variations in skin tone.

The process of melanin formation starts deep in the cell, where a gene makes an enzyme called tyrosinase. After that, chemical dominoes fall: tyrosinase changes tyrosine into dopa, which turns into dopaquinone— and dopaquinone forms either black-brown "eumelanin" or red-yellow "pheomelanin." These two types of melanin are formed as granules within structures called melanosomes, which are then shipped off to epidermal cells at the surface of the skin.

THE BIOLOGY OF BLEACHING

A well-rounded bleaching routine should not only eliminate excess pools of pigment but also prevent melanin from being formed. Inactivating tyrosinase, or interfering with its function, is the best way to prevent pigment production.

You can prevent tyrosinase activity by substituting another compound for tyrosine (a "false substrate"). You can strip tyrosinase of the sugars (glucose) it needs to function. You can block it from reaching its cellular receptors. You can reduce the factors that stimulate tyrosinase activity, like sun exposure.

Preventing skin discoloration is one part of the bleaching equation. The other is eliminating the undesirable blotches that are already present.

Multitasking Bleaches

In the dark ages of bleaching (no pun intended), products with a single ingrediant ruled. Nowadays, the bleaching mantra is "The more the ingredients, the merrier." You'll find many different ingredients used in nearly endless variations.

Before you read more about those ingredients, it's important to understand the official terminology of bleaching. Currently, the FDA recognizes only hydroquinine as a bleaching agent. Manufacturers must refer to the other ingredients as *lighteners* or *brighteners* or *whiteners*.

Hydroquinone. This is the most commonly used bleaching agent in the United States. It interferes with tyrosinase activity, shutting down melanin production. Hydroquinone is found in both prescription (4 percent) and nonprescription (2 percent) strengths.

There are two main issues with hydroquinone. One is skin irritation. The other is ochronosis, a highly unusual side effect of long-term use, afflicting mostly people of color, in which the treated area darkens or takes on a bluish cast. I have treated hundreds of patients with 4 percent hydroquinone, but the only person I have ever seen with ochronosis was at a teaching convention for dermatologists. However, if you think your skin is darkening despite your best bleaching efforts, discontinue use of the hydroquinone-containing product and check with your dermatologist.

Additionally, research studies show that hydroquinone can cause mutations in salmonella bacteria and hamsters. Although is has a high safety rating in the United States, hydroquinone is unavailable for use as a bleaching agent in Europe and South Africa.

Mitracarpus Scaber Extract. This lightening agent is derived from the leaves of a tropical plant. Its active ingredient is harounoside, a derivative of hydroquinone. Like hydroquinone, it stalls the activity of tyrosinase, short-circuiting melanin production. However, harounoside is considered to be more effective than hydroquinone. And less irritating without the concerns of ochronasis.

Arctostaphylos Uva Ursi Extract. Derived from the leaves of the bearberry shrub, and commonly referred to as bearberry extract, its active agent is arbutin. It is another hydroquinone derivative, inhibiting tyrosinase activity—without the downsides.

Dithiaoctanediol. This agent prevents the chemical reaction in which a sugar (glucose) molecule is added to tyrosinase. In this novel way, it helps block the pigment-forming pathway.

Beta-Carotene. This vitamin A molecule blocks tyrosinase receptors on the melanocyte.

Licorice Extract. The main ingredient is glabridin, which prevents tyrosinase activation. It may also reduce inflammation.

Gluconic Acid. This "chelating" agent binds the copper molecules that are necessary for activating tyrosinase.

Azelaic Acid. This is a naturally occurring by-product of the yeast *Pityrosporum ovale* used in acne therapy. Dermatologists first noted and then employed one of its side effects: skin lightening. Azelaic acid works selectively on overactive melanocytes, bypassing normally pigmented skin.

Paper Mulberry. This is another plant extract shown to inhibit tyrosinase activity. It is not considered an irritant and is often incorporated into skin-lightening products.

Kojic Acid. Derived from a fungus, kojic acid is widely used in the Orient as a skin lightener. It inhibits tyrosinase activity and, with long-term use, also decreases the ability of melanocytes to pass residual pigment to keratinocytes.

Melatonin. Although not usually found in skin bleaches, some anecdotal reports say this pineal hormone, secreted in response to sunlight, can lighten hair follicles. It's theorized that it affects energy generation in the melanocyte, rather than interfering with tyrosinase.

Vitamin C. Several forms of vitamin C—L-ascorbic acid, magnesium ascorbyl phosphate, and sodium ascorbyl phosphate—can reduce melanin formation. Cellex-C and SkinCeuticals manufacture vitamin C serums that you can use both for skin rejuvenation and to round out your bleaching regimen.

Desquamating Discoloration Away. You can prevent skin discoloration. *And* you can eliminate undesirable, uneven blotches that are already there. AHAs, BHA, retinoids, papain, and sutilains all work to exfoliate discolored cells, revealing the clear skin underneath.

Tretinoin. The active agent found in medications such as Retin-A, Avita, and Renova, tretinoin increases cellular turnover, expediting exfoliation and eliminating pigment already pooled in the epidermis. Faster turnover time also means that melanocytes have less time to send melanosomes to keratinocytes.

Alpha Hydroxy Acids (AHAs). These agents expedite cellular exfoliation and are frequently incorporated into a bleaching regimen. Glycolic acid and lactic acid are most commonly used.

Sutilains. A member of the keratase family, which includes agents like papain (an enzyme in papayas), sutilains dissolve the intercellular cement that hold cells together, easing the shedding of skin (desquamation).

Multitasking Bleaches

Here are the top multitalented prescription players among bleaches:

- Lustra (4% hydroquinone, 4% glycolic acid)
- Lustra-AF (4% hydroquinone, 4% glycolic acid, SPF 15)
- Alustra (4% hydroquinone and retinol)
- Glyquin (4% hydroquinone, 10% glycolic acid, SPF 15, metabisulfite-free)

- Glyquin XM (4% hydroquinone, 10% glycolic acid, Vitamin C, Vitamin E, SPF 15, metabisulfite-free)
- Tri-Luma (4% hydroquinone, 0.05% tretinoin, 0.01% fluocinolone acetonide)
- Obaji (the prescription-strength version of this bleaching system combines generic 4% hydroquinone and generic tretinoin cream)
- Solagé (2% mequinol, 0.01% tretinoin)

TRI-LUMA: THREE INGREDIENTS ISN'T A CROWD

A recent and important development in melasma therapy is Tri-Luma, a prescription bedtime cream manufactured by Galderma. Tri-Luma contains the active trio of 4% hydroquinone, 0.5% tretinoin (the active agent in Retin-A), and fluocinolone acetonide 0.01%, a potent topical steroid.

Studies show that Tri-Luma is safe and dramatically effective. I consider it a kick start to successful melasma management, as a way to start reducing the problem as quickly as possible. It is applied every night for no more than eight weeks. The reason for the time limit is that if used too long, a high-potency topical steroid can cause thinning of the skin.

If you still require further treatment after the eight weeks, you should continue a nonsteroid-based method of bleaching after stopping Tri-Luma. Talk with your dermatologist about switching to one of the combination prescription products listed above. Or add Retin-A or Tazorac to your routine, products that will also help rejuvenate your skin and clear up any acne. You may also want to consider Azelex, a prescription acne cream containing azelaic acid. A side effect you can use to your advantage is that it helps lighten skin. If you switch to one of those "super separate" products, you'll also want to use a primary bleaching ingredient like hydroquinone to help complete the process of restoring normal skin tone.

Nonprescription Hydroquinone

- M.D. Forté Skin Bleaching Gel (10% glycolic acid, 2% hydroquinone)
- Peter Thomas Roth Potent Skin Lightening Gel Complex (2% hydroquinone, kojic acid, azelaic acid, salicylic acid, vitamin C)
- ScarGuard Lightener Gel (2% hydroquinone, arbutin, kojic acid, retinoic acid)

Bleaching, au Naturel

Sometimes hydroquinone just isn't in the cards. Maybe you're sensitive or allergic to it. Maybe you're pregnant, nursing, or concerned about ochronosis. Whatever the reason, you still have many excellent options.

- DERMAdoctor Immaculate Correction Revitalizing Skin Tone Equalizer (arctostaphylus uva ursi leaf extract, mitracarpus scaber extract, azelaic acid, dithiaoctanediol, gluconic acid, beta-carotene, licorice extract, glucosamine-urea complex, glycosaminoglycans, glycopolysaccharides, sutilains)
- Peter Thomas Roth Potent Botanical Skin Brightening Gel Complex (kojic acid, azelaic acid, bearberry extract, ascorbic acid, salicylic acid)
- SkinCeuticals Phyto+ (kojic acid, arbutin)

Application Tips

Bleaches can't tell the difference between normal and abnormal skin tone. That means you need to carefully apply the bleach *only* to areas of abnormal color. Sometimes this can be difficult, so I recommend that you don't try to bleach every last minuscule freckle. Stay with the larger, well-defined sites. Bleaches are typically applied twice daily.

Don't expect results overnight; bleaching is not a speedy process. Depending on the disparity between normal and abnormal skin tone, it can take up to a year (and sometimes longer) for your skin to return to normal. Because of this extended time frame, I think using a combination product is best; using several ingredients that work synergistically speeds up improvement.

However, if you're already using a single-ingredient bleach and don't wish to give it up, consider broadening your routine by adding another product to your regimen. Glycolic acid makes a wonderful base for the hydroquinone. It draws the bleach more deeply into the skin. I start with M.D. Forté Facial Cream or Lotion I (15%) and work up in strength, as tolerated. Topical retinoids (tretinoin, tazarotene, adapalene, retinol) applied solo every other night work well to reduce skin blotchiness.

Azelex 20% Cream (azelaic acid is the active ingredient) is prescribed for acne. It has a potential side effect that can be used to advantage—it bleaches out skin color. It may be applied once or twice a day.

BLEACHING BASICS

Regardless of the cause of skin discoloration—whether melasma, old acne, bug bites, skin trauma, underarm irritation, or sun damage (such as freckles or "liver spots")—bleaching basics remain the same.

Basic Techniques

Apply the bleach only to the dark spot. Selecting well-defined areas to bleach can help improve the ultimate outcome. If you don't have well-defined areas, choose a skin brightener that is safe to use in more widespread areas: one based on a botanical ingredient, rather than one based on hydroquinone.

Don't apply the bleach to normal skin. This will slowly lighten regular skin tone too.

Twice is nice. Apply the bleach twice daily to the offending area.

Sun not. Sun exposure will darken the areas you are working so hard to bleach. Use sunscreen with a minimum SPF of 15 that protects against both UVA and UVB rays. Ideally, wear sun-protective clothing and a hat.

Be patient. Bleaching is not a fast process. The darker the area compared to your natural skin tone, the longer it can take. Six to twelve months is typical.

Declare victory. Stop bleaching when you achieve the desired effect. Otherwise, you can end up with areas of skin that are lighter than your normal skin.

Basic Helpers

Vitamin A Derivatives. Vitamin A creams, such as Retin-A, Renova, and Afirm, help exfoliate away unwanted skin discoloration, help active bleaches penetrate better, and seem to have a lightening effect of their own. To help minimize irritation, use them every other night, alone.

Azelex. This prescription topical acne cream can lighten skin. Dermatologists have taken this "side effect" and used it in a positive way, to help bleach out dark skin concerns like remnant acne discoloration and melasma.

L-ascorbic acid. This highly acidic component can help you treat or prevent wrinkles, along with getting rid of skin discoloration. Start with Cellex-C High-Potency Serum or SkinCeuticals Serum 20.

Glycolic Acid. A potent glycolic acid product, like M.D. Forté's Facial Lotion or Cream I, can help your bleach penetrate better, give you some light exfoliation, and also help treat conditions like acne or skin changes associated with aging. Many multitasking bleaches incorporate glycolic acid.

Basic Caution: Prevent PIH

Postinflammatory hyperpigmentation (PIH) is the result of irritation or inflammation of the skin. If a cream, gel, or lotion is irritating and you are prone to skin discoloration, get rid of it (unless it's a prescription agent you can't live without).

If you are continually getting irritated by every cream you use and have a history of overly sensitive skin, ask for patch testing. You may learn that you're allergic to an ingredient that is easy to avoid.

Basic Regimen

- Apply your AHA, vitamin C, Renova, Kinerase, or Azelex to the general areas of the face and then apply your bleach only to the dark spots. Apply sunscreen.
- Try to wait twenty minutes, if possible, between the application of your helper creams and your active bleach, in order to minimize potential irritation.
- If you experience irritation from layering, apply your products separately during the day, even if you end up with an every-other-day use of some of the products. Irritation can lead to more skin discoloration. Better to draw out the bleaching process a little.

PEEL POWER

Exfoliation hastens the resolution of melasma by removing superficial pigmented skin cells and easing the penetration of bleaching agents. You can use a variety of exfoliating agents, both mechanical and chemical. Whatever your weapon of choice, there's a fine line between exfoliation and excessive inflammation. The unwanted outcome of too much irritation can be an *increase* in skin pigmentation, known as postinflammatory hyperpigmentation. If you've used products that produce red, irritated, stinging skin, stop or use less of them—and always use common sense.

There are three main exfoliation procedures commonly used to treat melasma: chemical peels (glycolic, TCA, and Jessner's); microdermabrasion (performed by a physician or aesthetician, or at home with an over-the-counter product like DermaNew); and a light freezing of the skin with liquid nitrogen.

I have encountered several patients who were treated with liquid nitrogen for melasma by another physician and subsequently developed darkening of the treated area; for that reason, I avoid this treatment.

FINAL THOUGHTS

When it comes to treating melasma, results won't happen overnight; you need to stick with your program for the long haul. When you have finally achieved your desired results, stop bleaching but continue your sun protection. Should you see a recurrence, restart your bleaching routine before the problem gets out of control.

Ask the DERMAdoctor

QUESTION:

I have melasma and feel that the contributing factor might be the use of oral contraceptives. I was considering changing brands, to hopefully help this condition from recurring. Are Depo-Provera shots less likely to cause melasma?

The DERMAdoctor:

It is unlikely that changing estrogens will change your melasma. Usually, melasma triggered by birth control is a matter of using estrogen-based birth control versus not using it at all. However, most women do not have to give up their contraceptives to control melasma but, rather, should practice proper sun avoidance (in particular, wearing a good sunscreen and even a sun-protective hat) and should consider incorporating a "cocktail" of effective skin-bleaching agents into their routine.

QUESTION:

Could you tell me if using a self-tanner will make my melasma spots darker?

The DERMAdoctor:

A self-tanner essentially works as a temporary skin stain. It will darken all skin areas without evening out variations in shades. Should you wish to experiment with a self-tanner, try applying it *around* the discolored area. You may find that you can blend the borders, reducing the visible disparity between the tones. The worst thing that can happen is that the discolored area will be darker for a few days; fortunately, if the tanner is not continually reapplied, this darkness will fade within a week.

MOUTH PROBLEMS

See Your Dermatologist and Say "Ahhh"

Feeling a bit down in the mouth?

Many a skin disorder puts in an appearance somewhere inside the mouth. And so do many internal health concerns; in fact, oral changes can provide important diagnostic clues to what's really ailing you.

So don't be surprised if you hear your dermatologist tell you, "Open wide . . ."

CANKER SORES

Canker sores tend to be small, shallow ulcerations covered by a white membrane and circled by a minimal red rim. They can arise anywhere inside the mouth, including the gums, palate, inner cheeks, and tongue. They are usually few in number, occur three to four times a year, and last less than a week.

Don't confuse them with cold sores. Canker sores aren't found outside the mouth, don't form blisters, aren't contagious, and aren't caused by the herpes virus.

What Causes Canker Sores?

No one knows for sure. Microorganisms like bacteria, yeast, and viruses are probably not to blame. A prime suspect is an exaggerated inflammatory or immune response to minor trauma or irritation.

Other possible triggers include stress, smoking, nutritional deficiencies (vitamin B_{12}, zinc, folic acid, iron), and pernicious anemia (the inability to absorb vitamin B_{12}).

And while there is no proven link to food allergies, some patients blame acidic foods like citrus fruits and tomatoes, as well as chocolate and nuts.

Give Your Toothpaste the Brush-off

Perhaps up to 80 percent of canker sores could be prevented—if everyone prone to them switched to an irritant-free toothpaste! The ingredients that might be doing the damage include detergents (sodium lauryl sulfate and cocamidopropyl betaine), tartar-control agents (pyrophosphate), bleach (calcium peroxide and hydrogen peroxide), and flavorings (in particular, cinnamon and spearmint).

If you suffer from canker sores (or any other form of oral ulceration), try Squigle Enamel Saver Toothpaste, which is free of these potential irritants.

Squigle's ingredient list also includes a potential helper: natural xylitol, which dramatically reduces dental plaque. Not only does plaque promote tooth decay and gum disease, it also generates irritating acids that can initiate canker sores.

Treatments for Canker Sores

When it comes to canker sores, you don't have to frown and bear it. There are a number of effective treatments.

Orabase. A standard in dermatology and dental care, this cream is formulated to stick to slippery oral mucosa. It provides a shield against further trauma, helping canker sores heal more quickly. It also helps reduce inflammation. Orabase paste with 20% benzocaine contains a topical anesthetic to rapidly reduce discomfort.

Many dermatologists will have the pharmacist compound two other medicines into the Orabase: a topical anesthetic and a topical steroid, which helps speed healing.

Aphthasol 5% (amlexanox). This anti-inflammatory oral paste, which became available in 1999, is the only prescription medicine specifically indicated for canker sores. Studies show that it speeds healing and reduces pain. In some patients, it completely eliminates pain after three days of regular use.

Tetracycline. Twice-a-day tetracycline rinses seem to be beneficial when used with other topical therapies. I have patients thirteen and older open a 500-milligram capsule of tetracycline, mix it with a small amount of water, rinse, and spit. (A rinse of warm salt water can also help control discomfort and speed healing.)

Steroids. In my practice, I find that applying a prescription-strength topical steroid gel or ointment three to five times a day helps speed the healing of an occasional painful canker sore.

When all else fails, and canker sores are destroying the quality of your life, consider a prescription systemic steroid (prednisone). Steroids help shut down the exaggerated immune response thought to be responsible for the development of canker sores. Oral steroids can have many serious side effects, however, and shouldn't be used on a frequent, long-term basis for recurrent canker sores.

When Sores Might Be More
If your sores won't heal (make two weeks your cutoff) or if you're plagued by never-ending bouts of apthous ulcers, check with your dermatologist. Sometimes chronic canker sores are the symptom of an underlying health problem.

GUM PROBLEMS
Gum Bleeding
If your gums bleed when you bite into a crispy apple or when you brush your teeth, check with your dentist. Poor dental care is unquestionably the most likely cause. But there are other gum problems where the cause isn't so obvious.

Discolored Gums
African-Americans and other people of color can have naturally dark gums (or gums that darken slowly with aging). But if your gums have always been pink and you notice a sudden change in coloration, check with your doctor—you may have a medical problem. Some possible causes are:

Smoking. Five to 22 percent of smokers suffer from smoker's melanosis—darkening of the gums. Smoking stimulates the pigment-manufacturing cells (melanocytes) to deposit melanin in the gums and the inner cheeks.

Medications. Bismuth (an ingredient in ulcer medications) and the anti-HIV drug zidovudine (AZT, Retrovir) can discolor the gums. Minocycline, an antibiotic, can discolor teeth and bones, which appear blue through the gums.

Heavy Metals. Poisoning with various heavy metals can discolor the gums. A sign of chronic lead poisoning is the presence of a blue-black line (Burton's line) at the gingival margin.

Dental fillings can contain mercury, silver, and tin. If minute amounts of filling material become accidentally lodged within the gums, the result is a bluish-gray, spotty discoloration, known as an amalgam tattoo (localized argyria).

Hormonal Problems. Abnormalities of the endocrine system can darken the gums. Addison's disease, an adrenal problem, can turn gums a fairly even brown or black.

Gum Overgrowth

It's not a typical problem. But if your gums become enlarged and puffy—and even reduce the visibility of your pearly whites—it's time to see a dermatologist or a dentist. Causes of gum overgrowth (gingival hypertrophy) include:

- Medications, such as the antiepileptic drug Dilantin (phenytoin sodium), cyclosporine (an immune suppressant, used in transplants), nifedipine (a calcium channel blocker, used to treat heart disease), and oral contraceptives
- Leukemia or lymphoma
- Hormonal states, like puberty and pregnancy
- Trauma from braces
- Systemic diseases, including tuberous sclerosis (a genetic disorder), sarcoidosis (an inflammatory disease), Melkersson-Rosenthal syndrome (a rare neurological disorder), Crohn's disease (a bowel ailment), and scurvy (caused by a vitamin C deficiency)

TONGUE PROBLEMS

Sometimes it isn't that hard to lick tongue problems. They may reveal a treatable medical concern or be the side effect of a drug.

Other times, medical science is tongue-tied—the problem is a lot harder to figure out and to treat.

And that's exactly the case with burning tongue.

Burning Tongue

You might not see anything, and the doctor might not either, but somehow patients with burning tongue inevitably *do* see the dermatologist.

Burning mouth syndrome (BMS) is a poorly defined disorder that primarily affects postmenopausal women. Areas most commonly affected include the tip of the tongue, the hard palate at the top of the mouth, and the inside of the lower lip.

Drs. Walter and Dorinda Shelley combed the medical literature looking for possible causes for this disorder. In their book *Advanced Dermatologic Diagnosis,* they recommend the following workup for burning tongue patients:

Have blood work to check for anemia, serum ferritin, and vitamins B_1, B_2, B_6, and B_{12}. Supplementation with vitamin B complex, B_{12}, and iron has helped many patients.

Get checked for glucose intolerance, a possible precursor to diabetes. Correcting diabetic tendencies can sometimes help with nerve problems like burning tongue.

Get a salivary gland stimulation test. In one study of nineteen patients, artificial saliva helped.

Check for low-grade thrush. (You'll learn about that tongue problem in the next section.) Antiyeast therapy can improve symptoms.

Get a specialist's opinion on your dentures. Do you have an allergy to the acrylic in your dentures? Do you have teeth grinding, tongue thrusting, or other mechanical oral disorders? If you have any of these concerns, fixing them can alleviate the problem.

If the symptoms are intermittent, perform a patch test for food-related products, including ascorbic acid, propylene glycol, benzoic acid, and cinnamon. Dietary avoidance cures the problem for some patients.

Are there menopausal symptoms? The doctors didn't mention whether estrogen supplements, soy, or similar treatments help with burning tongue, but keep them in mind as an option.

Do you have esophageal acid reflux (heartburn)? Eliminating gastric acid damage to the tongue can reduce inflammation.

Don't be shy about getting a complete psychological examination, to rule out stress, anxiety, depression, and sleep disorders. Having emotional difficulties doesn't mean you're imagining your symptoms. Rather, it's helpful to deal with any psychological condition that might be contributing to BMS or might have developed due to the stress of BMS.

Antidepressants can help reduce discomfort from neurological concerns (like postherpetic neuralgia) and are worth discussing with your doctor.

Above all, don't give up hope.

Thick, Heavy White Coating

A thick, heavy white coating on the tongue can be an infection known as thrush, caused by the yeast *Candida albicans*. This is quite different from the thin white coating seen first thing in the morning, after eating, or during a mild illness. Thrush is mostly an annoyance, but some patients develop a sore throat or shallow ulcerations when they have the infection.

The most common causes of thrush are medications: antibiotics, inhaled steroids (commonly used for asthma), and chemotherapy. It is also seen with diabetes and with immunosuppression, as with AIDS.

Treatment of thrush consists of rinses with prescription Nystatin Oral Suspension, three times daily. Rarely, a systemic antiyeast medication like Diflucan (fluconazole) is necessary.

Bright Red Tongue

Your lipstick should be glossy, not your tongue.

A tongue that looks bright red, glossy, and smooth (the taste buds are flattened out and barely visible) could signal a vitamin B_{12}, zinc, or iron deficiency, or pernicious anemia.

A blood test can usually confirm the diagnosis, and vitamin supplementation can fix a nutritional deficiency.

Black Hairy Tongue

Black hairy tongue is typically a side effect of an antibiotic. Tetracyclines and penicillins are the primary culprits. Discontinuing the antibiotic usually clears up the condition immediately.

Hairy White Tongue

Hairy leukoplakia (a hairy white tongue) is often associated with Epstein-Barr virus, HIV infection, or some other cause of immunosuppression. The only patient I have ever seen with this condition presented with advanced AIDS, in the days when medical science did not fully understand the HIV infection.

Treatment for hairy white tongue consists of addressing the underlying condition and using an oral medication to try to remove the debris.

I have read reports that cigarette smoking can also cause hairy white tongue, which resolves upon cessation of smoking.

DRUG ERUPTIONS

Question: What symptom automatically changes a drug-caused rash into a medical crisis?

Answer: The development of sores in the mouth or other mucosal areas.

Known as Stevens-Johnson syndrome, this sign moves an allergic reaction into a serious status, requiring systemic steroids, supportive care, and much closer monitoring.

If you are at home nursing a "simple" rash caused by an antibiotic (or other medication) and develop ulcerations inside the mouth, let your dermatologist know *immediately*.

LICHEN PLANUS

A disorder known as lichen planus can cause delicate, lacy, white streaking on the buccal mucosa (insides of the cheeks). Lichen planus can also cause painful erosive sores on the gums, tongue, and throughout the mouth.

Rarely, long-standing sores from lichen planus progress into squamous cell carcinoma; if you have this condition, an oral examination once or twice a year is a good idea.

(For more information, please see the chapter "Lichen Planus" on page 148.)

PAINLESS NODULES

When I perform a complete skin examination, I always include an examination of the oral cavity. Not only does the mouth hold important clues from a dermatological perspective, but oral cancer can present as painless nodules, which the patient has come to accept as "normal." (If you're a smoker, you have an increased risk for developing oral cancer.)

Another cause of painless nodules and ulcerations of the hard palate is systemic sporotrichosis, a fungal disorder that can be seen in immunosuppressed patients.

FRECKLES

A freckle or freckles on the mucosal (inside) surface of the lips, the gums, or the inner cheeks can be a random, normal mole, a normal variant in dark-skinned patients, a hallmark of a potentially cancerous gastrointestinal disorder (Peutz-Jegher syndrome), or even a malignant melanoma.

If you have brown spots within the mouth, have a dermatologist examine them. Better safe than sorry.

FINAL THOUGHTS

Who would have thought there was a world of dermatology inside the mouth? If you are experiencing skin concerns near your pearly whites, visit your dermatologist, and just say "Ahhh."

Ask the DERMAdoctor

QUESTION:

I've noticed that my mouth is dry much of the time and, needless to say, this really, really bothers me. Why is this happening?

The DERMAdoctor:

The most common cause of dry mouth is an adverse response to one of many medications, ranging from antihistamines to antidepressants. The good news is that most patients will acclimate to this change within a few weeks.

But if you're not in the midst of medication changes and can't get past uncomfortable cotton mouth, consult your doctor. Autoimmune diseases, including Sjögren's syndrome, can cause oral dryness.

Right now there is no perfect therapy and no true "cure" for dry mouth. Two prescription medications, however, Salagen (pilocarpine hydrochloride) and Evoxac (cevimeline hydrochloride), are able to help stimulate saliva production. Here are some useful tips that may help: Avoid caffeine and alcohol. Stop smoking. Chew sugarless gum or suck on sugarless hard candy. Use a humidifier in your bedroom at night. Finally, avoid harsh irritants found in regular toothpaste by trying Squigle Enamel Saver Toothpaste.

NAIL PROBLEMS AND DISEASES

What Your Nails Are Saying About Your Health

Your eyes may be the windows to your soul, but your nails can be windows to your overall health.

More than just a canvas for polish, your fingernails can tip off a savvy observer to whether or not you have a nutritional deficiency, a skin disease like psoriasis, a recent injury, or many other possible health concerns.

The nail itself is dead tissue made of a durable protein called keratin (the same protein that forms hair). But the nail matrix (the area under the cuticle, where the nail is formed) and the nail bed (the tissue beneath the nail itself) are alive—and often reflect your health.

What are your nails trying to tell you?

BRITTLE NAILS
Possible Culprit: Water Damage
You immerse your hands in water a couple of times a day to scrub dishes or you often wash your hands to banish germs, and each time you put your hands in water, your nails swell and then shrink as they dry. The possible result: brittle, chipped, and split nails.

Combat the problem by regularly slathering on and working into your nails a rich, protective moisturizer, like TheraSeal Hand Protection or AHAVA Dermud Intensive Nourishing Hand Cream. Nail treatments to help strengthen and harden nails, like Nailtiques Formula 2, are also beneficial.

Possible Culprit: Biotin Deficiency

Biotin is a member of the B-vitamin family. If biotin-rich foods are missing from your diet, your nails can become brittle. One study found that 80 percent of people with brittle nails who switched to a biotin-rich diet had normal nails within a few months. Good food sources include brewer's yeast, corn, barley, soybeans, walnuts, peanuts, molasses, cauliflower, milk, egg yolks, and fortified cereals.

A supplement might help, too. In a study from Switzerland, published in the *Journal of the American Academy of Dermatology*, people who took a biotin supplement grew fingernails that were 25 percent thicker and had less splitting. Taking their cue from the Swiss study, doctors in the Department of Dermatology at Columbia University in New York looked at thirty-five patients who had visited a nail-consultation practice and had been prescribed biotin; after the treatment, 63 percent had nails that were far less brittle.

A multivitamin containing biotin, like DermaVite Dietary Supplement, can help you maintain the levels of nutrients vital to nail health.

Possible Culprit: Iron-Deficiency Anemia

Ask your doctor to test you for iron deficiency, which deprives every part of your body of oxygen-rich red blood cells—including your nails. If you're anemic, your doctor will prescribe an iron supplement. And make sure to include iron-rich foods in your diet, like beef, beans (and soy products), pumpkin seeds, and leafy, dark green vegetables like kale.

PITTED NAILS

Possible Culprit: Psoriasis

Psoriasis is a chronic skin disease that shows up as red, scaly patches on the body—and sometimes as pitted nails. A psoriasis-afflicted nail might also change in shape (rippling), color (reddish brown), or separate from the skin. Inflammation of the nail bed, hidden beneath the cuticle, can lead to nail pitting. Therapy here is very difficult because it needs to be aimed at what's going on beneath the surface, making creams and ointments essentially ineffective.

LOOSE OR DETACHED NAIL

Possible Culprit: Fungal Infection

Loosening (onycholysis) is frequently due to a fungal infection of the nail plate. (For more information on fungal infection, please see the box on page 182.) Thick debris often seems to collect under these nails as they lift away from the nail bed, but it's really fungi happily proliferating. Nail plates may further discolor as they detach, frequently because of bacteria taking advantage of the situation. These infections are tough to treat but not impossible. See your dermatologist, who can prescribe an antifungal medication.

HORIZONTAL FURROWS
Possible Culprit: Systemic Illness or Stressors
Sudden illness (like a heart attack), malnutrition, and even the pain and stress of carpal tunnel syndrome can stop nail growth. When the nail starts growing out, it can have horizontal, depressed furrows, called Beau's lines.

A WHITE SPOT (LEUKONYCHIA)
Possible Culprit: Injury to the Nail Bed
Your manicurist may be pushing those cuticles back too harshly. Fingernails grow just one-eighth of an inch per month. An injury to the nail bed won't show up for months, until the nail grows out. You might not remember minor events that traumatized the nail folds months ago—but your fingernails remember.

DARK STREAKS
Possible Culprit: Malignant Melanoma (Skin Cancer)
Dark streaks running the length of the nail could potentially be melanoma, so get to the dermatologist as soon as possible to have them checked out. Additional signs of danger are streaks that spread to the surrounding skin under the nail or the cuticle, or change in color and size. Fortunately, not all streaks are abnormal. They may be nothing more than a normal mole. And African-Americans can have natural dark, vertical streaks beneath the nail; however, it's always wise to have these identified by your dermatologist. As with any routine mole, any changes should be examined by a physician.

Possible Culprit: Injury
Sometimes a dark streak is just a fine, splinterlike hemorrhage caused by an injury to the nail matrix.

Possible Culprit: Clotting Disorder or Heart Infection
Sometimes these hemorrhages are the sign of an underlying clotting disorder (anticardiolipin antibody syndrome) or, even more rarely, due to a bacterial infection of the heart valve.

NAIL FUNGUS

Yellow, thickened, splitting nails often signal the presence of nail fungus, a contagious infection caused by several members of the fungus (dermatophyte) family. The problem can affect both fingernails and toenails, and afflicts many Americans. Which isn't all that surprising: fungi are everywhere, though you're most likely to pick up the infection in a bathroom, locker room, poolside, or gym. If you've had a fungal infection, you've probably tried several different over-the-counter remedies and maybe even some topical prescription products. It's not unlikely, however, that you've still got the problem. A fungal infection is tough to get rid of. But not impossible.

THE BEST TREATMENT: SYSTEMIC TREATMENT

The most effective nail fungus treatments available include three systemic, prescription antifungal medications and one prescription topical therapy. (Unfortunately, there aren't any topical over-the-counter medications that can penetrate the nail plate and cure a fungal infection.) But the most recent entry into the category—Lamisil (terbinafine)—is, in my opinion, far superior to the others.

Unlike griseofulvin (Gris-PEG, Grifulvin V, Fulvicin), Lamisil remains in the nail bed, significantly reducing the time of therapy. Toenails require three months of treatment, while fingernails require only six weeks— instead of as much as two years with griseofulvin! And unlike Sporanox (itraconazole), Lamisil doesn't usually interact negatively with a number of other medications. Lamisil is also easier on the body than the other medications, though it still has a low risk of systemic effects, such as bone marrow and liver problems.

For the safety of my patients, I perform blood work before and during the therapy (this is an absolute must with the other systemic antifungal medications): once every three weeks when treating fingernails, once a month for toenails. Occasionally, my patients experience diarrhea, and I have seen one drug reaction, but in my practice Lamisil has basically been a well-tolerated medication.

Penlac 8% solution (ciclopirox) remains the sole prescription topical antifungal therapy effective for nail fungus. Penlac works best for early nail fungus, limited to a very few nail plates. Consistent daily application and immaculate nail grooming are necessary to maximize results.

YEAST AND BACTERIAL INFECTIONS

Yeast and bacterial infections are usually the result of microscopic damage to the nail plates. (Yeast and fungus infections may *sound* similar, but the organisms are entirely different and respond to entirely different therapies.) The nails will either form a white discoloration at the tip that extends toward the cuticle or will take on a greenish black color. In neither case does the nail plate thicken or form subungual (under-the-nail) debris.

Amorese Thymol—a mixture of 4% thymol in alcohol—is excellent for yeast and bacteria infections of the nails. Use it twice daily, until the affected area has grown out. I also advise patients that diminishing exposure to water and soil can help significantly.

DIABETICS

Diabetics with toenail fungus are at higher risk of developing cellulitis, a bacterial skin infections of the lower legs. Patients who are not candidates for oral antifungals should be given a topical antifungal cream—like Lamisil or Spectazole—to use on their toenails daily. This helps prevent the fungus from spreading onto the foot, creating microscopic breaks in the skin through which bacteria can enter.

ARTIFICIAL NAILS

People who wear artificial nails are at a higher risk for developing fungal or yeast infections of the nail, due to the microscopic damage to the nail plate. Fastidious practices by the nail technician go a long way to help cut down on the development of these infections.

NAIL GROOMING

Nail grooming is important. Cut or file healthy nails first, followed by infected ones. Use a metal nail file that you can easily disinfect (along with the clippers) in a solution of dilute ammonia or bleach, or with rubbing alcohol. These procedures are critical in preventing the spread of the infection to other nails. A good antifungal cream will also help contain (but not clear) the infection.

Recurrent, inexplicable, purplish black hairline vertical lines beneath the nail plate, especially if combined with a history of recurrent miscarriages, Raynaud's disease, joint pain or swelling, or in association with intermittent low-grade fever, should be evaluated by your physician.

REDNESS AND SWELLING
Possible Culprit: Bacterial Infection
A nick at the manicurist's, a paper cut, or any trauma or injury to the cuticle can set you up for a bacterial infection called paronychia. Keep the area clean and speed healing with Polysporin ointment, an over-the-counter antibacterial preparation.

Sometimes a yeast infection of the nail—which appears as either a thin white discoloration at the tip that extends toward the cuticle or a greenish black color—can cause microscopic breaks triggering a bacterial infection. Applications of the over-the-counter medication Amorese Thymol can stop a yeast infection of the nail. But if the problem doesn't resolve or gets worse, see your doctor. (For more about yeast infections of the nails, see the box accompanying this chapter.)

CLUBBING
Possible Culprit: Systemic Disorders
Nails (and fingertips) that swell at the end can be caused by a wide array of diseases, including emphysema, lung cancer, heart disease, and disorders of the thyroid, liver, or bowel. (At times, it can also occur in healthy people.) If you notice clubbing, see your doctor for a thorough checkup.

BLUE OR WHITE NAILS
Possible Culprit: Illness
Discolored nails can indicate a health problem. Lack of oxygen in the bloodstream can cause nail beds to appear blue. White nail plates can signal liver disease. Pale nail beds may indicate anemia. If the nail is half pink and half white, you may have kidney disease.

Obviously, any dramatic change in the color of your nails should be a green light to see your physician.

YELLOW OR ORANGE NAILS
Possible Culprit: Illness
Diabetes can show itself as yellowish nail beds that are pink near the cuticle.

Possible Culprit: Lymphedema

Yellow nails can be associated with chronic lymphedema (swelling) of the arm, due to alteration of or damage to the lymph nodes under the arms, such as in a mastectomy.

Possible Culprit: Lung Disease

If your nails yellow, seem to stop growing, and thicken, you may have lung disease.

Possible Culprit: Medication Side Effect

Penicillamine, tetracycline, and fluorescein (a dye used in certain medical tests) can cause nails to appear yellow.

Possible Culprit: Smoking

Nicotine can stain the nail plate yellow.

Possible Culprit: Iron

Orange nails can be caused by excessive iron in well water.

DISCOLORED LUNULES
Possible Culprit: Illness

The lunules are those half-moon shapes that peek out from the base of the nail plates. Typically a pale pinkish white, lunules can turn dusky red due to many internal conditions, including lupus, congestive heart failure, alopecia areata, arthritis, and dermatomyositis.

Possible Culprit: Silver Poisoning

Azure blue lunules may tip off the doctor to the presence of argyria (silver poisoning).

FINAL THOUGHTS

Nails should be smooth, glossy, and beautiful. When they're not, it may have little to do with having missed a manicure. If your nails don't look healthy, what are they revealing about your health?

Ask the DERMAdoctor

QUESTION:

I am concerned about the ingredients used in some acrylic nails. I understand that the methyl methylacrylic acid used in some formulations is not approved for use in acrylic nails. I came across several nail products that contain polymethylacrylic acid. Are these safe?

The DERMAdoctor:

In chemistry, there are certain general, common molecular formations, like alcohols, esters, and aldehydes, that can be confused with a single, identifiable end ingredient that sounds similar. The polymerized form of methyl methacrylate (PMMA) is not the same thing as the free form of the molecule methyl methacrylate (MMA). PMMA is considered safe to use in acrylic nail application and nail care products.

Methyl methacrylate was commonly used in the past as an agent to help bond acrylic nails to the natural nail plate. MMA bonds well and remains attached to the surface over a prolonged period of time, but it can be toxic. Side effects include suppression of the central nervous system, irritation to the skin, eyes, and mucous membranes, and lung damage. High doses of MMA may actually cause pulmonary edema. Today, several acrylic nail manufacturers have reformulated acrylics that do not contain MMA.

The FDA has banned MMA, but some states still allow its use. Signals of the chemical include a strong, almost fruity odor emitted from the liquid being used, and masks being worn by most or all of the technicians in the shop. (These signals don't necessarily prove that your nail technician is using a product with MMA, but they are fairly reliable indications.) If you are not sure, ask what product the shop is using and what the chemical content of the product is. There should be a bottle that provides this information.

MMA goes by a variety of names. According to a list from the National Toxicology Program, the various synonyms by which free MMA is known include: 2-methyl-2-propenoic acid; methyl ester methacrylic acid; methyl ester; 2-methyacrylic acid methyl ester; methyl methacrylate monomer; methyl methylacrylate; methyl alpha methylacrylate; methyl 2-methyl-2-propenoate; 2-methyl-2-propenoic acid methyl ester; diakon; methyl methacrylate monomer, inhibited; methyl methacrylate monomer, uninhibited; MME; monocite methacrylate monomer; NA 1247; NCI-C50680; RCRA waste number U162; UN 1247; 2-methyl-2-propenoic acid methyl ester; acrylic acid, 2-methyl, methyl ester; 2-propenoic acid, 2-methyl, methyl ester.

OILY SKIN

Solve the Problem—
but Don't Go Too Far

Perhaps you have been wishing that your oil-laden T-zone would suddenly vanish and be replaced with a healthy, radiant complexion.

Your wish *can* come true: changing skin from oily and shiny to fresh and glowing is not an unattainable goal.

The key is confronting the predicament without giving in to skin-traumatizing temptation.

WHY OILY ME?

Microscopic sebaceous glands hidden beneath the surface of the skin are the source of all this trouble. Concentrated on the face (particularly in the notorious T-zone), back, scalp, and midchest, these glands lubricate the skin and hair with oil (sebum), providing protection from environmental challenges like dehydration and helping maintain health and luster. But as anyone who suffers from oily skin knows, too much sebum is a real problem.

Surplus sebum leaves the skin greasy and shiny, which is both uncomfortable and cosmetically unacceptable. Oily skin can take a toll upon its victim, generating a negative impact on body image and self-esteem. From a medical standpoint, excessive sebum blocks pores, providing nourishment to bacteria that live on the skin (*Proprionibacterium acnes*) and triggering acne flare-ups.

Why do sebaceous glands go into overdrive? The culprit (along with your genetics) is the hormone dihydrotestosterone (DHT). DHT is first formed at the onset of puberty, in both boys and girls. This metabolite of testosterone triggers the sebaceous glands to produce sebum. Too much DHT results in too much oil.

Hormonal fluctuations during the menstrual cycle affect DHT levels, which rise after ovulation, along with progesterone. Ever wonder why your skin becomes oilier and acne-prone just before menstruation? Blame DHT.

CLEARING UP . . . THE MISCONCEPTIONS

There are so many wrong-minded ideas out there about how to clear up oily skin. So let's clear those up first.

Using oil-control products will lead to an increase in sebum production. Let's not mince words: this is absolutely false.

Blotting facial oils helps reduce the production of sebum. While blotting temporarily removes oil, it doesn't control the source of the problem.

Oily skin is not a concern for those with rosacea. Rosacea sufferers are more likely to have drier, sensitive skin because of the natural aging process, but I've seen more than my share of tremendously oily rosacea patients.

Accutane fully eliminates ("cures") oil production. Accutane normalizes the glandular lining, which helps repair a faulty mechanism contributing to the formation of cystic acne. A "side effect" of this repair is a reduction in sebum production. But oiliness is not eliminated entirely—a person on Accutane can remain oily, or oiliness can return after the treatment ends.

You can't wear makeup while using oil-control products. Yes you can, but the makeup should be labeled "oil-free" or "noncomedogenic." You can also apply oil-free makeup on top of products that help control oily skin conditions or acne. (For those affected by excess oils in spite of using oil-control products, a powder base can help. Rice powders—like those used in T. LeClerc or mineral-based powders like Jane Iredale Mineral Cosmetics—feel light, don't plug pores, and help absorb excess oils.)

Oil-control products cause unpleasant dryness and irritation. While many products that reduce facial oil can cause these problems, it's not true across the board. And product overuse or misuse can be responsible for skin irritation, not just the products themselves.

OIL-CONTROL PRODUCTS: HOW TO CHOOSE WHAT'S RIGHT FOR YOU

After all that myth busting, it's time to do some oil busting. Here's a complete overview of some products intended to help oily skin.

DERMAdoctor Tease Zone Oil Control Gel

Oil-reducing skin care products generally fall into one of three less-than-desirable categories. They may be loaded with fragrance, the leading cause of sensitivity in facial products; be fragrance-free, but retain a strong chemical odor; or have a pore-smothering silicone base.

DERMAdoctor Tease Zone Oil Control Gel doesn't fit into any of those categories. Tease Zone relies upon polymer technology—Sebum-Sequestering Micro-Particles—that work to surround and absorb excessive surface skin oils. As a result, Tease Zone is so light-weight that it literally disappears upon application, without leaving any residual scent, odor, or tackiness. Oil already present on the skin or deep within the glands is soaked up, and as oil is formed through-out the day, it continues to be absorbed, keeping skin matte and foun-dation intact. Eliminating excess surface skin oils also deprives the bacterium *P. acne* of nourishment, reducing acne formation (and reducing visible pore size, since the presence of more bacteria widens pores). Another benefit: Tease Zone absorbs only *excess* oils, so it doesn't dry out your skin. That makes it an appropriate product whether you're plagued by oily or combination skin.

You can use DERMAdoctor Tease Zone Oil Control Gel in con-junction with other acne products, including topical antibiotics, gly-colic acids, and topical retinoids; and with makeup. Tease Zone is also an ideal product to use post-Accutane, for those with remnant oil production. It is safe to use while pregnant or nursing.

And because it is dye- and fragrance-free, and has been both der-matologist- and allergy-tested, those prone to sensitive-skin issues, like rosacea, seborrheic dermatitis, or perioral dermatitis, can benefit from using Tease Zone.

Synthetic Topical Retinoids

This category includes prescription Retin-A, Retin-A Micro gel, Differin, Tazorac, and Avita, as well as over-the-counter retinols like Afirm.

Using synthetic topical retinoids unquestionably improves oily skin. However, despite appropriate use, a sizable minority of patients still develop redness, flaking, and irritation. I always encourage my oil-plagued or acne-prone patients to use these treatments sparingly: no more than every other night, at least to start. (Retin-A, Retina-A Micro gel, Differin, and Avita have all been touted as being gentler to the skin than other options, but I find they are all quite similar in irritancy.)

Using gentle products for routine skin care can help stabilize a too dry situation. Consider M.D. Forté Replenish Hydrating Cleanser and M.D. Forté Replenish Hydrating Cream, particularly during cold weather, when skin dehydration is more likely.

You can combine other oil-control products in your regimen, including glycolic acids and/or DERMAdoctor Tease Zone Oil Control Gel, but always apply your retinoids solo. Applying other topicals at the same time as a synthetic retinoid increases the potential for irritation.

In addition to oil reduction, prescription synthetic retinoids help eliminate blackheads and other acne lesions. Personally, I find that Tazorac Cream is the best prescription retinoids option for those with incredibly oily skin accompanied by acne.

Accutane

I don't feel that oily skin alone justifies the use of Accutane. (And neither does the FDA, which hasn't approved this prescription agent for the control of oily skin.) Accutane is a great medication for treating severe cystic acne, but it also can have significant side effects. While some clients with oily skin tell me they wish they could take Accutane for controlling excess sebum production, I remind them that it's not a medically indicated use, and for good reason.

Glycolic Acid

Glycolic acid, a popular form of the alpha hydroxy acids (AHAs), is often formulated in bases that are more effective for those with oily skin. Remember, however, that while glycolic acid does help exfoliate the skin, cutting through surface oils and cleaning out pores, it is a temporary oil reducer. It does not actually stop or "cure" the overproduction of oil within the gland.

M.D. Forté Glycare products—including their M.D. Forté Glycare Cleansing Gel, M.D. Forté Glycare I, and M.D. Forté Glycare Perfection Gel—are great, and I try to have my patients with oily skin or acne patients incorporate them into their skin care regimen. You can use M.D. Forté Glycare Cleansing Gel once or twice a day, then apply M.D. Forté Glycare I and DERMAdoctor Tease Zone Oil Control Gel. (After your skin accommodates to the level I strength, you can advance up to level II.)

The application of these and other glycolic acid products also helps acne medications penetrate more deeply into the skin and be more effective. However, I *do not* recommend applying glycolic acid at the same time as products containing benzoyl peroxide (which kills *P. acne*) or retinoids; this can cause irritation. (Using a glycolic acid cleanser with these products is fine.)

There are certainly individuals in whom glycolic acid will cause too much irritation or exfoliation. If you're one of these, try switching to a product with the same level of glycolic acid but in a gentler, less drying base, like M.D. Forté Facial Lotion I or M.D. Forté Facial Lotion II. Occasionally, that strategy doesn't work and less concentrated products are necessary to eliminate the irritation.

Salicylic Acid

Salicylic acid—or, as it's more trendily known, beta hydroxy acid (BHA)—functions similarly to the glycolic acids: it helps in the exfoliation process and in removing surface oil but does not treat the underlying condition.

To reduce facial oiliness, consider cleansers like Sal Ac Wash or Peter Thomas Roth Beta Hydroxy Acid 2% Acne Wash.

Salicylic acid can cause dryness or irritation if it's overused. Its use is not recommended while pregnant or nursing.

OC Eight Mattifying Gel

OC Eight Mattifying Gel is an aqueous (water-based), nonirritating gel containing oil-absorbing microbeads that mechanically sequester surface skin oils. Studies show that it is effective in reducing oiliness for up to eight hours; you can apply it up to three times a day. It is compatible with prescription acne treatments.

Clinac BPO is a prescription option; it blends the microbeads with benzoyl peroxide.

Astringents and Toners

Astringent agents—including alcohol, witch hazel, and acetone— dissolve skin oils. But they provide only a temporary, short-term fix that doesn't tend to last throughout the day. Still, there continues to be considerable loyalty to this daily grooming ritual. I view toners as an incomplete approach for those with problematic oily skin. For better results, use them in concert with a cleanser and oil-absorbing agent. Some options include:

- Ionax Astringent Skin Cleanser.
- Peter Thomas Roth Conditioning Tonic contains both benzoic acid and BHA. It helps strip away grease and grime and kills bacteria.
- Neova Balancing Toner contains silica beads, which absorb ten times their weight in oil, leaving the skin refreshed.
- Cellex-C Betaplex Facial Firming Water contains moderate levels of AHA and BHA, to gently remove oils and surface debris.
- Seba-Nil Cleanser.

Astringents and toners can cause redness, dryness, or irritation, so avoid overuse.

Masques
Masques can effectively reduce oiliness on the skin for several days. I recall being in college and wearing a clay masque every few evenings. Not really an attractive approach, but it helped at the time.

Peter Thomas Roth Therapeutic Sulfur Masque is a product I really like to use. It also contains therapeutic additives that deal with some acne-causing issues.

Another oil-reducing masque is Cellex-C Betaplex Clear Complexion Mask, which helps draw out excess oils and keep them at bay for several days This masque not only reduces oils but also helps exfoliate materials lodged deep within the glands. It's my personal favorite.

Oil-Blotting Papers
There are a variety of oil-blotting papers on the market. Some people erroneously think that they aggravate oily skin conditions, which isn't true. But neither do they control oiliness. They simply reduce the shine that can develop on the skin throughout the day. Agents that reduce the presence of oil on the skin's surface in the first place provide a more comprehensive solution to the problem. But having blotting papers on hand for an oily emergency shouldn't cause any harm.

FINAL THOUGHTS

So now you know all about how to improve your oily skin condition. There is a wide range of options for you to take advantage of. Remember, too, that your dermatologist is the perfect resource for prescription options that can help with unrelenting oil production and acne outbreaks.

Ask the DERMAdoctor

QUESTION:

I am forty-two, very fair, and have very oily, sensitive skin, I have tried Retin-A and other retinol products, and M.D. Forté. They all make my skin very irritated and almost burned. I also have fine lines under my eyes from sun damage. Please recommend something that is gentle enough for my sensitive skin but will also control the oiliness and help with sun damage. Am I asking for a miracle?

The DERMAdoctor:

With oily, sensitive skin you are walking a fine line. The point is to reduce the oil while not overly drying out your skin and irritating it. So you may find that you have to reduce your frequency of use of glycolic acid products. You may want to consider trying this regimen: Wash with Seba-Nil Cleanser once or twice a day. In the morning, apply Neova Mattifying Facial Lotion, followed by DERMAdoctor Tease Zone. At night, try applying M.D. Forté Facial Lotion I and DERMAdoctor Tease Zone. That way, you will be able to use an antioxidant in the morning and glycolic acid at night for skin rejuvenation, in bases that are appropriate for (and can help with) oily skin.

QUESTION:

I have a very oily nose and forehead but a very, very dry chin and cheeks. I want to get that flawless look that all the models have, but every time I put on powder, my skin either looks greasy (if I don't use enough) or dry and peeling (if I use enough to cover the oil). Please help me get that flawless look!

The DERMAdoctor:

First of all, you need to realize that models have skin just like you and me. They use an incredible amount of makeup to improve any imperfections, and then the photos are touched up. Your ideal should be your own skin—at its best.

It sounds like you have combination skin, which is very common. It is difficult to apply multiple products, on various portions of the face. I usually recommend skin care products that are made for dry, sensitive skin, then apply an oil-absorbing product to the trouble zones. Try cleansing with M.D. Forté Replenish Hydrating Cleanser or Vanicream Cleansing Bar.

It's likely that you will want a moisturizing cream. Try M.D. Forté Replenish Hydrating Cream or Cellex-C Sea Silk Moisturizing Cream. Apply to the entire face. Then apply DERMAdoctor Tease Zone to your problematic areas, most likely the T-zone. Don't forget your sunscreen. DERMAdoctor Body Guard helps balance the skin's moisture and is not only oil-free but also oil-reducing.

QUESTION:

Can I use a moisturizing cream if I have oily skin?

The DERMAdoctor:

Probably the most overused step in skin care is applying moisturizers. Hydrating the skin when it's dry is unquestionably important to both heal and protect against dehydration. But using a moisturizer just for the sake of including a moisturizer is not an essential part of daily facial skin care.

The skin derives moisture from whatever is applied to it. So treatments, topical medications, skin rejuvenation products, and sunscreen all lend moisture to the skin. If your skin still feels dry, then apply a moisturizer. The need for a moisturizer may also vary with the seasons.

Make certain to select a moisturizer that is labeled as noncomedogenic. If your skin looks oily, either you don't need a moisturizer or you need to select a lighter base, probably a lotion or gel. Again, this selection may vary with the seasons.

Don't hesitate to apply an oil-absorbing product either beneath or on top of your moisturizer, like DERMAdoctor Tease Zone.

PERIORAL DERMATITIS

Treat It Right and It's Gone Forever

Perioral dermatitis is a common yet curious skin condition that takes its name from its location. *Peri* means "around" and *oral*, of course, means "mouth." Perioral dermatitis, therefore, is an eruption in the area surrounding the mouth.

The condition looks like a cross between acne and eczema: there are acnelike lesions within eczema-like areas that are red, rough, scaling, and very sensitive. But perioral dermatitis doesn't affect everyone the same way. Some eruptions look more like acne, others more like eczema, and some a little bit like both.

The good news: if perioral dermatitis is treated appropriately, it's usually a onetime event.

For patients with no contraindications (like a drug allergy), my favorite therapy (because it's the most effective) is a combination of two medications: 500 milligrams of oral tetracycline twice a day, along with DesOwen Lotion, a low-potency topical steroid, applied twice a day.

SKIN THAT'S ADDICTED TO STEROIDS

Unfortunately, that's often not the therapy a patient gets. Many patients with perioral dermatitis have seen another physician for their condition before they see a dermatologist. And if they've been prescribed a high-potency topical steroid cream (and that's often the case), it is difficult to convince them to stop using the cream. It's not that most haven't tried to stop. But whenever they did, the condition flared up.

What's going on? Well, skin can literally become addicted to a high-potency topical steroid cream. Once a patient has used the cream and stops, perioral dermatitis "rebounds" for at least two weeks.

Besides miring you in this chronic cycle, regular use of a high-potency topical steroid can lead to atrophy (thinning) of facial skin. And atrophy can lead to lightened skin color, spider veins, and stretch marks.

So if you have perioral dermatitis, it is really in your best interest to give up the offending cream.

REDUCING THE REBOUND

Once you stop the cream, my counsel is for you to wait out the rebound. If at the same time you start the therapy described above—oral tetracycline and a mild topical steroid cream—you'll reduce the intensity of the rebound.

Treatment typically lasts six weeks. At that time, I see the patient again to evaluate her progress. If she is clear, I gradually reduce the dosage of her two medications over the next few weeks.

IS IT ALL ABOUT LIFESTYLE?

Yes, there are patients who struggle with a chronic case of perioral dermatitis who have tried everything and just never clear.

An astounding 90 percent of perioral dermatitis patients are women. Because of this, cosmetics and skin care products may potentially factor into this disorder. Bases containing paraffin, petrolatum, or isopropyl myristate have been implicated as flare-causing factors.

You are what you eat and, in some instances, what you put in your mouth. The use of toothpaste containing SLS (sodium lauryl sulfate), cocamidopropyl betaine, pyrophosphates, bleaches, and strong flavors is also thought to play some role in triggering perioral dermatitis. If you are battling perioral dermatitis, it may be time to switch to Squigle Enamel Saver Toothpaste, which is free of these potentially irritating ingredients.

A FEW MORE TIPS

If you have perioral dermatitis, you probably have very sensitive skin and a burning sensation in the affected area. General skin care can include gentle washes like Cetaphil Gentle Skin Cleanser or Vanicream Cleansing Bar and moisturizers like Cutanix Dramatic Relief Sensitive Skin or Wibi Dry Skin Lotion.

Zinc pyrithione is a favorite therapeutic ingredient of mine. I often incorporate it into dandruff and psoriasis therapy. It works thanks to its antibacterial and antiyeast actions. And since the yeast candida is implicated somehow in flare-ups of the disorder, I have found that antidandruff cleansers containing zinc pyrithione are beneficial when incorporated into the treatment plan for my perioral dermatitis patients. FYI, this is considered an "off-label" use (meaning not approved by the FDA). Consider adding a therapeutic wash like DERMAdoctor Born To Be Mild Medicated Cleanser or ZNP bar to your perioral dermatitis regimen.

FINAL THOUGHTS

Perioral dermatitis is common, it's sometimes chronic, and it's most definitely controllable. If you can't seem to get anywhere with your treatments, taking a hands-off approach may be that final treatment option for you to consider. Eliminating all skin care products, cosmetics, prescription medications, and just about anything else you can think of avoiding may just get you the relief you seek.

Ask the DERMAdoctor

QUESTION:

I've recently been diagnosed with both acne rosacea and perioral dermatitis. I have red bumps not only around my mouth, but also in between my eyebrows and on my nose and cheeks. If it's not just around my mouth, is it still considered perioral dermatitis?

The DERMAdoctor:

I would presume that you have only one condition: acne rosacea. It is not uncommon for early rosacea to resemble perioral dermatitis. The dermatological rule of thumb is that what looks to be perioral dermatitis and continues to recur may be rosacea in disguise. More than one patient of mine has looked as if she had the perfect case of perioral dermatitis, but inexplicably it did not clear up and, in fact, continued to flare. Eventually, such a patient tends to develop full facial symptoms—as in your case—and the real diagnosis is apparent.

QUESTION:

I have a mild case of perioral dermatitis. Can I use makeup to disguise the problem while it gets better?

The DERMAdoctor:

In a pinch for a special occasion, try a mineral-based makeup, such as Jane Iredale. But ideally you should keep the makeup off as much as possible during this time. Fortunately, the problem shouldn't last that long, though. With the right treatment, perioral dermatitis usually goes away in about six to eight weeks.

PITYRIASIS ROSEA

Relief for a Little-Known Rash

Its initials are PR, but it's got bad PR—most Americans have never heard of it.

PR is pityriasis rosea, a pink, itchy, annoying, and all too common rash that peaks in the fall and spring. Anyone can develop the rash (though it's most prevalent among those ten to thirty years old), and a lot of people do. It hasn't been unusual for me to see more than twenty PR patients each season. Multiply that by all the dermatologists and primary care physicians—and add in all the people with PR who never see the doctor—and you get a feel for how prevalent it is.

Like chickenpox, PR usually afflicts patients only once in a lifetime. But unlike with chickenpox and most other rashes, no one is certain what causes PR. It's not a bacterial infection, nor is it contagious. (Someday I'll regret saying this, but . . . I've seen hundreds of patients with PR over the years, and I've never developed it.) The onset of the rash is often preceded by a recent low-grade temperature or upper-respiratory illness, so most dermatologists suspect that PR is triggered by a viral infection. But scientists have yet to isolate the responsible virus.

HERE A SPOT, THERE A SPOT, EVERYWHERE A SPOT, SPOT
The vast majority of patients develop a solitary "herald patch" or "mother spot" a few days or weeks prior to the rest of the outbreak. The herald patch is often the largest spot, measuring up to several centimeters in diameter. When the rest of the rash makes an appearance, it's far showier.

Small, salmon pink oval patches about one centimeter in size, each with a "collarette" of scale, form rapidly on the torso, stopping abruptly at the neck and the hips. The spots arrange themselves in an angular pattern on the chest and the back that looks very much like a Christmas tree.

It's not unusual, however, to see stray patches develop on the extremities, neck, and face. And there is always the unfortunate patient who is covered from head to toe.

Pityriasis rosea can have a somewhat different appearance in patients with darker complexions. The rash can seem bumpy, both in texture and look, and the tiny bumps can coalesce into oval patches. There can be less scale, and the centers of the oval may have a duskier hue. Nevertheless, it is the same skin disorder, and treatment remains the same.

Characteristically, the rash has a duration of six weeks, arising over the first two weeks, remaining stable for another two weeks, and resolving over the final two weeks. A very few patients have long-term PR. If a case hasn't cleared within eight to ten weeks, I'll usually perform a workup to verify that no other possibility has been overlooked.

Diagnosis

Typically, pityriasis rosea is a straightforward clinical diagnosis that doesn't require testing. However, the presence of the thin, white scale can result in a misdiagnosis of ringworm, a fungal infection. A doctor can solve a confusing case with a simple skin scraping, called a KOH, which will show the presence or absence of a fungal infection. Rarely, a skin biopsy is performed.

In adults, secondary syphilis can mimic the appearance of pityriasis rosea, so I routinely order a blood test for the disease, called an RPR (rapid plasma reagin). Generally, syphilis is clinically obvious, but I don't want to miss a case.

If you're pregnant and get PR, don't worry. To my knowledge, there are no reports of fetal anomalies when a pregnant woman has had PR or been exposed to it.

CONTROLLING THE DISCOMFORT

Regrettably, there is no treatment available to clear the rash. It's one of those occasions when you just have to leave it alone and let it go away by itself. Fortunately, after the rash vanishes the skin returns to normal. The possible exception: those with darker complexions may find that some postinflammatory hyperpigmentation (brown skin discoloration) remains for several months. But that, too, fades over time.

While there's no treatment for the rash itself, there is something you can do about the itching.

Itching is by far the most common complaint of people with PR. (A close second is the appearance of the rash itself.) Therapy is aimed at controlling the discomfort.

Itching is always worse at night. I suspect this is because during the day we're distracted by work, family, school, and a bevy of other commitments. But once your head hits the pillow, there's no escaping the itch. There's simply nothing else to think about!

Itch control isn't always easy. But there's certainly no lack of options to try.

Over-the-Counter Topical Relief
Some of the best anti-itching products for PR include:

- Prax Lotion, a moisturizing lotion that temporarily relieves itching.
- Caladryl Clear Lotion, which is not the bright pink product you might remember from when you were a kid and had chickenpox or poison ivy. It now has a colorless base containing the anesthetic Pramoxine instead of Benadryl (a potential skin sensitizer when applied topically), and also contains camphor, which cools the skin.
- PrameGel, also a topical anesthetic.
- L.M.X. 4 Topical Anesthetic Cream, which contains 4 percent lidocaine. Health professionals use lidocaine preparations to numb the skin prior to inserting IV lines or obtaining blood specimens, for example. Following the application of this product, you might notice a slight cooling sensation, followed by an increasingly numb feeling in the area covered by the cream.

You can also soothe your itchy skin by taking a bath in Aveeno Oatmeal Bath Treatment or adding approximately one-third of a box of baking soda to the bathwater.

Antihistamines
Oral antihistamines, including over-the-counter Benadryl and prescription Atarax (hydroxyzine), can help alleviate itching and are particularly useful at bedtime to help you sleep.

A prescription topical antihistamine cream, Zonalon (doxepin), can rapidly reduce the itching. However, it isn't intended for full-body use, particularly on a long-term basis. Should Zonalon be absorbed through the skin (this potential increases with more widespread use), it can actually cause drowsiness. Use it sparingly, according to your doctor's directions.

Topical Steroids
Topical steroids can help reduce the inflammation associated with the rash, reducing itching. The highest-potency over-the-counter options contain 1% hydrocortisone, like Aveeno Maximum Strength Anti-Itch Cream or Sarnol-HC.

UVB LIGHT
Some dermatologists will treat patients once or twice with ultraviolet light (UVB), which can help reduce itching. This isn't for everyone, but it offers an option in cases where nothing else works.

FINAL THOUGHTS
All in all, PR is an annoying, itchy rash that dermatologists see seasonally—and that goes away without a trace.

Ask the DERMAdoctor

QUESTION:
I am a thirty-one-year-old African-American woman. I was diagnosed with pityriasis rosea by my dermatologist. I read that it never attacks the face, but it attacked mine. I am also covered with a rash on my neck, shoulders, torso, arms, and thighs. I was prescribed Benadryl for itching and a medicated lotion. Is there some type of makeup or cream that can camouflage this rash on my face? (It is bad enough that it is all over my body!) Please help.

The DERMAdoctor:
Pityriasis rosea can most definitely affect the face, especially for African-Americans. (I have no idea why. It just seems that this particular rash has a very different presentation in blacks, compared with Caucasians and other races.) You want to keep the inflammation to a minimum with your

Benadryl. (If that oral antihistamine doesn't work, ask the doctor for a stronger medication, like Atarax.) For facial areas, you may want to use a low-potency topical steroid cream, which will help minimize remnant discoloration after the rash is gone. Try over-the-counter Cortaid Steroid Cream, or ask your doctor for a prescription cream or lotion, like Des-Owen. And as for makeup, Covermark makes an excellent array of concealer foundation shades, which can be used individually or mixed to match your specific skin tones.

POISON IVY, OAK, AND SUMAC

Don't Let Them Ruin Your Great Outdoors

How much oil from poison ivy would it take to give everyone on Earth a rash?

One-quarter of an ounce.

That's right: urushiol, the oil (a.k.a. resin) found in poison ivy, poison oak, and poison sumac, is powerful, nasty stuff. But with a little botanical knowledge—and a quick therapeutic response—you can keep these "poisonous" plants from ruining your experience of the great outdoors.

A RASH MOVE

Poison ivy, poison oak, and poison sumac are sneaky plants. (They're also similar plants—same urushiol in each; same type of rash caused by each—and I refer to them interchangeably through this chapter.) Because their oil isn't noticeable, you don't know when it has gotten onto your skin. But soon—one to two days for someone who's had a previous bout of poison ivy; up to nine days for a first-timer—you'll begin to experience the characteristic eruption. Itching. Swelling. Redness. And, finally, groups of watery blisters.

The rash often appears in streaks, mirroring where each leaf or branch has touched the skin. The spot where the most resin contacted your skin is where the rash will start and where it will probably be the worst. Areas exposed to smaller amounts can continue to break out, sometimes over a three-week period. (Just when you thought it was safe to go back in the woods . . .)

The two most common misconceptions about the rash are that touching it spreads it, and that scratching the blisters makes it contagious. It's the *resin* that causes the allergic reaction—and most people wash it off long before the rash breaks out. (Another reason to wash immediately after coming indoors.)

DELAYED REACTIONS

Even when it's off the plant, urushiol can cause a rash for up to five years.

Can't figure out how you got poison ivy in January? How about those logs you carted in for the fireplace?

Did your garden tools sit untouched (and unwashed) throughout the winter, only to be taken out eagerly for springtime gardening—giving you the season's first bout of poison ivy?

Did you play with the family cat or dog after they romped gleefully in a patch of poison oak?

Too many moms find themselves with poison ivy after doing laundry that was drenched in resin and then sat in the hamper for a couple of days. Train yourself and your family to immediately toss dirty clothing into the washing machine. And wash them immediately too—regular detergent in a hot-water wash cycle will get rid of the oil.

BOTANY LESSON

"Leaves of three, let them be."

That instruction for identifying poison ivy seems pretty straightforward. Both poison ivy and poison oak have three leaflets per stalk. On the other hand, poison sumac can have anywhere from seven to thirteen leaves. If you live on the East Coast, where you are far more likely to encounter poison sumac, be wary! The rest of us in the United States and Canada are more likely to stumble across poison ivy or poison oak.

These plants are usually red in early spring, green later in the season, and (just like deciduous trees) change to autumn hues.

Poison ivy can flower and make berries. The leaves can vary in size on the same plant, be straight or scalloped, and look shiny or dull. It can creep along the ground, climb like a vine, or look like a shrub. (Both poison oak and poison sumac are shrubs, but their appearance can vary, too.)

But whatever the appearance of the plant, your rash will look the same.

BLOCK THAT POISON

What can you do about it?

If you know you're going to be in an area where there might be poison ivy . . . prepare! Try the product Ivy Block, which contains the active ingredient bentoquatum.

Studies show that applying Ivy Block to the skin at least fifteen minutes before contact with urushiol can prevent or diminish the rash.

A JEWEL OF A WEED

Jewelweed has long been touted as a natural remedy for washing away plant oils after exposure and reducing itching from the rash. Jewelweed is thought to contain tannin, the active ingredient in tea leaves that helps reduce swelling and inflammation. (Remember those tea bag compresses for puffiness under the eyes?) It's way back in the medical history books, but a study published in 1958 showed that of 115 patients treated with jewelweed, 108 responded well to treatment.

The FDA hasn't evaluated jewelweed as an active therapeutic agent for treating poison ivy. But if poison ivy is the bane of your summertime existence, it might be worthwhile to wash with an inexpensive, jewelweed-based soap after participating in "high-risk" outdoor activities like gardening or hiking.

Burt's Bees Poison Ivy Soap contains a blend of jewelweed, clay (used in a variety of poison ivy remedies, to try to lift the urushiol off the skin), and pine tar (to help gently cleanse the skin). The goal is to wash away some of the unwanted plant oils.

However, this is *not* the time to take a bath. The last thing you want to do is soak in a tub full of urushiol that has been rinsed off one area of your skin and is now contacting the rest of you!

SELF-CARE COMFORT

But what if for some reason your preventive steps didn't work out or weren't taken—and you find yourself itching on a Friday night when seeing a doctor isn't possible? Here are some ways to make it through the weekend in relative comfort.

Dry It

There's a old medical saying about dealing with blistery rashes: "If it's wet, dry it." Domeboro Astringent Solution helps dry out blisters quickly and is also antibacterial. Follow the package instructions for mixing, and apply a compress to the blistered area for twenty minutes, twice a day. Your compress should be damp, not sopping wet. But always dip a fresh cloth into the mixture; that prevents contamination, allowing you to reuse the solution. And skip the eye area; you don't want to risk getting the astringent in your eyes.

Try a Topical Steroid

Over-the-counter steroid creams contain 1% hydrocortisone, which is usually too weak to be of much benefit against poison ivy. But applied twice a day, it can help get you through the weekend. The best choices for the rash are Sarnol-HC 1%, which also contains menthol and camphor to help soothe the itching, or plain Cortaid 1% cream. When you see your dermatologist, she'll probably prescribe a much stronger topical steroid, like Temovate Gel. The gel base aids your efforts at drying out weeping blisters.

Take an Oral Antihistamine

An oral antihistamine like Benadryl can help stop the itching. The downside: most women get so drowsy after taking a single 25-milligram dose of Benadryl that they can barely function. Here's a secret: if you use the syrup form of Benadryl—like Benadryl Allergy Dye-Free Liquid—you can take a smaller dose, which will help prevent drowsiness.

Use a Topical Anesthetic

To temporarily blunt the itching, try products like PrameGel, Caladryl Clear Lotion, or Prax Lotion.

Skip topical anesthetics that contain topical diphenhydramine; they can cause a contact allergic dermatitis.

PREVENT INFECTION

To prevent infection, apply a topical antibacterial ointment to any raw, denuded areas. I usually suggest Polysporin ointment or Bacitracin.

PREDNISONE PREDICAMENT

Here is my pet peeve about professional poison ivy care.

The majority of poison ivy patients make their way initially to the ER or their primary care physicians, where they are given either steroid shots or five-day dose packs of the steroid Medrol (methyl-prednisolone), or both. Systemic steroids used for treating poison "tease" the system. Once the temporary, anti-inflammatory effects are over, the rash can come back worse! This is called the "rebound phenomenon."

So the poor patient goes back to the doctor and is given another round of short-term treatment. And possibly another, when the cycle repeats again. By the time a dermatologist is consulted, the patient is experiencing the Rebound Phenomenon of the Year.

It's not unusual for me to have at least twenty patients a summer suffering through this situation.

Bottom line: If your poison ivy is bad enough to deserve systemic steroids, you need a *high* dose of prednisone, followed by a long-term tapering of prednisone, going from 60 milligrams to zero, over at least two weeks. (See page 88 for the schedule I use.) That's the same treatment you'll need to get off a rebound cycle.

Z Last Word in Home Therapy; or, Z Is for Zanfel

The rash forms because of an allergy to urushiol, which has bound to the skin in the areas it contacted. If you could somehow lift the urushiol out of your skin cells, you could reduce the severity and/or duration of the rash.

That's what Zanfel Poison Ivy Cream claims to do.

For minor cases, rub Zanfel into the active areas of rash, then rinse off after one minute. After the first wash the itching is supposed to abate, and ideally the rash should improve over the next twenty-four hours.

If you need additional itch relief or have widespread poison ivy, don't hesitate to incorporate other poison ivy therapies along with Zanfel.

IMMUNE TODAY, NOT IMMUNE TOMORROW

Some people have the luck of the draw and are naturally immune to poison ivy; others become so over time. Others are the opposite—they *lose* their immunity, for no apparent reason. I know an avid gardener who began developing her annual case of poison ivy after she turned forty! Our systems change, so don't take your immunity for granted.

GET RID OF THE PLANT

If you have poison ivy, oak, or sumac lurking in your yard, by all means, try to get rid of it! You can do this at any time of year, but the best time is May through July, so you can actually identify what you're trying to kill off.

However, you can't get rid of poison ivy by mowing or weed whacking. You'll end up with hundreds of tiny pieces of toxic plant material, each one of which can make you break out—and which are likely to sprout into new plants!

Instead, look for a weed killer that contains the active ingredient glyphosate, like Roundup. Read the directions and follow them. Do not spray what you don't want to kill. Take it from me; I've lost more than one plant with less than vigilant treatment.

If your ivy is acting like ivy, climbing high up trees or tangled hopelessly in your prize shrubs, cut it close to the ground. The portion above the cut will die off. Treat the part still in the ground with weed killer.

Stay vigilant for regrowth in that area and try to catch it early. It is not uncommon to have to re-treat an area (more than once!) in order to get poison ivy under control.

And keep in mind that all parts of the poison ivy plant are poisonous year-round. Once you've pulled or sprayed your unwanted plants, do *not* burn them. The oil will literally go up in smoke. You can get it in your lungs, causing a systemic reaction that can last as long as five weeks.

FINAL THOUGHTS

Don't let your summers be overshadowed by a plant. Always remember: "Leaves of three, let them be"—and do it! Plan ahead when you're going to be outdoors. But also know that there are options to help you obtain comfort and peace of mind (along with a good night's sleep) should you stray into a patch of poison ivy.

Ask the DERMAdoctor

QUESTION:

My son has poison ivy really badly on his face. He is on prednisone from the doctor. I bought Zanfel, and we used it last night. It took away the itching, but he is swollen now. From the beginning his left eye was pretty swollen, and this morning his right eye is swollen, too. Any ideas on how to get the swelling to go down?

The DERMAdoctor:

Swelling typically accompanies severe facial poison ivy. It may take the systemic steroids a few days to radically reduce the edema. I find that adding an oral antihistamine and a topical steroid lotion or cream for significant facial poison ivy helps reduce this tendency toward swelling. Keep the steroid lotion out of the eyes.

PREGNANCY AND YOUR SKIN

Keeping the Glow

Pregnancy is a time of great joy. It's also a time of transition for your body—and your skin. Certain skin conditions may inexplicably flare up; others may just as surprisingly go away. Knowing what your options are for those troublesome moments can help you keep the "glow of pregnancy."

ACNE: A PROGESTERONE PROBLEM

The hormone progesterone puts you in a "pro" gestational state, preparing and maintaining the uterine lining for a successful pregnancy. But it also causes fluid retention and tissue swelling. We are all familiar with premenstrual bloating. You can thank progesterone for that monthly puffiness.

You can also thank it for the formation of monthly blemishes during the end stage of the menstrual cycle and the first half of pregnancy. As levels of progesterone rise and the skin swells, the pores are compressed. This "tourniquet effect" causes sebum (the oil on the skin that for some produces a healthy glow and for others a chronic oil slick) to build up beneath the skin's surface. The result: continuous formation of extra blemishes during the first four to six months of pregnancy, when progesterone surges.

And not only is the sebum trapped, but there's also more of it. Progesterone has qualities of both estrogen and androgens (like testosterone). Androgens activate sebaceous glands to make more sebum.

Treating Acne Cysts

I know that whenever I have been pregnant one of the very first signs was the development of some rather ugly acne cysts. If necessary, your dermatologist can deflate terribly painful or large acne cysts with an injection of steroid solution. Or they can be lightly treated with liquid nitrogen. Freezing an acne cyst is a rather old-fashioned treatment and not one I typically use, but sometimes there aren't other options.

Antibiotics

Unfortunately, few acne medications are safe during the first trimester. One exception is the antibiotic erythromycin. Erythromycin is not typically the most effective oral drug for controlling acne, but at least it helps. Unfortunately, it often causes nausea, something most pregnant women don't need more of. And purists might argue that no drug should be used during pregnancy. However, I feel perfectly comfortable prescribing topical erythromycin.

Antibiotics related to tetracycline are not to be used during pregnancy; they can permanently discolor the baby's teeth and possibly contribute to skeletal malformations. For women who are actively trying to conceive, I avoid prescribing oral tetracycline derivatives (tetracycline, minocycline, and doxycycline) or topical retinoids.

Needless to say, Accutane and spironolactone—very powerful drugs used for acne—are also off the list of potential treatments.

Self-Help

To cope with pregnancy-induced acne, I favor skin care products that contain glycolic acid, which is in the AHA (alpha hydroxy acid) family. AHA helps keep the oils down and the pores somewhat clean.

A dab of DERMAdoctor Tease Zone Oil Control Gel, which contains sebum-sequestering microparticles that surround and absorb excessive surface oils, can also help reduce some of that exaggerated pregnancy "glow."

SKIN REJUVENATION AND PREGNANCY

I had my first child when I was thirty-five. That's no longer unusual. Just the way women don't want to worry about fighting wrinkle formation while having acne, they don't want to worry about forming wrinkles while pregnant. Surprisingly, there is a wide variety of safe options that allow you to continue your rejuvenation regimen while pregnant. And there are some ingredients you should definitely stay away from.

Ingredients to Avoid

These include: vitamin A derivatives (retinol and retinyl palmitate and the prescription options); vitamin K (phytonadione); gotu kola, also called *Centella asiatica;* and BHA (salicylic acid). Carefully read the labels of individual products to make sure you are avoiding these ingredients.

Safe Ingredients

These include: L-ascorbic acid (for example, Cellex-C or SkinCeuticals); AHAs, including glycolic acid (M.D. Forté); N6-furfuryladenine (Kinerase); amino acid peptides (DERMAdoctor Wrinkle Revenge Face Cream); and GHK copper peptide (Neova).

Using a gentle soap, a daily moisturizer applied immediately after bathing, and an SPF 30 sunscreen will also help keep your skin in good condition.

Your Daily Routine

If you are pregnant and skin rejuvenation is a priority, start a routine that requires only a once-a-day approach. Trying to begin a complicated new schedule of skin care products now will simply make it less likely that you will be able to follow through after the baby is born, when there's just not enough time—for anything!

If you're already using a rejuvenation routine, cutting back on your favorite treatment to once daily will yield some results, yet provide the freedom to take care of that little bundle of joy.

There will be a chance later—once you find more time for yourself again—to add in other steps.

WHY AM I COVERED WITH UGLY GROWTHS?!

Hormonal epidermal growth factors (EGFs) are on the rise, helping form the baby's integumentary system (skin). However, they're also responsible for unwanted skin growths on the "pregnancy host"— namely, you. Other hormones that help form the baby's blood vessels (VEGFs) can also cause skin lesions on the mother. Skin tags, seborrheic keratoses, moles, cherry angiomas, and pyogenic granulomas are all skin growths that can (and often do) arise during pregnancy.

Removal: Now or Later?

Typically I wait until after the baby is born before I worry about removing these unsightly spots for patients. Periodically, though, a patient presents with a symptomatic or bleeding growth, and I will happily remove it for her.

If you've been pregnant before, were you told that all those ugly spots would magically disappear after the pregnancy? I haven't found that to be true. Once they've appeared, they're usually there to stay until you do something about them.

Viral Warts

A woman's immune system naturally regulates itself downward during pregnancy. After all, we don't want our bodies rejecting the baby. However, infections can take hold more easily, and that includes viral warts.

I have found that no matter how hard I try, I usually can't get warts to resolve on a pregnant patient until she's done breast-feeding and her immune system has returned to normal. I periodically try to control larger, symptomatic lesions with liquid nitrogen. But I always tell my patient that the wart will remain to some degree until breast-feeding is completed.

PUPPP AND HG

Two skin eruptions are unique to pregnancy. One is PUPPP, which stands for pruritic urticarial papules and plaques of pregnancy. The other is herpes gestationis (HG). These eruptions typically arise for the first time during the third trimester. They can cause intolerable itching, and their appearance is truly displeasing.

PUPPP

Of the two conditions, PUPPP is the more benign, albeit annoying. Statistically, you have a 1-in-240 chance of developing PUPPP. I usually see about ten women a year with it.

Beginning in the third trimester, a hodgepodge of tremendously itchy, red bumps forms on the stomach, along stretch mark lines, and around the belly button. At its worst, the rash covers the torso and the extremities.

PUPPP begins to fade almost immediately after delivery. A few unlucky patients may continue to itch for a month or more postpartum. PUPPP characteristically returns with each subsequent pregnancy, appearing in earlier trimesters.

Medication can't clear PUPPP, but you can definitely control the itching. Benadryl is appropriate, and a syrup form allows you to take it in less-sedating doses. Benadryl Allergy Dye-Free Liquid is an ideal choice.

The prescription antihistamine Atarax (hydroxyzine) is permitted during the third trimester of pregnancy. I frequently prescribe a topical steroid cream for short-term use, which helps diminish itching and inflammation. And a variety of over-the-counter remedies temporarily relieve itching, like PrameGel, Prax Lotion, Aveeno Oatmeal Anti-Itch Concentrated Lotion, and Caladryl Clear Lotion.

As with all conditions that arise during pregnancy, it is very important to check with your obstetrician. I also recommend consulting with a dermatologist, who will be well versed in the various pregnancy rashes.

HG

Herpes gestationis got its name because it resembles herpes, but it's neither viral nor contagious. It's an autoimmune disorder: antibodies formed during the second or third trimester of pregnancy attack the skin, causing blisters clustered on a red base.

Herpes gestationis is one of the more common of the skin disorders associated with pregnancy, but it's still rare, arising in just one in every sixty thousand pregnancies. In over ten years I have seen only one patient with HG.

The doctor should perform a skin biopsy, along with special staining (DIF) upon the biopsied specimen, to help differentiate it from PUPPP (which usually does not blister) and other disorders not related to pregnancy.

The goal of treatment is to prevent further blisters and secondary bacterial infection and to control itching. Usually that involves oral and topical steroids and good wound care, with Domeboro Astringent Solution and Polysporin ointment.

Herpes gestationis resolves within a few months following delivery. Recurrences are typical with future pregnancies; there have also been infrequent reports of HG flare-ups during menstruation and oral contraceptive use.

Babies born to mothers with active HG may be premature or small for their gestational age.

YOU'RE SO VEIN

Varicose veins and spider veins. Need I say more?

All that leg swelling during pregnancy puts pressure on the circulatory system, leading to varicose veins.

An increase in "growth factors" that influence circulation can create spider veins on the legs. (It's practically unheard of for a woman not to form at least a few wispy spider veins during pregnancy.)

Compression can prevent both types of unsightly veins, so wear some form of support hose. Think they're too ugly? Fortunately, Jobst makes a variety of high-fashion knee-highs, athletic socks, and fashion hosiery that help provide high style and reduce your venous worries. Additionally, try to avoid tight shoes and high heels, which can cause fluid to pool in your feet and lower legs.

Don't underestimate the power of sclerotherapy—an injection that causes the veins to disappear after a few months—to get rid of these smaller vessels. Once you've had the baby, stopped breast-feeding, and most of the weight is off (six to twelve months postpartum), consider treating yourself to a few sessions.

MELASMA: WHO IS THAT MASKED WOMAN?

Melasma literally means "mask of pregnancy." It is a darkening of the facial skin, commonly affecting the apples of the cheeks, the mid-forehead, the jawline, and areas around the mouth. Overachieving melanocytes are to blame. These pigment-producing cells become stimulated by the estrogen surge during pregnancy and trigger the production of melanin, resulting in unwanted patchy discoloration. For complete information, please see the chapter "Melasma: (Mask of Pregnancy)" on page 158.

STRETCHING: THE TRUTH

Stretch marks are often mistakenly blamed on the rapid stretching of the skin associated with life events like pregnancy and growth spurts, but this isn't true. They're caused by an increased level of glucocorticoids in the bloodstream. This hormone, secreted by the adrenal glands, becomes elevated during pregnancy. For complete information, please see the chapter "Stretch Marks" on page 272.

SKIN CARE PRODUCTS AND PREGNANCY

If you think that all pregnant women actively avoid the use of all medications, think again. According to a report by CNN, of the six million women who get pregnant every year in the United States, 60 percent use at least one prescription drug at some point during their pregnancy. And almost all of them use at least one over-the-counter medication. With these statistics in mind, how can one make an intelligent, informed decision about using such products while pregnant or breast-feeding?

I have compiled information about many different ingredients in over-the-counter and prescription skin care products, based on data from Medline Plus (the database of the National Institutes of Health and the U.S. National Libraries of Medicine) and from the *Physician's Desk Reference (PDR)*.

However, this information is *not* prescriptive advice. You should discuss the use of any product—whether prescription or over the counter—with your obstetrician.

Alcohol and Acetone, Topical. Nail polish remover, antibacterial wipes, rubbing alcohol, antiseptic hand gels.

> *Pregnancy:* No reports of birth defects or other concerns in human use.

> *Breast-feeding:* No reports of problems in nursing infants.

Anesthetics, Topical and Local. Products to soothe itching, sunburn, bug bites, and the like. This category includes ingredients like benzocaine, menthol, butamben, dibucaine, lidocaine, pramoxine, and tetracaine. Some examples of brands containing these ingredients are PrameGel, Prax Lotion, and L.M.X. 4 Topical Anesthetic Cream.

> *Pregnancy:* Studies haven't been performed in pregnant humans, but there have been no reports of problems in pregnant patients. In animal studies, lidocaine has not caused birth defects or other problems. Animal studies have not been performed on the other topical anesthetics.

> *Breast-feeding:* Topical anesthetics have not been reported to cause problems in nursing infants.

Antibiotic Ointments. This category includes triple-antibiotic ointment as well as Polysporin ointment, Neosporin, and Bacitracin.

Pregnancy: No studies have been performed on pregnant women, but no known birth defects or other problems have been seen in humans.

Breast-feeding: It is not known if these topicals are present in breast milk, but no reports exist of problems with nursing infants.

Antihistamines. Mainly oral itch relief, although topical Benadryl also falls into this category.

Pregnancy: Atarax (hydroxyzine) is not recommended for use in the first trimester of pregnancy. It has been shown to cause birth defects in animal studies if given in doses much higher than normal human use.

For desloratadine (Clarinex) and fexofenadine (Allegra): no studies have been performed on pregnant women. But animal studies show that birth defects or other concerns exist when doses were given that are much larger than typical human patient dosing.

For azatadine, brompheniramine, cetirizine (Zyrtec), chlorpheniramine, clemastine, cyproheptadine, dexchlorpheniramine, dimenhydrinate, diphenhydramine (Benadryl), doxylamine, loratadine (Claritin), and tripelennamine: no studies have been performed on pregnant women, but no known causes of birth defects or other concerns have been demonstrated in animal studies. In this category, guidelines vary by drug manufacturer.

Breast-feeding: Antihistamines can be found in breast milk in small concentrations. Use is not typically recommended, since sedation, irritability, or hyperactivity in babies can result. In some patients, antihistamine use can also result in a reduction of breast-milk flow.

Benzoyl Peroxide. Primarily used for acne relief, benzoyl peroxide comes in a variety of strengths and combinations with other active ingredients.

Pregnancy: No studies on humans or animals have been performed. Benzoyl peroxide can be absorbed through the skin.

Breast-feeding: Benzoyl peroxide may be absorbed through the mother's skin. The presence of benzoyl peroxide in breast milk is unknown. A search of Medline shows no reports of problems in nursing babies.

Capsaicin. Used in pain management, such as in the relief of postherpetic neuralgia. Can be found in Zostrix HP Stick.

Pregnancy: No reports of birth defects or other concerns in human use.

Breast-feeding: Unknown if capsaicin can be passed through breast milk. No reports of problems with nursing infants. It is important to remember that topical use of this medication in an area coming into contact with the nursing infant should be avoided, to spare the baby severe skin irritation.

Coal Tar. Usually an ingredient used in dandruff and psoriasis shampoos, as well as topical psoriasis-treatment products.

Pregnancy: No human or animal studies reported. But due to its effect of reducing or stopping cellular turnover, it is probably wise to skip this during pregnancy.

Breast-feeding: Unknown if this topical can make its way into breast milk. No reports of problems in nursing infants.

Hydrocortisone. Used to treat skin irritation and inflammation. Over-the-counter versions include 0.5% and 1% of the active ingredient. Found in products like Cortaid Steroid Cream.

Pregnancy: Used under proper controlled situations, hydrocortisone has not been shown to cause problems. No studies on pregnant women have been performed. Birth defects have occurred in animal studies using large amounts or prolonged use of topical corticosteroids.

Breast-feeding: There are no reports of problems in nursing infants.

Nystatin. A treatment for candida yeast of the skin.

Pregnancy: No reports of birth defects or other problems in pregnant humans.

Breast-feeding: It is not known whether nystatin passes into breast milk. There are no reports of problems with nursing infants.

Miconazole. Treats yeast and some fungal infections of the skin.

Pregnancy: Topical miconazole preparations have not been shown to cause birth defects or other problems in humans.

Breast-feeding: There are no reports of problems with topical miconazole causing problems for nursing infants.

Minoxidil. Used topically in the treatment and prevention of hair loss. Commonly known by the brand name Rogaine.

Pregnancy: No studies in pregnant women. But some studies in animals have shown that oral minoxidil can cause problems during pregnancy. (These concerns do not include birth defects.) Use not recommended if pregnant or nursing.

Breast-feeding: Not recommended.

Permethrin. One percent is found in home lice treatments, including Nix Lice Treatment Creme Rinse. Five percent is found in prescription strength Elimite, for scabies treatment.

Pregnancy: No studies have been done on pregnant women. Animal studies have not shown birth defects or other concerns.

Breast-feeding: It is unknown whether permethrin can be found in breast milk. However, animal studies have shown that permethrin can cause tumors. Skip it unless you discuss it with your doctor and have good reason for use.

Pyrithione Zinc. A favorite in dandruff shampoos and treatment soaps for seborrheic dermatitis, like DHS Zinc Shampoo. Also used in products for tinea versicolor, like the ZNP Bar.

Pregnancy: There are no reports of birth defects or other problems in pregnant women.

Breast-feeding: Unknown if present in breast milk. Pyrithione zinc has not been reported to cause problems in nursing infants.

Resorcinol. While commonly thought of as a component in certain chemical peels, this agent is often combined with sulfur for treating blemishes, as in Rezamid Acne Treatment Lotion.

Pregnancy: Resorcinol may be absorbed through the mother's skin. However, combination topical resorcinol and sulfur has not been shown to cause birth defects or other problems in humans.

Breast-feeding: The combination of topical resorcinol and sulfur has not been reported to cause problems in nursing babies.

Salicylic Acid. Trendily termed a BHA (beta hydroxy acid), salicylic acid is found in products for skin rejuvenation, acne, dandruff, and corn and wart relief.

Pregnancy: Salicylic acid can be absorbed through the skin. There have been no studies on pregnant women. Animal studies show birth defects when given systemically in doses six times those recommended in topical use for human patients. Applied on large areas or in high concentrations, salicylic acid may be of concern. I consider it an ingredient to avoid during pregnancy. Use only under the recommendation and supervision of a physician.

Breast-feeding: The product is absorbed through mother's skin. While there are no reports of problems for nursing infants, it's best to avoid salicylic acid during this time.

Selenium Sulfide. Often included in dandruff shampoos. Also found in Selsun Blue shampoo, for tinea versicolor.

Pregnancy: When used on the scalp, no reports of birth defects or other concerns in human use. But selenium sulfide can be absorbed through the skin when applied in a widespread manner. It is not recommended for this use while pregnant.

Breast-feeding: No reports of problems in nursing infants.

Sulfur. Used in acne treatments and in dandruff shampoos.

Pregnancy: Sulfur has not been shown to cause birth defects or other concerns in humans.

Breast-feeding: There are no reports of problems for nursing infants.

Terbinafine. An antifungal ingredient found in the brand Lamisil AT.

> *Pregnancy:* No studies have been done on pregnant women. There are no reports of birth defects or other concerns in animal studies.

> *Breast-feeding:* Oral terbinafine passes into breast milk; it is unknown if topically applied terbinafine can pass into breast milk. Do not apply to the breast if nursing.

Sunscreen. Sixty-four active ingredients or combination of ingredients are used in sunscreen products.

> *Pregnancy:* Studies are lacking on pregnant women and animals. But with the increased risk of developing melanoma during pregnancy, as well as the cosmetic concerns of melasma, the use of sunscreen to help prevent sun damage and resulting future skin cancer appears to far outweigh any unknown risks at this time.

> *Breast-feeding:* There are no reports of problems with sunscreen use affecting breast milk or nursing infants.

Other Important Safety Concerns
Depilatories. The use of hair-removal products during pregnancy can be of concern. Both of the active ingredients found in depilatories have not been proven to be safe during pregnancy. It is probably best to avoid their use while nursing, as well.

Hair Dye. Permanent hair dyes may contain naphtylamine, phenylene-diamines, or toluene diamines. Temporary dyes may contain silver, mercury, lead, arsenic, bismuth, and pyrogallol. Other troublesome ingredients may also be present. Because of the side effects these ingredients can cause, the rule of thumb is to avoid hair color during pregnancy. Hair stains that are not applied to the scalp itself may in some cases be fine. Vegetable-based temporary stains, such as 100 percent henna, are considered safe. But don't just take someone's word for it; check the ingredients yourself.

Vitamin A. The use of topical medications and skin care products containing vitamin A during pregnancy and nursing is *not* recommended.

This includes prescription treatments such as Avita, Avage, Differin, Retin-A, Renova, and Tazorac, as well as any over-the-counter retinol or retinyl palmitate product. Generic names for the prescription medications include adapalene, tretinoin, and tazarotene. Oral use of large amounts of vitamin A and its derivatives, such as Accutane, is known to cause birth defects.

FINAL THOUGHTS

Pregnancy is a great time to try to pamper yourself, particularly if this is your first baby. Consider getting yourself started on a good skin care regimen that you can perform quickly. Once the baby comes along, lack of sleep can take a toll on the skin. And if you don't look your best, you won't feel your best, either. You should anticipate that the first six months or so will be a blur. Plan to keep things simple!

Pregnancy is one of those passages of life. You deserve to enjoy this time without blemishes, without rashes, and with the great expectation of welcoming a new addition to your family. So baby your skin and look great. After all, pregnant women are supposed to have that glow!

Ask the DERMAdoctor

QUESTION:

I just had a baby a few months ago and have lost all the weight. Is there any way to help my skin firm back up a little faster?

The DERMAdoctor:

Understand that the skin has stretched quite a bit and, depending on the individual, may never return to its prepregnancy status.

For general skin firming, L-ascorbic acid (a form of vitamin C) and GHK copper peptides are great. They both help to boost collagen production, which is responsible for the structure and firmness of the skin. I recommend trying Cellex-C Body Smoothing Lotion or Neova Body Therapy Lotion.

Exercise is important, and not just the aerobic kind. Lax skin responds best to toning exercises and weight training.

PSORIASIS

Many Wonderful Therapies

What would happen if there was a "short circuit" in the way your skin cells are manufactured?

Unfortunately, we know what happens. It's called psoriasis.

In this skin disorder—the second most common, affecting 4.5 million Americans—there is an increased rate of skin-cell turnover. When this occurs (with sheer unpredictability), the skin becomes thickened, flakes, cracks, bleeds, and itches—and, as you might imagine, can also hurt. Although no area of the body is immune, the sites most commonly affected include the elbows, knees, sacrum, scalp, nails, palms, and soles.

Several factors can make psoriasis flare up. They include: lack of light exposure (the disease is often worse in the fall and winter); infections like strep, staph, and mycoplasma; and hormonal extremes (like pregnancy).

Psoriasis strikes women and men equally. Every age group is a potential target. And it can affect every aspect of daily life. How do you explain it to your friends, children, coworkers? What do you wear at the beach? Should you go on that date? And—since some sufferers can spend more than two hours a day applying creams to the affected areas, called plaques—how do you manage your time?

YOUR THERAPEUTIC OPTIONS

From soaking in the Dead Sea to using the drug Tazorac, the search for the most effective psoriasis therapy has gone on for centuries. However, it has been only in the last fifty years that medical science has achieved any real success in treating the disorder. And it's only in the last decade or so that many new treatments—more effective, safer, and easier to administer than previous therapies—have become available.

Topical Steroids: A Mainstay

Topical steroids are one of the mainstays of psoriasis therapy. They diminish inflammation, stop the itching, and help cut down on cellular proliferation. They are available as creams, ointments, lotions, and liquids, so you can tailor the delivery method to the area being treated. Strengths range from over-the-counter 1% hydrocortisone to prescription Temovate.

Steroids have drawbacks, however. Overuse can lead to atrophy (thinning of the skin), with associated stretch marks, spider veins, and even acne. Also, there is the risk of developing pustular psoriasis, a dermatological emergency. Or the area being treated can become "addicted" to the steroid: when the steroid is stopped, the condition "rebounds," becoming much worse . . . until it's treated with more steroids.

That is why other topical medications, including Tazorac and Dovonex (discussed next), are excellent options; not only do they help improve clearing, but they also allow you to use far less steroid.

Systemic steroids, delivered orally or by IV, are an effective treatment for psoriasis patients with a severe condition called exfoliative erythroderma, in which 100 percent of their body has turned bright red and the skin is peeling terribly. Otherwise, they're best avoided by patients with psoriasis.

Tazorac (Topical Vitamin A): A Uniquely Effective Treatment

I have been amazed by the effectiveness of Tazorac. In fact, I have not had a single patient treated with Tazorac fail to improve. I consider it one of the best therapies for moderate plaque psoriasis.

However, I ask my patients to alter their treatment from the normal, daily recommended use. I ask them to use it the way that experience has taught me is the best way for skin to tolerate a topical vitamin A cream: every *other* night, very sparingly, on very dry skin.

Plus, I add a second element to the treatment regimen. Every morning, I have the patient apply the steroid Temovate (clobetasol) to her psoriasis (except for thinner areas of skin: the face, groin, flexures like the elbow crease, and the neck). Every other night, they use Tazorac. I start with the stronger 0.1% Tazorac Gel, unless the affected areas are in the same thin regions I don't treat with Temovate (in which case I choose the lower-potency 0.05% in a cream base). Within four to six weeks, clearing is seen. For stubborn areas, I increase the Tazorac to every night, if the patient's skin can tolerate it. Children have more delicate skin, and I prescribe Tazorac 0.05% cream only on a case-by-case basis.

The biggest problem with Tazorac has been irritation or initial enlargement of the involved sites; this routine is great at preventing that problem.

Again, I have to say that Tazorac has been one of the most impressive therapies for psoriasis that I have ever prescribed. Of course, there may be situations where it is not appropriate: for pregnant women, for a person with generalized psoriasis, napkin dermatitis (atypical psoriasis), or pustular psoriasis. Ask your dermatologist if it is right for you.

Dovonex: Great for the Scalp

In the early 1990s—when there had been no new psoriasis treatment for a decade—the introduction of Dovonex represented a turning point in the fight against psoriasis and a new hope for dermatologists. Dovonex is a vitamin D derivative that helps normalize cellular turnover. I have found Dovonex to be helpful for scalp and body psoriasis, but it often requires the coadministration of other medications, like topical steroids. In fact, including betamethasone diproprionate with Dovonex use has been documented in studies to be more effective than either active ingredient alone.

Dovonex is available in a liquid formulation (Dovonex Scalp Solution), making it a potent treatment for psoriasis of the scalp. I base my treatment recommendations on what I would like to be treated with. I like liquids for the scalp, while the thought of rubbing an ointment into my hair doesn't thrill me. It's great to have a clear liquid available as a potent option for psoriasis of the scalp.

Biologics: A Major Breakthrough

Approximately 1.4 million Americans with psoriasis—about one in every three patients—have a severe enough case to warrant the use of biologics, a new class of drugs. How do they work?

Research shows that the abnormal immune responses believed to cause psoriasis are triggered by the activation of T cells, a type of white blood cell. Once T cells are activated, they release cytokines, chemicals that send messages throughout the body. In psoriasis, the cytokines tell epidermal cells to reproduce at an abnormally fast rate. Biologics block either T cell activation or the release of cytokines.

In early 2003, the FDA approved one of these drugs—Amevive (alefacept)—for the treatment of moderate to severe psoriasis. It works by destroying activated T cells. A study by researchers at the University of Utah and other institutions found that half of the patients who received weekly doses of Amevive had a 75 percent improvement in their symptoms. Amevive is given intravenously.

In October 2003, the FDA approved Raptiva (efalizumab). Raptiva neutralizes the T cells' ability to function and communicate with other cells. In studies of more than two thousand patients, Raptiva lessened the scope and severity of psoriasis symptoms by an average of 75 percent. It is self-administered as a once-a-week injection.

Enbrel (etanercept), another biologic, was approved in 2003 for the treatment of psoriatic arthritis, a chronic inflammation of the joints that afflicts about 10 percent of those with psoriasis. Enbrel blocks the cytokine TNF (tumor necrosis factor) from telling the epidermal skin to overreproduce. It is also a self-administered injection.

And preliminary studies have shown that yet another biologic—Onercept (TNF binding protein–1)—improves both psoriasis and psoriatic arthritis.

Additionally, scientists are conducting studies on topical creams, sprays, and even bath beads that block immune cells from causing psoriasis plaques.

Biologics don't come cheap. A year's worth of treatment can run more than $10,000. Medical insurance should cover most of the cost of these therapies.

Keratolytics: Soften and Exfoliate

These agents soften and exfoliate thickened, often cracking psoriatic scales, making them thinner and smoother. This can relieve discomfort and improve overall skin aesthetics.

There are many options to try. Bland creams and ointments create a barrier, moisturizing the skin and protecting against dehydration. Think Vanicream, Moisturel, Eucerin, and Aquaphor. Those with "active" ingredients help soften and exfoliate scales, in addition to hydrating the skin. AHAs, BHAs, and urea are good examples of "active" ingredients. This category includes M.D. Forté Hand & Body Cream (20% glycolic acid compound), DERMAdoctor KP Duty (glycolic and urea blend), Amlactin (lactic acid), Carmol 10 and 20 (contain urea; there are also prescription-strength Carmol 30 and 40), and Lac-Hydrin 12% (prescription lactic acid formulation).

Apply one of these hydrating agents immediately after washing your hands and after bathing. If you start a hydrating agent when psoriasis first appears, along with your dermatologist-prescribed medication, you can really reduce the severity of your symptoms.

Nizoral: Beat the Yeast

What a surprise to learn, early on in my training, that the normal yeast and bacteria that live on our skin can actually aggravate psoriasis (and seborrhea), particularly in hair-bearing areas like the face and scalp. Now I *always* include antiyeast therapy for psoriasis patients with eruptions in these regions. It makes a big difference.

Nizoral cream is an impressive antiyeast treatment for the face. Bear in mind, however, that it can occasionally irritate already sore, sensitive skin.

Nizoral cream quickly morphed into a shampoo that is very helpful for treating psoriasis of the scalp. Try either over-the-counter Nizoral A-D Shampoo, which contains 1% ketoconazole, the active ingredient, or prescription-strength Nizoral 2%. Use the shampoo twice a week.

The use of Nizoral alone is usually not going to control psoriasis, but it is amazing how helpful it is when used in combination with other agents in your regimen.

Sometimes, however, you think you should use Nizoral when you shouldn't. There is an unusual presentation of psoriasis called napkin dermatitis (a.k.a. inverse or atypical psoriasis). It arises in moist regions: under the breasts, between the legs, or under heavy abdominal folds. Most nondermatologists (and some dermatologists as well) mistake it for a fungal infection and don't understand why it doesn't go away when treated with an antifungal. It is actually psoriasis. In these areas, a combination of a mild topical steroid *and* Nizoral cream is often the best treatment.

For really moist areas, the use of prescription Mycostatin powder or over-the-counter Zeasorb-AF powder can help dry out the skin and kill fungi and yeast. Do *not* use cornstarch-based powders; they are food for yeast and bacteria.

Other Options for the Scalp

Cutting through thick crust requires tough treatment. You can apply P&S Liquid at bedtime, put on a shower cap, and wash it out the following morning. Phenol helps cut through the crusts and reduces discomfort. A three-night cycle is often performed. You may also apply DermaSmoothe F/S Oil Solution at bedtime. The steroid base reduces itching and inflammation. Rotating these two scalp treatments is a highly effective regimen for freeing the scalp from its shell.

To halt psoriasis of the scalp, you can rotate a group of medicated shampoos. These include: steroid-based, prescription Capex (formerly called FS Shampoo); glycolic and salicylic acid, flake-removing shampoos, including AquaGlycolic and Meted; DHS Zinc Shampoo, for zinc pyrithione; and, Pentrax, one of the best cell-stopping tar shampoos.

At the height of the flare-up, when shampoos can't provide adequate control, topical solutions can come to the rescue. Just five to eight drops (or sprays), randomly scattered on the scalp twice a day, of either prescription cortisone Dovonex or over-the-counter zinc pyrithione (as in DermaZinc) quickly augment medicated-shampoo therapy. Steroid solutions vary widely in their strength; I select one based on the severity of the condition. When the scalp is clear, the drops are shelved until the next out-of-control bout of psoriasis.

XTRAC Excimer Laser: For Resistant Plaques

XTRAC is the first FDA-approved laser for the treatment of psoriasis. It emits a high-intensity beam of ultraviolet (UVB) light that is less than one inch in diameter, so it can be directed at select areas of the skin, sparing uninvolved areas. It's a real blessing for people with small patches of psoriasis that don't respond to other treatments. It usually takes four to ten sessions to see results. Each session lasts just a few minutes.

Researchers from Massachusetts General Hospital gave eighty psoriasis patients ten treatments or more with XTRAC. Seventy-two percent achieved at least a 75 percent improvement, which lasted for eight months or more after the therapy ended.

A laser is a worthwhile treatment to consider if you have one, two, or three big plaques. But if you have psoriasis on multiple areas of your body, biologics are probably a better choice.

The Dead Sea: Mud, Fun, Salt, and Sun

Every year, thousands of patients descend on the psoriasis spas of Israel's Dead Sea, hoping for an improvement in their skin condition. Studies refute therapeutic claims for any long-term effect, but that hasn't slowed the trade.

Salt water's ability to soften the scales, the exfoliating and palliative nature of Dead Sea mud (which contains up to ten times more minerals and salts than other types), and the UVA and UVB sun exposure (sunlight helps prevent excessive reproduction of skin cells), combined with the serenity of a vacation (stress is a major flare factor) probably do help improve psoriasis for many people on a *temporary* basis.

Those looking for some of the benefits of Dead Sea treatment without a trip to the Middle East can use AHAVA skin care products, which include the mud and salts found in the Dead Sea. These very nice products include AHAVA Dead Sea Mineral Mud and AHAVA Dead Sea Bath Salts.

Tar: Reformulated and Effective

In the 1800s, someone realized that tar had a healing effect on the skin. Since then, it has been used for psoriasis, seborrhea, eczema, and atopic dermatitis.

Tar works by interfering with mitosis, the division and reproduction of skin cells. It's been dirty work, however—tar smells, stains, and is aesthetically unappealing. But in the 1990s, drug companies reformulated tar, eliminating some displeasing qualities while retaining its effectiveness.

A soak in Balnetar Therapeutic Tar Bath is a popular choice for treating widespread psoriasis. It helps slow down or stop scale formation and softens thickened crusts.

For the scalp, there are many tar shampoos. (Look for a *T* in the name.) Just remember that if you have blond or gray hair, tar shampoo can cause some discoloration.

LIGHT THERAPY (PUVA): A POWERFUL LAST RESORT

This therapy combines the medication psoralen (P) with exposure to UVA light. UVA wavelengths reduce the rate of cellular turnover in the skin. Psoralen is taken up by skin cells and makes them highly sensitive to UVA light, improving psoriasis. This therapy is reserved for patients with widespread disease who have not responded to other treatments. I see approximately ten patients a year in this category.

PUVA definitely has a downside. You have to go two to three times a week for weeks or months until clear. For twenty-four hours after each treatment, you have to wear goggles when awake to protect the eyes, which are also sensitized by the drug. Since the treatment markedly increases sunburn potential, you also need to protect your skin during that time. And light therapy can damage cellular DNA, increasing one's future risk of skin cancer.

Still, patients with large, generalized plaques find it worth the annoyance and the side effects.

Tar and Light: A Healing Tradition

Known as Goeckerman, this was a highly popular psoriasis therapy in the 1930s. Patients bathed in a 5 percent coal-tar solution and slept in it overnight. It was removed in the morning, and they were treated with light therapy. The tar cut down on cellular turnover and helped attract light to the skin (this was the era before psoralen). In the early 1980s, medical insurance began limiting hospitalizations for Goeckerman, which resulted in the establishment of a number of outpatient centers. The treatment is still available today, but it's not as likely to be recommended.

Goeckerman deserves its place in the Dermatology Hall of Fame as one of the first psoriasis therapies to give positive results.

Antibiotics: For Guttate Psoriasis

Anyone with psoriasis who has experienced strep throat may have found herself covered with literally thousands of small psoriatic plaques. Called guttate psoriasis, this condition looks like many water droplets were flicked at the skin. It is typically seen in association with bacterial infections, so oral antibiotics are often given.

SYSTEMIC THERAPIES

Systemic therapy agents are for treating generalized, severe, or pustular psoriasis. Although highly effective, they have a limited patient base because of their possible side effects. These medications should be used only under close supervision by a dermatologist.

Methotrexate: Low Dose, High Impact

When I was just out of residency, I received my first "thank you" gift basket after treating a patient suffering from overwhelming psoriasis with methotrexate. It had been difficult to convince her to try the drug, but within a month she was clear for the first time in years. This made a big impression on me as to how aggressive therapy can be crucial to a psoriasis patient's well-being.

Methotrexate, which disrupts cell reproduction, is given as three oral doses, twelve hours apart, once a week until the psoriasis clears. The number of pills used for each therapy is how we describe its use. For instance, 1:1:1 refers to a patient taking one pill every twelve hours for three doses. 2:1:1 refers to two pills taken as the first dose, then one pill for each of the remaining two doses. This system of dosing allows the dermatologist to closely monitor and adjust the amount required for each individual patient.

Methotrexate is a "big gun" medication. (Its primary use is as chemotherapy for cancer.) As such, it is associated with several side effects. However, the once-weekly, low-dose regimen rarely causes hair loss, nausea, vomiting, or other side effects often associated with chemo therapy.

When the drug is used on a long-term basis, it requires frequent monitoring of blood counts and liver enzymes. While methotrexate is still widely prescribed, other more recent therapies like the biologics are cutting into its use.

Cytoxan: For Psoriatic Vasculitis

Cytoxan is traditionally used in cancer therapy. I typically reserve its use in psoriasis therapy for rare cases when white blood cells that destroy joints (as in psoriatic arthritis) become focused on blood vessels, causing significant ulceration of the skin. (Medically, this is known as psoriatic vasculitis.) This major complication requires immediate and aggressive therapy, often in a hospital setting.

Oral Vitamin A: Help with Keratinization

Accutane (isotretinoin), the first prescription oral vitamin A derivative for the treatment of severe cystic acne, was found to help normalize severe psoriasis.

Newer variations included Tegison (etretinate), which was taken off the market with the advent of Soriatane (acitretin), which, unlike

Tegison, does not pose a long-term risk of birth defects. Accutane is not nearly as effective as Soriatane for psoriasis, which is why it is not a typical substitute when an oral retinoid is required. Neither is used unless there is overwhelming exfoliative erythroderma or pustular forms of psoriasis.

For now, however, Soriatane is the primary vitamin A–related psoriasis therapy prescribed. Blood work is done every few weeks to monitor blood counts, liver enzymes, triglycerides, and general chemistry. Two methods of contraception are required during and after treatment, until the drug clears from the body and the risk of birth defect (three years) is over. Blood donation is not allowed until after the drug is no longer present in the system, due to the risk to the blood recipient. Alcohol is specifically not allowed while taking Soriatane, as it can cause the drug to be broken down into etretinate (a metabolite that can last in the body indefinitely).

Neoral (Cyclosporine): From Transplant to Psoriasis

Initially used for preventing the rejection of transplanted organs, cyclosporine has been found to be very helpful in many overwhelming skin conditions, including generalized exfoliative psoriasis. Its main drawbacks include the need for frequent monitoring, potential kidney damage (less likely with the lower dosing used for skin conditions), and a very low risk of lymphoma. Most psoriasis patients will never need to consider this drug as a therapeutic option.

FINAL THOUGHTS

Psoriasis has many wonderful therapies, several of them new in the past five years. While there is still no cure, almost everyone has the potential to clear stubborn plaques. If you suffer from psoriasis and have not yet seen a dermatologist, I urge you to do so. These days, there is no reason to allow it to go unchecked.

Ask the DERMAdoctor

QUESTION:

My nine-year-old daughter has been diagnosed by a dermatologist as having psoriasis of the skin and nails. The doctor gave us a sample of steroid cream to use and it seemed to help, but the psoriasis is now spreading to her toenails. It obviously doesn't hurt my daughter, but it sure is ugly. Do you have any suggestions I might use to make her nails look better?

The DERMAdoctor:

Therapy for nail psoriasis is still quite limited, particularly for a child. The reason is that topicals just do not penetrate down under the nail fold and are therefore unable to reach the nail bed, where the psoriasis is actually doing its damage (and disfiguring the nail plate). And those big-gun systemic therapies (methotrexate, Neoral, biologics) that could correct the problem are not appropriate for treating minor cases, especially in young children. Unfortunately, while I understand that this isn't a minor concern to a patient, "mere" nail psoriasis does fall under this restriction.

Do you recall those spray-jet vaccinations that were popular in schools in the 1960s, which had the advantage of rapidly treating numerous children without the nurses' having to fuss with needles? This procedure has recently been used to inject steroid solution (Kenalog) into the nail fold. The drawbacks are that it is not a cure (although with multiple treatments it does help and can be used on a maintenance basis), and it *really* hurts. If your daughter is highly motivated and able to tolerate pain fairly well, it may be worth considering.

Another option would be to try to add Dovonex Scalp Lotion to the steroid. (I presume you are using the liquid.) Theoretically, solutions have a better chance than creams or ointments of reaching the nail bed, where they can be effective. Realistically, however, the odds of their effectiveness remain slim. Still, it is better to hope and try than never to have tried at all.

Topical local PUVA would be another option worth considering. Many dermatologists do not like performing PUVA on children, as cumulative light-therapy damage early in life can increase the risk of developing skin cancer later on. There is a new form of PUVA called narrowband that has fewer risks associated with it. You may want to ask your dermatologist about it.

ROSACEA

Addressing All Your Concerns

Rosacea (a.k.a. adult acne) is a skin condition about which many people—both those who get it and those who treat it—have misconceptions. For example, I personally encounter many "overdiagnosed" patients who have been told they have rosacea, but don't! On the other hand, a Gallup Poll shows that 78 percent of Americans have no knowledge of rosacea—how to recognize it or what to do about it. My goal in this chapter is to help clarify rosacea for you: its diagnosis, its treatment, and what you *really* need to know.

WHO GETS ROSACEA?

Every year, fourteen million Americans—most of them between the ages of twenty-five to fifty-five, and three times as many women as men—have to deal with rosacea. Heredity plays a role. You're more likely to get it if you're fair-skinned and of northern European descent (English, Scottish, Welsh, Irish, German, or Scandinavian). Ditto if you have a family history of rosacea or severe acne. (Or if you yourself have had significant acne.) But those are just statistical probabilities. Anyone can develop it.

HOW DO I KNOW I HAVE ROSACEA?

Rosacea isn't limited to blemishes. It's a constellation of skin symptoms. And while not everyone has every symptom, it's typical to have a few. These include:

- Redness of the face
- Flushing

- Skin sensitivity and/or dryness
- Oiliness
- The presence of small, "broken" blood vessels (telangiectasias, spider veins)
- Enlarged oil glands (sebaceous hyperplasia)
- Acne in all its forms—blackheads, papules, pustules, and cysts
- Occasional surface irregularities of the nose (rhinophyma)
- Eye symptoms, including redness, irritation, or the feeling of "grit," and sometimes clear discharge (ocular rosacea)

PRESCRIPTION ACNE CONTROL

Blemishes are often the easiest symptom to control. And there are many powerful, effective prescription therapies available. As with teenage acne, treatment is aimed at stopping the formation of blemishes.

Topical Metronidazole

Metronidazole is a topical antibiotic (also known as Flagyl) that eradicates the bacteria that trigger acne. The "Metros" (MetroLotion, MetroCream, and MetroGel) dominate this category.

MetroGel was the first prescription topical rosacea medication, and it was highly effective. However, rosacea patients often have exquisitely sensitive skin, and gel formulations frequently exacerbate irritation. Fortunately, a gentler cream and lotion are now available.

Noritate contains the same active ingredient as MetroCream but is free of certain potential irritants and requires only once-daily application.

Oral Antibiotics

Just as with regular acne, tetracycline and its derivatives minocycline and doxycycline are the best family of oral antibiotics for controlling the severe or resistant inflammatory acne of rosacea, particularly when cysts are present.

Topical Sulfur and Sodium Sulfacetamide

This prescription therapy incorporates two active ingredients: sulfa (an antibacterial agent that has no relation to sulfur) and sulfur (which clears clogged pores and removes "keratotic plugs" lodged deeply within oil glands). This therapy is *not* an option for anyone with a sulfa allergy. But remember, while the names sound similar, being allergic to sulfa does not mean you are allergic to sulfur.

Plexion led the way with both a lotion and a cleanser containing these ingredients; several more products have followed.

As a nonprescription alternative, you can find over-the-counter sulfur in products like Rezamid and Sulforcin acne-treatment lotions.

No matter whether prescription or over-the-counter, sulfur can be drying. Use it sparingly and moisturize as necessary.

Something Old Is Something New

Sometimes old-fashioned is best. Three percent precipitated sulfur, blended into a low-potency steroid cream like DesOwen, is an old-fashioned (and time-proven) concoction that I fall back on whenever I encounter a case of rosacea that simply refuses to go away. The lower-strength prescription topical steroid helps alleviate the redness and inflammation and rounds out the benefits of sulfur. I limit this to short-term use because chronic application of steroids to the skin poses the risk of atrophy. This thinning of the skin may include signs like the loss of skin color, the appearance of spider veins, easy bruising, and even stretch marks. A month should be adequate to gain control with this "quick fix."

You can create a homemade version of lower-potency cortisone and sulfur by layering equal parts Rezamid Acne Treatment Lotion on top of over-the-counter-strength Cortaid, which contains 1% hydro-cortisone. As with the prescription treatment, I recommend that you use this "off-label" approach for a month to two weeks. Avoid contact with the eyes.

Accutane

When all else fails and the cystic acne is severe, scarring, and resistant to all other options, Accutane may be necessary. This twenty-week therapy with a prescription vitamin A derivative is the closest thing there is to an acne cure. However, treatment with this drug (which can cause birth defects) must be closely monitored, with blood work and mandatory pregnancy prevention both during and thirty days following therapy.

TARGETING ALL THE CONCERNS AND SYMPTOMS

I can't tell you how many times I've received e-mail from women with rosacea concerned not only about their blemishes but about having to deal with acne *and* wrinkles. Often they were also struggling with a host of other rosacea symptoms not addressed by their prescription therapy—problems like dry or sensitive skin, oil spots (yes, the skin can go both ways in rosacea), and redness.

Clearing the skin of acne is a fundamental therapeutic goal of rosacea treatment. However, most over-the-counter medical approaches to rosacea address only the acne; specifically, they are antibacterial. And, many times, prescription therapy for acne inadvertently aggravates other skin complaints. Ideally, effective treatment would address the *entire* spectrum of concerns, including blemishes. Is there a way out of this dilemma?

I decided to develop 2n1 rosacea cream to be an effective, multifunctional treatment that could stand alone for some patients and be complementary to prescription therapy for others. This product translates scientifically proven skin care technology into an effective, multifunctional treatment that targets all the symptoms and concerns experienced by those with rosacea. Using a sophisticated complex of ingredients, it controls oil production, reduces inflammation, fights blemishes, lessens cellular buildup, minimizes bacteria production on the skin—and also helps diminish signs of aging.

Two distinctive ingredients found in 2n1 rosacea cream are nordihydroguaiaretic acid (NDGA) and oleanolic acid. Together they improve the appearance of blemishes and redness. NDGA is a natural, plant-derived lipooxygenase inhibitor; it reduces inflammation. Medical journals report that NDGA possesses the ability to reduce 5 alpha-reductase activity. That is the enzyme necessary for converting testosterone to its active metabolite, DHT (dihydrotestosterone). DHT is responsible for all those undesirable masculine skin traits like acne, facial hair growth, and female pattern alopecia. The idea is, if you can interfere and lower the DHT, the blemishes should improve. And this would round out taking aim at acne with other methods such as antibiotics.

Oleanolic acid reduces sebum lipid (fatty acid) levels in the skin, creating an environment hostile to normal skin bacteria that contribute to rosacea, and also helps reduce rosacea-related inflammation.

In many cases, 2n1 rosacea cream may supplant the need for additional therapy. However, it was designed to complement all prescription rosacea regimens, working synergistically against rosacea symptoms and delivering the ideal rejuvenation factors for rosacea-riddled skin.

FOR SENSITIVE SKIN

Patients with rosacea often live with the discomfort of very sensitive skin. This can make it difficult to use "typical" acne medications, which may dry and/or irritate.

Washing with M.D. Forté Replenish Hydrating Cleanser, Free & Clear Liquid Cleanser, or Vanicream Cleansing Bar gently removes makeup, oils, and other debris without further irritating the skin.

Cutanix Dramatic Relief moisturizing formulations contain Quadrinone, an ingredient that helps reduce inflammation. Cutanix is available in three different varieties of hydrating bases.

Other moisturizers appropriate for those with rosacea include M.D. Forté Replenish Hydrating Cream, Wibi Dry Skin Lotion, and Nutraderm Therapeutic Lotion (Original Formula).

Whenever applying any product to the skin, remember that it also provides moisture. So your sunscreen, skin care treatment, or medication may make an additional moisturizer unnecessary.

GET RID OF THE RED

Redness is caused by many factors, such as spider veins, flushing (when blood vessels deep within the skin dilate), and skin irritation. Here is a partial list of factors that can temporarily increase facial redness:

- Exposure to sun, wind, or cold weather
- Physical exertion or becoming overheated
- Stress
- Hot foods and beverages
- Spicy foods and beverages
- Alcohol
- Foods: liver, citrus fruits, tomatoes, soy sauce, vinegars, and some cheeses

Spider Veins: Redness That Sometimes *Isn't* Rosacea

I often see patients with wispy facial blood vessels who are convinced that they have rosacea. However, the presence of telangiectasias (a.k.a. spider veins) alone does *not* mean that you have rosacea. Certainly, rosacea patients are more prone to forming spider veins, which are an unnecessary proliferation of superficially placed, minute blood vessels. But not all spider veins are due to rosacea.

A variety of factors can cause telangiectasias, including a history of sun damage, a fair complexion, aging, steroid use (topical on the face or systemic), and a family history of telangiectasias. (However, none of these factors "breaks" the blood vessel. Although telangiectasias are often called "broken," there is nothing broken about them.)

How do you know if your problem is merely limited to spider veins or if you actually have rosacea? You don't, and neither does your doctor. If telangiectasias are the sole complaint, I will treat them. But I don't label the patient with the diagnosis of rosacea *unless* other symptoms develop.

Spider veins respond well to physical destruction. Procedures include electrocautery, pulsed-dye laser eradication, and IPL (intense pulsed light).

Electrocautery is the ideal first treatment: most cases respond, and it is the most cost-effective. It is performed with a tiny needle that literally zaps the length of the blood vessel, killing it. Doctors typically don't use anesthesia during the procedure because it can cause transient skin whiteness, concealing the location of the veins. But, when necessary, the doctor can apply L.M.X. 4 Topical Anesthetic Cream or Betacaine to improve the patient's comfort.

Typically, only one or two treatments are required to eradicate blood vessels, depending on how many spider veins are present. Each treatment lasts fifteen to thirty minutes and costs approximately $200. There may be some swelling and redness for a day or two.

For resistant cases, or when confronted by an inordinate number of spider veins, the pulsed-dye laser and the IPL are options. Laser and IPL usually require a series of treatments (sometimes up to twelve) and can cost $1,500 or more.

Facial redness is also a common symptom of lupus, an autoimmune disease. If you have a significant number of spider veins or redness, don't be alarmed if your doctor asks you to have a simple blood test known as ANA, used to eliminate lupus as a possible diagnosis.

For Persistent Redness

Persistent, general redness often improves with 500-milligram doses of oral tetracycline, taken twice daily. (This is not an option if you are pregnant or nursing.)

DERMAdoctor's own 2n1 rosacea cream can quickly help reduce redness. Oleanolic acid and white tea extract assist in this process.

Topical vitamin K can often help reduce facial redness (and spider veins) in many cases. Try K-Derm gel twice a day.

Other remedial therapy includes Neova Calming Green Tea Serum and Cutanix.

Medications for Flushing

Flushing is by far the most difficult aspect of rosacea to control. Your doctor might prescribe a beta-blocker, a type of medication typically used to lower blood pressure, but this can be tricky in patients with normal blood pressure. Nicotinamide and calcium channel blockers—agents that are used to control circulatory problems—have also been prescribed to help reduce this annoying condition.

Sun Protection Is a Priority

Sunscreen is essential for anyone with rosacea. Whether you require both ultraviolet and visible-light protection (as from Total Block), or are looking for the lightest oil-free, oil-reducing, rejuvenating, and rehydrating product you can find, like DERMAdoctor Body Guard Exquisitely Light SPF 30, make sure you wear your sunscreen daily. This will go a long way in helping minimize your redness!

Camouflage

When topical treatments and procedures aren't enough to handle the redness (or perhaps they just haven't had time to kick in), you may want to consider strategic camouflage.

Green neutralizes red. This explains why neutral shades of concealers allow redness to peek out from beneath your foundation. And it explains why green-based T. LeClerc Liquid Concealer-Tilleul is so effective at in hiding redness. For more stubborn redness, try layering it with T. LeClerc Liquid Concealer-Beige, prior to applying your foundation.

If your skin is oily, apply DERMAdoctor's Tease Zone or other mattifying product to help absorb excessive oils. Sebum breaks up foundation, so reducing the amount of oils helps extend the daily length of wear time for your makeup.

Rice-powder-based foundations, like those made by T. LeClerc, are incredibly absorbent and won't clog your pores. If fact, the strict use of powder foundation is a good idea in general; it is less likely to aggravate your acne. Mineral makeups, such as Jane Iredale, are also for anyone who is rosacea-prone.

WILL I LOOK LIKE W. C. FIELDS?

Rhinophyma—a surface irregularity that can form on the nose—is occasionally seen in rosacea. (And rarely seen in women.) Picture W. C. Fields. Everyone thinks he looked that way because of his drinking; in fact, it was due to rosacea. Early treatment helps prevent rhinophyma from worsening. And the condition responds in part to surgical repair.

THE EYES HAVE IT

Ocular rosacea can leave the eyes feeling irritated and gritty. Patients can experience redness, tearing, or crusting on the lashes. Many mistakenly think they have allergies. The use of steroid-based prescription eyedrops will usually help improve this condition. For more severe cases, I have found that oral tetracycline or minocycline is necessary as well.

FINAL THOUGHTS

If you have rosacea, there is definitely something you can do to look your best. And you may find comfort in knowing that millions of women also face the same concerns. But when it comes to having rosacea, only your dermatologist needs to know!

Ask the DERMAdoctor

QUESTION:

I have rosacea and have just received your DERMAdoctor's own 2n1 rosacea cream. Where does this fit in my skin care routine? Currently, I use MetroGel, then my skin rejuvenation product, then a sunscreen, occasionally a light moisturizer, and finish with a vitamin K cream for redness.

The DERMAdoctor:

With the launch of DERMAdoctor's own 2n1 rosacea cream, rosacea patients can really cut their routine down to just a few products. 2n1 rosacea cream addresses redness and blemishes, balances moisture needs, and targets skin rejuvenation. I would continue to use your MetroGel twice daily. In the morning, follow this by applying 2n1 rosacea cream and a sunscreen like DERMAdoctor Body Guard Exquisitely Light SPF 30. In the evening, you may either layer 2n1 rosacea cream on top of your MetroGel or alternate it with other skin rejuvenation, as desired.

SCABIES

The Family Skin Problem

Its nickname is "the seven-year itch." But scabies don't really strike in cycles. Every year, three hundred million people worldwide are affected by this parasite. If you or your family are among the unfortunate many, here's what you need to know—and do.

BUGOLOGY

Scabies is caused by a microscopic mite capable of producing itching so severe that victims can stay up all night scratching. The eight-legged parasite burrows into the top layers of the skin (epidermis), seeking shelter and nourishment. Once there, it lays its eggs, ensuring more mites—and more itching—to come. But for all the discomfort they can cause, only ten to twenty mites live within the skin at any one time!

Overcrowding in poor areas makes a scabies infestation more likely. But, contrary to popular belief, getting scabies does *not* imply a lack of cleanliness.

The highly contagious mite is passed strictly by skin-to-skin contact between people. (Pets are not affected—they neither give nor receive the mite.) Contact essential for passing scabies can vary from holding hands to hugging to sharing a bed. When trying to determine how your child got it, think of sleepovers and day care centers. Scabies is also rampant in nursing homes and facilities that care for the mentally disabled.

DON'T BE RASH

Once itching begins, it is widespread and overwhelming. However, there's no rash—at first. The "rash" of scabies is a consequence of uncontrolled scratching, and consists of innumerable scratch marks and small open sores. This self-inflicted skin trauma can lead to a secondary bacterial infection. Small red bumps may also form, part of the allergic reaction produced by the body in response to the infestation.

Itching may be pervasive, but scabies mites actually seek out cooler areas of the body in which to live. Scratch marks tend to center around the soft portions of the wrists, the finger and toe webs, the belly button, and the groin and buttock area. However, infants can have eruptions on their scalp and in other areas that are atypical for adults.

A textbook description of scabies inevitably mentions visible linear burrows on the skin. Despite having treated hundreds of scabies patients, I've rarely seen this.

A simple office test that undeniably confirms the diagnosis is the scabies prep. The dermatologist gently scrapes the skin with a small blade coated in mineral oil and transfers the exfoliated cells onto a glass slide. This is then looked at under the microscope. The presence of the mite (or its droppings) is unquestionable confirmation of the diagnosis.

Remember, there are only ten to twenty mites present at any one time. That makes it quite difficult to find them. Oftentimes, a strong patient history (or ongoing family history of scabies), combined with classical clinical signs, determines the diagnosis and treatment.

KILLING THE MITE

Itching begins approximately thirty days after exposure. That is why it is crucial that *all* family members be treated at the same time, even if they do not exhibit symptoms. You may have scabies and just not know it . . . yet.

Prescription Elimite cream (5% permethrin) is my favorite scabies treatment. Only one Elimite treatment is necessary to kill both the mites and their eggs, compared to multiple treatments with lindane (found in Kwell). That makes it both easier to use and safer. Here's a six-step process for effectively treating scabies:

All household members should be treated. Your physician will discuss any exceptions or modifications for infants and pregnant women.

Apply Elimite from your neck down to your toes at bedtime (don't overlook the webs between the fingers and toes), and wash it off in the morning. This is a onetime treatment.

You'll also have to do a lot of laundry. All clothing worn the previous day, all pajamas worn the night of the treatment, and all bedding, down to the mattress (but not the mattress itself), must be washed. Dry the laundry for an hour in a hot dryer.

Place any unwashable items in a closed plastic bag for two weeks. The eggs will hatch in about ten days, but scabies aren't able to live away from human skin for more than twenty-four hours, so the mites will die.

It is not necessary to treat objects like the sofa or fog the house. Scabies mites must burrow into the skin of their human host in order to survive. They don't live in carpeting or furniture; they are slow moving and have no wings, and cannot jump up and latch on, as fleas can.

Leave pets alone. They cannot get human scabies.

Once and Done

As you can see, the good news is that scabies is easily treatable.

The bad news is that you can continue to itch for six weeks following treatment. You would be amazed at how seldom this information is conveyed to the scabies patient.

Persistent itching does not mean that you should continue to use antiscabies medications. The bugs and eggs are long dead. If you do so, the only thing you'll accomplish is enormous skin irritation.

Patients who misinterpret itching as ongoing infestation may try every conceivable home remedy—including some very unsafe ones—in an attempt to "kill the scabies mites that didn't die from the medicine." Bad idea.

STOPPING THE ITCH

Six weeks of discomfort *after* you've finally figured out why you were itching in the first place is a long time to wait for relief. It is just as important to address the itching as to kill scabies mites.

It's fairly obvious that scratching isn't good for the skin. It can lead to further skin inflammation (and itching), open wounds, bacterial infections, and even scarring. But when you have scabies, displaying self-control and refusing to scratch is almost impossible. Anyone who tells you otherwise is greatly lacking in empathy.

Itching from scabies is essentially a two-part problem. An allergic reaction occurs in response to the parasite, releasing histamine into the skin. Conquer the histamine and much of the problem is controlled.

Inflammation drives itching, too. White blood cells swarm into the skin, in response to the infection and the disruption caused by all that scratching.

In order to get a reprieve from your discomfort, treatment should target the allergic reaction, the inflammation, *and* additional complicating factors. To enhance success, I don't limit therapy to a single option. Rather, I may combine antihistamines (oral and topical), topical anesthetics, cortisone (topical and, rarely, oral), bath treatments, and bacterial-infection control.

Antihistamines Are a Lifesaver

For seemingly uncontrollable, generalized itching, oral anthistamines provide relief. The goal in antihistamine use is to put an end to the discomfort yet not produce drowsiness. Unfortunately, I find that nonsedating antihistamines (those often used for hay fever) do not adequately stop itching. I like to prescribe hydroxyzine in a small, 10-milligram dosage that can be increased in 10-milligram increments. This helps balance maximum effectiveness with minimum drowsiness.

An over-the-counter option that can work for you is Benadryl. Here's a secret: by using Benadryl allergy syrup (made for children) instead of the adult 25- or 50-milligram tablet form, you can dispense a smaller dose.

Zonalon is a prescription topical antihistamine cream. It's great for treating limited areas of itching for short periods of time. Head-to-toe use, however, may cause drowsiness. If your dermatologist prescribes it, understand its place in the overall treatment regimen.

Numb with Relief

There's a lot to be said for the simplicity of numbing an area that itches like mad. Topical anesthetics don't last long and they don't solve the cause of the itching, but they certainly offer a constructive alternative to scratching.

There are a bevy of topical over-the-counter anesthetics on the market. Pramoxine and lidocaine are two commonly used active ingredients. My favorite products containing those ingredients continue to be PrameGel and L.M.X. 4 cream, respectively.

Cortisone Control

Inflammation drives itching. Cortisone reduces inflammation within the skin. So it makes sense to include steroids in the treatment. My preference is to avoid systemic steroids (pills or shots) if at all possible and to rely upon topical steroid creams, applying them to the nastiest areas. While prescription-strength cortisone creams are the most effective at reducing the intensity of scabies-induced itching, in a pinch you can use over-the-counter Cortaid, which contains 1% hydrocortisone.

Bath Time

Sometimes a good soak in the tub will help reduce stress and take your mind off the discomfort. Adding baking soda or Aveeno Oatmeal Bath to the water can do more—they help soothe the skin and lessen the itch. Try adding a packet of Aveeno or one-third of a small box of baking soda to your bathwater—and relax.

INFECTION PROTECTION

Open wounds simply beg for bacterial invasion. Not only is this undesirable, but infection also worsens itching. It's vital, therefore, to keep open wounds (scratch marks included) clean. Twice a day, dab these areas with hydrogen peroxide. Let it bubble, gently pat dry, and apply an antibiotic ointment like Polysporin.

Golden crusts, drainage, and redness extending from wounds are warning signs of infection. I prescribe an oral antibiotic if any of these symptoms develop.

RESISTANT SCABIES

Recently, I have seen a few cases of patients with scabies resistant to treatment. A one-time oral dose of Stromectol (ivermectin) was required to eliminate the mites. This is considered an off-label use for this medication, which is currently approved for the treatment of other parasite infections, including some forms of intestinal worms. However, ivermectin has been shown to be highly effective for treating scabies resistant to treatment, as well as in overwhelming, crusted scabies infestations (a condition known as Norwegian scabies) of immunosuppressed patients.

FINAL THOUGHTS

The next time your child complains of relentless itching at night, pay attention—before you end up itching, too!

Ask the DERMAdoctor

QUESTION:

Following the treatment for scabies, how do you know if you are going through the six-week itching period or have become reinfested with scabies?

The DERMAdoctor:

If you did everything properly—following the prescription therapy; washing your clothing you wore the day of the treatment, along with your bedding and pajamas; and getting everyone in the household treated—you should have eradicated the scabies. If you are still having problems after the six weeks, return to your dermatologist and request a scabies prep. (See page 243.)

QUESTION:

What is the best and most effective dose of ivermectin for resistant scabies?

The DERMAdoctor:

The use of ivermectin to treat scabies is considered an off-label use of this prescription medication and, as such, there are no *PDR* (*Physicians' Desk Reference*) or FDA-approved dosing guidelines. However, from many articles I have read, a single dose of 200 milligrams per kilogram of body weight is typically considered effective. In the few patients I have treated for resistant scabies, a single treatment was adequate. A few cases of scabies resistant to this dose have been reported, and some doctors are advocating raising the single dose to 250 milligrams per kilogram; others recommend giving a second dose of 200 milligrams per kilogram ten days after the first dose. (This is the dose for adults, not children.)

Significant toxicity has been associated with ivermectin; there have even been a few suspected fatalities. So while there is no question that it can be helpful in the treatment of resistant scabies, I would not recommend it as a first-line treatment. Hopefully, over time there will be studies comparing dosing and other procedures, and should future FDA approval for this use of ivermectin occur, we will have more definitive guidelines.

SHINGLES AND CHICKENPOX

Skin Infections for Adult and Child

Shingles is the nickname for herpes zoster (a.k.a. zoster), a blistering, frequently painful rash. Shingles is normally (but not always) a one-time event.

It used to be thought that shingles affected only those who were incredibly ill or had cancer, but this is now known to be incorrect. With ever-increasing life spans, most people have had shingles by the time they hit eighty.

Despite the medical name, the herpes virus is *not* to blame. Rather, shingles is caused by the chickenpox virus, *varicella zoster.*

After the last chickenpox scab disappears, the virus persists, setting up residence within the spinal column. The virus remains there, dormant, until at some future time, for no apparent reason, it becomes reactivated.

Nerve fibers extend from the spinal canal, organized much like the branches of a Christmas tree. Each fiber or branch supplies a single bandlike area on its side of the body. As the viral particles reactivate, their activity is limited to a single nerve branch (dermatome). This explains why the rash has a bandlike distribution restricted to one side of the body.

Intense pain, corresponding to the affected dermatome, commonly precedes the rash. There are many stories of patients with left-sided chest pain who mistakenly feared a heart attack and rushed to the emergency room. Days later, shingles appeared across that area. (By all means, if you ever have chest pain in that area without a rash, don't self-diagnose shingles! Go to the emergency room and let the experts tell you that your heart is healthy.)

The distinctive red band, strewn with clusters of blisters, forms within a few days to two weeks following the onset of pain. The skin may become even more sensitive to touch at this point, and the blisters may weep.

Remember, a shingles rash is a single well-defined band that extends from the midline of the back (or scalp, for facial shingles) and "wraps itself" around to the front (or down a limb). The presence of blisters on *both* sides of the body is another problem entirely.

Getting Serious

Disseminated zoster, where blisters develop well outside the dermatomal distribution, is customarily limited to immunosuppressed patients. It is a potentially life-threatening condition and requires hospitalization and IV therapy.

Shingles in the trigeminal nerve dermatome (which extends across the eye) is another serious situation. If it's left untreated, blindness can rapidly ensue, as the blisters cause corneal scarring.

For the trained dermatologist, even a single blister on the tip of the nose is an immediate, early clue to this condition. If I suspect that my patient has any form of trigeminal nerve shingles (an early clue or a full-blown eruption), I arrange for the patient to get an immediate ophthalmology consultation.

STOPPING SECONDARY INFECTION

All shingle blisters will inevitably rupture, leaving the denuded area vulnerable to secondary bacterial infection.

To prevent infection and dry out blisters or weeping, I ask my zoster patients to use a product called Domeboro Astringent Solution, which they apply as a moist compress for fifteen minutes, two to three times daily. To help prevent bacterial infection, after removing the compress use an over-the-counter antibiotic like Polysporin on the open sores. I am not fond of the antibacterial ingredient neomycin (which can also be found in triple-antibiotic ointment), as there is a risk of developing a contact dermatitis.

CONTROLLING PAIN

Use of anti-inflammatory medications like ibuprofen or naproxen will help relieve much of the discomfort associated with shingles. You can use over-the-counter products that contain these ingredients, like Advil, Motrin, or Aleve, or get a prescription for versions containing higher levels of these drugs. It is uncommon for me to ever have to resort to a mild prescription narcotic, like Tylenol with codeine.

POSTHERPETIC NEURALGIA

Postherpetic neuralgia is a debilitating, life-altering condition that can result from shingles. It is a nerve inflammation that remains or intensifies after the rash resolves. Fortunately, the majority of patients escape postherpetic neuralgia.

Taking prescription antiviral medication during the active phase of shingles can not only help prevent the condition but is a foundation of shingles therapy that helps hasten the resolution of the outbreak itself. The original medication used for this purpose was Zovirax (acyclovir), taken in large doses of 800 milligrams, five times a day, for ten days. That's a lot of medication!

Postherpetic neuralgia has been addressed with a variety of treatments ranging from antidepressants to antiseizure medications. Local nerve blocks, TENS treatments, and even acupunture have been tried.

A relatively new prescription product called Lidoderm (lidocaine 5% patch) is indicated for the treatment of postherpetic neuralgia.

Fortunately for the many people who suffer from postherpetic neuralgia, these therapies have been mostly successful.

CHICKENPOX: WHAT YOU NEED TO KNOW

Chickenpox is unquestionably the best-known viral infection of childhood. What isn't so well known is that countless adults also develop it each year. But child or adult, the infection is definitely seasonal, peaking during late fall and early spring.

It's Very Contagious

Chickenpox is *highly* contagious, and it is spread primarily via small airborne droplets that are coughed or sneezed by infected individuals. However, blister fluid also contains viral particles that are capable of spreading the infection by skin-to-skin contact, often through tiny breaks in the skin. Wash your hands well after caring for your child.

Chickenpox is contagious from twenty-four hours before the blisters appear (so you have no idea you're spreading the virus) until the last lesion has crusted over. The incubation period—from exposure until the first signs of illness appear—ranges from ten to twenty-one days.

The Symptoms

Ordinarily, a twenty-four-hour, flulike phase precedes the rash. Symptoms may include low-grade fever, malaise, and muscle aches.

Tiny, fragile blisters, characteristically described as "dewdrops upon the rose petal," first form on the scalp and face, then spread to the torso and limbs. The severity of the rash and the fever go hand in hand. The higher the fever, the more blisters are likely to form. (Whatever the cause, a childhood temperature over 101°F is reason to notify the pediatrician.)

New blisters continue to form in crops for about three days. Chickenpox is one of the few dermatological conditions in which all stages of the rash are simultaneously exhibited: newly formed, fragile vesicles; recently ruptured lesions; and crusted scabs.

TREATING CHICKENPOX

What's important to have on hand to help treat the rash and soothe the skin?

Not aspirin! In those eighteen years old and younger, it can cause a potentially fatal condition called Reye's syndrome.

Baking soda and Aveeno Oatmeal Bath Treatment are very soothing. If your child is amenable, you can bathe him or her as often as you like during the day.

A compress with Domeboro Astringent Solution can quickly dry out blisters. I recommend using a damp washrag as a compress, leaving it on for fifteen to twenty minutes, twice a day. Make sure you keep it out of the child's eyes.

I like applying Polysporin ointment to the worst-looking or open spots, to prevent secondary bacterial infection.

Tylenol or ibuprofen can help control the fever and other symptoms of the illness.

I was never much of a fan of pink calamine lotion. I don't like being covered in pink; nor did I find it effective. However, there is now a colorless version that contains pramoxine, an effective topical anesthetic. I find that topicals containing this ingredient, like Caladryl Clear Lotion,

Prax Lotion, and PrameGel, help provide temporary local relief from itching. They may be applied to children ages two and up. Check with your pediatrician for use on younger children.

Oral nonprescription Benadryl (Benadryl Allergy Dye-Free Liquid or Benadryl Allergy Liquid) or prescription Atarax (hydroxyzine) are very helpful at controlling the itching.

Don't scratch! The more scratching, the more likely it is that scar formation will occur. Invasive beta strep is a major cause of hospitalizations every year for chickenpox patients. The major cause is scratching open blisters.

Oral Zovirax

The use of oral antiviral medications like Zovirax (acyclovir) is not normally recommended for run-of-the-mill cases of chickenpox in otherwise healthy children. However, in certain high-risk categories such treatment is recommended, to reduce the possibility of a more complicated case. These categories include:

- Anyone thirteen and over (nonpregnant)
- Anyone one year or older with chronic skin or lung conditions
- Those on long-term aspirin therapy
- Children who are on systemic steroids (including asthma inhalers)

For maximum benefit, acyclovir should be started within the first twenty-four hours of the rash. Acyclovir may cause harm to the fetus, so it is not normally given to pregnant women.

VZIG

Varicella zoster immune globulin (VZIG) is an emergency treatment to help prevent or reduce the severity of chickenpox after known exposure. It is recommended for patients at extreme risk of developing a life-threatening case of chickenpox. These include:

- Pregnant women
- Newborns whose mothers had chickenpox within a seven-day span of their birth (ranging from five days prior to two days after)
- Patients with cellular immunodeficiencies
- Anyone whose immune system has been suppressed through drugs

(including steroids) or other disease states (HIV, AIDS, transplant patients, and some cancer patients)
- Unvaccinated children with lymphoma or leukemia

As with acyclovir, VZIG should be given as soon as possible but must be given within four days of exposure to chickenpox.

Vaccination

The chickenpox vaccine is now widely accepted by the medical community. Prior to its introduction, there were four million cases of chickenpox a year, eleven thousand hospitalizations, and one hundred deaths.

It is now recommended that all children between the ages of twelve and eighteen months be vaccinated. For children below the age of twelve, a single vaccination is given. For anyone thirteen and older, two injections are given, four to eight weeks apart.

Due to the risk of serious complications associated with adult-onset chickenpox, all adults without a past history of the disease should also be vaccinated.

Those who cannot take the vaccine include:

- Anyone with an allergy to neomycin or gelatin
- A person ill at the time of the planned vaccination (low-grade fever, cold, etc.)
- Long-term steroid users
- Anyone who has received blood products within the past five months
- Pregnant women
- Immunosuppressed patients (there are certain exceptions, so discuss this with your doctor)
- Children on salicylates (aspirin), as they run the risk of Reye's syndrome (aspirin should be discontinued for six weeks prior to vaccination)

Truly, chickenpox is one of those childhood diseases best gotten as a child. Adults with chickenpox have a much higher risk of developing a much more severe case of the infection, as well as such serious complications as varicella pneumonia, encephalitis, and systemic spread.

IMPETIGO: A BACTERIAL SKIN INFECTION

Impetigo is a bacterial infection of the skin, typically caused by either *Staphylococcus aureus* or strep. It is very contagious through direct contact; hand washing goes a long way to help cut down on the spread of this infection. Usually it takes about twenty-four to forty-eight hours of treatment before you are considered no longer contagious.

A bacterial culture can verify the presence of impetigo, which usually looks like oozing, golden-crusted sores and/or blisters. Impetigo is treated with prescription oral antibiotics like Keflex (cephalexin), Cipro (ciprofloxacin hydrochloride), or erythromycin. The area itself is treated with prescription Bactroban ointment. Supportive home care includes compressing any oozing areas with Domeboro Astringent Solution for ten to twenty minutes before applying Bactroban.

FINAL THOUGHTS

Chickenpox should be taken seriously, so don't be chicken about seeking treatment. High fever, extreme lethargy, vomiting, severe headaches, shortness of breath, and red streaks extending from an area of the rash are reasons to seek medical attention quickly.

PREGNANCY MATTERS

Developing chickenpox while pregnant puts the baby at risk for developing the infection in the womb, which can be quite serious and even life threatening. Most women contemplating pregnancy have a simple blood test to see if they have had chickenpox in the past. For those who have not and are planning a pregnancy, the vaccine is recommended.

When a woman who has already had chickenpox becomes exposed, her maternal antibodies should protect the unborn fetus. Once the baby is born, maternal antibodies will provide protection for three months.

Ask the DERMAdoctor

QUESTION:

I am thirty-one years old and just had chickenpox. I am planning to spend time with my family, and they have all had chickenpox many years ago. Can someone with chickenpox give someone shingles? And what about my children, who have had their chickenpox vaccines? Are they at risk?

The DERMAdoctor:

There is no evidence that being exposed to someone with chickenpox stimulates an eruption of shingles. If you have never had chickenpox and you are exposed to it, you may develop chickenpox. If you have shingles and expose someone who has never had chickenpox to the virus (this is tough to do, as shingles is not spread through the respiratory organs, as chickenpox is), they could develop chickenpox, not shingles. If your children have had their vaccines, theoretically they should be immune to chickenpox or get a very light case. Basically, it sounds like you are fairly safe.

SKIN CANCER
Awareness Is Half the Battle

Skin cancer is now the most common cancer in America: rates of newly diagnosed cases are rising by 4 to 5 percent a year, with 1.3 million people affected last year. But unlike other cancer epidemics, the cause isn't a mystery. Blame the sun.

Ultraviolet rays from the sun create cellular DNA damage. Under normal circumstances, the skin's repair system literally cuts out damaged DNA and replaces it with new, healthy code. (Heredity plays a role in your ability to repair that damage.) But too much ultraviolet damage can overwhelm the system, leading to skin cancer.

Obviously, lighter skin is more prone to sun damage, which is why redheads and fair blonds with blue eyes so often develop skin cancer. (However, anyone can develop skin cancer, regardless of race.) A long-term history of sun exposure also places you at higher risk. That includes people raised on farms, veterans of World War II who were stationed in the South Pacific, construction workers—basically, anyone who has spent a lot of time outdoors. In addition, immuno-suppressed patients (especially transplant patients) are likely to see the early and rapid development of skin cancer.

There are three types of sun-induced skin cancer: basal cell carcinoma (BCC), squamous cell carcinoma (SCC), and, of course, malignant melanoma.

BASAL CELL CARCINOMA
Most people have never heard of this form of skin cancer, but it is the most common, with an estimated 800,000 Americans newly diagnosed each year.

The slow-growing basal carcinoma is so named because it forms within the basal (basement) layer, deep within the epidermis. BCCs can grow quite large and invade adjacent spaces, but they rarely spread to other areas of the body (metastasize).

Early basal cell carcinomas—superficial spreading basal cells— resemble reddish, dry skin patches that don't heal, lasting for a month or longer. BCCs slowly rise above the skin's surface as pink or flesh-toned bumps. (It's not unusual for patients who think they've had an acne bump for years to find out that it's really a BCC. Acne resolves spontaneously; skin cancer does not.) BCCs often look "pearly," and it's this quality that gives them away. Given enough time, a basal cell carcinoma may form a central ulceration, or sore.

A skin biopsy—a shave biopsy or a deeper punch—can easily diagnose BCC. Unlike with a melanoma, there's no risk of a biopsy spreading the cancer or affecting its diagnosis or prognosis.

Treatment of a basal cell carcinoma is relatively straightforward.

Simple Excision

The skin is numbed with a local anesthetic and the visible area of the cancer, along with a small margin of normal skin, is excised and sutured close. The removal of very small amounts of nearby normal skin allows the pathologist to determine if the entire cancer was excised.

ED&C × 3

This is an abbreviation for electrodesiccation and curettage. After being numbed with a local anesthetic, the affected area is cauterized and scraped three times.

A quick and simple method, ED&C × 3 is ideal for larger skin cancers on the torso (because there's less skin excised) and for treating skin cancer in elderly or infirm patients who may not be able to adequately care for a large sutured area.

The downside is that there is no pathological confirmation certifying 100 percent eradication of the skin cancer. Typically, ED&C × 3 has a 75 to 80 percent rate of successfully eliminating the BCC.

Given their slow growth rate and the tendency for BCCs to remain localized, ED&C × 3 is an excellent option under the right circumstances.

Mohs Micrographic Surgery

Named for its creator, Dr. Frederick Mohs, this treatment combines surgical excision with immediate confirmation that the tumor has been fully removed. Typically, Mohs surgeons are dermatologists who have undergone an additional one to two years of training in this procedure.

In the specialist's office, the visible cancer is removed under local anesthetic and microscopically accessed for pathology. Should any skin cancer remain, the edges are gradually shaved away and evaluated. These steps are repeated as necessary—in the office, during the surgical procedure—ensuring complete removal of the skin cancer and preservation of the maximum amount of uninvolved, healthy tissue. Mohs is now the standard of care for a BCC involving the central face, where preserving such cosmetically important areas like the nose is vital.

Aldara (Imiquimod)

Aldara is a topical immune response modifier used to treat genital warts. The drug's ability to provoke local tissue production of tumor-fighting interferons and tumor necrosis factor–alpha has taken this medication to the forefront of basal cell carcinoma treatment.

Multiple studies have demonstrated the ability of topical imiquimod to resolve early SBCCs and more advanced basal cell carcinomas, and in 2004 the drug was approved to treat both superficial basal cell carcinomas and actinic keratosis.

Patients who are unable to undergo surgery and have very small BCCs may be potential candidates for this therapy.

Other Treatments

Less commonly used treatment options include:

- Laser destruction
- Cryosurgery
- Radiation therapy
- Topical chemotherapy with 5-fluorouracil
- Photodynamic therapy (Levulan Kerastick, for early BCCs)

Follow-up

Patients who have been treated for basal cell carcinoma should have a follow-up skin exam every six months for five years after treatment, then at least once a year thereafter. It's during that five-year time frame that BCC is most likely to recur. (I often follow up ED&C sites every three months for a few visits after the treatment, to monitor for recurrence.)

It's important to note that skin in the region of the removed cancer is also sun damaged and at a higher risk for developing a new skin cancer—a BCC, SCC, or melanoma. That's why a complete skin examination is recommended, not just a spot check of the surgery site.

SQUAMOUS CELL CARCINOMA

Every year, SCC affects about 200,000 Americans. It's a more dangerous form of skin cancer than BCC because it can spread to other parts of the body. Metastasis occurs in less than 1 percent of cases, resulting in approximately 2,000 deaths a year.

Squamous cell carcinoma arises on sun-exposed, sun-damaged skin—and the more sun exposure there has been (even from routine tanning), the higher the risk of developing SCC.

SCC can also form on areas of skin subjected to chemicals, thermal burns, and radiation. Occasionally, it even arises within vaccination scars.

Arsenic exposure is another (although uncommon) risk factor. Arsenic was found in "old-fashioned" cough and cold remedies, which were sold predominantly in the South. More recently, arsenic exposure has been associated with pesticides.

Typically, SCC looks like a hard (sometimes scaly or crusty) red bump or nodule. The cancer can form an open sore, itch, and bleed. It continues to grow in height and diameter until removed.

SCC can also arise from a precancerous skin change called actinic keratosis, which is a chronic, reddish brown, scaly patch on sun-exposed skin. (For more information on actinic keratosis, please see the chapter "Age Spots" on page 25.)

Treatments

Because SCC can spread, the best procedures guarantee complete removal. Excision and Mohs micrographic surgery are both appropriate.

As with BCC, other options may be appropriate for patients unable to undergo a full excision. These include laser destruction, ED&C × 3, radiation therapy, cryosurgery, and treatment with 5-fluorouracil. And as with BCC, there are ongoing clinical trials using biologic therapies alone and with retinoids.

Follow-up

Follow-up for SCC mirrors that for BCC. However, quarterly rather than twice-a-year checks are best, because of the greater potential for metastasis.

It's important to remember that if one form of skin cancer has developed, a level of sun damage has been reached where the patient is at a higher risk to develop any skin cancer—or all of them. Vigilance is the best bet for early detection and intervention.

MELANOMA

Melanoma is by far the most lethal of these three skin cancers. According to the Melanoma Research Foundation, every hour of every day of the year an American dies of malignant melanoma, totaling seventy-four thousand deaths a year.

Early detection is key: melanoma is almost 100 percent curable if discovered early. Famous people who have survived melanoma include the former Dallas quarterback Troy Aikman, the TV broadcaster Sam Donaldson, and Senator John McCain.

Beauty Marks

Some call them "beauty marks," others call them unacceptable, yet moles have long been associated with many a diva. Because the word "mole" has become so generalized to refer to any number of skin growths, it's appropriate to clear up any confusion. True moles (nevi) are benign colonies of reproducing skin pigment–forming cells (melanocytes).

Moles can vary in location. Those limited to the epidermis are flat and include those cute frecklelike moles and café au lait spots.

Moles that arise from melanocytes residing along the bottom layer of epidermis are responsible for those bumps protruding above the surface of the skin.

Moles formed by nests of melanocytes trapped solely within the dermis include the Mongolian spot and blue nevus.

Understanding moles is critical because they can turn into melanomas. The vast majority of moles are visible on the skin and are brown in color. Rarely, moles lack pigment (are amelanotic) and appear pink or red. And there are even hidden, internal moles, including at the back of the eye, in the spinal column, and in the colon.

Under certain conditions, moles can begin to change, a situation referred to as dysplasia. While a dysplastic mole does not guarantee the formation of cancer, the more severe the degree of dysplasia the more it is of medical concern. Of course, the worst-case scenario is a mole that fully transforms into a malignant melanoma.

Fortunately, moles don't change into melanomas overnight. Moles go through a gradual series of changes (some faster than others) called dysplasia. The greater the degree of dysplasia, the more likely it is that the mole may turn into melanoma.

Even though they're easy to see, many symptomatic moles are ignored. Knowing four symptomatic warning signs—the ABCD's of melanoma—can save your life. They are:

A: Asymmetry. The mole is not completely even in appearance.

B: Border. The margins should be even and smooth, without ratty or projecting edges.

C: Circumference. The mole should be nice and round, without jagged or sharp edges.

D: Diameter. The mole should not measure more than 6 millimeters across. This is the size of a pencil eraser.

Other signs to pay close attention to include rapid mole growth, formation of a sore, and itching or bleeding within the mole.

The above signs and symptoms do not automatically mean that the mole is malignant or even dysplastic (prone to forming cancer). But they are *definitely* a reason to be evaluated by a dermatologist, and the sooner, the better.

TREATMENT
A state-of-the-art biopsy of a suspicious mole consists of a full excision around the area. (The unusual exception is a mole so large that full excision is impossible.) The excision is performed under local anesthetic, and the area is closed with stitches. If melanoma is diagnosed, a reexcision is performed. (The exception might be an original excision of a very early melanoma in situ, in which a 5-millimeter area surrounding the border was found to be clear of cancer.)

The prognosis for melanoma is based on how deeply the mole has grown into the skin. Further workup and treatment are based on this very important measurement. That is why simply shaving through a suspicious mole or lasering it off without a pathology report is inappropriate.

Follow-up

If the excision took care of the problem, the patient should have a complete skin examination (CSE) every three months for five years. At that point, she should have a CSE once or twice a year. My follow-up also includes an ophthalmology appointment (checking for hidden moles at the back of the eyes), a chest X-ray, blood work, and sometimes a CT scan (depending on the patient's history).

There can be a genetic predisposition to melanoma. If your parents or siblings have had the disease, you should have a CSE and eye exam once a year. Those with a large number of moles or dysplastic nevus syndrome (multiple, changing moles) should be screened more often.

PREVENTING SKIN CANCER

When it comes to preventing skin cancer, you're probably more than familiar with the standard, sun-avoiding tips. Let me recap those steps you simply must do:

Sun Avoidance. Try to avoid being outdoors during the hours of eleven A.M. to three P.M., when the sun is strongest.

Sunscreen Use. Use only broad-spectrum screens or blocks that protect against UVA and UVB rays. An SPF 15 is minimum protection, and SPF 30 is preferable; disregard products with an SPF less than 15.

Tanning Bed Avoidance. Skip the tanning beds—they're far more dangerous than an unprotected day at the beach.

UV-Treated Sunglasses. Protecting the eyes makes sense. It helps prevent the ultraviolet damage that can cause melanoma and it helps save your sight.

SPF-Treated Clothing. Throw a packet of Rit Sun Guard Laundry Treatment UV Protectant in with your laundry and give your clothing an SPF 30 (compared to a mundane SPF 4).

Complete Skin Examination. Don't have access to a dermatologist? Take advantage of any number of free skin cancer screenings performed across the country every May, during Skin Cancer Awareness Month.

Protect Your Children. UV damage and sunburns before the age of ten are more likely to cause skin cancer later in life. One in seventy-five children born in the year 2000 will develop melanoma. Protect them!

Awareness. Being aware of the signs of skin cancer is half the battle. Don't ignore symptoms.

FINAL THOUGHTS
Rapid growth of a mole and itching, bleeding, crusting, or sore formation within any skin lesion should be checked. The good news is that when most patients follow up on these signs, either the spot isn't skin cancer or they get their condition diagnosed in the early stages, when it's curable. It's easier than you think to help save your life.

Ask the DERMAdoctor

QUESTION:
I am a forty-seven-year-old female living in Australia. I am faced with a decision about whether to have surgery to remove a BCC on the tip of my nose or to try Aldara. I have seen two specialists—a dermatologist who wants to try Aldara and a plastic surgeon who wants surgery. Obviously, I want the best outcome in terms of scarring. My thoughts are to try the Aldara first; if that doesn't work, I can then have the surgery. I would really appreciate some help with this decision.

The DERMAdoctor:
There is no question that getting rid of the skin cancer as soon as possible is crucial. On the tip of the nose, with so little skin available to close, you don't want to have a large carcinoma that will result in noticeable scarring when removed.

However, I do believe that Aldara has a role in the treatment of basal cell carcinoma in certain situations. While only the doctors involved in your care can determine what is best for you, I do not fault your dermatologist for wanting to try this therapy before the surgery. Certainly if the Aldara is successful in even shrinking the BCC, the scar should be smaller.

As for the surgery itself, make sure you have Mohs, in which only the visible portion of the skin cancer is removed and is immediately checked by frozen-section pathology. If the margins are involved, then additional minute portions are removed and checked, until the entire tumor is removed. This helps preserve as much healthy tissue as possible, which is important in an area without much room to spare.

SPIDER VEINS

They're Not Broken—
but They Are Fixable

They may look like broken blood vessels and they may be called broken blood vessels, but they aren't actually broken at all!

Telangiectasias (facial spider veins) are a weblike proliferation of the tiniest superficial veins of the epidermis. They can be red to purple, lacy to threadlike, few and wispy or numerous and tangled. Some groupings have large feeder veins beneath the skin that look like the "body" of a spider amid the "legs" of the veins; hence, spider veins.

Preventing new spider veins and eradicating those already present can help keep your facial skin looking creamy smooth.

(For information on spider veins of the legs, see page 269.)

WHY ARE THEY THERE?

The most likely cause is a blending of genetics with the natural aging process of the skin. Sun damage is another contributor—the more sun damage you've had, the more likely it is that telangiectasias will form. Other reasons include:

- Rosacea (adult acne)
- Steroid atrophy of the skin, from topical or systemic use
- CREST syndrome (a form of scleroderma, an autoimmune disease)
- Lupus (an autoimmune disease)

IS IT ROSACEA?

Patients with blood vessel growths on the face frequently ask me if they have rosacea.

You can have facial spider veins without having rosacea, and you can have rosacea without having facial spider veins.

If you're aging, have very fair skin, have had sun damage, and have a family history of telangiectasias, you're fair game for spider veins. This has nothing to do with rosacea, which has many symptoms, like facial redness, blemishes, flushing, and dryness. I refrain from making a broader diagnosis should the case be limited to spider veins.

EMBARRASSINGLY RED
Whenever a spider vein (or any blood vessel) dilates, more blood flows to the skin's surface, producing redness. Factors that can cause veins to dilate include:

- Exposure to sun, wind, or cold weather
- Physical exertion
- Becoming overheated
- Stress
- Hot or spicy foods and beverages
- Drinking alcohol
- Foods like citrus fruits, tomatoes, soy sauce, vinegars, some cheeses, and liver

At a party involving alcohol, hot food, cheese-filled hors d'oeuvres, spicy food, or just an overheated room, you may catch a glimpse of yourself in a mirror looking unflatteringly flushed. At that moment, you suddenly find the motivation to eradicate that tangled web of spider veins.

TREATMENTS FOR SPIDER VEINS
Getting rid of spider veins is not only appropriate but is becoming very popular. You can get rid of the redness by physically destroying the blood vessels, as well as by dealing with the redness itself.

Electrodesiccation
Spider veins are easily electrodesiccated with low-voltage electricity; a tiny needle attached to the machine literally zaps along the length of the blood vessel, destroying it.

Depending on the number of blood vessels present, one or two sessions are usually adequate, with each session typically lasting fifteen to thirty minutes. The procedure is simple and highly effective. And it's very economical, with costs running approximately $200 per session.

Injected anesthesia isn't used because it causes the veins to blanch and become difficult to see. I have a pharmacist-mixed concoction called Betacaine Plus that I apply in the office fifteen minutes before treatment; it does a wonderful job of numbing the area. Talk to your dermatologist about this treatment. Or consider using an over-the-counter topical anesthetic, like L.M.X. 4 Topical Anesthetic. Topical anesthetics don't entirely deaden the area, but they do dramatically raise your pain threshold.

There may be some swelling and redness of the treated area for a day or two.

Just as with other "age-related" growths, if you're prone to telangiectasias, you'll probably continue to find new ones arising periodically. Expect maintenance treatments every now and then.

Intense Pulsed Light (IPL)

If you're resistant to electrodesiccation, or if you have such an overwhelming number of telangiectasias that this procedure seems out of the question, IPL (FotoFacial) is another option.

IPL is not a true laser but an intense pulsed-light therapy that helps destroy spider veins; it can also treat brown skin discoloration. It requires five thirty-minute treatments, performed every three to four weeks. The cost for a full course of treatment is around $2,500. Plan on one-session maintenance treatments every three to twelve months.

Vitamin K

The topical use of vitamin K has become very popular in dermatology for helping improve the appearance of a number of conditions: bruising, dark circles, ruddy skin tones—and facial redness and spider veins. (For more information on bruising, please see page 271.)

If you have large or numerous telangiectasias, you may find that vitamin K diminishes the intensity of the redness but that you still require a procedure to reach your intended goal.

Topical vitamin K products generally range from 2% to 5%. K-Derm is useful when applied twice daily. K-Derm Gel is preferable for oilier skin, K-Derm Cream for drier skin. They are usually well tolerated when applied simultaneously with other skin care products.

DERMAdoctor's Own 2n1 Rosacea Cream

DERMAdoctor's own 2n1 rosacea cream contains oleanolic acid, a lipoxygenase inhibitor that helps reduce inflammation within the skin. This product also contains white tea, which contributes two crucial ingredients: a potent antioxidant (the most potent of the tea extracts) and EGCG, which has anti-inflammatory properties. 2n1 rosacea cream helps reduce facial redness caused by the presence of spider veins—and it does so immediately after application.

Red Plus Green Equals . . .

There's nothing wrong with simply hiding the redness and the veins. However, you may not feel like wearing a layer of makeup comparable to spackle. So consider your color wheel when trying to hide those veins.

Green counteracts red. Dust with a green powder like T. LeClerc Loose Facial Powder-Tilleul, and you'll find that the intensity of the redness is countered automatically. If necessary, you can always use the liquid form, T. LeClerc Liquid Concealer-Tilleul, on the larger veins, then apply a flesh-toned concealer or liquid foundation on top.

REJUVENATION OPTIONS FOR WOMEN WITH SPIDER VEINS

If you have spider veins, you have a few issues to consider when choosing rejuvenating skin care products.

Topical Retinoids

It is known that the topical use of vitamin A (including tretinoin, tazarotene, and even over-the-counter retinol) may increase spider vein formation in a *very few* individuals. I am not suggesting that everyone with spider veins dump their retinoid of choice. However, for that rare consumer who is convinced that their veins are multiplying faster than they can track, it may not be their imagination. You may want to contemplate this possibility and discuss it with your dermatologist.

But remember: it's likely that anyone with spider veins will continually form new telangiectasias. So it could be a hard call to determine whether the drug is causing the problem.

Low-pH Topicals

The second issue involves the use of skin care products that have a low pH. These acidic products, like some AHAs (alpha hydroxy acids) and vitamin C treatments, may cause spider veins to dilate and temporarily redden the skin.

The choice is yours. They won't "worsen" your skin or cause spider veins to multiply. But if your skin seems more sensitive to these ingredients or you simply dislike that transient redness, skip them in favor of gentler, yet still highly effective rejuvenation options.

Try GHK copper peptides like Neova; white tea extract and superoxide dismutase, in DERMAdoctor's own 2n1 rosacea cream; or N-6 furfuryladenine, in Kinerase.

And don't forget to wear your sunscreen! It will help prevent the further photodamage that can contribute to spider vein formation.

SCLEROTHERAPY: RELIEF FOR SPIDER VEINS OF THE LEGS

Twenty-five million Americans have spider veins of the legs. The precise cause of this proliferation of weblike veins remains unclear, but they are thought to develop due to a combination of heredity, aging, gravitational forces (pooling of fluid in the legs), and hormonal changes.

What is your best move to get rid of the veins? Find a board-certified dermatologist or phlebologist (vein doctor) who is skilled at the nuances of sclerotherapy—which the American Academy of Dermatologic Surgery states is the "the gold standard of spider vein treatment."

Sclerotherapy involves injecting a chemical directly into the unwanted spider veins (most commonly, a highly concentrated saltwater solution), which causes irritation of the inner venous lining. Ultimately the vein dissolves and becomes reabsorbed by the body.

The effects of sclerotherapy are not immediate. Expect to see vessels fade in approximately two weeks (some sources say up to six). Only at this point can you determine if you'll need to undergo further treatments. I always tell patients to expect at least two treatments, and they are pleasantly surprised if only one is required for full resolution of the veins.

The procedure works well with busy schedules. I schedule a thirty-minute session and treat as many spider veins as I can possibly get to in that time. For the average patient, that is typically long enough time to get all of the vessels (as well as an end point to their tolerance level).

There may be a slight burning and stinging sensation associated with each injection. After the procedure, patients need to care for any visible injection sites with hydrogen peroxide and Polysporin ointment (antibiotic) twice daily until healed.

Some patients complain about leg cramps either during the procedure or later that day. Discomfort can be alleviated later with the use of Tylenol. I always caution my patients to take it very easy the next day and to avoid exercise and excessive walking or standing. Routine movement is certainly allowed. I have patients avoid the use of aspirin and NSAIDs (Advil, Motrin, etc.) two days before and twenty-four hours post-op because of the risk of increased oozing or bruise formation.

The multiple injection sites will often be puffy, bruised, and possibly tender for several days. Don't get this procedure done just before you need to make an entrance to a social event in a short skirt or before you plan to go on vacation. You'll want to make sure that you keep the sun off your legs so that you discourage darkening at the injection sites. You'll also want to make sure that you take some baby aspirin before any long car rides or plane flights (within a month posttreatment) to discourage unlikely (yet possible) blood clots.

Sclerotherapy is generally not covered by medical insurance; it's considered a cosmetic procedure. Those with significant leg pain may find a way to get medical insurance to help cover costs (with a lot of demanding). Although pricing may vary, you can expect to pay a few hundred dollars a session.

While sclerotherapy is a fairly patient-friendly procedure, those who should avoid it include diabetics, patients with known circulatory problems, and those with blood-borne infections such as hepatitis and AIDS. If you are pregnant, it is recommended you wait at least six months after delivery before contemplating sclerotherapy.

It is important to remember that once a spider vein is dead, it's gone for good. However, those prone to forming spider veins are probably going to continually form new ones. For these patients, periodic maintenance treatments may be required. Fashionable compression stockings (Jobst) may slow up spider vein formation. I certainly suggest that repeat work be done when fewer vessels are present to maintain increased comfort and ideal cosmetic appearance.

FINAL THOUGHTS

Spider veins can easily be made obsolete. By eliminating veins, reducing ruddiness, and keeping a clever concealer on hand, you too can face facial redness.

Ask the DERMAdoctor

QUESTION:

My skin is thinning with age, and I have developed both spider veins of the face and chronic bruising on the rest of my body. I am treating the spider veins as you recommend, but what can I do about those bruises?

The DERMAdoctor:

A variety of problems can cause chronic bruising, including medications (daily aspirin, blood thinners, and steroids), blood disorders like leukemia, chronic sun exposure, even the normal aging process. And, of course, a genetic predisposition can play a role.

Vitamin C deficiency (scurvy) can also lead to bruising. While scurvy is an unlikely cause in this day and age (in med school I thought *no* one experienced it anymore), I have seen two cases while in practice. Malnourished individuals or those making poor dietary selections without vitamin supplementation are at higher risk. If you're considering vitamin C supplementation to help reduce bruising, the recommended dosage is 1,500 milligrams daily. One caveat: your kidneys must be fully healthy and functional; check with your doctor if there is any question.

For many people, K-Derm Gel may be used to help prevent or expedite the resolution of bruising. Pregnant or nursing women and patients on Coumadin (warfarin) should avoid the use of topical vitamin K.

Sun damage is an important contributing factor. Cumulative sun damage thins the skin, and tiny blood vessels are more easily ruptured. This is why elderly patients frequently complain of bruising. Sun protection can help prevent further photoaging of the skin.

STRETCH MARKS

Color-Coded Treatment

Most people think stretch marks form when the skin stretches, such as during pregnancy and growth spurts.

Well, that's not just stretching the truth. It's simply wrong.

Stretch marks (referred to medically as *striae distensae*) are caused by increased levels of glucocorticoids circulating in the bloodstream. This adrenal hormone is elevated during adolescence and pregnancy, and with obesity, weight training, and Cushing's disease (a disorder of the adrenal glands).

Steroids can also cause stretch marks—either oral steroids, high-potency topical steroids, or even chronic use of low-potency steroids and ointments, particularly if after application they are covered with plastic wrap, which drives the steroid more deeply into the skin.

STRETCHING 101

Stretching may determine where the stretch marks will appear and in which direction they will run, but stretching alone doesn't cause stretch marks, as long as there is support within the dermis.

Glucocorticoids rob the dermis of that support. They prevent fibroblasts from forming the collagen and elastin fibers that keep rapidly growing skin taut. The result: a lack of supportive material, leading to dermal tears. Glucocorticoids also affect the epidermal cells, so that the epidermis becomes thin and flattened, allowing for increased visibility of the defects below.

Stretching Under a Microscope

Stretch marks are most commonly seen across the abdomen, buttocks, hips, breasts, and thighs. If you were to look at one of those stretch marks under a microscope, you'd see that the collagen fibers have been pulled apart from each other, and the elastin fibers are broken and lie clumped along the edges of the stretch mark. And there is no elastin within the heart of the tear.

As the stretch mark ages and turns white, collagen bundles mix with abnormally thin elastin fibers but are unable to fully realign themselves. Normal elastin fibers are still absent.

Treatment is aimed at trying to fix this subcutaneous disarray.

CUSTOMIZED TREATMENTS

Early in the life cycle of a stretch mark, wrinkled and crinkled strips of skin develop a red and often raised appearance. If your skin is dark you may not see a red tone to the skin, but it's there. Over time, stretch marks turn to a dusky purple or brown, and finally into flattened white bands.

Therapy is based on what your stretch marks looks like, which is determined by their phase of development. And, happily, there is a lot of new medical information on the effective treatment of stretch marks.

Red Alert

Red-colored stretch marks are medically known as *striae rubra*. This phrase offers is your best chance of really making an impact on the ultimate demise of your stretch marks. The idea behind early intervention is limiting the amount of damage. Your options include:

Mederma. Apply it three to four times daily, for six to twelve months. Mederma has shown good results in helping treat red, raised stretch marks; we still don't really understand why. It is certainly as "natural" as one can get—the active ingredient is nothing but onion-juice extract. It is safe to use while pregnant and nursing.

L-ascorbic acid. You can find this ingredient in such products as Cellex-C or SkinCeuticals. Apply a 15 or 20 % serum daily for six to twelve months. L-ascorbic acid helps stimulate fibroblasts to produce collagen and elastin fibers, which are essential in helping prevent stretch marks.

Prescription 0.1% Tretinoin or Tazarotene (Retin-A or Tazorac Cream).
Apply it nightly (start out every other night until your skin adjusts) for
twelve months. A nonprescription option is Afirm 3X and SkinCeuticals Retinol 1%. Retinoids have long been suspected of stimulating
fibroblast activity. In addition, exfoliation will occur, helping create a
more uniform surface.

If you're pregnant or nursing, items in this category are not
appropriate. Wait until afterward.

A 585-Nanometer Pulsed-Dye Laser. This procedure is *not* recommended for anyone with a dark skin tone (Fitzpatrick skin type IV, V,
or VI), because of an increased risk of skin discoloration. This is
another option to skip while pregnant or nursing.

White Out

Most women reading this chapter are probably far past their adolescent growth spurts, and even postpartum concerns may seem like
ancient history. In other words, your stretch marks are probably not
red but white, or what doctors call *striae distensae alba*.

I have received many a hopeless letter from women with older,
white stretch marks who have been told by their doctors, "You needed
to do something when they were red, and there's nothing you can do
now." Au contraire. The DERMAdoctor's First Rule of Skin Care is
Never give up. And there's no reason to. There are many ways to take
an aggressive approach to these types of stretch marks and try to
greatly improve their appearance.

Glycolic Acid and Vitamin A Creams

In the late 1990s, a study was published in the *Journal of Dermatology*
that looked at the best way to handle white stretch marks. Doctors in
the Department of General Surgery at Portsmouth's Naval Medical
Center studied several groups of women for twelve weeks. One group
applied M.D. Forté Hand & Body Cream once daily, using Cellex-C
High Potency Serum on their stretch marks at another time during
the day. Another group also used M.D. Forté, but used 0.05% tretinoin
(Renova 0.05% cream) for their second application.

The doctors found that both groups had a definite visual improvement. And there was also microscopic improvement: both groups

increased the thickness of the epidermis, and the thickness of the dermis within the stretch mark approached that of normal skin.

Unbuffered glycolic acid at a concentration of 20% can be highly irritating to the skin. The choice of M.D. Forté—which contains buffered 20% glycolic acid—was ideal, since it offered therapeutic effectiveness with a minimum of irritation.

Renova is a prescription item. If you are unable to obtain it from your doctor, you can try substituting a potent over-the-counter retinol, like Afirm 3X. (As indicated earlier, avoid these products if you are pregnant or nursing. Go with Cellex-C instead.)

Implementing any topical vitamin A cream is tricky because of the potential for irritation. Start out every other night, using a pea-sized amount on each treatment area (a pea-sized dab per hip, for example). Wait thirty minutes after washing before application, making certain the skin is dry.

Both glycolic acid and Vitamin A creams can cause an increase in photosensitivity, so wear your SPF 30 sunscreen daily.

In which order should you apply the creams?

If you're using M.D. Forté Hand & Body Cream and Cellex-C High Potency Serum: Apply Cellex-C in the morning (this provides antioxidant benefits during the daytime) and M.D. Forté at night.

If you're using M.D. Forté Hand & Body Cream and Renova or a retinol, apply M.D. Forté in the morning and the vitamin A cream at night.

This study I just discussed was conducted for twelve weeks, which means the women experienced *initial* improvement. Plan for a twelve-*month* course of therapy to see maximum results.

Microdermabrasion

Microscopic studies support the effectiveness of microdermabrasion as a helpful procedure for stubborn, older white stretch marks. Personally, I don't think it is a solution, but in combination with a proven regimen it may help hasten improvement.

In microdermabrasion, tiny particles are "sandblasted" against the skin, gradually removing scarred or discolored epithelial tissue. Typically, the procedure is done in a series of six or more treatments, and can be performed in a variety of settings, from dermatologists' and plastic surgeons' offices to some spas and high-end aesthetician clinics. Or you can try it yourself, with DermaNew Microdermabrasion Total Body Experience.

Nonablative Lasers

A final option for the treatment of older stretch marks is a nonablative laser like N-Lite. Lasers in this category do not burn the skin, as they do with ablative laser resurfacing.

This off-label use of these lasers revolves around their ability to stimulate fibroblasts, which produce collagen fibers. If you plan to try this procedure, you will need at least three sessions before you and your doctor can determine if it has been effective.

The XTRAC Laser

The XTRAC laser helps restore skin color. In fact, it's FDA approved to treat vitiligo. For stretch marks that are merely areas of white coloration, repigmentation may be possible with this laser, which was originally developed to treat psoriasis.

PREGNANT PAUSE

It's estimated that among Caucasians, nine out of ten pregnant women will develop stretch marks. (Women of color tend to fare better but are still at risk.) That's a huge number!

During pregnancy, glucocorticoids circulate in high concentrations. While they are the major culprit, it is thought that other hormones, such as estrogen, may also play a role.

As always, genetics is at work, helping to determine whether you'll be in that lucky 10 percent who don't get stretch marks, and also how severe they'll be. If your mother has really bad stretch marks, odds are that you will too.

Stretch marks formed during pregnancy can improve without intervention, but they never seem to fully go away.

The next time you go to a baby shower, consider taking a tube of Mederma or a bottle of Cellex-C or SkinCeutical serum. The mother-to-be will welcome the opportunity to do something constructive for her rapidly changing form. And rest assured: Mederma, Cellex-C High Potency Serum, and M.D. Forté Hand & Body Cream are all safe to use while pregnant or nursing.

An Herb You Should Avoid

In the mid-1990s, a study by G. L. Yang and D. Jewell was published titled "Creams for Preventing Stretch Marks in Pregnancy." In it, doctors looked at one hundred women who had been pregnant at least once, had developed stretch marks, and were pregnant again. Some of the women used a cream composed of the herb gotu kola (*Centella asiatica*), combined with vitamin E (alpha-tocopherol) and collagen-elastin hydrolysates. Others received an inert look-alike cream (a placebo). The group of women getting the cream with active ingredients had a 59 percent lower incidence of developing stretch marks.

As you can imagine, I was pretty excited about this study—until I did some of my own research on gotu kola. It turns out that when taken as a supplement it has a narcoticlike effect—and can cause a miscarriage! Obviously, it should not be used if you are pregnant or nursing. In addition, it is known to cause increased sun sensitivity or a rash when applied topically.

I would be incredibly hesitant to advise a pregnant woman to apply any cream with an ingredient known to be dangerous if taken orally. Currently, we go to great lengths to discourage the use of topical vitamins A and K for pregnant woman. I would add gotu kola to that list.

For you ingredient readers, other names for gotu kola include *Hydrocotyle asiatica*, Indian pennywort, Indian water navelwort, and marsh penny.

GROWING, GROWING, GROWING, GONE!

Approximately 35 percent of girls and 15 percent of boys develop stretch marks during puberty. The cause of these stretch marks is an increase in blood levels of the glucocorticoid 17-ketosteroids. You can't do anything to stop that, of course, but you can be aware of the problem and help your teenagers plan ahead.

It's likely your teen isn't going to talk to you about her (or his) concerns; a teen is usually far too self-conscious about her body to talk to a parent, let alone request help. So you need to bring up the subject. Ask her if she is seeing red or white streaks on her skin. She probably has no idea what is happening and will be thrilled to try anything to clear it up.

I think if parents were better educated about stretch marks, teens could treat their stretch marks early on and prevent much of the aftermath coursing across their skin.

I suggest taking the pregnancy approach: prevention with topical vitamin C serums like Cellex-C High Potency Serum. Or begin applying Mederma as soon as the stretch marks start to form.

As with all white stretch marks, if yours are from a growth spurt long gone, you need to handle them exactly as detailed above in the section "White Out."

FINAL THOUGHTS

It's no longer a stretch of the imagination to think you can ameliorate the look of your stretch marks. Be thankful that researchers are constantly finding new options to help improve the appearance of those "badges of life" we wear upon our skin.

Ask the DERMAdoctor

QUESTION:

I have stretch marks on my legs and want to cover them up. What should I apply?

The DERMAdoctor:

Any kind of waterproof makeup will work for the leg area. If your stretch marks are fairly new and still have color, you may wish to use a concealer like Covermark.

QUESTION:

I would like to know why my stretch marks itch sometimes. I have heard that it's because I'm either gaining weight or losing weight. Is that true?

The DERMAdoctor:

Science hasn't figured out why stretch marks tend to itch, but it is certainly a reality. A topical anesthetic like PrameGel or Prax Lotion may help control the intermittent itching.

SUN ALLERGY

When Ultraviolet Is Ultra-Itchy

You might think you're allergic to the sun. Why else would the parts of your body exposed to the sun break out in a rash every spring, when sunlight starts to become more intense?

Well, most so-called cases of sun allergy really *aren't* a true allergy, in which the immune system reacts to an allergen, like pollen. Rather, they are a *hypersensitivity* to the sun, called polymorphous light eruption (PMLE).

This condition is most commonly seen in parts of the world that have four seasons, and it's most commonly triggered by springtime sun exposure. The rash forms only on parts of the body exposed to the sun, usually one to four days after exposure. The sensitivity of the skin and the severity of the rash gradually lessen as spring changes into summer and the skin becomes adjusted to ultraviolet rays.

There is nothing specific about the rash caused by PMLE. Red blotches appear that may be raised, bumpy, or hivelike.

Polymorphous light eruption equally affects women and men, adults and children. Typically, it begins between the ages of twenty and thirty-five. (Native Americans have a high rate of PMLE, and there is some evidence of a genetic predisposition.)

An Accurate Diagnosis

Because the rash is so nonspecific, a very important diagnostic feature is that its presence is limited to areas exposed to the sun. And it spares areas out of reach of sunlight, like skin folds, the jawline, and below the chin.

Ruling Out Autoimmune Disease

A rash triggered by sunlight is not a guarantee that you have polymorphous light eruption. Patients with autoimmune diseases (lupus, rheumatoid arthritis, and many others) often have a heightened sensitivity to the sun. When I work up a sun-induced rash, I always rule out the possibility of an autoimmune disease masquerading as PMLE.

A simple blood test called an ANA (antinuclear antibody test) helps determine the true diagnosis. A positive ANA does not always indicate autoimmune disease, however; many healthy people test positive. A true positive result has a significantly elevated level of ANA and has the proper "pattern" of ANA, as recognized by the lab.

A Skin Biopsy

The patient who doesn't improve as the summer progresses may want to pursue a more in-depth workup. A skin biopsy might be in order to confirm the diagnosis of PMLE. What else might be going on? Perhaps the ANA was normal but an autoimmune disease is nonetheless present. Perhaps it's another skin disorder mimicking PMLE. It's time to find out.

If your sun-induced rash doesn't get better as spring changes to summer, ask your doctor about a skin biopsy. Make certain that the doctor also intends to order a second test on the tissue, called a DIF (direct immunofluorescence). This is an essential test whenever an autoimmune disease is even remotely considered in the diagnosis. For this test, the dermatologist must have a special fixative on hand at the time of biopsy. Don't presume it will be there—it's better to ask.

Light Testing

In difficult-to-diagnose cases, light testing provides a useful option. An area of unaffected skin is exposed to a medical ultraviolet B light. Approximately three out of four people with PMLE will respond to the light exposures with a rash.

TREATING PMLE

Itching is the main symptom that people with PMLE complain about.

Oral antihistamines like over-the-counter Benadryl or prescription Atarax (hydroxyzine) can effectively control the itching. Other over-the-counter remedies for soothing discomfort include anti-itch preparations like Sarnol-HC 1%, PrameGel, L.M.X. 4 cream, and Aveeno Oatmeal Anti-Itch Concentrated Lotion.

Topical steroid creams also help reduce itching and can hasten resolution of the rash. Prescription-strength cortisone creams are more potent and effective. However, Cortaid, a nonprescription 1% hydrocortisone cream, is a useful home treatment, particularly when PMLE strikes you unprepared.

Unresponsive, prolonged, or severe forms of PMLE may require Plaquenil (hydroxychloroquine) or Atabrine (quinacrine). These medications, used in the prevention and treatment of malaria, have also been used with great success in PMLE. For some, the medication may be used on a limited basis, like during a vacation in a sunny clime. For others, it may be a year-round necessity.

The use of medical-grade ultraviolet light provides another treatment option. Called "hardening," this form of desensitizing light exposure helps patients who are very sensitive to seasonal fluctuations in sunlight stay comfortable. Risks associated with UV light exposure (skin cancer, premature skin aging, and cataracts) make it vital to precisely control exposure and monitor for future problems. In other words, it's not a treatment you should try on your own at the local tanning salon.

SUN PROTECTION

Sun protection is important for everybody—but it's uniquely important for those with chronic PMLE.

Use a sunblock that has both UVA and UVB blockers with a high SPF. Total Block Clear SPF 65 and Total Block Cover-Up/Makeup SPF 60 are great products that completely block both UVA and UVB, as well as infrared and visible light rays.

Treat clothing with Rit Sun Guard Laundry Treatment UV Protectant. Add it to your washing machine along with the detergent. It boosts the ultraviolet protection factor (UPF) of normal cloth from 4 to 30!

A wide-brimmed hat is also a smart choice.

FINAL THOUGHTS

Should you find yourself with an odd little "sun allergy" you simply can't explain, consider the possibility of PMLE.

Ask the DERMAdoctor

QUESTION:

The rashes that I get on my body when exposed to the sun are just as you describe, only they appear within ten to fifteen minutes after I'm exposed, rather than after twenty-four hours. Do I have PMLE, or is it something else?

The DERMAdoctor:

Although it's unusual, you can most definitely develop PMLE within only fifteen minutes of sun exposure. You should also see a dermatologist to have a workup that rules out an autoimmune disease or other photosensitive disorders.

SWEATING PROBLEMS

No-Sweat Solutions

Anxiety can make you sweat. But sweating can also make you anxious.

Hyperhidrosis, or excessive sweating, is a condition that causes significant anxiety for those who suffer from it. Sweat glands on the palms, soles, underarms, and forehead are most commonly involved. Social interactions and first impressions can be adversely affected by extreme perspiration.

While hyperhidrosis can be the result of genetics, problems including neurological conditions (multiple sclerosis, paralysis, stroke) and head trauma can also cause excessive sweating. I had a patient involved in a car accident who sustained a head injury and, as a result, developed hyperhidrosis. Frostbite causes damage to nerve endings within the dermis and can also lead to hyperhidrosis.

DRYING OUT

Treatment often begins with drying agents. The ingredient traditionally used in antiperspirant deodorants, aluminum chloride, is incorporated into prescription medications like Xerac AC (contains 6%) and Drysol (contains 20%, for recalcitrant conditions). These are applied to the offending areas at night, three to four nights in a row, until excess perspiration is controlled.

It is crucial that treatment sites be very dry before applying the product. The aluminum chloride needs to be reapplied as needed to control perspiration. Typically this is once to twice a week.

FINDING A SKIN-FRIENDLY ANTIPERSPIRANT (AND SOLVING UNDERARM DISCOLORATION)

Delicate underarm skin is almost set up to experience a bad reaction to many antiperspirant products. Three major complicating factors involve the architecture of the underarm area. First, the epidermis is thinner in this region, making it vulnerable to a host of contact allergens. Second, the underarm area is warm and moist, the ideal site for bacteria and yeast to thrive, which complicates the control of body odor. Finally, this area is under occlusion, meaning that skin lies upon skin, driving any product or treatment deeper into the epidermis and making seemingly mild treatments more potent and potentially more irritating.

Who's at risk for developing a reaction to an antiperspirant? Anyone who is prone to eczema; has sensitive-skin concerns; suffers from razor burn, regional friction, acanthosis nigricans, or diabetes; has a contact, fragrance, or dye allergy; or has a history of irritation caused by aluminum chloride.

THE NEWEST-GENERATION INGREDIENT

Traditionally, aluminum chloride and aluminum chlorohydrate have been the active ingredients du jour in antiperspirants. However, aluminum in these forms can be irritating to the skin, cause acne, and aggravate razor burn.

Years of complaints from consumers and patients about the lack of acceptable options inspired me to develop DERMAdoctor Total Non-Scents Ultra-Gentle Antiperspirant, my solution for the thousands of consumers searching for a truly skin-friendly antiperspirant.

It contains the newest-generation ingredient, aluminum zirconium tetrachlorohydrex glycine, which is much more effective at controlling perspiration and far less likely to cause irritation or acne.

The number of other ingredients in Total NonScents is small, thereby limiting exposure to potential irritants. It is free of fragrances and dyes, is in an aqueous base (unlikely to parch or inflame delicate skin), and doesn't leave an unsightly white residue.

Naturally, it has been thoroughly tested by dermatologists and for allergens to ensure that it is suitable for even the most sensitive patients.

SOLVING UNDERARM DISCOLORATION

But what about all of those patients who've already experienced irritation and inflammation due to aggravating deodorant or antiperspirant choices and ongoing skin concerns? Irritation and inflammation routinely yield undesirable dark skin discoloration. And the odds that you'll develop discoloration go up the darker one's baseline skin tone and the more prolonged the condition.

Anybody suffering with unsightly underarm darkness usually avoids wearing clothing that exposes the area, so it's unlikely that the condition is commonly seen in public. Embarrassment prevents discussion about this problem. But underarm discoloration, the aftermath of poor product selection and/or ongoing skin concern, is incredibly common.

Most prescription options for bleaching hyperpigmented skin are more irritating when used in the underarm area, making the discoloration worse. And they don't address what to do about an antiperspirant. So I chose to blend my Total NonScents antiperspirant with something to help brighten discolored skin.

Kojic dipalmitate is a powerful known botanical skin brightener. Unlike traditional kojic acid, kojic dipalmitate remains stable and effective in an aqueous (water) base.

DERMAdoctor Total NonScents Ultra-Gentle Brightening Antiperspirant addresses, improves, and helps eliminate embarrassing underarm discoloration. It's a unique concept for solving this dilemma.

Powders

Moisture trapped in hot dark areas, like under skin folds and between toes, creates an ideal environment for yeast and fungi to flourish, a condition known as intertrigo.

Absorbent powders like Zeasorb powder (three times more absorbent than regular talcum powder) help reduce this moisture. Zeasorb is also available with an antifungal agent, as Zeasorb-AF.

Air and Astringents

Simple air drying (try a handheld dryer set on "cool") reduces the moisture buildup in the skin that can otherwise leave skin soft, peeling, and white.

Local over-the-counter astringents, like Burow's solution, or products with potassium permanganate, like Colorless Castellani's Paint, can do the same.

Oral Medications

When topical treatments aren't enough, oral prescription anticholinergic medications are tried; these drugs diminish the activity of acetylcholine, a chemical that helps regulate the nervous system. Pro-Banthine (probantheline bromide) is the medication of choice. As with all drugs in this category, potential side effects include dry mouth and possibly blurred vision.

Antisweat Machine

Although I have never had a patient who required one, there are portable "iontophoresis" machines that can help with hyperhidrosis. Electrical current is used to diminish the productivity of the sweat glands. One of the best-known devices is called the Drionic unit.

Surgery

A more radical approach to this problem is surgical removal of the nerves supplying overactive eccrine sweat glands, a procedure known as sympathectomy. This has been used with variable levels of success for the worst cases.

Botox

Botox is an exciting option for controlling excess sweating. Tiny injections randomly placed into the affected area can shut down the problem for up to six months at a time.

A large number of units of Botox are required to achieve dryness, making this a rather costly procedure. Yet for someone looking to avoid daily therapy or messy options or who has been resistant to all other forms of treatment, Botox is well worth the price.

FINAL THOUGHTS

Remember, there's simply no reason to sweat about sweating. There are now more highly effective treatment options than ever. Ask your dermatologist about which therapy is ideal for you.

Ask the DERMAdoctor

QUESTION:

I have severe eczema and can't use regular creams because I also have severe hyperhidrosis in the same area. What do you recommend?

The DERMAdoctor:

When your doctor is prescribing a topical steroid, make sure you request a trial of the gel formulation. Clobetasol gel is the strongest prescription topical steroid on the market and, depending on the area being treated, may be a worthwhile option to try.

Should you require a moisturizer, consider giving M.D. Forté Advanced Hydrating Complex-Gel Formula a try. It is very hydrating without being heavy and occlusive. In fact, it is something I routinely suggest for my oily, acne-prone patients.

And, of course, you need to get your hyperhidrosis under control. You are going to be walking a fine line between drying out the excessive sweating and making certain you do not overdry your eczema. This is a situation where Botox may be beneficial.

TINEA VERSICOLOR

Coming This Spring . . . TV

Perplexed by the sudden appearance of spots each spring or summer? Perhaps it's tinea versicolor (TV).

Malassezia furfur, a yeast that grows on everyone's skin, is responsible for causing the characteristic, noncontagious rash of TV. The rash is composed of an odd assortment of flat, scaling patches, which polka-dot the upper torso, shoulders, neckline, and sometimes the lower face. Edges of the dime-sized patches may coalesce, merging into larger patches.

Sunlight makes the rash far more noticeable, explaining why so many TV patients seek out the dermatologist each summer. The phenomenon is similar to having a bad tan line, or having had a Band-Aid on your skin, so the sun darkened everywhere but where the Band-Aid sat. TV produces the same effect, creating lighter patches. Additionally, *M. furfur* can produce a mild acid, exaggerating the lightening effect.

TV DINNER

The yeast doesn't always cause a rash; if it did, we'd all walk around spotted. But when *M. furfur* flourishes and reaches a critical mass, it becomes visible to the naked eye. Why does it multiply?

One leading theory is that certain individuals have a higher level of fatty acids exists in their sebum or sweat. This nourishes the yeast, triggering more growth.

DIAGNOSING THE PROBLEM

Diagnosis is usually obvious to the trained eye of the dermatologist. However, if there's any doubt, the doctor can perform a test called a KOH.

The doctor does a light, painless skin scraping with a small blade. The scales are placed on a glass slide with a droplet of liquid (potassium hydroxide) and then examined under the microscope. A positive test shows what we dermatologists fondly call the "spaghetti and meatballs" sign under the microscope; the yeast's hyphae (stringy, cellular filaments) and spores (seeds) provide that appearance.

TREATING TINEA VERSICOLOR

Treatment is aimed at constant control of the condition. If it's not controlled, it's likely to come back. Ease of treatment is a must, as well as trying to keep it aesthetically pleasing.

My Favorite Routine

The two-week routine I recommend to my patients consists of the following:

- Wash in the shower with a therapeutic cleanser, like ZNP Bar soap (2% zinc pyrithione) or DERMAdoctor Born to Be Mild Medicated Cleanser. Do this daily for two weeks.
- Towel dry.
- Choose one of these antifungal creams: DERMAdoctor Feet Accompli or Lamisil AT cream for athlete's foot (or use the spray formulation, Lamisil AT athlete's foot spray). Apply it to the upper torso, arms, and neck. Treat your face, too, if it is also involved, avoiding the eyes. Don't worry about trying to polka-dot the rash— apply the cream to the entire affected area.
- Once a week, on a maintenance basis, wash with your medicated cleanser. This keeps the yeast under control.
- Repeat this two-week cycle any time you note a recurrence and before exposing skin to the sun in early spring or prior to a tropical vacation.

Dealing with Discoloration

Once the two-week cycle is complete, the yeast is gone—but it's likely the rash isn't. What is left is residual skin discoloration. Just as with a bad tan line, it takes time for the skin tone to even out.

Avoiding sunlight helps speed the process of achieving a more even complexion. Sunscreen, therefore, is important. Because *M. furfur* feed on skin oils and sweat, I favor an oil-reducing sunscreen, like DERMAdoctor Body Guard Exquisitely Light SPF 30.

Restoring an even skin tone may take six months or more, depending on how uneven the problem was initially. This is the perfect reason to follow through with your maintenance preventive therapy. You don't really want to continually play catch-up with skin discoloration, do you?

Nizoral Tablets

Some dermatologists will prescribe an oral medication, Nizoral tablets, for the treatment of tinea versicolor. This is given as a one-time dose. However, these pills do have a rare, unpredictable side effect of liver failure. This therapy also doesn't address the issue of maintenance. For these reasons, I personally don't prescribe this therapy for tinea versicolor.

FINAL THOUGHTS

Tune in to what's happening with your skin and "turn off" TV. This is one program you can follow on your own.

Ask the DERMAdoctor

QUESTION:

I just moved to Atlanta and my tinea versicolor, which I've had all my life, is definitely worse. Does the move have anything to do with this?

The DERMAdoctor:

Tinea versicolor is unquestionably more common in a hot, humid climate. While only 10 to 15 percent of the population in the northern United States experiences TV, 50 percent of those living in the South may develop this condition. Figures run even higher (75 to 85 percent) for those who live in the tropics.

No one expects you to contemplate moving because you're developed tinea versicolor. But there are things you can do to reduce recurrences. First, try following the TV treatment cycle I recommend in this chapter. Next, reduce the humidity in your environment. Consider adding a dehumidifier to your home. Keep cool—turn on your air-conditioning.

And prevent yeast from getting what they want: nourishment. Reduce oily skin by applying an oil-absorbing treatment or wearing an oil-reducing sunscreen.

WARTS

HPV, Begone

You won't turn that toad into a prince by kissing it—but you won't get warts either! In spite of the classic misconception that lays blame upon the lowly toad, warts are a viral infection that afflicts strictly us humans.

Warts result when the human papillomavirus (HPV) infects the skin, causing unsightly, sometimes painful growths. These can be flat or raised and hard, soft, or crusty. (When most people think of warts, they think of the variety that are hard and crusty.) Most warts will be raised, especially as they age.

Warts do not have "seeds," as many people think. The "seeds" are blood vessels; you see them as seedlike flecks because you're looking at the wart head-on, as if you were looking at the open end of a pipe. They're black because of small clots within the blood vessel.

Nor do warts have roots, another common misconception. They never grow deeper than the thickness of the epidermis.

WHY AM I WART-PRONE?

Why do warts infect only certain individuals? I think a major reason is that some people's immune systems don't recognize the existence of the wart on the surface of the skin. That doesn't mean if you're wart-prone you have a major immune deficiency; it simply means that you have a genetic predisposition to warts. Think of people who always have sinus infections or strep throat or fungal infections; it's the same type of thing.

People with atopic dermatitis and red-haired individuals seem to be predisposed to chronic reinfection with warts.

Pregnant women have reduced immunity. They tend to pick up warts more easily and have a more difficult time getting rid of them.

DIFFERENT TYPES OF WARTS

Technically, warts are categorized by families. There are groups of warts within each family, but this is a highly technical distinction that doesn't make any difference unless you're conducting scientific research. Here are a few of the different types of warts.

Plantar Warts

Everyone has heard of plantar warts. They get their name from their location: they are on the plantar (bottom) surface of the foot. They seem deeper than other warts, but that's only because the skin on the bottom of the foot is thicker.

Periungual Warts

Periungual warts affect the skin surrounding the nail. The wart can get under the skin fold or even the nail plate, and sometimes the nail becomes deformed. And they can cause further complications. I have seen several patients who developed yeast or fungal infections of the involved nail because of breaks in the nail created by the wart's growth. If caught early enough, before damage occurs to the nail fold (where the nail is made), periungual warts usually resolve with time. However, they can be terribly difficult to get rid of and often require prolonged treatment.

Flat Warts

Flat warts are tiny, smooth warts, often only two or three millimeters in diameter. Many women are familiar with them on areas that get shaved, like the legs. (Shaving through a wart easily spreads the virus, sowing it into every microscopic nick.)

I like treating these very gently, with liquid nitrogen. But in stubborn or widespread cases I have found that topical Retin-A solution or a chemotherapy cream called Efudex (neither are recommended for children or pregnant women) can help.

Retin-A and similar topical vitamin A derivatives should be applied once a day. Efudex may be applied once or twice daily, depending on what your doctor thinks is appropriate.

Whatever treatment you use, make certain to keep it away from your eyes. (Do *not* apply any of these treatments to warts on the eyelids.) And pay attention to what your skin is telling you. If too much irritation develops or you see sores, back off or stop use altogether.

Mollusca

Mollusca, also known as soft warts, are highly contagious. They are very common in children and often spread to adults. (If a family member has mollusca, don't share towels; this is a great way to spread the warts throughout the household.) Mollusca are flesh colored or almost clear and often have a central depression, like a belly button. Growths are usually small, at just a millimeter or two.

There are several ways to treat these warts, from liquid nitrogen to physical removal with curettage, a simple and relatively painless (I didn't say pain-free) method. The doctor uses an instrument that resembles a bobby pin and literally pops the warts out of the skin. Mollusca are self-contained, so they basically come off in one piece, as if they were scooped out of a shell. They may ooze, and Drysol is often applied to the base to help stop the small amount of bleeding.

In cases where children won't cooperate with curettage, the doctor can apply a medication like podophyllin to kill the wart. Over-the-counter salicyclic acid–based wart medications don't get rid of mollusca.

You will probably continue to see new molluscum for up to six months after the initial treatment; it takes that long for invisibly infected skin cells to form new warts. Keep up with new growths a few at a time. (Children find this much easier and less traumatizing.)

WART, WART, GO AWAY . . .

There are hundreds of old wives' tales about eradicating warts. One of my favorites: rub the wart with a piece of raw potato and then bury the spud at night under a full moon on the east side of the house. An entertaining idea—but it's never gotten rid of a wart!

In fact, warts are contagious and should be treated *seriously* before you develop further lesions. One of my pet peeves is the patient who presents with twenty, thirty, forty, or more warts because a friend or health professional told them that treatment was unnecessary. ("Warts go away on their own, you know.") Although this occasionally may be true, it's far more likely that they will increase in number.

If you want serious treatment, consider these facts.

Physical or Chemical Destruction

For the most part, the treatment of warts still involves physical or chemical destruction. There are no topical antiviral agents that can kill the wart on contact, nor are there oral antiviral drugs for warts that are the equivalent of antibiotics for bacteria.

Liquid Nitrogen

Liquid nitrogen sprayed onto the wart (or applied with a cotton swab) is still one of the most effective and easiest wart therapies. It usually takes three treatments to kill the average wart. Huge warts could take much longer. I usually do a treatment every two weeks. This allows the treated area to heal for the next round. An area treated with liquid nitrogen is usually pink and puffy for a day or so, and the discomfort is typically minimal. However, liquid nitrogen can cause a blister, a blood blister, or a superficial sore, as it is basically controlled frostbite.

Compound W Freeze Off Wart Removal System is a home-version cryotherapy spray for the treatment of warts. Follow the directions carefully. The goal is success, not a cold-induced injury.

Over-the-Counter Medication Helps

Often, I have patients use an over-the-counter wart medication (on a nonblistered site) at home in conjunction with liquid nitrogen therapy; this helps exfoliate much of the infected tissue. My favorites contain 17% salicylic acid as the active ingredient, like Occlusal-HP and Duofilm. Usually two coats of the medication are applied to the treated area. As treatment goes on, the wart will become soft, white, and moist.

To help kids comply with therapy, there are topical wart medications imbedded into brightly colored plastic bandages, like Dr. Scholl's Clear Away 1 Step for Kids.

To maximize the effectiveness of over-the-counter antiwart medications, make sure the area is moist; then lightly rough up the surface with a pumice stone (like Tweezerman Eco Stone), an emery board, or even a piece of fine-grade sandpaper. Caution: the viral particles will remain on the roughening object, so don't use it elsewhere. Better still: use a metal buffer like Diamancel Callus Rasp and disinfect it after use with rubbing alcohol. But regardless of which instrument you select, you're just roughing up the surface to enhance absorption of the medication; you're not trying to rub off the wart.

A final caution about over-the-counter treatments: they're not for use on the face or by diabetics, except with a doctor's recommendation and supervision.

Methods Other Than Liquid Nitrogen

Physical destruction with methods other than liquid nitrogen, like electrodesiccation and curettage (ED&C) or carbon dioxide laser, have also been used.

Statistics show that ED&C for wart removal is about as effective as liquid nitrogen. However, it tends to be a somewhat messy procedure, with more discomfort and healing time involved, so I hold off on this therapy if possible.

There's no question that destruction by carbon dioxide laser, which simply evaporates the wart tissue, or by Tunable Dye Laser, which kills the blood vessels that feed the wart, are effective. But they can also cost more than other treatments.

Periodically, I use Bleomycin, an injectable chemotherapy agent, for troublesome, recalcitrant warts. Bleomycin kills the blood vessels that support the wart's growth, and the lesion turns black within a day or two. This therapy is not appropriate for warts on the fingers or toes; it may cause diminished blood flow to these areas. Also, the injections can be rather painful (with more than one treatment usually required), and it's a costly therapy.

A method not approved by the FDA but long recognized as effective at treating recalcitrant warts (and other dermatologic conditions) is topical application of a liquid called DNCB, which always causes contact dermatitis (an allergic reaction). The theory is that if you stimulate the body to recognize the DNCB, by first applying it to the forearm, and later apply it to a recalcitrant wart, the body will destroy the treated area, wart and all. This has proven to be a reliable method when all else fails.

Oral Medications

Oral medications have long been rumored to help fight warts. I have tried stimulating patients' immune systems with oral vitamin C and vitamin A. To be honest, I have not been impressed with this treatment.

An ulcer medication, Tagamet, in combination with another medication known as levamisole, seems to have an effect on some warts. An article in the *Australian Journal of Dermatology* reports more than a 70 percent reduction in the size or number or both of warts with this therapy. I would reserve this therapy for that occasional impossible-to-treat wart.

FINAL THOUGHTS

It's much better to be proactive and prevent infection in the first place! Public areas like pools and locker rooms are common places to pick up warts. Protect your feet by wearing sandals or other footwear.

Don't wait for lots of warts to develop or for your wart to be the size of a quarter before you seek medical attention. This will only make your treatment more difficult.

By all means, if you know you have a "regular" wart, go ahead and start treating it with an over-the-counter wart medication like Occlusal-HP while you're waiting to see the dermatologist.

Ask the DERMAdoctor

QUESTION:

I have been applying Occlusal-HP for about seven weeks, according to the instructions. How do I know when to cease application of the product? I can't tell if I am treating the wart or burning the skin where the wart was previously located.

The DERMAdoctor:

You can use Occlusal-HP for up to twelve weeks. If your wart(s) are not reduced or gone by that point, you may want to make an appointment with your dermatologist. I think that using a product like Occlusal-HP is a great start for helping with warts, particularly while waiting to get in to see a dermatologist, but I also think that most warts, particularly when more than one are present, respond more rapidly to having liquid nitrogen treatments in addition to using the at-home product. Caution: do not overuse any home-wart treatment to the point where a deep sore forms in place of the wart! Salicylic acid is more potent than most people realize, so one needs to be observant and careful.

PART II

BEAUTIFUL SKIN
IS ALWAYS IN

AGING AND YOUR SKIN

The Anatomy of a Wrinkle: Cause and Repair

Now more than ever, attitudes about aging are being redefined—literally, right before our eyes. Baby boomers know there is a possibility for a healthier, longer life span and want to look the part. But a youthful appearance isn't only about the surface of the skin. Time and sun damage take their toll on each layer of the skin and its supportive tissues. To meet our expectations of ongoing youthfulness, rejuvenation must take into account *all* of our skin, outermost to inmost.

THE FOUR ZONES OF AGING
With the passing years, changes occur simultaneously in four vastly different "aging zones."

The Epidermis
Dryness, dullness, blotchiness, and fine lines are the definitive aging concerns occurring in this outermost layer.

By age thirty, the skin is becoming drier, as less sebum is produced. This escalates at menopause. Dryness may also be the source of increased skin sensitivity during this time.

The pigment-producing cells called melanocytes live in the basement layer of the epidermis. It is here that our skin color is produced. Over the years, the cumulative effects of the sun cause the melanocytes to become more active. The resulting overproduction of melanin leads to blotchy discoloration and those large freckles (lentigos) that frequently appear as we age.

Closer to the surface, the corneocytes (superficial epidermal cells) accumulate and the epidermis thickens. The final result: a dull, sallow, lifeless complex.

An Anatomical Prescription:

- Skin bleaching, as necessary
- Fine-line therapy (AHAs, BHA, retinoids)
- Restoration of the protective ceramide barrier (humectants, free fatty acids)
- Exfoliation
- Chemical peels
- Microdermabrasion

Sunscreen use and a change to a more hydrating, calming moisturizer are daily essentials.

The Dermis

Below the epidermis, the dermis is a busy place. There are tiny veins called capillaries, which bring blood flow to the skin. There are sweat glands, hair bulbs, and nerve endings. And, of course, there are collagen and elastin fibers, which give strength and support to skin. Like the epidermis, the dermis undergoes major changes related to the aging process. After the age of forty, 1 percent of the skin's collagen is lost each year.

Collagen and elastin fibers begin to break down, leading to sagging or "crepiness" of the skin. (Envision a chain-link fence—with the links coming apart.) Compounding this, the collagen- and elastin-producing cells called fibroblasts become far less active and reduced in number. Your skin can't make the amount of collagen fibers necessary to maintain your skin's status quo, let alone repair damage.

Sunlight also takes its toll on the dermis, damaging cellular DNA. This can lead to an increased formation of blood vessels, like spider veins on the face; to the skin becoming more fragile and easily bruised; to thinning of the GAGs (glycosaminoglycans), the dermal milieu that surrounds the cells, blood vessels, etc.; and to thinning of the extracellular cement, which holds cells together.

Certain age-related freckles are caused by melanin deposited into the dermis, similar to what is seen with some birthmarks. That is why the bleaching process can be so difficult (or even impossible) for some women.

An Anatomical Prescription:

- Antioxidants, to neutralize skin-damaging free radicals, stimulate fibroblast activity, and help maintain and rebuild the dermis and the extracellular cement
- Nonablative lasers, to help stimulate collagen production
- Fillers (topical and injectable), for deep lower-facial lines and lips
- Peptide therapy to stimulate production of collagen
- Thermage, to contract and tighten collagen fibers

Topical vitamin A derivatives, like Renova, Retin-A, or their cousins the retinols, also have some of these fiber-stimulating properties, in addition to their exfoliating effects.

The Fat Layer

Below the dermal layer is a layer of fat. As we age, the fatty layer on the backs of the hands, the neck, and the face becomes noticeably thinner. (We tend to add some weight with aging—but never where we want it!) The results: more noticeable blood vessels on the backs of the hands; dark circles exacerbated by loss of the fat-pads beneath the eyes; and overall thinning of the skin, allowing for increased fragility.

Fat will accumulate, however, along the jowls, creating the wattle (double chin) and heavy-looking, sagging lower cheeks.

An Anatomical Prescription:

- Fat transplants
- Filler agents (injectable and implantable)
- Liposuction of double chin

The Muscle Layer

Below the fat lies muscle. Deeply grooved wrinkle lines on the face are caused by the buildup of facial muscles through overuse, typically smiling and frowning. Chronic puckering from smoking can cause deep lines to form around the mouth. But even a nonsmoking lifetime of puckering can eventually form these deep, crevice-like lines, particularly if there has been quite a bit of additional sun damage.

An Anatomical Prescription:

- Botox
- Topical line relaxers (also known as TLRs or TMRs)
- Laparoscopic brow lift
- Filler agents, for vertical lip lines
- Feather lift

FINAL THOUGHTS

Understand what you are treating and what you are trying to accomplish. By doing this, you can match the therapy to the underlying problem. Don't let someone tell you that there is a single fix-it-all solution that tackles every mature skin issue. There isn't. Targeted treatment takes education and the ability to read between the lines. Otherwise, continuous bombardment by overhyped products may leave you with just a bottle of dreams.

Ask the DERMAdoctor

QUESTION:

I am twenty-five years old and don't have any wrinkles, but I am interested in what I could use to help prevent future wrinkles, besides just using sunscreen.

The DERMAdoctor:

That's a great question. Too many times women wait until they have really advanced skin changes before they think to do something about them. And it is much tougher to try to reverse these changes than to try to do something preventative. A woman's twenty-first birthday is the perfect time for her to start a rejuvenation and preservation regimen for her skin.

However, it's ideal to implement an amino acid peptide treatment with an every-other-night retinoid. Procedures really don't have much of a role, unless perhaps you have already formed some blotchy skin discoloration (melasma) and want to consider a series of microdermabrasions or chemical peels to round out your therapy.

Needless to say, continued sun avoidance—by wearing a broad-spectrum, high-SPF sunscreen and a wide-brimmed hat—will go a long way in helping slow down those skin changes associated with aging.

COSMETIC DERMATOLOGY

Make an Appointment with Beauty

Ultimately, you may have to come to terms with the fact that your favorite products just can't resolve those newly formed deep frown lines between your brows. Or perhaps you just noticed a crease the depth of a small canyon developing alongside your mouth.

I am a big fan of the nonsurgical approaches to skin rejuvenation covered in this chapter: quick-fix skin treatments, Botox, chemical peels, microdermabrasion, and injectable fillers. These procedures are easy to undergo, highly effective, and work synergistically with your skin care regimen. And they are just a phone call to your dermatologist away.

BOTOX: STRONG MEDICINE FOR DEEP LINES

Remember when your mother told you to get that look off your face or it would freeze in that position? She wasn't wrong—she was just ahead of her time.

Over the past thirty years or more, each and every time you smiled, frowned, or raised your brows in surprise, you were building those muscles of facial expression, just as if you were building a biceps from lifting weights. If you overwork a biceps, it becomes bulky and inflexible. In much the same way, decades of everyday emoting "overwork" the muscles of facial expression until they thicken, leaving deeply grooved wrinkle lines.

These aren't the fine little wrinkle lines that respond to topical skin rejuvenation products. These are industrial-strength lines. And that's where a potent medicine like Botox comes into play. Botox provides a long-term improvement by paralyzing the muscles, literally smoothing out deep wrinkles, lines, and creases.

Zoned for Wrinkle Reduction

There are three zones of facial expression most commonly treated with Botox: 1) crow's-feet (both eyes form a single zone); 2) deep frown lines between the eyes (in the glabella); and 3) lines across the forehead.

There is another zone that I prefer *not* to treat with Botox: around the mouth. Remember, Botox paralyzes muscles. That's great if you don't want frown lines. It's not so great if the doctor treats deep lines around the mouth and you suddenly find that you're drooling or can't smile. Yes, some doctors will inject these so-called smoker's lines. But before you undergo that procedure, I urge you to verify that only an infinitesimal amount of Botox will be used—less than 1 unit per 0.1 ml of Botox per injection site.

Doctors are also experimenting with yet another zone: the muscular bands that run the length of the neck (*platysma*). This area can really show your age. But your doctor could do some serious damage using Botox to correct the problem: an injection that's too deep or a dosage that's too high could result in difficulty swallowing or breathing. Just as with the area around your mouth, ask your doctor to approach the muscles of your neck with extreme caution.

The Lunchtime Face-lift

The treatment itself is a simple, quick series of injections with a tiny needle into the unwanted wrinkles. Most doctors charge by the zone, with costs for injections usually running about $400 per zone.

First, your doctor will ask you to make the undesirable expression. (Strange as it seems, you may find yourself having to force a smile in order to say good-bye to crow's-feet!) Then it's time for the wrinkle-banishing jabs.

Extra Care, Before and After

Let's face it: nobody likes shots—even when they're for the sake of beauty. To minimize the pain, I find that it helps to apply an ice pack for one or two minutes to the zone about to be injected. An ice pack can also help reduce possible postinjection swelling and bruising.

Afterward, to help minimize the appearance of any slight redness at the site of each injection, I apply a dusting of green powder to neutralize redness. To camouflage any immediate bruising, I apply DERMAdoctor Eye Spy Concealer and Treatment (which has a yellow tint, neutralizing purple).

After your Botox injections you can return to your normal routine. However, it is crucial that you keep your head upright for the next four hours. This prevents the Botox from spreading to adjacent muscles, where you don't want it to go. That means: no naps, no lying down, no exercise—and, sorry to say, no shoe shopping. (Just think of all the time you spend looking down at your feet when trying on the latest pair of heels!)

Fast Results

The fastest result I ever saw from Botox took just eight hours. I treated the patient in the morning and her wrinkles were gone by five that evening. I've never seen anything like it, before or since. However, anyone with fair, paper-thin skin may find that results are quite rapid—a few days to a week. For those like me, who have thicker, oilier skin, it's typical to wait two weeks to see improvement.

Touch-ups

Nobody's face is perfectly symmetrical. After your first treatment, you may infrequently find that you have a hint of a frown, or that one brow goes up a bit more than the other, leaving you looking somewhat quirky. Such experiences aren't typical, but they're not unheard of.

If this happens to you, I recommend that you hold off on a touch-up until two full weeks after the initial treatment. This period of time will allow you and your doctor to judge how fully the treatment took, and to decide on the adjustments necessary for future treatments.

Many women want to avoid the plastic, expressionless appearance that excessive Botoxing can create. Working with your doctor to undertreat can help smooth out your skin without eliminating all signs of life. A less-is-more approach, followed by a touch-up if necessary, may be just what you're looking for.

Avoiding Side Effects

Fortunately, side effects from Botox are relatively minor and temporary. They can include temporary paralysis of adjacent muscles, such as those in the eyebrows or eyelids, resulting in a drooping of the eyelids (*ptosis*). This usually lasts only three to six weeks. And it's a very unlikely result if your doctor kept the injections at least one centimeter away from your eyebrows. Prescription eyedrops like Iopidine can help improve the symptoms while the side effect wears off.

Local bruising or temporary swelling of the treated area is also possible.

Pregnant or nursing women or those with neurological conditions should not use Botox.

Repeat Treatments

You can expect the wrinkle-smoothing effects of Botox to last three to six months. Be happy with three—and be thrilled if you're one of the lucky ones who can go up to a year!

The good news: repeat treatments may extend the time between future injections. That's because, over time, paralysis of the facial muscles of expression due to Botox helps soften those muscles. Going back to the biceps analogy: lack of use results in a soft, flabby muscle. In this case: *Don't* use it (the muscle) and lose it (the wrinkle). This is a rare and welcome instance when *not* toning a muscle makes you look younger!

Topical Line Relaxers (TLRs)

Okay, Botox is the hottest rejuvenation trend of the new millennium and unquestionably the most effective treatment to relax tight muscles and smooth away deep wrinkle lines. But sometimes you just need a *quick* fix. And there may be other reasons why Botox isn't for you: fear of needles, expense, health risks, or just personal preference.

Or maybe your Botox is wearing off and you are looking for that extra "something" to buy you some time between treatments.

That's where topical line relaxers (TLRs) are useful. (They're also called TMRs, or topical muscle relaxers.) TLRs are a short-term, quick fix to smooth out crow's-feet, frown lines, and other wrinkle lines that years of smiling, laughing, squinting, and frowning have left behind.

Essentially, Botox works by preventing the release of the chemical neurotransmitter acetylcholine from the nerve ending, blocking the relay of the information that encourages the muscle to contract. It is target-specific and obviously highly effective.

But physiology doesn't happen in a vacuum. There are many potential steps to interfere with in order to get uptight muscles to relax. DERMAdoctor Immobile Lines does just that, targeting *three* physiologic events (not just one, like other options) within the pathway that leads to deep wrinkle lines, instantly relaxing up to 90 percent of these lines for as long as twenty-four hours following application.

Immobile Lines accomplishes this goal because it contains naturally derived (rather than synthetic) GABA (gamma aminobutyrate), harvested and biotransformed (a process that further increases its effectiveness) from a botanical source, combined with other neurotransmission inhibitors.

The end result: you look beautifully relaxed.

CHEMICAL PEELS: RETEXTURIZE AND RESTORE

Chemical peels are one of the most popular procedures in cosmetic dermatology. A peel can give your skin a healthy, "just refreshed" look, or it can be aggressive, taking years off your appearance.

Just as with other cosmetic procedures, a wide range of chemicals and techniques exists, and deciding which is best for you can be overwhelming. Which goals are realistic? Which aren't? What can you do for yourself? What should your doctor do that your aesthetician shouldn't? Let's find out.

Realistic and Unrealistic Goals

Realistic goals include: Correcting sun damage. Reducing mild scarring. Reducing or eradicating wrinkles. Improving dark skin discoloration. Removing excessive or stubborn blackheads. Temporarily reducing excessive oiliness.

Unrealistic goals include: Removing or reducing the appearance of blood vessels on the skin. Changing pore diameter. (However, when you remove blackheads, the pores may appear less pronounced.) Getting rid of keloidal scars. Improving dark skin discoloration in people of color. Expecting a "chemical face-lift."

Active Ingredients Used in Peels

A variety of different chemicals are used in chemical peels. An active agent is selected based on the desired depth of the peel. If the skin concern is predominantly superficial, a milder, less caustic ingredient is selected. If there are deeply placed conditions, a far stronger product (with matching levels of potential complications) may be necessary.

Active ingredients used alone or in combination for mild- to moderate-strength chemical peels include:

- Glycolic acid (AHA)
- Salicylic acid (BHA)
- Lactic acid (another AHA family member)
- Jessner's peel (a combination of salicylic acid, resorcinol, and lactic acid mixed in ethanol)
- Resorcinol
- TCA (trichloracetic acid); TCA is used in a variety of peeling regimens, such as AccuPeel and the Obagi Blue Peel

For deep chemical peels, the active ingredient is Baker's phenol.

The Four Levels of Peeling

There are four levels of chemical peels: very superficial, superficial, medium, and deep.

Very Superficial. Most chemical peels have a two- to four-week preoperative regimen of exfoliating agents such as Renova, Tazorac, or a strong glycolic acid cream. This itself is a very superficial chemical peel, removing or thinning the most superficial layers of the stratum corneum (the top of the epidermis). It helps the peeling agent penetrate more deeply and evenly.

Superficial. These are the "refreshing" skin peels. Their effects are limited to the epidermis. They can also help cleanse pores and reduce the appearance of very mild blotchy skin discoloration and remnant acne discoloration. The superficial peel is the most common type performed in a spa or by an aesthetician. Typically, these peels utilize glycolic acid, AHA blends, or BHA as the active ingredients.

Home peel kits usually fall somewhere between very superficial and superficial. They can help freshen the skin, eliminate blackheads, improve symptoms of oiliness and/or acne, and renew texture. Home peels usually rely on glycolic acid (AHA) or a blend that includes salicylic acid (BHA). They can be fun to use, effective, and safe.

Medium. A medium-strength chemical peel allows the acid to penetrate through the epidermis, down into the uppermost portion of the dermis, known as the papillary dermis. This category comprises TCA (trichloroacetic acid) and more potent levels of glycolic acid. It is far more likely to be associated with complications, both temporary and permanent. It should be medically performed, rather than done in a spa by an aesthetician or facialist.

For more aggressive forms of these peels, or for patients who already suffer from skin discoloration, a bleaching agent, such a 4% hydroquinone, and a broad-spectrum sunscreen may be added to the prepeel skin care regimen a month prior to the procedure. Noticeable postprocedure peeling may be visible for two weeks. Use bland emollients, like Moisturel or Vanicream, and gentle cleansers, like Cetaphil Gentle Skin Cleanser.

Inflammation from this peel may temporarily produce darkening of the skin tone. (Medium peels are typically not appropriate for people of color or those with darker skin tones, due to the risk of irregular pigmentation.)

Dealing preventively with infection is key. For anyone with a history of cold sores who is undergoing a nonbuffered glycolic acid or a TCA peel, it is helpful to use antiviral medication before the peel is performed. For some peel patients, antibiotics are also used. And it is *crucial* that you not pick at the peeling skin during the healing phase—that is a sure way to end up with an infection and long-lasting problems, like scarring or skin discoloration.

Deep. This peel goes through the epidermis, the papillary dermis, and into the deeper portion of the dermis known as the reticular dermis. These peels are not simple procedures. Absorption of the active ingredient, phenol, has been known to cause cardiac arrest and even death. Patients who undergo phenol peels should be placed under general anesthesia and on full cardiac and pulmonary monitoring.

This procedure must be performed in a surgical setting, not just a room adjacent to the doctor's office. The downtime from this procedure is obviously the longest: generally, it will be two to three weeks before you want to be seen in public. The skin will peel dramatically during this time. Infection, permanent skin discoloration, and scar formation are potential risks.

All chemical peels can increase sensitivity to the sun. Sunblocks that offer UVA, UVB, *and* visible light protection, such as Total Block, are ideal.

MICRODERMABRASION: FRESHENING UP YOUR SKIN

Microdermabrasion is literally a superficial sanding of the skin, resulting in exfoliation of thickened epidermis and a smoother, radiant, more even skin texture and tone. It involves the use of tiny, rough particles, which are blown onto the skin and vacuumed away, in a closed system.

Microdermabrasion requires a series of treatments. When it is repeated every week or two, for anywhere from six to sixteen weeks, the cumulative results can be significant. And it is easy to undergo. It doesn't require local or general anesthesia; while you certainly feel the sanding, it is basically painless.

Treated skin looks slightly pink, but there should be no obvious skin wounds, weeping, oozing, or blistering. For deeper microdermabrasion procedures, your skin may be slightly red and swollen for a day or two.

Microdermabrasion is used for: Hyperpigmentation. Uneven skin tone or texture. Reducing skin "dullness" that accompanies aging skin. Temporary smoothing out of keratosis pilaris. Allowing easier and more effective penetration of topical treatments. Some stretch marks. Opening blackheads and keeping pores clean. (This is not acne therapy, though several companies make this claim.) Softening mild saucerlike acne scars and some other forms of scarring. Smoothing out fine wrinkle lines. The procedure doesn't make a huge difference on advanced, deep wrinkles.

Microdermabrasion shouldn't be used for: Keloidal scaring; it may stimulate further scar formation. Jagged ice-pick scars. Removing skin growths. Precancerous actinic keratoses (AKs). Skin cancers.

Selecting a Machine and a Technician

I can't tell you how many times I've been asked which microdermabrasion machine is "perfect," or how a particular machine compares with another brand.

Microdermabrasion is a very nice procedure when it is performed by the proper professional upon the appropriate client—but there is often very little difference between brands of machines.

There are two levels of machines; most manufacturers produce both levels. Gentler machines with less power are marketed to aestheticians. More powerful machines with the ability to give more aggressive results are marketed to physicians.

If you are considering microdermabrasion, you need to know about a number of factors that are *not* machine-driven.

Is the technician adequately trained in the use of the machine? Powerful machines have no business being used by an aesthetician. They result in deeper removal of tissues, with more potential for wound formation and resulting hyperpigmentation, and are meant to be used under a physician's supervision.

Is the machine being used in a sanitary manner? Crystals should never be reused. And there are now machines that offer sterilizable or disposable handpieces (the part that contacts your skin), improving sanitary conditions.

Does the use of aluminum oxide crystals concern you? The FDA states that there is no concern relative to the use of aluminum oxide crystals, known as corundum, which is supposed to be a different compound from the aluminum powder implicated in (but proven not related to) the development of Alzheimer's disease. However, the use of these crystals has been controversial, not because of Alzheimer's but because of the problems associated with any inhaled particles. (Remember asbestos?) Many manufacturers have made several changes to their equipment to minimize the particulate matter that escapes into the air, especially during disposal and refilling of the containers. And a few manufacturers are coming out with machines that utilize salt crystals instead of corundum.

INJECTABLE SKIN CARE

Sometimes nature, gravity, genetics, and perhaps some skin neglect may work together to form deep wrinkle lines, sagging nasolabial folds, thinning lips, or other undesirable skin flaws. Injectable fillers are one way to solve this dilemma. They instantly improve the appearance of wrinkles and scars. There has been a recent influx of new filler agents deluging the marketplace both here and abroad. Each comes with its own unique benefits and individual quirks.

Animal-Derived Collagen

Almost everyone has heard of collagen. Collagen fibers support the skin, keeping it taut and youthful. However, collagen breaks down over time, a process worsened by excessive sun damage. With the loss of these supporting fibers, the skin begins to show fine lines and sag. So the theory of reintroducing collagen to the skin in order to correct these problems was born. Topical collagen creams can't penetrate the skin's surface. (They do, however, trap moisture and hydrate the skin nicely, if only temporarily.) In the 1970s an injectable form of collagen was found. It is derived from bovine (cow) tissue. Used to treat wrinkle lines, as well as depressed scars from acne and chickenpox, injectable collagen is considered a safe and effective treatment.

Collagen is reabsorbed fairly quickly by the body; the effects will last anywhere from six weeks to about four months. Collagen is not inexpensive; however, thousands of patients happily keep up with their maintenance therapy.

Women who are pregnant or nursing or have an autoimmune disease should not undergo injectable collagen treatments.

Manufacturers have been very proactive in creating safeguards to prevent mad cow disease from infecting their product. The cows used to create Zyderm and Zyplast come from a closed herd in northern California; their genealogies are documented, and testing is diligently performed.

Everyone wants to know whether these injections are painful. Yes, they will hurt, but the product contains a local anesthetic and the areas being treated go numb quickly. The numbness lasts for a few hours. Each treated area receives several serial injections along the length of the wrinkle line. The only exception is the edge of the lips, where a single long injection is done along the length of the lip. The doctor typically massages each treated area after injection to disperse the collagen evenly.

Zyderm I (Bovine Collagen).

Uses. Very fine lines around the eyes (periocular) and mouth (perioral).

Allergic potential. Requires skin testing four weeks prior to use; 3 percent of tested patients experience a positive reaction. As with all forms of bovine-derived collagen, it is more likely to cause allergic reactions than human-derived collagen.

Cautions and downsides. Because of the collagen fiber structure and high water volume of the product, the physician overcorrects treatment sites by 200 percent. Immediately after the treatment the injection sites are puffy and swollen for a few days, until the surrounding tissue absorbs the saline.

Zyderm II. A more concentrated form of Zyderm I.

> *Uses.* Deeper wrinkle lines, such as those of the glabella (the space between the eyebrows) and the nasolabial folds (lines that extend from the nose to the edge of the mouth).
>
> *Allergic potential.* Same as Zyderm I.
>
> *Cautions and downside.* Zyderm II contains more collagen fibers than Zyderm I, so the physician overcorrects the treated area by only approximately 150 percent. Redness and puffiness should resolve within a few days.

Zyplast. A larger-fiber product than Zyderm I and II.

> *Uses.* Ideal for deeper tissue defects, such as the nasolabial lines and oral commissures (the creases at the edges of the mouth).
>
> *Allergic potential.* Same as Zyderm I.
>
> *Cautions and downside.* Zyplast is not to be injected into the glabellar lines (between the eyebrows), because of the risk of clotting in blood vessels in this area.

Artecoll. Approved in the United States under the brand name Arte-Fill. Spheres of an artificial material, PMMA (polymethyl methacrylate), are surrounded by bovine-derived collagen fibers. Promoted as a permanent filler agent, as opposed to the other types of bovine-derived collagen, which are considered temporary.

> *Uses.* Acne scars, nasolabial folds, neck folds, inverted nipples, and vertical lip lines (smoker's lips). Filling various depressions, such as sunken areas under the eyes.
>
> *Allergic potential.* Anyone with known bovine collagen or lidocaine sensitivities is unable to use this product.
>
> *Cautions and downside.* If there is a reaction to the PMMA, you could be stuck. Difficult-to-treat granulomas may form what the

skin perceives as foreign matter. The FDA states this product should not be used for lip augmentation.

Fibrel. Three ingredients are combined to make up Fibrel: porcine gelatin, e-aminocaproic acid, and plasma obtained from the patient being treated. Fibrel is supposed to stimulate inflammation and the deposition of the patient's own collagen.

Uses. Acne scars, deeper wrinkle lines, and furrows. Not recommended for scars that are not easily stretched or fine wrinkle lines.

Allergic potential. Testing must be performed four weeks prior to treatment.

Cautions and downside. Bruising. Other side effects are comparable to those of animal-derived collagen products, including delayed allergic reaction and granuloma formation.

Synthetic Fillers

Restylane (Hyaline Gel). Approved by the FDA in 2003. Comes in three particle sizes for "tailored" tissue augmentation: Restylane, Restylane Fine Lines, and Perlane. (The latter two are available only outside the United States.) The active component, hyaluronic acid (HA), is a natural polysaccharide found in all tissues. HA fills areas between cells, known as the extracellular space, and is a critical portion of the dermal matrix in which collagen and elastin fibers are suspended. Restylane is longer lasting (six to nine months) than other non-HA options. It is absorbed over time, and maintenance touch-ups are done as desired.

Uses. The most common areas for Restylane treatment are the glabellar lines (between the eyebrows), the nasolabial folds (from the wing of the nose to the angle of the mouth), and the lips, but other sites can also be treated. Giving a puffy, pouty look to the lips and accentuating the border of the lips is also done.

Allergic potential. Pretesting is not required. This is virtually no potential for allergic reaction.

Cautions and downside. Expect temporary redness/puffiness for the first day or two. (Occasionally, this can last up to two weeks.) More significant reactions are rarely reported.

Restylane Fine Lines and Perlane. Companion products to Restylane. Injection method, allergic potential, and cautions and downside are similar.

> *Uses.* Restylane Fine Lines: most delicate lines, such as crow's-feet, frown lines (including any left behind after Botox), and vertical lines around the mouth. Perlane: Deep wrinkle lines; cheek, chin, or lip augmentation.

Other Brands. Hylaform is another FDA-approved hyaluronic acid filler agent very similar to Restylane. Hylaform, however, is produced from avian sources and may contain remnant protein. Anyone allergic to eggs or poultry should avoid using Hylaform.

Other hyaluronic acid filler agents currently available in Europe include: Rofilan, Juvéderm, MacDermol, Hyal 2000, Hyacell (contains embryonic tissue and various other elements), Hyruan, and AcHyal. Macrolane, an even larger form of Restylane-type particle made by the same manufacturer, is also on the horizon.

Human Cadaver-Tissue Fillers

Another category of filler agents includes those derived from human cadaver tissue. Not only do most of these not require testing a month in advance (a major benefit for patients), but they also tend to have fewer problems associated with them than bovine material. Most of these products are obtained from cadaver tissue, much of it donated through tissue banks. Cadaver collagen is regulated by the FDA and must meet criteria established for extensive testing against infectious agents such as hepatitis B and C and HIV, as well as diseases like cancer. To date, there have been no reports of transmission of such diseases through tested cadaver tissue. In fact, the Musculoskeletal Transplant Foundation estimates that your chance of acquiring AIDS through such tissue is 1 in 1.67 million.

Cymetra Micronized, Injectable AlloDerm. The primary cadaver-harvested injectable product on the market, Cymetra is acellular, which means that the building blocks of the dermis are present, but intact human cells are not. This milieu of fibers forms the necessary network for the repopulation of the area with the patient's own cells and thus the rebuilding of the dermis. And as the body does not identify the material as foreign, there is a slower rate of reabsorption of the material than is seen with bovine or porcine collagen. Two to three treatments over a three-month period will typically provide long-lasting results, although patients should see good improvement after the initial treatment.

Uses. Improvement of wrinkle lines and acne scars. Areas appropriate for Cymetra include facial creases, depressed scars, nasolabial folds, and lip restoration.

Allergic potential. Because this form of treatment is not derived from animals, it is far less likely to cause allergic reactions, granulomas, or inflammation. Avoid it if you have a lidocaine allergy.

Cautions and downside. Contains trace amounts of a variety of antibiotics, limiting use in patients with certain drug allergies.

Fascian. An injectable agent derived from a different source of human tissue, known as the fascia, a fibrous layer that surrounds muscles. Fascian takes several months to be reabsorbed; once it is, your own tissue may have been re-formed in the area.

Uses. Skin defects such as depressed scars, regardless of their cause. Wrinkle therapy.

Allergic potential. No testing needs to be done prior to use. Fascian may contain trace amounts of polymyxin B sulfate, bacitracin, and/or gentamycin, so if you are allergic to any of these antibiotics, you may want to try a different product. Reconstituted with lidocaine.

Cautions and downside. May leave the area feeling lumpy for a while, as it is a very thick mixture. Bruising may be an issue.

Human Living-Tissue Options

Filling a void (pun intended), these entries offer a novel injectable beauty option. Available in the United States and parts of Europe, this collagen filler is derived from a single living, human cell, grown in a tissue culture. These products offer an excellent option for people squeamish about the use of harvested tissue from cadavers.

CosmoDerm and CosmoPlast. Well-blended, smooth fillers contained within prefilled syringes. Contain 1% lidocaine to help reduce discomfort. This is a tremendous benefit for patient comfort, but those who are allergic to lidocaine cannot use it.

Uses. Deeper wrinkles and skin defects, as well as lip augmentation.

Allergic potential. Requires no skin testing. Not for those with a lidocaine allergy.

Cautions and downside. Minimal.

Fat

Fat transplantation has been used for years and has the advantage of utilizing a patient's own resources. Fat is removed by a small cannula (liposuction tube) or large bore needle from the patient's fatty areas, such as the thigh, buttock, or stomach, after the area has been locally anesthetized. The fat cells are then washed and reinjected into places like the sunken areas under the eyes, the lips, or the backs of the hands. Approximately 20 to 30 percent of the fat cells will take; further periodic treatments are required. The advantages of this treatment are that it makes use of something you may not want, and it uses your own tissue. The drawbacks include bleeding, bruising, and infection. Rarely, a fat embolus (the fat equivalent of a blood clot) occurs.

Sculptra

Fat loss doesn't occur only with aging. Lipoatrophy is a disorder associated with HIV (human immunodeficiency virus) infection. Critical facial fat is lost, leaving cheeks appearing sunken and creating hollows under the eyes. Sculptra is the first synthetic filler specifically approved to restore facial contours lost to lipoatrophy.

Sculptra is an injectable synthetic polymer composed of micro particles of poly-L-lactic acid, from the AHA family. Before being used as a filler, this agent was used in medicine for several years as a component of dissolvable sutures and sustained-release injectable medications. Because it is a synthetic product, no skin testing is necessary prior to use. Unlike other filler substances, improvement is seen gradually over a two-week period, so it is not unheard of to see the deep hollows temporarily reappear soon after treatment.

A side effect more specific to Sculptra is the occasional delayed formation (several weeks or more after injection) of lumps that are not visible but can be felt when pressing firmly on the skin.

Sculptra lasts up to two years, giving it the distinction of being one of the longest lasting fillers on the market.

Maximizing Your Experience

Little steps to maximize comfort during a filler session (regardless of brand or type of filler) help the patient feel more relaxed and comfortable during the procedure.

Typically, I apply a 4% or 5% lidocaine product to the skin, such as Betacaine or L.M.X. 4, and allow the skin to numb before I begin the procedure. The additional application of prescription Viscous Xylocaine to the upper gums also helps blunt discomfort. For a true lip augmentation, the added measure of a painlessly performed dental block can make all the difference to the patient, regardless of the filler being used.

Anytime the skin becomes distended from the introduction of a filler, there may be some skin discomfort or tenderness and perhaps minor bruising. Avoid strenuous activity for twenty-four hours after the procedure.

The use of aspirin and NSAIDs like Advil should be avoided, as they may increase possible bleeding. Ask your physician if Tylenol would be appropriate for you.

Patients who've undergone lip augmentation may find that their lips look extremely puffy for up to forty-eight hours postinjection. Don't plan on having a lip augmentation and showing up to a fancy function that night. Always undergo this procedure in advance!

Topical Line Fillers

Anyone who fears needles, isn't keen on injecting artificial substances, wants to avoid the high cost of traditional filler treatments and maintenance, or simply wants to try something else now has another option.

DERMAdoctor Faux Fillment is the first-of-its-kind quick fix for deeper wrinkle lines such as smile and lipstick (a.k.a. smoker's lines), and for softly depressed acne scars.

This instant topical line filler works by driving hyaluronic acid into dermal defects through a sophisticated chemical process. Microscopic spheres (nanosomes) encapsulate hyaluronic and fulvic acids, isolating them from each other until the cream is applied to the skin.

Upon application, the spheres break, and, as the two components meet, the fulvic acid propels the hyaluronic acid into the skin, effectively plumping up lines and scars within twenty minutes of application. Up to 80 percent improvement can be seen, and results last up to twenty-four hours. Faux Fillment may be used in conjunction with DERMAdoctor Immobile Lines, a quick-fix "topical line relaxer" that helps smooth out crow's-feet, frown lines, and other wrinkle lines for twenty-four hours.

FINAL THOUGHTS

Face-lifts can be fabulous. But they aren't a minor procedure, they are costly, and you can expect to have a new one every decade. If your skin is just beginning to give away your age, cosmetic dermatology may be exactly what you need to help turn back the clock.

Ask the DERMAdoctor

QUESTION:

I just read in a magazine that there are "nonsurgical" face-lifts that use radio waves. That sounds too good to be true. Can you tell me more about this?

The DERMAdoctor:

ThermaCool, more commonly referred to as Thermage, uses a radio frequency to heat the collagen fibers located within the dermis, causing them to contract and tighten. The result: the skin becomes firmer. Lasers have long been used to produce this very effect; Thermage differs in the type of energy used, but compared to a nonablative laser, the treatment is very similar.

A topical anesthetic is applied; a sedative may be given as well. A small handpiece blasts a cold spray at the skin, followed by a quick feeling of warmth, followed by a cold blast.

Thermage averages a 25 percent increase in skin firmness. Results don't happen right away; two to five months are necessary to notice a difference. While the treatment is currently approved for the upper one-third of the face, physicians are trying it "off label" elsewhere on the face, neck, and body to determine what type of result they can achieve.

Thermage is unlikely to tighten skin that has simply succumbed to gravity. If your skin is sagging significantly, contemplate a brow lift, face-lift, or feather lift or use fillers to help create a more youthful, refreshed look.

COSMETICS

Deciphering Labels, Understanding Ingredients

As we learn more about our skin, we're all becoming more ingredient conscious. And that's a positive thing.

Understanding the substances contained in skin care products can provide useful information. It can help you determine what makes particular products greasy, irritating, aggravating to acne, or drying, and also why some ingredients are particularly effective. In addition, if you have a known allergy, your dermatologist or allergist can help you determine related ingredients that you should avoid.

This chapter isn't meant to be a compendium of ingredients. But it does attempt to cover the most pertinent issues raised by the labels of the products you use. Consider it a handy guide to the world of skin care products.

HOW TO READ A LABEL

The government's Food and Drug Administration (FDA) oversees cosmetics: their claims, their safety—and their labeling. Every manufacturer must meet certain label requirements set by the FDA.

In Fair Order. The Fair Packaging and Labeling Act set guidelines regulating the order in which ingredients are listed. In cosmetic products, ingredients lists must begin with the ingredient present in the largest concentration—typically the vehicle, like water or SD alcohol 40—and move downward, oftentimes to trace elements. Colors are typically listed last. (The vehicle creates the suspension that carries the other ingredients, so even though water may constitute most of a product, it's usually for a good reason.)

Double-Duty Labeling. Should the cosmetic also act as an over-the-counter drug (like an antidandruff shampoo or a makeup with sun-protection claims), the primary therapeutic agent is called the active ingredient and is listed before all other ingredients. But that doesn't mean it's the ingredient present in the highest concentration. Take sunscreen, for example. Titanium dioxide might be listed first as the active ingredient, not because it is present in the greatest concentration but because it is what screens the sun's rays. Package labeling for products containing over-the-counter drugs must now display a special box with information specific to that drug.

The FDA also requires that the components that aren't the active ingredient be termed either "other ingredients" or "inactive ingredients." The latter term is somewhat confusing, since these secondary ingredients may not be truly inactive.

The 1% Rule. Any ingredient present below a 1% concentration may be listed in any order, as long as it is listed after all the other ingredients present at or above 1%. The only problem: there is no guideline regarding where the 1% cutoff exists on the label! And some ingredients *should* be present below 1%, for reasons of efficacy range or potential irritation.

The Name Game. Confusion can abound when ingredients have more than one name, equivalent botanical names, or more than one molecular variation. In those cases, the ingredient may be listed in a multitude of different ways on different labels. Because of changing European Union guidelines, botanicals are now listed by their Latin name, followed by their more recognizable English name, in parentheses. Ingredients are most commonly listed according to their name in the CTFA (Cosmetic, Toiletry, and Fragrance Association) cosmetic ingredient dictionary.

Take Your Vitamins. Vitamins in skin care products are required to be listed by their chemical name (i.e., phytonadione, instead of vitamin K), to prevent the misperception that the vitamin is providing nutritional supplementation.

Trade Secrets. When shopping for a product, I've found that an ingredient a brand claimed was present wasn't listed on the label. Why not? In certain circumstances, the FDA will grant a product "trade secret" status, allowing the special ingredient to be left off the ingredient list. However, this is very rarely granted. And when it is, at the end of the ingredient list you should see the phrase "and other ingredients." Buyer beware: if you don't see an ingredient listed, odds are it's not there.

Terms That Describe How Ingredients Work

Binding Agents. Hold products together, preventing the separation of water and lipid components.

Emollients. Smooth and soften the skin. There are literally hundreds of emollients, each providing its own individual texture to the product and affect on the skin.

Emulsion. The formulation contains a blend of oil and water, resulting in a single, smooth product.

Humectants. When placed on the skin, these ingredients attract water, usually from the air. By definition, all humectants are also moisturizers. Urea is a classic humectant used in dermatology to treat markedly dry skin conditions.

Lubricants. These ingredients reduce friction and make the skin feel smoother to the touch. Silicone, dimethicone, and cyclomethicone are excellent lubricants.

Preservatives. Kill detrimental bacteria, yeast, and/or molds, preventing spoilage. Without them, products become rancid more quickly. Examples include: parabens (methyl-, ethyl- butyl-, propyl-), DMDM hydantoin, phenoxyethanol, methylchloroisothiazolinone, quaternium-15, imidazolidinyl urea, formaldehyde, EDTA, sorbic acid, and BHT.

Solvents. These substances, such as alcohol, oil, or water, dissolve the other ingredients.

Surfactants. Also known as surface-active agents. These are commonly thought of as ingredients used to improve the lathering ability of skin cleansers, soaps, and shampoos. Technically, the term refers to ingredients that help cause lather or foam, that emulsify or make soluble, or that cleanse or wet the skin. Examples include sodium lauryl sulfate, laureth sulfate, sodium cocoyl isethionate, sodium cocoate, lauryl sarcosine, and decyl polyglucose.

Vehicle. The base that carries the active ingredients; the vehicle and solvent are often the same. An aqueous base is composed of water; a lipid base, of oil. A gel base is often formulated with an alcohol.

COMEDOGENICITY: DETERMINING THE CLOG FACTOR

Everyone looks for a product that says it is oil-free—but is it non-comedogenic?

Comedogenicity refers to the chance that an ingredient or combination of ingredients will cause your pores to clog. This results in blackheads or whiteheads, officially called comedones. Comedogenicity is rated on a scale of 0 to 5. The lower the number, the less likely that the ingredient *used by itself* will clog your pores.

But if an ingredient is comedogenic, that doesn't mean that everyone who uses it will automatically develop acne or clogged pores. Most people will tolerate the presence of that ingredient in the product just fine. It simply means that those who have a real problem with clogged pores are more at risk when using that ingredient.

Again, it boils down to the amount of the ingredient in the product (where it falls in the ingredients list) and to what other ingredients are present that may negate the comedogenicity.

So why even include an ingredient known to be comedogenic? The ingredient may serve an essential purpose in the formulation, necessitating its inclusion.

The real question to ask is, Did the product make it through comedogenicity testing? If so, don't sweat the presence of a single comedogenic ingredient.

Oil and Wax

In the cosmetics industry, "oil" and "wax" are three-letter words, not four-letter words. They may sound bad, but many oils and waxes are not necessarily bad for the skin.

Much of the naming process has to do with chemical structure. Mineral oil is a good example of such an ingredient. Many people avoid it like the plague—but its comedogenicity rating is zero!

When you're looking for a noncomedogenic product, keep in mind that the label must make that claim. "Water-based" and "oil-free" mean just that, and may not have any bearing whatsoever on comedone formation.

HYPOALLERGENIC . . . OR HYPEALLERGENIC?

You'll be surprised to learn that the time-honored term "hypoallergenic" has little to back up its claim! A product labeled "hypoallergenic" suggests that it is less likely to cause an allergic reaction. But cosmetics manufacturers are not required to substantiate their claim. A reputable company will have an independent verification, resulting in one of the following labelings:

Allergy Tested. Patch testing with the final product was performed on a statistically significant number of human volunteers in an independent third-party testing facility.

Dermatologist Tested and Approved. A dermatologist independent of the manufacturing company assisted and evaluated the patch-testing procedure and the final results.

Ophthalmologist Tested and Approved. This test is performed only for products specifically intended for the eye area. And only after a product has been allergy tested may it pass on to the stage of ophthalmologist testing. Here, the product is applied to the delicate skin around the eyes and eyelids on human volunteers for a specified length of time. An ophthalmologist monitors and approves the testing, watching for reactions that may have been absent on the tougher skin of the torso.

"Hypoallergenic" products that are fragrance-free and dye-free are less likely to cause a contact dermatitis. But the reality is—despite testing and the manufacturer's best intentions—that at some point, someone will experience an allergic reaction to the product.

FRAGRANCE: I SMELL AN ALLERGY

Everyone loves a pretty fragrance—unless you're on the receiving end of a fragrance allergy. Whether natural (the scent from an essential oil) or synthetic, the fact is that many consumers are allergic to fragrance. It is unquestionably the personal care additive that is responsible for the most cosmetic allergies.

According to the Allerderm T.R.U.E. Test patch-test kit information, the key eight fragrance ingredients that may cause a contact dermatitis are:

- Geraniol
- Cinnamaldehyde
- Hydroxycitronellal
- Cinnamyl alcohol
- Eugenol
- Isoeugenol
- Alpha-Amylcinnamaldehyde
- Oak moss

A fragrance added to scent a product is typically a blend of many ingredients. These blends are often considered a "trade secret" and are listed as "fragrance" on the label. For someone with a known allergy to a particular fragrance ingredient, this makes shopping for scented products a challenge. And the challenge doesn't end there.

Fragrances That Aren't Listed

An ingredient added to a product specifically to add scent *should* be listed as "fragrance." However, an ingredient added for its botanical benefits may still provide the product with fragrance. The classic example is lavender, which is added to many skin care products for its perceived astringent benefits; the classic scent of lavender pervades the product. In this case, there are no rules mandating that "fragrance" be listed. You need to learn that certain botanicals possess a scent and, if it is a problem, to steer clear of them.

"Odor-Free" Isn't Necessarily "Fragrance-Free"

A product that claims to be fragrance-free suggests that fragrance was purposely *not* added for aesthetic purposes. On the other hand—and quite surprisingly—"odor-free" or "unscented" doesn't necessary mean the product is fragrance-free. Sometimes ingredients have a naturally displeasing aroma; sulfur is a good example. A masking fragrance may be added to help make the product more acceptable—and "odor-free." An example of a masking fragrance is linalool.

ALCOHOL: THE MOST MISUNDERSTOOD INGREDIENT

If I had to pick a single ingredient as the most misunderstood, it would be alcohol. I can't tell you how many times I've heard "I can't use that product—it contains alcohol and will dry, irritate [fill in the blank] my skin." Is this true? Probably not.

If "alcohol" is listed on a cosmetics label, it refers to ethyl alcohol (a.k.a. ethanol). Used most commonly as a solvent, an antiseptic, or to cut through grease, ethyl alcohol may *occasionally* cause dryness or irritation issues—when present in very high concentrations or when the product is unintentionally misused.

But how much ethyl alcohol is in the product, anyway? Recall from the section on label reading that an ingredient mentioned early in the list is present at a higher level. You may have an issue with the ingredient when it's the solvent, but not when it's used in smaller amounts as a degreaser.

Plus, not all ingredients that have the word "alcohol" within them are ethyl alcohol. Nor do they inherently possess negative attributes.

Yes, I can empathize with the consumer who is concerned by high alcohol levels in a product (even when that concern isn't warranted). But the true problems arise when ingredient confusion interferes with product selection. Here's the real skinny on alcohol.

A Friendly Family

Think of alcohols as a family of organic compounds with an –OH (hydroxy) group attached. Now think of antibiotics. You would never avoid all antibiotics simply because you were allergic to penicillin. The same holds true for avoiding all "alcohols" because of ethyl alcohol. In fact, most cosmetic ingredients that are alcohol family members do *not* possess the attributes of ethyl alcohol.

For example, cetyl alcohol and its close molecular cousins are derived from vegetable sources, usually coconut or coconut oils. (They may be made synthetically, too.) They function as emulsifiers, thickening agents, moisturizers, and stabilizers, allowing formulations to have the silky-smooth bases that we all look for in skin care products. In other words, cetyl alcohol is well behaved. Don't blame the family for the dysfunction of one of its members. (And remember that ethyl alcohol usually doesn't even deserve that "dysfunctional" label.)

A list of some (but not all) misunderstood alcohols:

- Cetyl alcohol (emulsifier, thickener)
- Cetearyl alcohol (emulsifier, thickener)
- Cetostearyl alcohol (emulsifier, thickener)
- Cetyl alcohol 40 (emulsifier, thickener)
- C12-15 alcohols benzoate (emulsifier used in sunscreen)
- Lanolin alcohol (emollient and moisturizer derived from sheep-wool oils)
- Stearyl alcohol (emulsifier, lubricant)

A last fact you should know about the ingredient alcohol: ethanol is frequently denatured in processing, so that when it is supplied in bulk to the manufacturer or added into skin care products, it won't (heaven help us) be consumed by someone looking for a cheap buzz. Denatured alcohol is listed with an "SD" preceding the word "alcohol" and often has a number following it. Examples: SD alcohol 40, SD alcohol 40-B, and SDA alcohol-40. (There are others.) "Alcohol denat." is a blanket term for the group and is often found on labels on European products.

FINAL THOUGHTS

Product labeling isn't meant to just be the "pretty face" on your package. Everything you need to know is there in black and white (or purple or blue or green). Read between the lines and you'll be the epitome of the informed skin care consumer.

Ask the DERMAdoctor

QUESTION:

I have an allergy to cocamidopropyl betaine. I am having trouble finding shampoos and conditioners that don't contain this. I saw the ingredient cocamidopropylamine oxide listed on a hypoallergenic shampoo and was concerned. Is there any relation between these two ingredients, or can I use the shampoo?

The DERMAdoctor:

Both cocamidopropyl betaine and cocamidopropylamine oxide are derived from coconut oil. So if you are allergic to one, I suspect that they are similar enough in molecular structure that you could potentially be allergic to the other. Surfactants originating from coconut are added to many shampoos, soaps, and conditioners because they help increase the silky texture and the lathering ability of the products. Unfortunately, the vast majority of surfactants are derived from either palm or coconut oils, which are essentially the same with respect to a coconut allergy. Decyl glucoside also comes from palm oil.

In fact, every cleanser and shampoo I have looked at contains an ingredient related to coconut or palm oil. You may need to take a creative approach to cleansing. For the face, you can use a toner to remove excess grime. Or use a face or body scrub in the shower, rather than a cleanser or shampoo. Consider mixing water, glycerin, aloe vera, and a touch of olive oil. You can add in your favorite essential oils, cucumber extract, or oatmeal (which makes a good scrub). Remember, it is really the water that is cleaning you, and any exfoliation you may be doing. The cleanser is an additional helper to further break down fats and oils and leave a pleasant scent.

HAIR REMOVAL

Many Painless Options

Concerned about trying to grow hair? Well, far more women are concerned about *removing* unwanted hair growth!

The medical term for excessive facial hair growth is hirsutism. While many women presume a hormonal imbalance has led to their excessive hair growth, this isn't typically the case. Often to blame are heredity or a natural, increased sensitivity to normal levels of testosterone. Certainly, some women do have a hormonal imbalance, often due to polycystic ovary disease, and your doctor can screen for this possibility.

A few, rare skin diseases are associated with hirsutism, like porphyria cutanea tarda.

Whatever the cause, the appropriate choice for removing excess hair will depend on several factors, including how much hair is present, where the unwanted hair is, and how much you can and want to spend.

OVER-THE-COUNTER DEPILATORIES: POPULAR AND EASY TO USE

One simple way to remove hair growth above the lip is with an over-the-counter depilatory like Nair or Neet. However, these products are made for tougher areas of the body, like the legs. So, if you plan to use a depilatory on unwanted facial hair, it is *very important* that you perform a spot test according to the package directions even if the package says the product can be used on facial hair. Depilatories chemically dissolve the hair, so you must rinse the product off, either at the recommended time or sooner, if you feel any stinging or burning.

REDUCING IRRITATION

Do you find that chemical depilatories work well for a while but eventually you experience increasing irritation? Mild topical steroid creams like Cortaid Steroid Cream, applied prior to using the depilatory, can help alleviate this problem, at least for a time. Or you can get a prescription from your doctor for an appropriate low-dose steroid cream. But once you reach the point where there is simply too much irritation, it's time to consider other options. And if you have a darker skin tone, remember that irritation may cause skin discoloration, which is especially undesirable on the face. Pay attention to what your skin is telling you.

BLEACHING: THE CASE OF THE BLOND MUSTACHE

There are several bleaches on the market for use on unwanted facial hair, and I tried several of them during college. The major problem with bleaching, besides the irritation, is that some women with hair above the upper lip may find that they don't end up with an invisible mustache but with a heavy blond mustache that looks more abnormal than what they began with! If this is happening to you, take my word for it—it *is* highly noticeable. Find a reliable method for *removing*, not bleaching, that unwanted hair.

WAXING: FOR THE WIDESPREAD OR WELL DEFINED

Waxing is great for removing hair, particularly if you are looking for results that can last a few weeks. Waxing allows you to treat widespread areas like the legs or torso, or very small, well-defined spots like the brows or above the upper lip. There is definitely an art to waxing. And it isn't exactly pain-free, which leads many women to see their aesthetician.

Home Waxing

Dermatologists often recommend avoiding waxing because of the low risk of developing problems like folliculitis or ingrown hairs or burning the skin from overly hot wax. Because of these concerns, I was a waxing virgin. But I am continually asked about waxing and decided it was time to give it a try. I am happy to report waxing is a great, albeit somewhat painful process.

As always, follow the directions! Use the prewaxing cleanser and lotion before waxing and then reapply the lotion after waxing. This will help prevent the formation of hair bumps, folliculitis, and tearing of the skin. There *is* a method to the madness.

A Warning to Accutane Patients

Avoid waxing with any product while on Accutane and for thirty days after coming off the medication. Accutane can make your skin much more fragile and prone to tearing when the wax is removed.

I am often asked if it is safe to wax while using topical vitamin A products like Retin-A. While there is a crossover theory that topical vitamin A products could cause the same type of problems as Accutane, I have not had any patients with this experience. Obviously, if you are using a topical vitamin A product, be all the more careful with waxing.

SHAVING: NOT FOR MEN ONLY

Simply shaving off facial hair above the lip with a Daisy razor every morning takes just a few seconds, but I find a lot of resistance to this procedure from women. I think there is a psychological aversion to having to resort to what is historically considered a male method of hair removal. However, you won't grow a masculine mustache (it is physiologically impossible), and while you may have to shave daily, it is quick and easy.

THE PRESCRIPTION OPTION: MULTIPURPOSE PILLS

Sometimes that hair growth just doesn't want to respond to routine forms of removal, or you may have a hormonal imbalance due to a condition like polycystic ovary disease. For these situations, there are prescription pills that help diminish hair growth, like spironolactone and Tagamet.

Often, my patients don't care for spironolactone, a diuretic, because it throws off the menstrual cycle or makes them light-headed. But it is effective and can also help cut down on acne due to excessive testosterone levels.

Tagamet, an ulcer drug, also helps cut down on hair growth.

You'll need to discuss the "off-label" use of these prescription drugs with your dermatologist. And neither medication makes the hair fall out, so you'll have to keep removing the hair until the medication kicks in and you start to see results.

MAKE UNWANTED HAIR "VANIQA"

A prescription cream called Vaniqa (eflornithine hydrochloride) helps prevent hair growth in the first place. It's approved by the FDA for unwanted facial hair in women. Vaniqa takes eight weeks to work. That's the time required for all of the hair follicles to rotate through their growth cycle.

Vaniqa stops unwanted hair growth, but it doesn't remove hair. You'll still need to perform your favorite method of hair removal during the first eight weeks of use. Eventually, you will notice that you need to remove hair less frequently, and in time you'll observe that hair growth has stopped completely. However, if you stop your Vaniqa, the hair will start regrowing in about eight weeks. While it's meant to be used only for areas on the face, I have no doubt that it will find its way into "off-label" uses on other areas of the body.

LASERS: FIND AN EXPERIENCED OPERATOR

Here are some guidelines if you're considering having excess hair removed with a laser.

The Ideal Candidate. If you have dark hair and light skin, you are the ideal candidate for hair removal with a laser. Otherwise, it's likely that you're not. One way to try to circumvent this is to ask the laser surgeon if they use Meladine, a temporary hair dye that helps improve laser results by up to 90 percent. Meladine is applied to blond, gray, or other light hair and darkens it. Dark hair absorbs laser light more effectively.

The Treatments. The process of laser hair removal usually requires three initial treatments. Although laser hair removal is not considered permanent, it does cut down on the amount of overall hair growth, and much of the future hair growth is a finer texture and lighter color, which is appreciated by the patient. Maintenance is typically required to keep the hair under control. Another benefit of laser removal is that any area can be treated, such as the bikini area, chest, back, shoulders, and so on.

Pain. Although it is marketed as "painless," laser hair removal is painful enough that topical anesthetics like L.M.X. 4 topical anesthetic and (at times) some oral sedation are used.

Choosing the Right Laser. There are several lasers marketed to physicians for hair removal. After attending a meeting that reviewed many of them, I got the impression that while some machines might have certain benefits, finding an experienced laser operator is your best bet at getting a good result.

Cost. Laser therapy certainly isn't cheap. I have heard quotes in the Kansas City area of $1,500 for the initial three treatments. I would presume it might be higher elsewhere in the country, as cosmetic procedures are typically less costly in the Midwest.

ELECTROLYSIS: ELECTRIFYING BEAUTY

Any chapter on hair removal wouldn't be complete without mentioning electrolysis. In essence, electrolysis is simply the destruction of the hair bulb with electrical current. No hair bulb, no way to make hair. The patient experiences the wire slipping into the hair follicle and the surprise twinge of pain as the current is discharged. The physics behind the process are a bit more complex.

Several sessions are likely required to treat the targeted area and achieve desired results. I personally recommend that any person of color who is interested in electrolysis have a test performed in an out-of-sight area of the body in order to make certain they do not develop keloid scarring.

Because electrolysis is notoriously painful, one way to make this a tolerable and rewarding experience is to apply L.M.X. 4 anesthetic cream prior to undergoing the procedure.

A word of warning: the American Society for Dermatological Surgery has issued a statement regarding laser and electrolysis hair removal procedures. Due to the increase in consumer reports of burns, discoloration, scarring, and other unsatisfactory results, they recommend that these procedures be performed only by an experienced physician.

SIDE EFFECTS OF HAIR REMOVAL

Are you prone to hair bumps, bikini bumps, folliculitis, or ingrown hairs, no matter what you do? Here are some solutions.

After shaving or hair removal, try Neova After Shave Therapy. The GHK copper peptides are very healing and soothing.

If you're prone to folliculitis or acne from shaving, Peter Thomas

Roth BPO 2½% Medicated Shaving Cream can help cut down on infection within the hair follicles. Prescription BenzaShave contains a slightly higher concentration (5%) of benzoyl peroxide blended into the foam.

Should you find you have folliculitis despite your best efforts, No Bump Rx or Peter Thomas Roth BPO Gel 10% and Sulfur can help treat this quite effectively. The use of prescription Azelex is also helpful, and a good reliable topical agent for anyone with chronic issues. Rarely, I have to prescribe an oral antibiotic for a raging case of folliculitis due to hair removal.

If you develop an ingrown hair, *gently* extract the hair from the follicle and allow it to straighten out. Do *not* forcefully yank it out; all you will end up with is more inflammation down in the hair bulb and perhaps some remnant broken hair as well.

FINAL THOUGHTS

Smooth skin is always in—and so is your dermatologist! If you are experiencing problems with excessive hair growth, you shouldn't hesitate to discuss this with your physician. There are definitely steps you can take to improve the situation.

Ask the DERMAdoctor

QUESTION:

I am light-skinned, and when I shave my bikini area I get reddish bumps. It's so embarrassing and I've dealt with it for so long. Is there something I can use to get rid of them?

The DERMAdoctor:

If you appreciate the always ready convenience of shaving, there are a few things you can do to minimize the "bikini bump" syndrome that often accompanies this home hair-removal method.

First, be sure to adequately wet the skin and the bikini hair. Since pubic hair is much more coarse than hair on other parts of the body, this saturating step is very important. Using a large amount of a moisturizing shaving cream, like Aveeno Therapeutic Shaving Gel, which helps soften the hair even more, makes shaving easier.

When you begin to shave, pull the skin tight with your nonshaving hand. Then shave in upward strokes. Make sure there is adequate shaving cream on the hair and skin before each stroke. Without this protection, you're likely to get red and bumpy after you shave.

Some experts recommend rubbing an ice cube over the shaved bikini area to reduce redness and discomfort. A nice application of a soothing aftershave product, like Neova After Shave Therapy, can help make you more comfortable. And if those nasty bikini bumps do appear, try M.D. Forté Glycare Perfection Gel, which is great for sending them packing.

To decrease the discomfort of the soon-to-return stubble, make sure to keep the area well moisturized between shaves.

MENOPAUSE AND YOUR SKIN

There Is Something You Can Do

Menopause isn't as bad as it's cracked up to be; however, it does create some interesting new dilemmas you need to figure out how to handle. How would I know? Well, it has been more than six years since I underwent surgical menopause (a complete hysterectomy) to help correct a medical condition. I thought it was a breeze awakening into menopause, but about a week later I began to discover the hidden "joys" of the experience. And I have to admit that, as a dermatologist, I was surprised to find out how quickly nuisance skin changes developed. I would like to share this experience with you and how I was able to work out solutions.

HORMONE REPLACEMENT THERAPY (HRT): THE ESTROGEN QUESTION

I am not a gynecologist, so I don't feel qualified to lecture on the pros and cons of HRT. However, I think many women now recognize the importance that estrogens play in protecting our bones from osteoporosis.

Estrogens have been implicated in increased rates of breast cancer, heart disease, stroke, and Alzheimer's disease. Undoubtedly, HRT is a controversial therapy, and one that should be carefully considered by a patient and her doctor. Extreme menopausal symptoms that affect the quality of life may be abated with HRT, especially early in menopause.

And for a woman who no longer has her uterus and ovaries, the use of HRT with low-dose estrogen without supplemental progesterone can be very helpful in decreasing the severity of many of the issues I will discuss below. I personally use the Climara transdermal patch, which I change weekly. This is not only convenient but also keeps me from having to metabolize oral estrogens through my liver. It has been suggested that estrogen breakdown in the liver may be riskier for those prone to blood clots; in my personal medical case, this is important for me. Anyone with a history of blood clots or clotting disorders may find this a way in which to at least contemplate a safer use of HRT.

PHYTOESTROGENS

Phytoestrogens are chemicals found in plants that act like estrogen. Phytoestrogens are of importance because it has been shown that they are capable of binding with certain estrogen receptors, acting as natural selective estrogen receptor modulators (SERMs).

Three groups make up the phytoestrogen family: the isoflavones (extracts from soy milk and soybeans), including soy extract, daidzein, and genistein; the lignans (from flaxseed, beans, and cereal brans); and the coumestans (from legumes like split peas, pinto and lima beans, and clover sprouts). It's been estimated that more than three hundred foods contain phytoestrogens.

A wide variety of soy-packed, processed foods on the market claim to make menopausal symptoms more tolerable. Many of them are cereals. If you do not want to take estrogen, or for some reason cannot, increasing the soy in your diet or taking a phytoestrogen supplement may be helpful. Discuss this option with your doctor. However, if you are already on estrogen or have a history of estrogen-receptor-positive breast cancer, you do not want to take additional large doses of phytoestrogens.

HORMONE-BASED WRINKLE CREAMS

We know that foods rich in phytoestrogens likely mimic SERMs, but what can they do topically? Research remains somewhat sketchy in this realm, but here is what we do know.

Soy isoflavones (soy extract, genistein, and daidzein) work as antioxidants, helping reduce cellular DNA damage due to free radicals, increase hyaluronic acid production within the skin, and help reduce unwanted skin pigmentation.

What about "natural progesterone" yam creams? In actuality, the Mexican wild yam (*Dioscorea villosa*) contains diosgenin, which, while not entirely without merit, is incapable of being converted to progesterone in the human body, and certainly is not converted when applied to the skin.

DRY SKIN

The loss of estrogen does cause a decrease in the amount of sebum that is produced, leading to drier skin. Postmenopausal women are "blessed" with this event—while the average male doesn't experience a decrease in sebum levels until approximately age eighty! Despite using HRT, I have found that my skin is somewhat drier (I have always been prone to terribly oily skin). Winter is the most troublesome time.

Personally, I find that the use of DERMAdoctor KP Duty or M.D. Forté Hand & Body Cream really cuts through the dry areas on my shins (my personal trouble zone) better than a plain bland emollient.

For really dry skin areas, I also use an exfoliating scrub or microdermabrasion cream to physically remove the scales before showering.

ANDROGENETIC ALOPECIA

Postmenopausal hair loss results in a receding hairline at the temples (a.k.a. a widow's peak) for most women as we age. In more extreme instances, women may thin in a diffuse, generalized pattern across the entire scalp.

In addition to hair loss on the scalp, all body hair can be affected, as the hair diameter decreases after menopause. This may result in a thinning of the eyebrows, pubic hair, and even underarm or leg hair. The hair that remains becomes coarser and more noticeable.

If you're not doing so already, I recommend you take a well-balanced multivitamin beginning around the time of menopause, to help supplement your baseline nutrition. This seems to help bolster hair and nail growth, as well as contribute to your overall health.

For complete information on androgenetic alopecia, please see the chapter "Hair Loss" on page 123.

FINE LINES

After years of constantly following a skin rejuvenation routine, I encountered something I had not anticipated, Actually, I was appalled by the fine lines on my face. However, I had become lax in my maintenance regimen for several months prior to my hysterectomy. Within a few weeks postop, I began noticing early signs of crow's-feet and forehead lines. I immediately restarted my products and have been happy with the results. However, I find that the lines are likely to return if I become lazy in my treatment.

Remember, you lose approximately 1 percent of your collagen per year after the age of forty, as well as in response to the loss of estrogens, despite HRT. Start your products now and do not let up once you are happy with the results. It is far easier to prevent lines than eradicate them!

Botox and wrinkle fillers hold a place in the hearts of millions of women. And now that nonablative lasers and radiofrequency Thermage are available—procedures to help treat crow's-feet and tighten skin—I anticipate a surge in preventive as well as fixative therapy.

UNWANTED FACIAL HAIR

Now I understand why fairy tales always depict the grandmother with that stray hair sprouting off her chin. And not only are these hairs sprouting, they become coarser. Yes, I too have had to deal with plucking in areas I *never* thought I would. Vaniqa has become a great way to help stop the growth of these unwanted strays when they're too numerous to pluck. Or consider laser hair removal.

WASHED-OUT COMPLEXION

With the aging process, the pigment-forming cells called melanocytes begin to die off. That means that by the time you're forty, your complexion is getting more "washed-out" looking. Since sun worshiping is out of the question, bronzers, self-tanners, or spray-on tanning can restore your glow.

Like skin, hair loses its color, leaving lashes, brows, and your beautiful mane of hair seemingly pale and lackluster. If you color your hair, reassess the hue. Dark shades look harsh against paler skin. A lighter color, combined with highlights, appear far more sophisticated and keeps you looking radiant.

INCREASED RATE OF GRAY HAIR FORMATION

At my age, I refuse to go gray! Unfortunately, when you have dark brunette hair, each and every gray hair stands out. So now I find I have to get my hair colored approximately every six weeks.

If your hair is dry, fragile, or prone to breakage, extending the time between color treatments can be a hair-saving strategy even if just an added week or two.

And try cutting back on dryer time. I no longer use the hair dryer unless I need my hair styled for a meeting or just want to look good. Instead, I rely upon my Aquis microfiber hair towel to dry my *very* thick hair; then I brush it out and go. This helps extend the length of time my color looks good, too.

INCREASED WEIGHT

My friends warned me that once I went through menopause I'd pick up a lot of weight. Actually, this didn't start to happen for about a year, but once it began, it was rapid, and seemed uncontrollable.

While the weight was spread around, my stomach (which had never been a problem) was suddenly showing a little bulge that just wouldn't go away, although I walked four miles a day.

I have since learned the harsh facts.

Studies have shown that after age thirty-five the average adult female loses about a half pound of muscle a year and gains one and a half pounds of fat. For women going through menopause, hormonal changes combined with the aging process worsen the situation. With the drop in estrogen, the fat cells begin to produce (and reproduce!) a natural supplemental source of estrogen. Naturally, these overactive cells are located in the abdominal area.

This is why our mothers and grandmothers often tend to have poochy tummies. In addition, women naturally store fat in their abdominal area. To make things even worse, our metabolic requirements drop significantly. Our daily caloric need drops by four hundred to five hundred calories a day.

How can you fight this? I was honestly at a loss, until I added two elements to my exercise routine: cross-training (aerobic exercise *and* strength training, which helps raise the metabolism); and the Pilates Reformer, which has made a big difference in my abdominal muscle tone.

Aerobic exercise, strength training, and Pilates have truly helped—but I do continue to yo-yo up and down, mostly because if I miss a few weeks of working out, the pounds simply reappear. I suspect I will have to fight the fat indefinitely. Yes, I dream of liposuction and tummy tucks, but it's unlikely I'll pursue either.

I don't know about you, but I'm a food lover. So I have decided that I am just going to have to somehow take the time to work out *and* do strength training with weights. I'd rather sweat a little bit more than have to watch every last morsel I eat!

SUBCUTANEOUS FAT LOSS

As we're getting plumper, we're losing fat in some very important areas under our skin. This loss of subcutaneous fat can drastically affect our skin and our appearance.

Hollows form under the eyes, creating dark circles. Skin becomes thin and crepelike and veins protrude, a major reason why bruising increases as we become older. Fat loss is also why our hands begin to "give away" our age.

Aging on the backs of the hands is difficult to treat. For slowing down the process and prevention, wear your SPF 30 religiously. Topical antioxidants and amino acid peptides stimulate collagen production, helping to add back some tone. For hands that are giving away your age, fat transplants have become the rage. Fat from an area with a bit more padding, like the hip or buttock, is removed with a syringe, treated, and reintroduced into the dorsal hand areas, instantly tenting the skin.

Sculptra, recently introduced into the market to refill areas of fat loss, may be a potential treatment for menopausal women struggling with subcutaneous fat loss.

For complete information on dealing with dark circles, please see the chapter "Dark Circles" on page 65.

HOT FLASHES AND FLUSHING

Nothing like a rosy glow to start out the day! Actually, I'm not really bothered by this new redness problem—I just skip my blusher, unless I happen to be wearing foundation that day. Remember, green counteracts red, so if you are looking for a way to mask the flush, try a nice green powder (like T. LeClerc) or cover-up stick.

It's the hot flashes that really get me. Despite HRT, these still occasionally catch me off guard. However, I have not yet felt it necessary to try blood-pressure medicines like clonidine to stop them.

Chilling out (literally) is a useful way to dial down one's internal thermostat. For squelching that flushed face, cooling masks can be useful and pampering. They can help put a chill onto your cheeks, which can rapidly constrict the blood vessels and reduce your redness. Make your experience a bit more frosty by keeping your favorite facial mask in the fridge. Keep these tricks in mind if you are getting anxious (and red!) about a big meeting or date.

FINAL THOUGHTS

Now you know the real scoop, from a veteran of the antiaging battle, about what to expect from your skin during menopause. The good news is that for most women, it's not nearly as bad as they feared. Furthermore, women's medical concerns are finally gaining the attention they deserve in the scientific community. Look for continued improvements in our knowledge base and therapy options in the near future.

Ask the DERMAdoctor

QUESTION:

I'm forty-one and postmenopausal and want to start over with my skin care products. I have a tendency to break out on my chin, and occasionally on my forehead and cheeks. I have dark circles, as well as wrinkles around the eyes and the lip area. Can you recommend a regimen?

The DERMAdoctor:

Most women who are postmenopausal have dry skin, despite their occasional breakouts. This said, using oil-free, noncomedogenic skin care products, in a cream base, helps address much of this. You can always add an oil-reducing agent if necessary.

Decide whether or not to use a moisturizer *after* any treatment and sunscreen layers are applied. You may find that you don't need a moisturizer, or that you need one on a seasonal basis only.

Wash with a gentle cleanser like Cetaphil Gentle Skin Cleanser or Vanicream Cleansing Bar. (If you have active acne outbreaks, try DERMAdoctor Born to Be Mild Medicated Cleanser.)

In the morning, you want to begin with an antioxidant-containing product that takes aim at rosacea. See pages 348–349 for a list of ingredients you should look for in a product. DERMAdoctor's own 2n1 rosacea cream helps treat the blemishes and addresses skin rejuvenation needs. The base is very hydrating, so you may not need a moisturizer. Naturally, you'll want to apply your sunscreen.

At night, try M.D. Forté Skin Rejuvenation Lotion I. While it says "rejuvenation" on the label, it contains glycolic acid and vitamin A, both of which can help your breakouts.

It's important to target the variety of issues that are causing your dark circles. To address fine lines, dark circles, and dryness, you may want to try DERMAdoctor Wrinkle Revenge Eye Balm.

For the lips, consider English Ideas Lip Refine AHA Exfoliating Cream nightly and DERMAdoctor Poutlandish Hyper Moisturizing Lip Paint & Treatment SPF 15 with Nanotechnology whenever required throughout the day.

SKIN REJUVENATION

Look Fresh and Healthy Every Day of Your Life

A patient I had a few years back defined my vision of aging and rejuvenation. Short like me, with dark hair, she gave me a hint of myself in maturity. But unlike the stereotypical grandmother, before me stood a pulled-together woman, sporting perfectly coiffed dyed hair, great makeup, and a chic, snugly fit little ensemble (often black jeans and a V-necked blouse). And each time she came to see me she had a different gentleman friend waiting in my lobby to take her to lunch. She was physically fit and mentally alert, with a fantastic attitude toward life.

Now, that's the way to be—at eighty-five!

Did she have wrinkles, you ask? Sure, but she had also taken great care of her skin throughout her life, and it showed.

THE SEVEN IDEAL INGREDIENTS

Making good decisions in rejuvenation isn't about having to use every product available or finding one that is "better" than all the rest. Rather, it's about trying to incorporate into your regimen at least two excellent ingredients—ingredients that work in a complementary fashion on the epidermis and the dermis, and are appropriate for your skin type.

(For a guide to the layers of the skin, and how each layer ages and can be rejuvenated, please see the chapter "Aging and Your Skin" on page 301.)

Currently, there are seven primary active ingredients that have been proven to be helpful in skin rejuvenation. There are also a variety of antioxidants, an array of ingredients that play a supporting role, and some new (and as yet unproven) entries into the rejuvenation scene. This list is in constant flux because of technological advances—and the claims of snake-oil salesmen. (When it comes to skin rejuvenation, distinguishing fact from fiction is practically a full-time job!) Let's take a look at the various ingredients you should know about.

I consider the following to be the ideal seven to look for:

- Retinoids
- Glycolic acid
- Idebenone
- Vitamin C (L-ascorbic acid)
- N-6 furfuryladenine
- GHK copper peptides
- Amino acid peptides

Add to this the array of supplements used to "boost" a product's claim for added effectiveness, and the permutations become endless. Information about skin rejuvenation could literally fill a book. But this chapter will help you successfully sort through the variety of creams, lotions, and other potions that make antiaging claims.

ANTIOXIDANTS: DISARMING FREE RADICALS

What They Do: As ultraviolet (UV) light contacts skin cells, a chemical reaction takes place that results in the formation of free radicals, molecules that damage cellular DNA. Antioxidants are molecules that work to neutralize free radicals.

Some antioxidants are purely antioxidants. Others also help stimulate fibroblasts to produce collagen fibers in the dermis. Examples of antioxidants:

- Alpha lipoic acid
- Beta-carotene
- Bioflavonoids
- Blackberry extract
- Blueberry extract
- Coenzyme Q-10 (a.k.a. CoQ10, ubiquinone)

- GHK copper peptides
- Grape-seed extract
- Green tea extract
- Idebenone (a variant of CoQ10)
- Lycopene
- Marine complexes or algae
- Pomegranate extract
- Superoxide dismutase (a naturally occurring enzyme within the skin that helps protect against free radicals; not technically an antioxidant)
- Vitamin C (L-ascorbic acid)
- Vitamin E
- White tea extract

A complete skin rejuvenation routine should incorporate a potent antioxidant. Doing so helps actively address the goal of reducing the rate of dermal degradation, as well as repairing and preventing some free-radical damage.

That doesn't mean you can apply a cream at age sixty and look twenty-five. Nor does it mean that severely droopy skin of the eyelids or jowls will snap back like a rubber band. But when you incorporate this strategy, noticeable firming and line reduction are certainly within reach.

RETINOIDS: EXFOLIATION PLUS

What They Do: Retinoids improve the appearance of fine wrinkle lines and blotchy skin discoloration and restore a healthier, more vibrant complexion. They also help treat acne, minimize the appearance of pores, and reduce oiliness. Studies suggest that they may also help firm the skin by stimulating fibroblast activity.

Retinoids are the granddaddy of the antiaging movement. With prescription Retin-A (tretinoin), medicine mated with beauty, and an entirely new industry was born.

Retin-A was originally formulated as an acne cream; it helps cells exfoliate, or shed, reducing the plugging in pores. As soon as it was medically proven to also help improve fine wrinkle lines, reduce skin discoloration (age spots), and restore a healthy, more youthful glow, Retin-A became the rage. However, many patients overused the product in the hope of more quickly finding their personal fountain of youth. The result was not that dermatologists suddenly saw far fewer wrinkled patients; instead, they found themselves triaging calls from overeager Retin-A enthusiasts who'd found out the hard way that the medication was formulated for oily teens and tended to be highly drying and irritating.

With age comes a reduction in the production of sebum, the oil that coats and protects the epidermal surface. As those early Retin-A users discovered, aging skin is drier and far less tolerant of creams purposely meant to reduce surface skin oils (among its other uses). Renova was developed in response to this need.

Renova

Renova contains 0.02% or 0.05% tretinoin, the same active ingredient in Retin-A, but in a moisturizing base. Don't get the wrong idea; Renova is great. But the base, made to hydrate drier, mature skin, is heavy enough to sometimes cause acne in middle-aged patients still dealing with oily skin. And Renova is still as potentially irritating as the original Retin-A formulation. Even the less concentrated formulation of 0.02% is still quite potent.

If you are unfortunate enough to find yourself with both wrinkles *and* acne yet want to stay with tretinoin, I recommend one of the Retin-A formulations instead of Renova. Renova is a wonderful product, but keep in mind that its heaviness could cause an acne flare in a woman with preexisting acne or prone to this condition.

Avage

Tretinoin isn't the only prescription vitamin A cream in use for skin rejuvenation. Tazorac (tazarotene), already approved by the FDA for treating both psoriasis and acne, has been shown in some medical studies to rival (and perhaps exceed) Renova in treating photoaging (sun damage to the skin). The FDA has given its blessing for the treatment of photoaging to this ingredient under the brand name Avage.

Retinol

The onslaught of prescription vitamin A wrinkle therapies essentially left the cosmetics industry out in the cold, so it turned to retinol—another vitamin A derivative—as the over-the-counter answer. Initially, the strength of retinol used in cosmetic products was quite weak. Currently, there has been a shift to stronger products at cosmetics counters.

Comparing retinol strengths can help you determine their relative effectiveness. Retinol is stronger than another vitamin A derivative, retinyl palmitate. They may be combined in certain formulations.

Retinols may not be as effective or yield results as rapidly as those of their rivals tretinoin and tazarotene, but they can be as irritating.

Use

Begin using any vitamin A cream—prescription or over the counter—only every other night. Use it sparingly (just a pea-sized amount), and wait thirty minutes after washing before application. These steps will help ensure tolerance, which in turn will help improve compliance.

Vitamin A creams, including retinols, increase one's sensitivity to the sun. Wear sunscreen!

And whether you've chosen retinol, retinyl palmitate, tretinoin, tazarotene, or adapalene—avoid using it while pregnant or nursing, and always wear your sunscreen during the day.

GLYCOLIC ACID: SMALL BUT POWERFUL

What It Does: Glycolic acid (and all AHAs) restores a fresh, glowing complexion, reduces skin discoloration, improves the appearance of fine wrinkle lines, minimizes the appearance of pores, and helps unplug sebaceous glands. It also helps other treatments better penetrate the outer layers of the epidermis.

When you hear the term *alpha hydroxy acid* (AHA), glycolic acid automatically tends to come to mind. Glycolic acid—derived from sugarcane and also sometimes synthesized—is indeed a member of the AHA family, along with lactic (from milk), citric (from citrus fruit), malic (from apples), and tartaric (from wine). Yet glycolic acid appears to be the most effective AHA for skin rejuvenation.

Glycolic acid works in a number of ways. Its small molecular size allows it to penetrate the skin more easily, which contributes to its effectiveness. It helps dissolve the "glue" that holds the skin cells together. This leads to exfoliation, its primary action. In addition, glycolic acid helps reduce surface skin oils, helps remove blackheads and other skin impurities, and smooths out fine wrinkle lines. Other benefits of glycolic acid include its moisturizing ability and the potential for it to help bleach unwanted skin discoloration. Glycolic acid is also thought to help stimulate collagen production within the dermis, to some degree.

SAFETY AND EFFECTIVENESS

AHAs are safe when used with caution and according to directions.

The amount of AHA in the product and the pH are the determining factors of a product's strength and the irritation you may experience. Don't forget: this is an acid. Too much can result in a chemical burn.

From a medical viewpoint, to provide effectiveness the free glycolic acid needs to be present in a minimum concentration of 8%. This is the baseline at which results begin to become obvious. AHA-containing products purchased at the drugstore, grocery, or department store are generally going to have far smaller percentages. The average over-the-counter AHA level is approximately 3%.

Glycolic acid compounds in a salt base are buffered (less acidic) and therefore better tolerated than "free" glycolic acids. The pH of a "free" glycolic acid is often around 2; the average pH of a glycolic acid compound is 3.8 to 4.5. The less acidic, the less potential irritation caused by the product. This can result in a 15% buffered glycolic acid being less irritating than the 3% solution from the grocery store. The best brand representative of buffered glycolic acid: the physician-only line M.D. Forté.

The buffering does not make the acid any less effective; there is simply less discomfort (burning sensation) and redness, and exfoliation takes place in a less visible manner.

A buffered glycolic acid compound also provides a time-release quality to the product. This prolonged effectiveness gives better long-term improvement than free glycolic acid. Applied to the skin, free acids quickly become neutralized, limiting their activity.

Dermatologists may use buffered glycolic acids to help boost a rejuvenation regimen that utilizes products notorious for causing flaking, such as prescription retinoids or over-the-counter retinols. Alternating a buffered glycolic acid product and a vitamin A cream every other night cuts down on the flaking, hydrates the skin, and provides an additional active ingredient to the regimen.

When using glycolic acid, it is important that you start at the lowest strength and work up to the highest, slowly. Don't think that using glycolic acid as a daily product or in a chemical peel must result in noticeable redness, dryness, and flaking in order for it to be effective.

There has been a trend for some companies or physicians to offer extremely high concentrations of free glycolic acid: 40% and up, some in home peel kits. The office of DERMAdoctor.com has received some frantic calls from panicked consumers who used such products (we don't carry them) and wanted to know what to do now that they were having serious side effects. These side effects may include burning, temporary or permanent skin discoloration, and even scarring. Buyer beware. You cannot be too careful.

Exfoliation due to any product, including AHAs, causes skin to be more susceptible to the elements. Sun protection is always important; when you are using an exfoliating agent, it is mandatory.

AHAs are typically considered safe to use while pregnant or nursing. As always, it is a good idea to discuss your use of all products with your doctor during this special time.

N-6 FURFURYLADENINE: NATURE'S CELLULAR PROTECTOR

What It Does: Reduces the appearance of fine lines and blotchy skin discoloration.

If you have tender, delicate skin and are unable to tolerate acidic or exfoliating rejuvenation products, or if you are looking for a product that doesn't encourage sun sensitivity, a little gift from Mother Nature may be just for you.

N-6 furfuryladenine is a naturally derived botanical growth hormone. This growth factor helps keep the plant green and healthy. It is formed as a self-protective response to oxidation created by photodamage and helps slow the cellular aging process. Used on the skin, it helps increase moisture retention and reduce the signs of aging.

A study on N-6 furfuryladenine from the University of California, Irvine, showed improvement of fine facial wrinkle lines and blotchy skin over a twenty-four-week period of use.

A Rejuvenator by Any Other Name

Not sure where to find this natural bounty? N-6 furfuryladenine, is better known by the names Kinerase and Kinetin.

Selection is based on your skin type. If you have dry skin or live in a dry climate, choose the cream base. If you have normal or combination skin or live in a warm or humid climate, select the lotion.

You can apply N-6 furfuryladenine under the eyes and to the crow's-feet areas, as well as to the rest of the face, neck, and décolletage. You can safely layer moisturizers and/or sunscreens on top of this ingredient.

While it may safely be used when pregnant or nursing, check individual product labels to verify that they do not contain other ingredients best avoided during this time.

GHK COPPER PEPTIDE: FOR DERMAL PROTECTION AND REPAIR

What It Does: Firms the skin, reduces inflammation, aids in wound healing.

A peptide naturally found in human skin and tissue, GHK (glycyl-L-histidyl-L-lysine) binds copper molecules, allowing them to arrive in an active state where needed. This peptide is now chemically synthesized in the laboratory. Known as prezatide copper acetate (Neova), it is capable of being used by the skin.

In the skin, GHK copper peptide helps to:

- Stimulate collagen formation, diminishing fine lines and firming the skin
- Stimulate elastin formation, cutting down on sagging and fine lines
- Stimulate the formation of the extracellular cement between cells, thus improving skin strength and cutting down on fragility
- Stimulate the formation of GAGs (glycosaminoglycans); this helps thicken the dermis, resulting in a lessening of sagging
- Increase blood vessel formation and oxygenation within the skin
- Act as a potent antioxidant, by stimulating the enzymatic function of superoxide dismutase

Studies are compelling regarding the effectiveness of copper when combined with a GHK protein peptide (GHK-Cu). A study of twenty volunteers showed that after thirty days, the formation of pro-collagen, a precursor of collagen, increased 70 percent (as shown by skin biopsy), compared with 50 percent with vitamin C and 40 percent with tretinoin. This means that GHK copper peptide is highly effective in the skin rejuvenation process.

VITAMIN C: CONVERTING ME TO SKIN REJUVENATION

What It Does: Firms the skin, reduces fine lines and under-eye bagginess, improves skin discoloration.

Discovering vitamin C was the turning point in my view of the effectiveness of certain specific skin rejuvenation products and the whole new world of antiaging.

Several years ago I was asked by a television station to speak on the benefits of Cellex-C. At that time, I was more focused on the treatment of difficult-to-solve skin conditions and, short of using some Retin-A and performing some sclerotherapy, was not really dwelling on the whole cosmetic and antiaging craze. After investigating the brand and its clinical research, as well as seeing what it could do clinically for my office staff, myself, and some friends, I was convinced.

Technically, vitamin C is an AHA (specifically citric acid), but it is also a potent antioxidant. L-ascorbic acid (the active form of vitamin C used in skin rejuvenation) helps stimulate fibroblast activity while simultaneously working as an antioxidant.

L-ascorbic acid requires a very low pH (less than 3.5; think lemon juice) to penetrate the skin and maintain its effectiveness. That is why there will be some tingling upon application. This acidity is the reason to use a vitamin C product just once daily. To make the most of its antioxidant abilities, apply it in the morning. My favorite, tried-and-true vitamin C lines are Cellex-C and SkinCeuticals.

Also, remember that the drier your skin, the more sensitive it may be to the acidity. To help circumvent this, select a cream base and precede it by the application of hyaluronic acid (such as Cellex-C Hydra 5 B-Complex or SkinCeuticals Hydrating B5 gel), which holds one thousand times its weight in water. This helps hydrate the skin and ameliorate some of this potential irritation.

Will an Orange a Day Keep the Wrinkles Away?

Even with adequate oral intake, the amount of a nutrient in your diet does not always correspond with its ability to reach the skin (or to do so in an active state). Vitamin C is the best-known example. Excess amounts of vitamin C in the diet are simply eliminated from the body, preventing higher dosages from reaching the skin. This necessitates the use of topical vitamin C for skin rejuvenation purposes. Topical vitamin C application is far superior to oral ingestion; the amount of ascorbic acid that can accumulate in the skin from Cellex-C is between twenty and forty times greater than what reaches the skin through the diet.

IDEBENONE: THE NEWEST ANTIOXIDANT

What It Does: Firms the skin, reduces skin discoloration, improves the appearance of fine lines, and improves skin texture.

Idebenone is the newest antioxidant ingredient. It is being promoted as the most potent, effective antioxidant used in skin care to date. Researchers have proven that it penetrates the skin, remains stable, and gets the job done.

Scientific data presented at the 2004 meeting of the American Academy of Dermatology showed that idebenone hydrated dry skin, improved the appearance of fine lines, and helped smooth skin texture—all without irritation, in as little as three weeks. In fact, the study showed that idebenone had double the strength and effectiveness of alpha lipoic acid, which was once touted as a potent skin rejuvenator but which was the weakest of the antioxidants tested in the study, scoring below N-6 furfuryladenine and vitamin C, among others. The only downside to the study was that neither pomegranate extract, green tea, nor white tea was included in the test. Green tea is a powerful antioxidant thought to be highly effective in skin rejuvenation. White tea is the most potent of the tea extracts.

In descending order of effectiveness, here is a list of how idebenone fared against five other antioxidants commonly found in skin care products:

1. Idebenone
2. Vitamin E
3. N-6 furfuryladenine
4. Ubiquinone (CoQ10)
5. Vitamin C (L-ascorbic acid)
6. Alpha lipoic acid

A variant of coenzyme Q-10, idebenone reduces mitochondrial DNA free-radical damage and helps prevent cellular DNA damage caused by the sun's harmful rays. (It is not a sunscreen; you still need to apply one.)

AMINO ACID PEPTIDES

When you cut your finger, collagen fibers within the dermis are broken. The end portion of the injured collagen fiber is composed of a chain of very specific amino acids (amino acid peptides) that send a chemical message out to fibroblasts (collagen-producing cells), enticing them to return to the area, make collagen, and repair the wound. This chemical message is known as chemotaxis.

Collagen destruction doesn't just happen when we're injured. It also takes place as we age: after the age of forty, 1 percent of our skin's collagen is lost each year. If you're twenty, you want to maintain skin firmness by keeping in place the fibroblasts that pump out lots of skin firming collagen. If you're forty-five, not only are you losing critical collagen levels, but the fibroblasts that are present are getting "lazy" and simply not working the way they used to.

Amino acid peptides used in skin rejuvenation are composed of the same end fragment that sends out the distress signal to those fibroblasts—in this case, chemically signaling skin to become firmer. DERMAdoctor Wrinkle Revenge Facial Cream and Eye Balm contain the Peptide-D58 Complex: a blend of the newest, most active generation of these amino acid peptides, created to maintain (or reclaim) firm skin. Wrinkle Revenge also contains the potent antioxidants white tea, pomegranate, and grape seed extracts, as well as other components to restore the protective ceramide barrier that is lost as our skin ages.

FINAL THOUGHTS

The good news is that we live in a time when science has merged with beauty. Aging skin isn't inevitable. There *is* something you can do for yourself to improve your skin and give yourself a healthier, fresher look.

Ask the DERMAdoctor

QUESTION:

I heard that skin cells are able to reproduce only a certain number of times and that the use of exfoliants like glycolic acid or retinol will use them up, speeding up the aging process. Is this true?

The DERMAdoctor:

This idea is frequently posted in cyberspace—and it's most definitely a myth. The theory is based upon some work performed in vitro (in a petri dish) in the 1960s and widely hyped about two years ago. The real threads of the story: glycolic acids/AHAs and retinoids thin the epidermis (what we *want* them to do), which can increase sun sensitivity. And overuse of either of these two potent treatment categories can irritate the skin. However, AHAs—including glycolic acid, retinoids, and other exfoliating agents—do *not* speed up skin aging.

SUNSCREENS AND SUN PROTECTION

Made in the Shade

It used to be that the number of sunscreens on the market was very limited and I had a few favorites from the handful of options available to my patients. However, there are now literally hundreds of sunscreens. It's become difficult to keep track of all the brands, so the consumer needs to know how to read the labels.

Not all sunscreens are created equal. Understanding what a sunscreen or sunblock is made of and why it is effective is very important. And that doesn't mean you need to overspend to adequately protect your skin!

LET THERE BE WAVELENGTHS

It's important to understand that light comes in a spectrum of different waves, categorized by length. Here are the various wavelengths of light, by category. "UV" stands for ultraviolet, of course.

UVC:	200 to 290 NM (nanometers)
UVB:	290 to 320 NM
UVA:	320 to 400 NM
Visible light:	400 to 760 NM
Infrared:	760+ NM

The wavelengths responsible for most skin problems are those in the UVA and UVB spectrums. These are invisible to the human eye.

Those with serious skin conditions such as lupus may experience sensitivity to visible light, too.

SUNSCREENS VERSUS SUNBLOCKS

While many people, including myself, often use "sunscreen" and "sunblock," interchangeably, there really is a technical difference between the two.

A true sunscreen is a chemical agent that absorbs and denatures the light, making the wavelengths incapable of causing damage.

Sunblocks literally establish a barrier that blocks UV rays from reaching the skin's surface.

Many "sunscreens" contain a mixture of these two properties.

THE BARE-SKIN MINIMUM

The following is what your sunscreen or sunblock *must* do in order to provide you with adequate, safe coverage.

Minimum SPF 15. It must contain a minimum SPF (sun protection factor) of 15 for routine sun exposure, with a higher SPF (preferably 30) for more intensive exposure, such as at the beach.

Broad Protection. It must provide broad-spectrum protection, meaning that *both* UVA- and UVB-protecting ingredients are present. If the label doesn't say they're there, odds are they aren't.

PABA-free. For those with sensitive skin, eczema, or a known PABA allergy, it must be PABA-free. Remember to check the ingredient list to make certain the vehicle (the base that contains the active ingredients) doesn't contain agents you're sensitive to. Individuals with known contact dermatitis allergies, eczema, or sensitive skin may find their skin better tolerates true sunblocks containing zinc oxide or titanium dioxide.

Reapply. Don't be fooled by the product's claims to be waterproof. Personally, I feel this phrase is both confusing and misleading. Many consumers simply apply a waterproof sunscreen early in the day and neglect to reapply it according to the fine print. You *must* reapply sunscreen or sunblock (whether it's labeled waterproof or not) after water exposure, toweling dry, or every two hours while outdoors.

ACTIVE INGREDIENTS

The following is a list of the different types of sunscreens and sun-blocks and their active ingredients.

UVB Screens: 260 NM to 320 NM

UVB, better known as the "burning" wavelength of light, is the cause of sunburns and skin cancers. Active ingredients in UVB blocks include:

- PABA (known to be a contact dermatitis allergen, and mostly avoided in current sunscreens)
- Padimate O
- Octinoxate (formerly known as octyl methoxycinnamate)
- Octisalate (formerly known as octyl salicylate or ethylhexyl salicylate)
- Homosalate

UVA Screens: 260 NM to 400 NM

UVA wavelengths are longer, capable of penetrating more deeply into the skin. UVA causes deeper tissue damage, wrinkle formation, and skin cancer. UVA chemical sunscreen ingredients include:

- Oxybenzone
- Avobenzone (Parsol 1789)
- Benzophenone
- Meradimate (formerly known as menthyl anthranilate; gives protection from the middle of the UVB range to the middle of the UVA range)
- Tinasorb (found in Rit Sun Guard; both UVA and UVB protection)
- Mexoryl SX and LX (available only in Europe; considered the most potent UVA screen)

Physical Blockers: 290 NM to 1,800 NM

Physical blockers block both UVA and UVB. They used to leave a heavy, white residue. But with the micronization process, they are now fairly innocuous. On darker skin, traces may still be seen. Active ingredients:

- Zinc oxide
- Titanium dioxide
- Iron oxide (also blocks visible light)

Pure physical blockers do not contain sunscreen ingredients, making them an ideal option for anyone prone to sunscreen allergies, eczema, or sensitive skin. Vanicream Sunscreen SPF 15 and Peter Thomas Roth Titanium Dioxide Sunblock SPF 30 contain a blend of titanium dioxide and zinc oxide.

I receive many questions regarding which is better, titanium dioxide or zinc oxide. Both provide similar, broad-spectrum coverage, although products containing titanium dioxide alone may have a gooier texture. The most common complaint about physical sunblocks is that their formulations often seem less lightweight.

ADDED ANTIOXIDANTS

Sunscreens and sunblocks are following the marketing trend of adding in a variety of antioxidants, like vitamins A, C, and E, to help neutralize cellular DNA damage where it starts (in this case, sun exposure that gets through your sunscreen) or help rejuvenate the skin. A little added benefit from these antioxidants is all well and good. Just don't feel this is all you need to do if you're actively trying to fix photodamage or eradicate smile lines.

Topical green tea extract, however, contains the active ingredient EGCG, known to possess anti-inflammatory properties. Green tea has been shown in many medical studies to be helpful in reducing UV damage and may play a role in skin cancer prevention. Green tea is an important ingredient in sunscreens like DERMAdoctor Body Guard.

For those looking to avoid vitamin A, particularly if you're pregnant or nursing, add sunscreen to the list of product labels you should read. The risk vitamin A in a sunscreen poses is purely theoretical, but for purists, vitamin A is vitamin A, no matter where it's found.

AVOIDING THE OIL SLICK

While it makes no difference in the effectiveness of the product, the aesthetic feel of the base is important to many sunscreen users. Although many products are labeled "oil-free" or "noncomedogenic," most consumers report that a common reason they skip their sunscreen is the residual greasiness, tackiness, or stickiness the product leaves behind. Add to that the complaint of sunscreen dripping into the eyes, and you can understand why sunscreens simply have not been embraced to their fullest extent.

Many women prone to acne or oily skin also notice a flare-up when they apply sun protection.

Oil-free sunscreens include DERMAdoctor Body Guard Exquisitely Light SPF, M.D. Forté Sun Protector SPF 20, and Peter Thomas Roth Ultra Lite Oil-Free Sunblock SPF 30. DERMAdoctor Body Guard additionally contains a polymer to absorb excessive skin oils and keep skin looking matte. All these products are safe for use on the face and body.

MAKEUP, MOISTURIZERS, AND SUNSCREENS

I'm often asked if the addition of sunscreen to a moisturizer or makeup is adequate protection. My standard answer: No. Many times, makeup and moisturizers are applied only to discrete spots rather than all over the face (not to mention other sun-exposed areas of skin like the neck), as a sunscreen should be, so I consider the presence of SPF in these products merely icing on the cake. And studies show that many of these mixed products don't have the all-day staying power of a typical foundation or moisturizer. If you can't live without sunscreen in your moisturizer, look to a product like Purpose Dual Treatment Moisture Lotion with SPF 15, and then apply sunscreen afterward.

On the flip side, there are several sunscreens with very moisturizing bases, an ideal combination for those with drier skin. Cellex-C Sun Care SPF 30+ and M.D. Forté Aftercare Environmental Protection Cream SPF 30 are examples.

ULTRAPROTECTION FOR THE ULTRASENSITIVE

Even the best routine sunscreen won't protect some women against sun-induced skin problems—those with lupus, transplant patients, postradiation patients, skin cancer patients, chemotherapy patients, or women who've had laser skin resurfacing. For these women, Total Block Clear SPF 65 is ideal. It contains eight different micronized physical blocker ingredients, including titanium dioxide and zinc oxide, and the visible light blocker iron oxide.

Total Block Cover-Up/Make-Up SPF 60 has the same protective qualities as Total Block Clear SPF 65, but it comes with a separately packaged colored iron oxide that mixes to lighten or darken the base. This provides a wonderful cosmetic cover-up for the most sun-sensitive women.

SPFASHION

Many people are unaware that regular T-shirt material has an SPF of only 4! UVA light is able to penetrate through the material and cause the nonburning, ultraviolet damage that can create wrinkles and lead to skin cancer down the road. And when the cloth is wet, the SPF is basically nil. Remember when you were sunburned and your mother told you to put on a T-shirt and go back into the pool? Unfortunately, she needn't have bothered. However, there are fabric options to help protect you and your family from unwanted sun exposure.

Sun-protective clothing definitely has an important role in sun avoidance. Numerous lines have made their way to the marketplace that offer a trendy, updated look for outdoor activities.

Lupus patients, in particular, need to be thoroughly protected from the sun. For them, there are sun-protective gloves and other specialty cover-up accessories.

Awash in SPF

These specialty clothing lines have made a huge contribution to the health of many a dermatology patient, but the costs can add up. And sometimes they're difficult to find. Now you can wear your own favorite items *and* have SPF 30 protection—by washing SPF right into them!

Simply add a single packet of Rit Sun Guard Laundry Treatment UV Protectant into your washer, along with your regular laundry detergent, and the clothing will be coated with a broad-spectrum SPF 30 that lasts through twenty additional washings. This is an easy, economical way to protect yourself and your family from the sun's damaging rays.

Another Excuse to Accessorize

This is the summer to add a chapeau to your wardrobe. Nothing protects your face, ears, and neckline like a hat with a wide brim (at least four inches).

If you choose a straw hat, remember that many of them are unlined and loosely woven, which allows the sun to go directly through the hat.

Baseball caps (assuming they're worn with the bill in front) don't protect the ears, the back of the neck, or even most of the face.

Sunglasses

Don't forget the importance of protecting your eyes from strong sunlight.

Moles that could potentially turn into melanomas can form at the back of the eye. (For anyone with a known history of dysplastic moles or melanoma or a family history of melanoma, I always advise an annual eye exam by an ophthalmologist. Don't forget to tell the doctor about what she or he should be looking for.) Sunlight can also cause problems like cataracts and macular degeneration.

You can find adequate eye protection at your local five-and-dime or spend big bucks on trendy frames. Either way, sunglasses should be marked as protecting against UVA and UVB.

And don't forget the kids! When you feel the need to put on your sunglasses, your children should be wearing them as well.

LAST BUT NOT LEAST: THE LIPS

When it comes to sun protection, the lips are often neglected. Many women believe that their lipstick will protect them, but this isn't true. The darkest shade of opaque plain lipstick (not containing an SPF additive) provides an SPF of only 5; the protection afforded by lip gloss is negligible. Also, not only can the sun more easily penetrate many lighter shades, but lipstick wears off throughout the day, leaving lips unprotected.

Consider carrying English Ideas Hint of Color SPF 18 Lip Balm during the summer, or applying it under your lipstick to provide a colorless layer of sun protection.

Poutlandish: The Ideal Lip Protectant

Lips that are chapped or cracked may be more prone to developing a contact dermatitis to the chemical sunscreen component. To create an ideal lip protectant, a physical blocker is essential. Yet zinc oxide and titanium dioxide may leave a trace of white residue on darker areas such as the lips.

By turning to nanotechnology, DERMAdoctor Poutlandish incorporates zinc oxide particles one-eighty-thousandth the diameter of a human hair, providing safe, effective broad-spectrum SPF 15 protection. It is available in clear as well as a variety of flattering shades.

FINAL THOUGHTS

When it comes to sunscreen, there are far more choices than meet the eye. I hope you will now feel more comfortable when out shopping for the product that is just perfect for you. And don't forget to apply your sunscreen daily!

Ask the DERMAdoctor

QUESTION:

I have recently been unable to use any sunscreen. When I do, I break out severely and it takes a long time to go away. I have tried various no-oil sunscreens, to no avail. I'm tired of wasting money on product after product. Please tell me what you recommend for a sunscreen.

The DERMAdoctor:

This is a very common problem. That's why I formulated DERMAdoctor Body Guard Exquisitely Light SPF 30 (for face and body), which is free from any of the common irritants and ingredients that would cause you to break out.

Body Guard is most definitely oil-free and noncomedogenic. But to make things even better, Body Guard is oil-reducing, incorporating a polymer technology that prevents skin from drowning in excess surface oils. Skin stays matte-looking without becoming dried out, making it ideal for any skin type.

Forty-five percent of individuals enrolled in comedogenicity testing of this product found their acne improved, presumably in response to a reduction in surface skin oils.

Body Guard also contains a comprehensive blend of powerful antioxidants like green tea and soothing botanicals.

After a day in the sun, an eight-hour window exists in which any free-radical damage or early sunburn or sun damage can be addressed. Consider Body Guard an ideal rejuvenating postsun treatment. Apply it after showering.

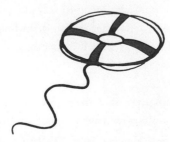

TATTOOS AND PERMANENT MAKEUP

The Canvas of You

Tattoos have definitely gone mainstream, as anyone who watches *Survivor* or MTV or spends a day at the beach is well aware. Recently, I went with my family to the local amusement park, and it seemed as if literally everyone there had a tattoo. I have had babysitters with tattoos, a myriad of young patients and neighbors, and was recently surprised to find that a good friend had a tattoo. Tattooing has a long and celebrated history. However, there are dermatological concerns that you should take into account if you are considering getting a tattoo.

The word "tattoo" literally means to puncture the skin. Tattoo pigment is placed into the layer of skin known as the dermis. It is a permanent placement, although over time some of the colors may fade. Tattoos may be for artistry, cosmetic uses such as permanent cosmetics, or reconstructive purposes. Tattooing of permanent makeup includes eyeliner, lip liner, full lip color, beauty marks, and eyebrow restoration, as well as scar camouflage. The use of tattooing for reconstructive issues includes the artistic replacement of the areola for some postmastectomy patients.

SAFETY RECOMMENDATIONS

Some of the "universal precautions" performed in a physician's office to avoid transmission of disease should also be performed in a tattoo parlor. From a medical point of view, here are some things to keep in mind to make tattooing as safe an experience as possible.

Reputable Parlor. Make sure the parlor is reputable. If you have doubts, check with the health department to see if there have been past claims against the parlor.

Sterilized Equipment. Does the artist autoclave multiuse items? (The autoclave is the best way to sterilize instruments.) Anything that is auto-claved for multiple uses must be sealed and dated to ensure sterility. Are sterile techniques used during the tattoo process? Does the artist wipe down surfaces with a viricidal and germicidal agent between clients?

Disposable Needles. Does the artist use single-use sterile disposable nee-dles and tubing? Are needles disposed of in properly labeled containers?

Other Single-Use Items. Does the artist throw away leftover ointments, tray, razors, and pigments after completing a tattoo?

Gloves. Does the artist wear gloves?

Vaccination. Has the artist been vaccinated for hepatitis B?

CARE BEFORE AND AFTER

Tattooing involves multiple punctures of the skin to instill pigment into the dermal layer, causing pain as well as some minor bleeding. To diminish discomfort, consider using topical anesthetics such as L.M.X. 4, freezing spray, or PrameGel. To stop the bleeding, your tattoo artist may try topical hemostasis liquid agents, like Monsel's or Drysol.

Initially, a tattoo results in a raw, open wound. Leave the bandage on for at least twelve hours. Gently wash off dried exudate. Apply a coat of Polysporin ointment (neomycin-containing antibiotic oint-ments have a higher rate of contact dermatitis). Do this until healed.

Don't immerse the tattoo in water; shower, but don't take a bath.

The area may get dry; a water-based cream like Moisturel Thera-peutic Cream or Vanicream Moisturizing Skin Care Cream is good to apply, if needed, until the tattoo is fully healed.

A scab or shiny skin patch will form over the tattoo and will remain for approximately three to seven days. Do not pick at the area!

Any sign of infection (redness, oozing, streaking, pus draining from the site, increased tenderness, or the formation of an ulcer) is *not* a good thing. Get yourself to a dermatologist right away.

CHOOSING THE RIGHT TATTOO

Select a symbol you can live with for the rest of your life. Remember that tattoos are still somewhat out of the mainstream in the professional world. Can you picture yourself as a lawyer in the courtroom wearing a skirt with a serpent going up the entire length of your leg? Can you picture yourself at eighty with the tattoo you have in mind? You may laugh at these images, but young people choose many tattoos before they are really out in the professional workforce, and this can turn into a future issue for them. So can having a lover's name on your arm, particularly when you end up with someone else!

Review the artist's portfolio and make sure that the tattoos have sharp lines and smooth edges.

Consider selecting a body surface that is more private.

Do *not* try to tattoo yourself. These are the types that not only turn out to look crude in appearance (remember those traumatic good old pencil lead tattoos from childhood?) but are also far more difficult to remove down the road. The pigment is often deposited at irregular depths within the skin. You also stand a greater risk of developing an infection.

INFECTION PROTECTION

Tattooing may potentially result in the accidental inoculation of infectious particles into the skin. The potential risk of an infection from a tattoo (particularly hepatitis B) is sufficiently high that pregnant women should avoid tattoos, to safeguard the health of the baby.

Here is a list of some of the most common infectious agents that may be transmitted via a needle stick:

Hepatitis B and C. The leading risks from a needle stick.

Tuberculosis. May definitely be transferred via a needle stick.

Mycobacteria. Other strains of mycobacteria (not just those that cause TB) may potentially be passed via a needle stick.

Syphilis. This epidemic venereal disease is contagious through exposure to infected blood, as well as to other bodily fluids.

HIV. While feared as the major risk to both client and tattoo artist, the virus responsible for this disease is very fragile and much harder to spread via a needle stick than a hardy virus like hepatitis B. Still, twenty-six medical workers have been reported as infected with HIV from accidental needle sticks, so there is a potential risk.

Malaria. More likely in indigenous regions. However, your artist (or client) may have been infected from previous travels.

Hansen's Disease (Leprosy). There have been reports of infectious spread via tattooing, primarily from areas in Asia where the disease is endemic.

SKIN REACTIONS
Some skin diseases may flare up when insulted by local skin injury. Psoriasis may form locally at the tattoo site. This is called the Koebner phenomenon.

Most tattoo inks are derived from metals that may cause a wide array of skin reactions. While these can be significant if you are the person affected, they tend to be unusual, affecting a limited percentage of the tattooed population.

Patch testing confirms eczematous reactions but is negative for granulomatous reactions. (For more on granulomas, see below.)

The following are problems that may be seen later on with tattoos, even years down the road:

- Lichenoid reaction (small bumps of reactive tissue)
- Sarcoidal granulomas (firm balls of reactive tissue beneath the surface of the skin)
- Keloids (raised scars)
- Scaling
- Itching
- Swelling (often due to a photosensitive or phototoxic reaction)
- Ulceration (the formation of a sore)
- Delayed hypersensitivity (a reaction separated by a significant period of time from the application of the tattoo, also referred to

within the trade as "the red reaction," since it is most commonly caused by red inks)

- Lymphocytoma cutis (a benign skin reaction that mimics lymphoma of the skin)

Let's look at some of these in more detail.

Granulomas

Granulomas—caused by an allergic reaction to a specific tattoo ink—are a commonly reported problem. For instance, you may find that a firm, localized swelling forms in the areas of the tattoo where a red pigment was introduced. These may be single granulomas, consisting of the entire color area, or multiple tiny granulomas within the affected color region. Granulomas are difficult to treat. Topical or injectable steroids can be used. If this fails, removal of the tattoo may be the only option.

Keloids

Following the procedure, large, raised scars (keloids) may develop. Tattooing is not recommended to known keloid formers. Keloids, while not easily removable, may be improved or flattened with the use of steroids injected directly into the keloid. (Topical steroid creams, ointments, or tape may help, but they do not tend to be as effective for keloids.) Injections may need to be repeated on an interval basis to keep the keloids flat. Medical insurance does not tend to cover this treatment, as scars usually fall into the "cosmetic" category on policies. Silicone gels and patches have become more available for use in keloid treatment and can help reduce scar visibility.

Delayed Hypersensitivity

In delayed hypersensitivity, local itching, scaling, and even redness and swelling develop suddenly within the tattoo—several years after you acquired it! The reaction can be to a specific color or generalized within the tattoo.

Treatment is limited to topical relief with steroid preparations and possibly some anti-itching lotions, like Sarnol-HC 1% or PrameGel. Systemic antihistamines may be useful.

The reaction may be self-limited. Or, if it's severe and ongoing, it may require the removal of the tattoo.

Sun Sensitivity

Photosensitivity and phototoxicity result from a reaction between the sun and the tattoo dye. Photosensitive reactions produce symptoms that mimic allergies, including local swelling, itching, scaling, redness, and so on. This is most commonly observed with yellow (cadmium) tattoo dye. Phototoxic reactions result in sunburn of the area.

Reaction to a MRI

Since most tattoo inks contain metal, MRI exams may cause burning or stinging within the tattoo. Redness may even occur. This should be temporary. The presence of a tattoo is not a contraindication to having an MRI.

TATTOO REMOVAL

What are you going to do if you ever decide that your tattoo needs to go the way of the old lover whose name is emblazoned upon your arm, or that a dragon on your leg just doesn't jive with your new corporate image? Remember, tattoos are forever—unless you actively try to have one removed. While there is no perfect remedy, there is a variety of options for eradicating an unwanted tattoo.

Cosmetic Cover-up

Specific cosmetics for camouflaging skin imperfections may be utilized to cover up the unwanted tattoo. Covermark by Lydia O'Leary or Dermablend are available.

A New Tattoo

If you still want a tattoo, cover the unwanted version with a more complicated overlay. Discuss this in depth with your tattoo artist to see if it is possible, and plan it out well. This is usually going to be customized, as opposed to an "off-the-shelf" pattern, so there may be more expense involved than you anticipated.

Excision

It works, but it's usually done in several stages, particularly for larger tattoos, and it most definitely leaves scarring.

Dermabrasion

Results are often better for professionally inked tattoos, as the pigment deposition should be at a fairly uniform depth within the dermis. Any time you abrade down into the dermis, there will be permanent discoloration and/or scarring. The skin is anesthetized, frozen, and sanded down until the pigment is gone. A complicated tattoo may require multiple sessions, and it's unlikely that you'll get 100 percent results.

Laser Resurfacing

Different tattoo ink colors require different wavelengths of laser light to break up the pigment. (Some lasers now have the ability to offer more than one wavelength of light, providing more versatility for the laser surgeon.) This technique is definitely improving as technology catches up with demand, but is not yet a perfected art. Expect several sessions.

The Q-switched lasers—Alexandrite, Nd:YAG, and ruby—are those used to help remove tattoos. Laser treatment is not inexpensive, but it may be worth it if you are looking for aesthetic results. The removal of blue and black tattoos yields the best results. The technique is less effective for lighter colors, like yellow or green.

Individuals with darker skin tones may be more prone to post-laser discoloration, potentially a permanent problem.

A Possible Side Effect: Keloids

All of these removal options may cause keloid formation (thickened, raised scars) in individuals prone to this condition. Those who have taken the drug Accutane should wait at least three years before considering any of these procedures.

PERMANENT MAKEUP

Permanent makeup, a form of tattooing, is a creative way to achieve that ready-to-go look all the time. A licensed permanent makeup technician injects a small amount of pigment into the skin, causing instant color and providing a look similar to that achieved with makeup. It is best for eyeliner and full lip color, and has been used to create beauty marks and hide scars. No more fussing with eye pencils or liquid liner. It's there. Forever. So before going ahead with a permanent makeup procedure, make sure it's something you are willing to live with for the rest of your life.

In addition to knowing what you want, you should be sure of what you're going to get. Make certain that the technicians are certified and follow the same fastidious habits required of all tattooists. After all, it's a permanent change to your face that you're going for.

What to Expect

As with any tattoo placement, there can be some swelling. Lips, in general, are prone to exaggerated swelling, so it comes as no surprise that they are typically swollen after tattooing, though the degree varies from client to client. Overall, experts say, the healing process is quite fast and requires little more than application of a gentle salve, such as A&D ointment or petroleum jelly.

Bottom Line

Permanent makeup doesn't come cheap. Clients can expect to pay $300 on the low end for eyebrows and $800 on the high end for lips. Don't forget: makeup colors and styles change, often by the season. Before proceeding with permanent makeup, be certain that your choice today will be one you will be happy with five or ten years down the road.

FINAL THOUGHTS

Tattooing has been an art form for more than six thousand years and is likely going to continue to increase in popularity. By understanding the process and knowing how to avoid infection as well as recognize reactions, you can achieve greater satisfaction from your tattoo.

Ask the DERMAdoctor

QUESTION:

Last week I finally got up enough nerve to get a small blue rose tattoo on the back of my shoulder. When the tattoo artist read my form, which said I was allergic to nickel, he told me it was risky to use any blue or purple ink for my tattoo but that he could use other colors. Is he correct? Is nickel the product used to make blue tattoo ink?

The DERMAdoctor:

Blue tattoo dyes are derived from a variety of cobalt salts and are notorious for causing deep granulomas, as well as localized hypersensitivity reactions, and there are a few reported cases of uveitis (an inflammation of the eyes). Light blue colors are also derived from cobalt and may also cause granulomas. Watch for the names cobalt blue and cobaltous aluminate, which are the terms for this blue pigment. There can be a cross-reaction to topical cobalt-containing products for some patients allergic to nickel, so I suspect that theoretically a patient allergic to nickel could have a cross-reaction to this tattoo ink as well.

YOUR SKIN CARE MEDICINE CABINET

What to Have on Hand

How many times have you had a rash or other skin problem and not been able to get into the doctor to get treatment right away? This has become much more common with the advent of HMO plans and the shortage of dermatologists.

Although none of the recommendations for care in this chapter should replace speaking with or seeing your doctor, they provide options for alleviating your discomfort in a timely, effective manner while you await your appointment. Too many times, I see patients who have complicated their condition with inappropriate over-the-counter selections.

So let me try to guide you about what to have on hand.

BLISTERS: DRY THEM OUT

Blisters can develop for any number of reasons—chickenpox, shingles, poison ivy, a drug rash, certain bug bites, or friction (like a too tight shoe).

There's a classic dermatology saying: "If it's dry, wet it, and if it's wet, dry it." So when it comes to drying out a blister, one of the quickest treatments is an over-the-counter product called Domeboro Astringent Solution. Not only does it help dry out the lesions quickly, it also helps prevent a secondary infection by bacteria.

It is available in tablet or powder form; both are equally effective. Mix according to the directions on the package. Use a compress on the blistered area twice a day, for approximately twenty minutes each time. Avoid using this product around the eyes.

Don't pull the top off a blister. Think of the skin as a natural alternative to a Band-Aid, but by all means feel free to cover the area with a bandage. If the blister causes you pain, you can take a sterile needle and gently pop it. Releasing the fluid quickly relieves the pain.

Anytime the skin is open, it is vulnerable to infection. Don't forget to apply a topical antibiotic ointment like Polysporin to denuded blisters, which will help prevent infection and help the raw, exposed area heal faster.

ITCHING: SOOTHE THE SPOT

Regardless of the cause, itching is dreadful. Who can't recall a sleepless night thrashing about and scratching for one reason or another? Dealing with itching inside *and* out helps hasten relief.

Over-the-counter Benadryl Allergy Dye-Free Liquid is very helpful at controlling itching. One of the best reasons to use the liquid version is that, unlike a pill, you can take as little as you need, which helps prevent drowsiness.

Be wary of sedation whenever you take an antihistamine. (I find that nonsedating antihistamines don't provide much relief for itching.) If you plan to take an over-the-counter antihistamine like Benadryl for bedtime relief, do so at least an hour before bed.

You can turn to your pantry for added relief by adding about half a box of baking soda to your bathwater. Or you can use Aveeno Oatmeal Bath Treatment.

Instead of scratching, apply something that will temporarily soothe the trouble spot. Topical antipruritic products like PrameGel, Prax Lotion, and Caldryl Clear Lotion can also help provide temporary, soothing relief from highly itchy areas.

Reasons to go see the doctor include: itching from head to toe (especially without cause); an isolated skin growth (like a mole) that continuously itches; and an unidentified rash.

HIVES: TRIPLE YOUR RELIEF

Instead of scratching like mad, take an antihistamine, apply Cortaid Steroid Cream, and rub in your favorite topical anesthetic.

Unfortunately, 95 percent of the time the cause of a bout of hives is impossible to determine. However, think about medications you're taking (especially those you've started in the past six weeks), recent or ongoing infections, and foods you've eaten. Strawberries, citrus fruit, seafood, shellfish, nuts, and peanuts are the top offenders. Remember, you have to have been exposed to something before in order to become allergic to it. For hives lasting more than six weeks, a workup is helpful.

Reasons to go the emergency room: difficulty breathing, swallowing or speaking.

Please read the chapter "Hives" on page 133 for more information on this annoying problem.

CUTS: KEEP THEM CLEAN

Keep those cuts and scrapes clean with hydrogen peroxide and Polysporin ointment. Do this at least twice daily.

Neomycin has a long tradition in wound care, but as a dermatologist, I discourage patients from using it. Several times a year, I see patients who are allergic to this ingredient, which is found in many antibiotic ointments, including "triple antibiotic ointment." The allergic reaction causes the treated area to become very swollen and red. The patient misconstrues this as a signal that the infection has escalated, applies more neomycin, and the cycle continues. It's best to avoid this situation entirely. I'd also avoid silver sulfadiazine cream, which can occasionally cause allergic reactions.

There are some reasons to make an emergency call to the doctor (even on a weekend): a wide area of redness around the wound, red streaking extending from the wound, extreme tenderness, or pus draining from the site.

SUNBURN: COOL IT

The best way to treat a sunburn is not to get one! In your medicine cabinet, keep a sunscreen with a minimum SPF of 15 (preferably 30) with UVA and UVB protection—and remember to use it! It needs to be reapplied every two hours while you're outdoors, as well as after swimming. Waterproof sunscreens also need to be reapplied after water exposure. (It usually says so in the fine print on the bottle.)

Also, wear sun-protective clothing, hats, and sunglasses with UVA and UVB protection. Hats need to have a four-inch brim. Baseball caps don't protect most of the face or the ears.

If you do get sunburned, over-the-counter ibuprofen (Advil) or naproxen (Aleve) will help relieve some of the discomfort and diminish the inflammation associated with the burn.

An old home remedy: my mother always rubbed distilled white vinegar on our sunburns, and it really did take the sting out of the burn, once the initial sting from the vinegar wore off. The reason it's effective is that the acetic acid in the vinegar works as a sort of topical NSAID (nonsteroidal anti-inflammatory drug). Of course we all smelled like salad!

Or you can brew up a batch of green tea, chill it, and make compresses. The EGCG found in green tea works as a natural anti-inflammatory ingredient.

DERMAdoctor Body Guard, a well-rounded sunscreen, contains green tea. This makes it the perfect after-sun treatment. Apply it after coming in from a long day outdoors.

Reasons to go see your doctor include: symptoms of heatstroke, such as nausea, vomiting, or fainting. Also consult your doctor if your burn blisters.

POISON IVY: AN OVER-THE-COUNTER ANTIDOTE

Poison ivy can now be prevented, or the development of the rash attenuated, with the use of Ivy Block. Applied fifteen minutes before going outdoors, Ivy Block works to neutralize urushiol, the rash-causing resin from poison ivy, oak, and sumac. But don't apply it to active poison ivy rashes.

If you've been outdoors with any risk of exposure, try to wash immediately with Burt's Bees Poison Ivy Soap, which contains jewelweed, a herb long touted as useful for poison ivy prevention. The soap economically and effectively washes away much of the resin responsible for the rash.

Poison ivy is unpleasant, and in an ideal world everyone would be able to get in to see the doctor right away, but reality dictates against this. Once you've gotten poison ivy, dry out the blisters with a compress of Domeboro Astringent Solution. Then apply Cortaid Steroid Cream. While a strong prescription steroid (preferably a gel like Temovate) is ideal and faster acting than Cortaid, on a Saturday night Cortaid may be all you can find in the drugstore. You may also consider applying Zanfel Poison Ivy Cream, which helps lift urushiol from the skin. Once more, you can rely upon oral Benadryl for the itching.

Reasons to call your doctor include blisters and swelling on the face, especially near the eyes, and blisters over a significant portion of your body.

Please see the chapter "Poison Ivy, Oak, and Sumac" on page 202 for more information.

ATHLETE'S FOOT: CREAM IT

Fungal infections of the feet are usually red, scaly, and very itchy. Lamisil AT and DERMAdoctor Feet Accompli provide antifungal options. Apply your cream sparingly. Too much of a good thing here can create more moisture, which drives the infection. In cases where oozing and weeping have occurred, try using Lamisil AT athlete's foot spray to kill the fungus, instead of the cream base. Treat any splits on the feet the way you would on your hands: fill with polysporin and apply DERMAdoctor Handy Manum twice daily.

Keeping the skin dry is essential to solving the problem. Hot, dark, moist skin folds are breeding grounds for fungus. Try dusting with medicated absorbent powders like Zeasorb-AF. Consider wearing special socks made to wick away perspiration. Jobst SensiFoot Unisex Athletic Support Socks are ideal. Trade in your leather athletic shoes for canvas. Leather traps moisture inside the shoes and prevents your feet from breathing. Kick off your shoes and socks when you get home and allow air to circulate around your feet.

Reasons to see the doctor include: spread of the infection to other areas, lack of response to topicals (sometimes oral antifungal pills are necessary), or involvement of toenails. Also, I recommend that diabetics or anyone who is immunosuppressed see their dermatologist. Fungi are capable of producing microscopic breaks in the skin, which for the healthiest patients may not be a problem but for anyone prone to infection can lead to a condition called cellulitis (bacterial infection of the skin). Seeing your doctor before this occurs can save you a possible hospitalization.

DANDRUFF: FIGHT FLAKES AND ITCH

Thick, greasy scale of the scalp, often known as dandruff, is highly responsive to over-the-counter medicated dandruff shampoos. To get better results, try alternating shampoos. Dandruff responds to zinc pyrithione (DHS Zinc Shampoo), glycolic acid (Aqua Glycolic Shampoo & Body Cleanser), and ketoconazole (Nizoral A-D Shampoo). Keep a few on hand and use whenever needed.

Both seborrhea and psoriasis can result in chronic dandruff conditions. Knowing how to keep them under control helps reduce flaking and discomfort due to itching. (For more information on these two conditions, see the chapter "Psoriasis" on page 222 and the chapter "Dandruff" on page 59.)

To help make hair feel silkier and restore its pH balance, after shampooing use the conditioner or cream rinse of your choice. Ionil makes a cream rinse that has long been a favorite recommendation of mine for users of dandruff shampoos.

Reasons to see the doctor include: resistance to treatment, spread of flaking onto the face or other areas of the body, or hair loss.

WARTS: ASSIST YOUR DOCTOR

Warts usually need some medical intervention to clear them, but if you know you have a wart, you may want to get started with either Occlusal-HP or Dr. Scholl's wart pads. These salicylic acid–based products are applied nightly to the wart, after you've soaked and lightly roughened up its surface with a pumice stone or emery board. They will help soften and debride the wart, making the area white, soft, and peely.

Another home option is freezing the warts with a product such as Compound W Freeze Off Wart Removal System.

Reasons to see the doctor include: the mere presence of warts. Warts are tough to treat, and their banishment often requires some medical help. While it's certainly possible that a single tiny wart will respond to persistent home treatment, if your warts begin to spread, make an appointment with your doctor. I feel bad for a patient who comes in with innumerable warts because she was incorrectly told that the warts would resolve on their own. This isn't usually true.

BUG BITES: INSTANT ITCH CONTROL

For mosquito or chigger bites, itch control is your biggest issue. Try applying a topical anesthetic. An effective selection includes PrameGel, Prax Lotion, and Caladryl Clear Lotion. Over-the-counter 1% hydrocortisone cream (such as Cortaid Steroid Cream) treats both the itching and the inflammation.

If you're scratching instead of sleeping, this is another time to consider a bedtime antihistamine. Scratching too vigorously can lead to a bacterial infection, discoloration, or scar formation. Always keep open skin wounds clean with hydrogen peroxide and a topical antibiotic ointment.

BEE STINGS: A KITCHEN REMEDY

Assuming you aren't highly allergic, once the stinger has been removed, apply an ice pack for at least fifteen to twenty minutes. Then mix up a paste of baking soda or meat tenderizer and water and apply it to the sore area. Leave the poultice on, uncovered, until it dries, which should be thirty minutes or so. This will help reduce much of the local inflammation and swelling.

Typically, I recommend taking an antihistamine like Benadryl, or perhaps some Triaminic syrup, to help with the swelling. The nice thing about antihistamine syrups, as opposed to pills, is that you can adjust the amount taken, so you can control your level of drowsiness.

Reasons to go to the emergency room include: extreme swelling of an extremity, any shortness of breath, or difficulty talking or swallowing.

SPIDER BITES: CALL THE DOCTOR

For any sort of spider bite, I'd call the doctor. I would also take a baby aspirin to help improve the circulation. Usually you need to take an antibiotic and watch the site carefully for the development of a sore.

TICK BITES: REMOVE IT RIGHT

While most ticks are harmless, concern about a potential infection harbored by the tick is understandable. But don't bother with the hot match, death by asphyxiation with Vaseline, or drowning with alcohol. These tricks don't work; worse, they can cause the tick to grab on more forcefully.

Personally, I've found that pulling the tick off gently but firmly with a pair of metal tweezers or forceps is the best method of removal. Clean the area with rubbing alcohol and apply a dab of Polysporin ointment.

Regarding calling the doctor: with the spread of Lyme disease, Rocky Mountain spotted fever, and ehrlichiosis, it's worth taking the time to call your doctor and ask if you require preventive antibiotics.

SWOLLEN EYELIDS: SEE YOUR WAY HEALTHY

For swelling caused by presumed pollen allergies or allergic contact dermatitis, try taking Benadryl according to package directions. Also apply some plain Cortaid Steroid Cream (1% hydrocortisone cream) ever so slightly to the eyelid, no more than twice daily, for only a day or two. Make absolutely certain you don't apply the cream so that it can get into the eye. Stop wearing makeup, and use a gentle hypoallergenic cleanser like Cetaphil Gentle Skin Cleanser or Vanicream Cleansing Bar.

Sometimes a contact dermatitis occurs only on the eyelids; a patch test conducted by a dermatologist can often detect the cause of the problem. Before you go to the dermatologist, please read the chapter "Contact Allergies" on page 53 to get some background on this essentially painless workup method.

Reasons to see the doctor: if the swelling lasts more than a day or two or is recurrent; if there is drainage; or if the eye itself or your vision seems affected.

CRACKED FINGERTIPS: THEY REQUIRE INTENSIVE CARE

Knowing how painful a tiny paper cut can be, can you imagine how debilitating chronically dry, cracking, splitting fingertips are? Once the skin is broken, whether because of cold weather, a contact dermatitis, or eczema, obsessive care can help expedite healing.

Fill the splits with Polysporin ointment at least twice a day. (Forget about the notion of using glue or rubber cement.)

Don't waste time with a hand lotion at this point; your skin needs a *massive* dose of moisture! Alternate hand creams like Theraseal and Vanicream. Keep a jar or tube of your favorite moisturizing cream at the office and reapply each and every time you wash your hands.

Once or twice daily, apply DERMAdoctor Handy Manum, which really helps soften those crusty edges and allows them to heal.

FINAL THOUGHTS

Sometimes it's just not possible to see the doctor. While nothing should replace your physician, I feel very strongly that patients will be more comfortable handling minor problems if they understand what to select on their own. Accurate information powers every good health care decision. After all, personal skin care begins at home.

INDEX